"In this sweeping and deeply researched study of Chinese miners in the world's nineteenth-century goldfields, Mae Ngai brilliantly reconstructs how race became woven into the fabric of international capitalism and wired into the politics of nations. A stunning, vivid, and indispensable history."

—Gary Gerstle, University of Cambridge

"This remarkable book takes the modern search for gold out of the old frames of transoceanic greed, violence, race, and migrant labor to enter the anglophone world of global politics. By so doing, it shows it was not surprising that the biggest rivals during the first decades of the gold rushes were the enterprising English-speaking and Chinese-speaking peoples. The author follows both groups around three continents and illuminates the rise of Anglo-American global power that turned Chinese adventures into 'the Chinese question.' This readable and exhaustive study of open-air and underground gold cuts through modern world history in a most refreshing way and contributes to our understanding of power rivalry that remains with us today."

—Wang Gungwu, National University of Singapore

"Ambitiously conceived, prodigiously researched, and engagingly presented, *The Chinese Question* weaves distant places, circumstances, and experiences into a compelling narrative that speaks to us today. *The Chinese Question* has deep historical significance but also pressing contemporary relevance."

—Gordon H. Chang, Stanford University, author of *Ghosts of Gold Mountain: The Epic Story of the Chinese Who Built the Transcontinental Railroad*

"During the high tide of western colonialism, Chinese peasants left their homes to enter into the vortex of a global gold boom that transformed large areas of the United States, Australia, and South Africa. Like other migrants, they worked hard, built new communities, and engaged in protracted political struggles. As gold diggers and local retailers, diplomats of the once powerful Chinese Empire, and masters of continent-spanning trade networks, they built new lives—only to be met by an escalating anti-Chinese racism. With unusual force and subtlety, Mae Ngai's beautifully crafted global narrative dismantles widely accepted, and deeply racist, tropes about Chinese migration. This is one of the few books that will make you genuinely rethink an important episode."

—Sven Beckert, Harvard University, author of *Empire of Cotton*

THE
Chinese
Question

THE
Chinese
Question

The Gold Rushes and Global Politics

MAE NGAI

W. W. NORTON & COMPANY
Independent Publishers Since 1923

Since this page cannot legibly accommodate all the copyright notices,
page 419 constitutes an extension of the copyright page.

For information about permission to reproduce selections from this book, write to
Permissions, W. W. Norton & Company, Inc., 500 Fifth Avenue, New York, NY 10110

For information about special discounts for bulk purchases, please contact
W. W. Norton Special Sales at specialsales@wwnorton.com or 800-233-4830

Manufacturing by LSC Communications, Harrisonburg
Book design by Chris Welch
Production manager: Lauren Abbate

Library of Congress Cataloging-in-Publication Data

Names: Ngai, Mae M., author.
Title: The Chinese question : the gold rushes and global politics / Mae Ngai.
Other titles: Gold rushes and global politics
Description: First edition. | New York : W. W. Norton & Company, [2021] |
Includes bibliographical references and index.
Identifiers: LCCN 2021008789 | ISBN 9780393634167 (hardcover) | ISBN 9780393634174 (epub)
Subjects: LCSH: Chinese—Foreign countries—History—19th century. | Gold mines and mining—
Social aspects. | Gold mines and mining—Australia—History—19th century. | Gold mines and
mining—California—History—19th century. | Gold mines and mining—South Africa—History—
19th century. | Chinese diaspora. | Race discrimination—History—19th century.
Classification: LCC DS732 .N43 2021 | DDC 331.6/251009034—dc23
LC record available at https://lccn.loc.gov/2021008789

W. W. Norton & Company, Inc., 500 Fifth Avenue, New York, N.Y. 10110
www.wwnorton.com

W. W. Norton & Company Ltd., 15 Carlisle Street, London W1D 3BS

1 2 3 4 5 6 7 8 9 0

FOR FELIX

What is the matter with foreignness?

—TONI MORRISON

Contents

PART I. TWO GOLD MOUNTAINS

PART II. MAKING WHITE MEN'S COUNTRIES

PART III. THE ASIATIC DANGER IN THE COLONIES

PART IV. THE CHINESE DIASPORA IN THE WEST

Illustrations follow page 136 and page 232.

List of Maps

World Gold Production and Discoveries

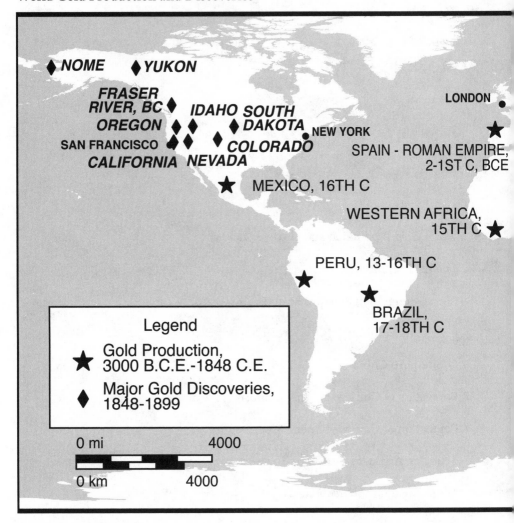

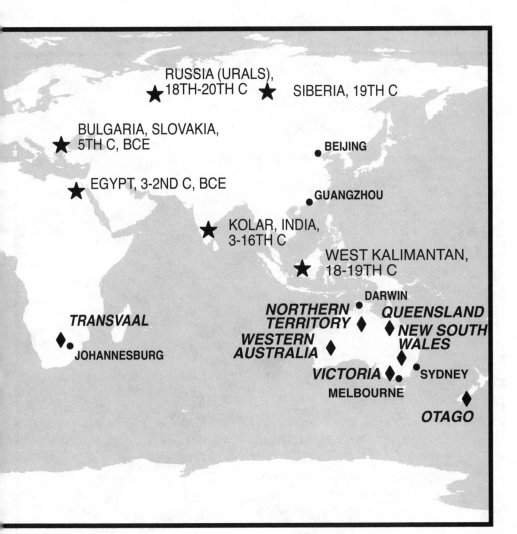

RUSSIA (URALS),
18TH-20TH C

SIBERIA, 19TH C

BULGARIA, SLOVAKIA,
5TH C, BCE

BEIJING

EGYPT, 3-2ND C, BCE

GUANGZHOU

KOLAR, INDIA,
3-16TH C

WEST KALIMANTAN,
18-19TH C

DARWIN

TRANSVAAL

NORTHERN
TERRITORY

QUEENSLAND

NEW SOUTH
WALES

JOHANNESBURG

WESTERN
AUSTRALIA

VICTORIA

SYDNEY

MELBOURNE

OTAGO

Map by Cailin Hong

The Asia-Pacific

Map by Cailin Hong

China, Emigration Sending Regions, 1850–1910

Northern China

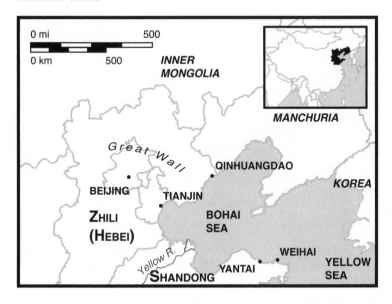

Map by Cailin Hong

Southern China

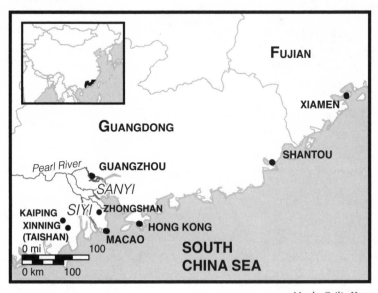

Map by Cailin Hong

Author's Note

This book has its origins in an interaction with a student who was writing a paper on nineteenth-century California politics. I attempted to correct the student's misimpression that Chinese workers were indentured workers, or coolies. The student could not be blamed for the error because the ill-founded claim dominated the existing historical literature. Evidence to the contrary was scattered or had been simply ignored by historians, who seemed invested in perpetuating the idea that Chinese workers were slavish, without individual personality or will, and pathetically oppressed. I vowed I would slay the coolie myth.

It has taken me more than ten years to complete the empirical research on the Chinese experience in the gold rushes and to think through the political dynamics that entrenched the racist coolie stereotype, not just in the United States but throughout the anglophone world. I had not, at first, intended to write a global history, but in 2005, while attending a conference of the International Society for the Study of Chinese Overseas (ISSCO) in Bendigo, Australia, I was struck by how the landscape of the Victorian midlands resembled that of northern California. I later learned that Edmund Hargraves, whom historians credit with discovering gold in Australia in 1851, had participated in the California gold rush and had had the same thought. A year later I went to the ISSCO conference in

Pretoria, South Africa, which piqued my interest in the experience of Chinese who worked as indentured workers in the deep mines of the Witwatersrand. These visits suggested a comparative study. But I had little idea what comparison would reveal.

It has been a long and fascinating journey to understand how the Chinese Question grew out of an alchemy of race and money in nineteenth-century global economic and political relations. My research was not unlike panning for gold—part hard work and part luck—which slowly yielded nuggets of insight and comprehension. The book involved research on five continents and challenged the limits of my knowledge, linguistic ability, and comfort zone. I am grateful to the many institutions and individuals who supported, encouraged, guided, and corrected me along the way. I thank them by name in the Acknowledgments.

I completed the writing of this book while sheltering in place during the coronavirus pandemic of 2020. During this difficult time, relations between the United States and China worsened. American politicians and pundits scapegoated China, and Chinese people in the United States—as well as Australia, Great Britain, and Europe—suffered racist insult and assault, including the well-worn epithet "go back to where you came from." The idea that Chinese do not belong, and can never belong, in the United States and other countries of the West has a long history, which begins in the gold rushes of the nineteenth century. This book opens a window into that deep history. My intention is to clarify racism's historical origins and reproduction as a strategy of political interests. I hope that might help us understand the potential for combating and eradicating it in our own time.

Mae Ngai
Accokeek, Maryland
August 2020

Note on Romanization and Currencies

Chinese proper names are given in pinyin with surname first, e.g., Yuan Sheng. In cases where individuals and organizations were known by their names in Cantonese transliterations or other romanization systems, the pinyin is provided in parentheses, if known, e.g., Lowe Kong Meng (Liu Guangming). Many ordinary Chinese people appear in Western records only by a familiar form of address, e.g., Ah Bu, with no indication of their full Chinese name.

Chinese place names are rendered in pinyin with the old Anglicized name in parentheses, e.g., Guangzhou (Canton), Xiamen (Amoy), Yantai (Chefoo), unless commonly known otherwise, e.g., Hong Kong. A glossary of Chinese proper names with pinyin, Cantonese, and Chinese characters may be found on page 319.

Currencies used in this book include the Chinese silver tael and yuan (dollar), the British pound sterling, the Mexican silver dollar, and the U.S. dollar. The value of taels varied by location in China. In 1875 the Imperial Maritime Customs Office introduced the Haikwan (*haiguan*) tael (HKT), or customs tael, an abstract measure used in official trade accounts. One HKT was the equivalent of 1.25 troy ounce of silver.

During most of the period covered in this book, £1 = 3.45 taels = $4.80. One Mexican silver dollar = 0.72 tael. The U.S. dollar was roughly equivalent to the Mexican silver dollar. In 1899 the Qing introduced the Chinese yuan (dollar) on par with the Mexican dollar.

The price of gold remained stable throughout the nineteenth century to World War I, with one troy ounce of gold = £3 17s.10d. = $20.67. Until the 1870s the silver-to-gold ratio was between 12:1 and 15:1. In the late nineteenth century, the gold-price of silver fell from 58d. per ounce in 1875 to 37.5d. in 1892 and to 27d. in 1899, a depreciation of more than 50 percent. The value of one HKT fell from six shillings in 1875 to two to three shillings in 1900–5. In 1905 one Mexican/U.S./Chinese dollar was about 27 pence, or slightly more than two shillings.[1]

Introduction

Yellow and Gold

Mountains of gold towered on high,
Which men could grab with their hands left and right.
Eureka! They return with a load full of gold,
All bragging this land is paradise.

Gold seekers from all over the world wrote tales of the nineteenth-century gold rushes, their imagery of riches and glory even grander when rendered in verse. These particular lines are from a long poem written in classical Chinese by Huang Zunxian, a Chinese scholar and diplomat. Huang served as general consul for the Qing government in San Francisco in the early 1880s, during the time of the great anti-Chinese agitation and the passage of the Chinese Exclusion Act. He was a reform-minded official who believed the United States was the most advanced nation in the world that held many lessons for the modernization of China. But while in America, Huang could not believe the oppression and violence meted out against the Chinese. He worked tirelessly on behalf of the emigrants, offering comfort to those who came to him and appealing to American officials for justice and fairness. Disillusioned and exhausted, Huang left the United States after three years. His poem, "Expulsion of the Immigrants," expressed his disappointment at Americans' betrayal of principles laid down by their nation's founders, where "all kinds of foreigners and immigrants,/ Are allowed to settle in these new lands."[1]

The consul's view from California extended to an understanding of the global consequences of the gold rushes:

Heaven and earth are suddenly narrow, confining;
Men and demons chew and devour each other.
Great China and the race of Han
Have now become a joke to the other races.

He wondered, too, whether other countries would follow the American example of Chinese exclusion: "Within the vastness of the six directions, / Where can our people find asylum?"

THIS BOOK EXPLORES the origins of Chinese communities in the Anglo-American world, locating their beginnings in the three largest gold-producing regions of the nineteenth century: California, Australia, and South Africa. It is a story about Chinese emigrants' dreams, labors, and communities, as well as their disappointments and sufferings, and their fateful marginalization and exclusion from self-described, self-anointed "white men's countries." It is the story about the making of the Chinese diaspora in the Anglo-American world during a tumultuous period in world history, during which gold fever and racial politics marked the closing of frontiers in the United States and in the British Empire; a time that saw the ascendance of British and American financial power and the inclusion of China in the world's "family of nations," but as an unequal and marginal player. It reveals that Chinese exclusion was not extraneous to the emergent global capitalist economy but an integral part of it. *The Chinese Question* is the story of how the Chinese communities in the West were born of a powerful alchemy of race and money—colored labor and capitalism, colonialism and financial power—across the nineteenth-century world.

THE CHINESE WHO WENT to the gold rushes were part of an expanding population of Chinese living abroad in the nineteenth century. Since at least the thirteenth century of the Common Era, people from China's southeastern coastal provinces had traded in Southeast Asia, from Indonesia and the Philippines to Vietnam and the Malay Peninsula to Thailand. But in the nineteenth century they traveled much farther from home, spurred by both need and opportunity. A quarter-million Chinese went as indentured laborers to European plantation colonies in the Caribbean as part of the notorious coolie trade that exploited Chinese and Indian workers after the abolition of slavery.[2]

An even greater number of Chinese, more than 300,000, went as voluntary emigrants to the United States and to British settler colonies in the nineteenth century, attracted first by the gold rushes. The Chinese gold seekers were not, of course, the first to cross the great ocean—that distinction is held by the Polynesian peoples whose seaborne migrations began over one thousand years BCE. In the sixteenth and seventeenth centuries, the Spanish ran a yearly galleon trade between Acapulco and Manila, the long middle leg of a journey that traded New World silver to China for silks, porcelain, and other luxuries for Europe. By the early nineteenth century, a budding U.S.-China trade of northwestern American furs and pelts and Hawaiian sandalwood drew new routes across the ocean.[3]

But the gold rushes were of another order. They exploded the early modern Pacific maritime world. Vibrant new routes and networks of trade and migration were established, nourished by gold first in California, then in Australia. Three new and lasting nodes of the transpacific rose to prominence: Hong Kong, San Francisco, and Sydney.

The goldfields were international contact zones on the frontiers of Anglo-American settler societies. The rushes attracted gold seekers from around the world—from the eastern and southern United States; from the British Isles and Continental Europe; from Mexico and Chile and Hawaii; from Australia and China. The gold seekers' arrival to the frontiers of white settlement made them participants, to one degree or other, in the elimination of indigenous peoples and in the formation of new communities and nations. How would these new polities reckon with the diverse character of the goldfield populations? Who would be included and who would be excluded? And who would decide, and by what means?

The gold rushes occasioned the first mass contact between Chinese and Euro-Americans. Unlike other encounters in Asian port cities and on Caribbean plantations, they met on the goldfields both in large numbers and on relatively equal terms, that is, as voluntary emigrants and independent prospectors. Race relations were not always conflictual, but the perception of competition gave rise to a racial politics expressed as the "Chinese Question."

In the nineteenth century, Americans and Europeans frequently described a thorny social problem as a "Question": "the Negro Question," "the Jewish Question," "the Woman Question." A "Question" usually referred to the political status of minority or subordinate groups in emerging modern nation-states. These problems, urgent and difficult, generated enormous controversies. They were also complex because they involved multiple contradictions and competing interests (for example, "we could use their labor but they are not fit to be citizens") and, not least, faced insistent claims made by the social groups in question themselves. Violence invariably accompanied debate (lynchings, pogroms, riots). The great Questions of the nineteenth century were all tied up with the development of capitalism and modern nation-states. They were challenges of democracy— defining who could belong, who could be a citizen, who could vote.[4]

The Chinese Question was simply this: were Chinese a racial threat to white, Anglo-American countries, and should Chinese be barred from them? Chinese exclusion was a radical idea at the time because it not only challenged liberal principles of equality but also sought to establish an exception in a world otherwise defined by free trade and free migration.

The Chinese Question arose differently in different places, produced by different local conditions. So in a sense, there were multiple Chinese Questions. But local political debates, whether in the United States, Australia, South Africa, or metropolitan Britain, were framed explicitly as the "Chinese Question," implying shared affinities across the Anglo-American world. And to be sure, local politics traveled and borrowed from each other. By the turn of the twentieth century, a global race theory about the dangers of Chinese immigration had emerged.

The United States and the British settler colonies (Australia, New Zealand, Canada, and South Africa) ultimately answered the Chinese Question with legislation excluding Chinese from immigration and citizenship. In the United States, the Chinese exclusion laws (1875–1943) were the first (and, to this day, the only) laws that explicitly named a group for exclusion. In Australia, immigration restriction aimed at Chinese, South Asians, and other non-Europeans was the cornerstone of an unapologetic White Australia policy (1901–73). In South Africa, the exclusion of Chinese (1880s–1980s) was part of the agenda of radical white supremacy and racial segregation. In each case, the Chinese Question played a central part in the making of white settler identity and the modern nation-state, of a piece with native dispossession and racial segregation. Not only were these laws consequential for emerging national identities—they also inaugurated a new way of imagining, organizing, and governing the world.

THE CHINESE QUESTION builds on historical research in subjects that have usually been pursued in separate research silos. Gold rush histories have noted racism against Chinese but usually as a side story. The histories of the gold rushes and gold are divided between social and political histories, on the one hand, and economic and monetary studies, on the other. They have little to say to each other, like ships passing in the night. The histories of Chinese immigration, exclusion politics, and China's economic development have touched only lightly upon the gold rushes. This book considers these various questions in one large historical framework, that is, the place of Anglo-American settler racism in the development of global capitalism. Such a framework not only enables us to make new connections between existing fields of scholarship; it considers how the gold rushes both expanded the world and brought its parts closer together: as Huang Zunxian wrote, "heaven and earth are suddenly narrow, confining."[5]

The Chinese Question also opens new horizons for thinking about how ideas and practices about race and money evolved in the nineteenth century. Race and money have long been symbiotically connected, but the relationship is neither fixed nor constant; rather, it is produced by history and politics. The nature of that relationship has been the subject of numerous inquiries and debates among historians. For example, what was the relationship between slavery and capitalism? Between colonialism, empire, and global finance and trade? Is capitalism inherently racist? This book contributes to our understanding of race and money by examining one of its specific expressions in the late nineteenth-century Chinese Question.

⚜

GOLD IS EVERYWHERE.

It is one of a few metals that can be found on all five continents. Typically, gold is found in the foothills of mountain ranges—not on flat plains or in mountains but in the areas in between. It is the only metal that exists in nature unalloyed, in pure metallic form; and it is one of only a few that does not oxidize when exposed to air—that is, it does not rust. It is both indestructible and malleable. Historically gold presented in the beds of streams, washed down from millennia of mountain erosion, easy to spot by its glimmer and to pick up by hand or by sifting it from river dirt and gravel. From time immemorial, humans have prized gold for its beauty, purity, and scarcity. Premodern societies—from ancient Egypt and Bronze Age China to Mesoamerica and medieval Europe—used gold chiefly as ornament, especially as a mark of high social rank.

After the disintegration of the Western Roman Empire, gold was often a store of value, but it was rarely used as a means of exchange (coined for use as money) in Europe until the early modern era. By the fifteenth century, though, as Europe emerged from its disastrous encounter with the bubonic plague, gold was, perhaps, more highly prized than ever. The Spanish conquest of the Americas in the early sixteenth century highlighted the discrepancy in the social value of gold. The Inca created gorgeous artifacts from gold in tribute to their kings, whom they believed personified the sun god. When conquistadores seized American gold in the early sixteenth century as ransom for the Incan emperor Atahualpa, they melted Incan artifacts into bullion, 13,000 pounds of 22-karat gold and 25,000 pounds of silver. The looting of American gold and silver continued. The latter proved to be an even greater treasure that gave rise to a fantastic global commerce in silver, mined in Spanish America, transshipped through Europe or across the Pacific, and sold in China at twice the price as in Europe.[6]

By the middle of the eighteenth century, Portuguese Brazil was producing 80 percent of American gold and more than half the world's supply. The Brazilian gold rush attracted 400,000 Portuguese emigrants, who brought with them as many enslaved Africans. Portugal used Brazilian gold to pay for British goods, which enabled the latter to transition to a de facto gold monetary standard and, in the early nineteenth century, facilitated its rise as an international creditor. Still, most European countries used both gold and silver monies, with silver being more common and more important. Not only was gold scarcer; silver was also the favored means of exchange in Asia, the engine of world trade in the early modern era.[7]

The next wave of gold rushes, the focus of this book, was truly stunning in scope and consequence. From the California gold rush of 1848 to the discovery of gold in the Yukon in 1896, gold miners and mining companies extracted from the earth some 435 million ounces of gold— more than the total amount that had been mined in the previous three thousand years, including the recent Brazilian gold rush. The sudden increase in world gold production resulted from Anglo-American settler colonialism and capitalist development. For although gold is everywhere, it is not everywhere *payable,* that is, possible to extract in a way that is profitable. Indigenous peoples on the settler-colonial frontiers of the United States and Australia were aware of alluvial gold deposits in their midst, but they did not value gold as the money-commodity.[8]

Sustained exploration and extraction for profit required not only a motive—the desire for wealth within an expanding imperial sphere where it was the monetary-commodity nonpareil; it also required private property rights, capital investment, deep-mining technology, mass labor migration, and long-distance transportation. The gold rushes transformed Anglo-American frontiers, accelerating the dispossession of indigenous peoples and the in-migration of nonnative peoples. Gold mining also gravely damaged the environment, leaving deep gouges in the earth, mounds of detritus, felled forests, and rivers choked with sediment and toxic debris. Corporations and financial investment followed individuals seeking gold, raising the stakes over control of land, property, and national and colonial territories.

In the late 1850s the British economists William Newmarch and Thomas Tooke waxed that the California and Australian gold rushes had, in just ten years, resulted in a 30 percent increase in the "Metallic Circulation of the leading portions of the Commercial World." Enthusiasts suggested that the new gold discoveries were a gift from nature, perhaps even from Providence, that would promote "intercourse between nations" and raise "the social condition of man." The economic historian Jean-Jacques Van Helten similarly argued, though without the fevered rhetoric, that the increase in the global supply of gold in the nineteenth century was a fortuitous meeting of the monetary demands posed by expanding world trade. But we might think of it also as a *stimulus,* a new stage of capital accumulation, that made possible that expansion and, in particular, the rise of Great Britain and the United States as the world's leading investor and creditor nations. In addition to promoting investment and trade, the increase in the supply of gold enabled more countries to adopt a gold monetary standard.[9]

In 1904 the United States and Great Britain controlled 88 percent of the world's yield of gold, at the time the highest yield on record, valued at about £71.5 billion. The British alone were responsible for two-thirds of it. Discoveries of gold in colonial territories did not create the British Empire. But the location of gold in Australia and South Africa dramatically elevated those colonies' strategic importance within the empire and helped consolidate Britain's power as global financial giant in the late nineteenth and early twentieth centuries. J. H. Curle, a British mining engineer who surveyed the world's gold mines at the turn of the twentieth century, did not exaggerate when he wrote, "Gold-mining is in reality one of our biggest national assets, mentally and materially."[10]

The discoveries of gold in the United States were directly consequential for American development and the increase in its foreign economic influence. While the Civil War had enabled the consolidation of a national market, gold increased the nation's wealth at myriad levels—that of individuals; in the development of California and the American West; for railroad, industrial, and finance capital; and for foreign investment. The United States was also a major producer of silver, with a booming silver-mining industry in Nevada and other western states. The country operated on a bimetallic monetary system until 1873, when Congress demonetized silver. The gold standard favored industrialists, bankers, and other creditors, and it disadvantaged those who depended on easier terms of credit, especially farmers. The money question—the demand for "free silver"—that rocked American politics in the 1890s expressed the growing alienation of small producers from the ascent of industrial and financial monopoly.[11]

⚌

AT THE TIME OF the gold rushes, China was already in the grip of European colonialism. China was never directly colonized by a Western power; in fact, by the mid-eighteenth century the Qing Dynasty (1644–1911) had built an empire of its own, having expanded China's boundaries to the west, most notably by annexing Tibet and Xinjiang. But in the mid-nineteenth century China was battered by European aggressions: the opium trade, gunboat diplomacy, and the forced opening to Western trade and missionaries. China's humiliation stood in stark contrast to the position it had once held, even relatively recently.

For two hundred years, from 1550 to 1750, China had been arguably the most important economic actor in the world. It was not only the single largest domestic economy; it was also at the center of global trade, both with its Sino-centric tributary and trading networks in East and Southeast Asia and as the premier destination market for silver produced in Spanish America and Japan. Europeans shipped silver to China not as "money" but as commodity arbitrage: the Ming Dynasty's (1368–1644) demand for silver for fiscal and commercial purposes fetched the highest silver prices in the world, double its price in Europe. China was the world's great "silver sink" that not only drew but also stimulated its production in the New World.[12]

Through the seventeenth century, Europeans traded silver for luxuries, including gold. For example, the British East India Company's first direct transaction with China in 1637 exchanged 60,000 Spanish dollars for sugar, silk, spices, porcelain, and "loose gould." Chinese traders also made handsome profits by buying low and selling dear, earning gross profits of 100 to 150 percent on silk and silk textiles sold to Europeans. Economic historians Dennis Flynn and Arturo Gilàldez describe these late sixteenth-century dynamics of global trade as "multiple arbitrage."[13]

Europeans began trading silver for tea in large quantities in the early eighteenth century. Like silk, tea was a luxury item in Europe, but it had greater potential for mass consumption. The creation of a mass market for tea in Europe coincided with the rise in consumption of sugar from the plantation-slave colonies of the Caribbean in the late seventeenth century. Indeed, tea and sugar, along with tobacco, undergirded a global trade in stimulants—"food drugs"—based on a symbiosis of colonialism and slavery, on the one hand, and new mass-consumption economies in European metropolitan societies, especially Britain, on the other.[14]

By 1800 silver's arbitrage advantage in China had ended. The British, now hooked on tea, looked for a different means of exchange. The East India Company had already drained India of much of its silver to sell in China; now it turned to India for the mass production of opium for export to China.

IN THE EARLY NINETEENTH CENTURY, opium ravaged both India and China—India, its producer; China, its consumer.

Farmers in the Bengal had traditionally grown a few clusters of poppies between their fields of winter crops, wheat, vegetables, and *masoor dal*. They pressed poppy seeds for oil and purified and sun-dried the sap drawn from the pod—the source of narcotic alkaloids—for *abkari*, black and hard, that was eaten during illnesses or at weddings, or sold to nobles. The British East India Company pushed Bengali peasants to the exclusive cultivation of poppies, forcing upon them cash advances and contracts in order to supply the company with tons of raw opium drawn from poppy seedpods. Not only did the East India Company destroy Bengali subsistence farming; the mass production of opium in its huge factories sucked the life from Indian workers. The fumes of opium permeated the factories and affected all who worked there, most pitiably those who, immersed to the waist in tanks of raw liquid opium, churned and tramped the dark ooze with their bodies and feet.[15]

As in India, Chinese had long used opium—called *wu xiang*, "black spice"—as a medicinal herb and as an aphrodisiac. An internal opium trade emanated from China's southwestern provinces and the western frontier. But in the early nineteenth century, massive imports by the British East India Company generated mass opium consumption and addiction in China. Americans also jumped into the lucrative business, importing into China opium grown in Turkey. The amount of opium imported into China increased from about 200 chests in 1729 to 1,000 chests in 1767 and to 10,000 each year between 1820 and 1830. The Qing government repeatedly banned the trafficking of opium, decreeing in 1810, for instance, "Opium has a harm. Opium is a poison, undermining our good customs and morality. Its use is prohibited by law." Ignoring Chinese laws, the East India Company cultivated networks of Chinese smugglers, clandestine merchants, and corrupt officials. By 1838 the company was importing 40,000 chests a year into China, reversing the balance of payment between China and Britain and feeding some 12 million opium users in China.[16]

Alarmed both by the spread of addiction and by the outflow of silver, the Qing court moved to aggressively crack down on opium smuggling in 1838. It sent a scholar-official, Lin Zexu, to Guangzhou to deal with the matter. As governor general of Hunan and Hubei provinces, Lin had already cleared those provinces of opium. Designated with the new title of Imperial Commissioner, Lin began by sending a diplomatic note to the British crown. He famously wrote to Queen Victoria that foreign traders "coveting profit to an extreme . . . have no regard for injuring others. Let us ask, where is your conscience? I have heard that the smoking of opium is very strictly forbidden in your own country; that is because the harm caused by opium is clearly understood. Since it is not permitted to do harm to your own country, then even less should you let it be passed on to harm other countries—how much less to China."[17]

There is no record that Queen Victoria received Lin's missive. But Lin, receiving no answer, arrested seventeen hundred Chinese opium dealers and confiscated seventy thousand opium pipes. He offered to exchange the foreign merchants' opium for tea, but to no avail. He then seized 2.6 million pounds of opium in Guangzhou's foreign section, mixed it with lime and salt, and threw it into the sea. Next, he blocked the Pearl River, trapping Westerners in Guangzhou. A series of failed diplomatic efforts and military feints on both sides led ultimately to war, the British claiming rights to property and free trade; the Qing, to protect its territory.

The Opium War (1839–42) rudely introduced China to Western

power. The Qing deployed ten thousand soldiers and fleets of war junks to defend its harbors, rivers, and cities. But ultimately they proved unable to resist British gunboats that were made of iron, powered by steam, and mounted with cannons far heavier than those of the Chinese. Chinese called them "devil ships." The Treaty of Nanjing extracted from China humiliating concessions including the island of Hong Kong, an indemnity of 21 million silver dollars, the opening of five ports to foreign trade, and extraterritorial rights for British citizens, which exempted them from Chinese law. France and the United States quickly demanded similar treaties recognizing them as "most favored nations" with the same access to the treaty ports and extraterritorial rights.

A second Opium War (1856–60), waged by the British and French, resulted in the Treaty of Tianjin, which was actually four simultaneous treaties made with Britain, France, Russia, and the United States. The treaties gave the foreign powers the right to establish diplomatic legations in Beijing; opened ten more ports to foreign trade; opened the interior to foreign merchants and missionaries; legalized the trade of opium; and imposed an indemnity of 8 million silver dollars for Britain and France.

By the time of the gold rushes, the European powers, especially Great Britain, had already inserted themselves into the East and Southeast Asian regional economy by mapping themselves onto the diplomatic and trade routes that had long connected China and Southeast Asia. The Opium Wars and unequal treaties enabled Europeans to force trading and missionary interests directly into China. China found itself thrust into a new system of international relations based on Westphalian sovereignty, with its principles of equality of nations, territorial integrity, and noninterference. Notwithstanding these high principles of equality, the shifts in the mediums of exchange—from silver to gold in the West and from silver to opium in China—meant that China entered into the evolving global economy and international relations in a position of extreme weakness and disadvantage. The Qing court would debate for several decades whether to refuse or adapt to Western diplomatic conventions and, more broadly, to Western knowledge and modern industrial development.[18]

After the second Opium War, the Qing established its first foreign office, the Zongli Yamen. Although begun as a temporary office to address practical emergencies imposed by Western encroachments, the Zongli Yamen was a major institutional innovation and grew as a center of power among reform-minded figures within the Qing bureaucracy. The Zongli Yamen conducted diplomatic relations and treaty enforcement in the treaty ports. It also sent several official missions abroad to learn firsthand about the West.[19]

Most Qing diplomats came from China's literati class, men who had passed the imperial examination and entered the government bureaucracy, the locus of social status, wealth, and power. Huang Zunxian was one such Qing diplomat. Huang came from northern Guangdong province, the son of a first-generation scholar-official. After Huang passed the imperial examination, he was posted to the foreign service, an assignment of low status that disappointed his parents. But Huang's experience abroad enabled him to see that China had stumbled not simply into a family of nations but also into a world marked by unevenness and big-power rapacity. He observed, "Just take a look at Poland, take a look at poor India; / Who knows what disasters loom in our future?"[20]

Depending on their posting, Qing diplomats also came into contact with local Chinese communities abroad. This augured a new relationship between Chinese overseas and the Qing government, which banned emigration on pain by death upon return, a policy that was first promulgated during the Ming Dynasty. The Qing had long dismissed those who left its realm as traitorous or irrelevant. The presence of Qing consuls abroad offered Chinese emigrant merchants and laborers unprecedented contact with their home government, indeed, a direct line to the central government and, with it, the hope and expectation that it would defend them. The Zongli Yamen came to understand the travails and sufferings of Chinese emigrants, which Huang memorialized in his long poem, as one of China's foremost international humiliations, along with the unequal treaties imposed upon it by the West.

The Zongli Yamen instructed Qing diplomats to keep journals, which they submitted monthly with their personal observations and experience, including "what is real in foreign countries, and what is bluffed." These journals—many of which were published contemporaneously—

contributed to a decades-long dynamic process of Chinese thinking about China's place in the world, debates that necessarily involved fundamental questions about the nature of Chinese state and society. Few in the nineteenth century were ready or willing to abandon Confucian tenets or imperial rule, but many thinkers wrestled with how to reconcile Western science and technology with their commitments to Chinese principles. Some, like the diplomat Xue Fucheng, argued that Western inventions such as printing, the postal system, and gunpowder were actually Chinese in origin. Zhang Zhidong, a powerful viceroy, famously coined the phrase "Chinese learning for the essence and Western learning for its utility" to both promote and constrain reform. Huang Zunxian admired Western technology and administration but was initially suspicious of democratic government. His thinking evolved such that by the 1890s he became a close colleague of China's leading radical reformers, Kang Youwei and Liang Qichao, who believed equality was central to progress. Kang and Liang, who were forced into exile by the Empress Dowager Cixi in 1898, also cultivated ties with Chinese living abroad.[21]

⊹

GOLD MINING IS famously risky, with high stakes, often compared to gambling. Driven by the desire for wealth, gold seekers took great risks that were explainable only by the potential for reward. Gold fever drove daring, hard work, technological invention, and political experimentation, as well as violence against humans and against the environment. The cold calculus of business, banking, and geopolitical interests harnessed gold fever for profit and advantage. For companies and nation-states, the desire for gold led to enormous expenditures of capital for digging and operating deeper and deeper mines. But the deeper the ore, the scarcer it was and the lower its grade, such that more and more rock had to be excavated for smaller and smaller yields of the precious metal. In the Witwatersrand gold mines in South Africa, for example, in 1905 it took on average 2.3 tons of ore to yield one ounce of gold worth $20.67. Hence the relentless drive for cheap labor in order to make gold mining payable.[22]

Thus, at the turn of the twentieth century, South Africa recruited sixty thousand indentured Chinese mine laborers to work in highly capitalized and industrialized, deep underground mines. Their indenture marked an important difference in experience from that of the independent prospectors who went to North America and Australasia. But there were also broad similarities in the patterns of Chinese workers' culture and resistance. This book tracks the migration of Chinese gold seekers to California, to the Australian colony of Victoria, and to the deep mines of the Witwatersrand. It considers how their experience and reception contributed to the evolution of their identity as "Chinese," to China's identity as a nation, and to their identification in the West as a global racial danger.

SURELY THERE IS something fantastical about the scale of capital and human endeavor expended in order to obtain a single ounce of gold. Yet it is precisely the value ascribed to gold-as-money that led individuals, companies, and nations to act in fantastical ways. Just as fantastical was the near-religious belief, cultivated by economists in the early twentieth century, that gold is the ideal monetary system. Their belief rested on the theory that a tight money supply generates both economic growth and stability, and that an international monetary system based on gold promotes equilibrium in the global balances of trade—a view that was more an ideal than it ever was a reality. The gold standard belied an inherent bias that favored creditors (banks, industrialists, rich nations) over debtors (farmers and workers, consumers, poor nations). The true believers promoted deflationary policies in times of economic downturn, "harsh medicine" in the form of high interest rates, wage cuts, and unemployment. These proved especially disastrous in accelerating the Great Depression.[23]

Thus during the 1930s John Maynard Keynes rejected gold standard orthodoxy and argued for government deficit spending to expand the money supply and stimulate the economy. Keynes famously wrote, "If the Treasury were to fill old bottles with banknotes, bury them at suitable depths in disused coalmines which are then filled up to the surface with town rubbish, and leave it to private enterprise on well-tried principles of laissez-faire to dig the notes up again . . . , there need be no more unemployment." He added, "It would, indeed, be more sensible to build houses and the like; but if there are political and practical difficulties in the way of this, the above would be better than nothing."[24]

Keynes further remarked, "Just as wars have been the only form of large-scale loan expenditure which statesmen have thought justifiable, so gold-mining is the only pretext for digging holes in the ground which has recommended itself to bankers as sound finance," signaling the arbitrariness of fiscal policy and linking money to gold. Indeed, gold is like all money in that its viability is based on trust—a shared belief that an abstract instrument of exchange represents something of "real" material value. The German sociologist Georg Simmel famously referred to trust in money as "a claim upon society." And trust is built on power, in particular, the power of sovereign governments that issue money and regulate its circulation.[25]

The dynamics of the gold rushes, gold mining, and the gold monetary system of the late nineteenth century informed Chinese emigration and China's unequal position in the world economy. Chinese emigrants suffered marginalization, violence, and discrimination, but they also adapted and persevered. They struggled to claim their place in the world, in their adopted countries, and as part of China. This book considers how the Chinese diaspora in the West navigated the webs—webs at once fantastical and brutal—spun by gold and the tumult of a new world come into being, a world newly imagined, organized, and governed by the powers of race and money.

PART I

TWO GOLD MOUNTAINS

When the Chinese first crossed the ocean,
They were the same as pioneers.
They lived in straw hovels, cramped as snail shells;
For protection gradually built bamboo fences.
Dressed in tatters, they cleared mountain forests;
Wilderness and waste turned into towns and villages.
Mountains of gold towered on high,
Which men could grab with their hands left and right.
Eureka! They return with a load full of gold,
All bragging this land is paradise.
· They beckon and beg their families to come;
Legs in the rear file behind legs in the front.
Wearing short coats, they braid their queues;
Men carry bamboo rainhats; wear straw sandals.
Bartenders lead along cooks;
Some hold tailors' needles, others workmen's axes.
They clap with excitement, traveling overseas.
Everyone surnamed Wong creates confusion.

—HUANG ZUNXIAN,
"EXPULSION OF THE IMMIGRANTS"

Chapter 1

Two Gold Mountains

C alifornia gold arrived in Hong Kong at Christmas, 1848.

It came as a packet of gold dust sent by George Allan, the San Francisco agent of the Hudson's Bay Company. The envelope contained a small sample taken from a payment that Allan had made for a shipment of goods, sent from the company in Hawaii to San Francisco—$6,720—payment that was made entirely in gold dust, about 420 ounces of it (two and a half cups in volume). Allan wrote to his counterpart in Honolulu, "No one here seems to doubt for a moment the purity of the Gold Dust," but he asked that the sample be sent "forward with all dispatch" to British experts in China for evaluation.[1]

The same ship that brought gold dust to Hong Kong also carried recent issues of the *Polynesian*, a Honolulu newspaper. Hong Kong's English-language weekly, *Friend of China*, often reprinted articles from the *Polynesian* for local consumption. In the January 6 edition, Hong Kong readers learned that six thousand people had taken gold valued at $4 million out of the earth in the six months since its discovery in California. The account predicted at least twenty thousand more arrivals in the coming year and the production of $62 million of gold in 1849, one-third of the world's total product of gold and half of the world's silver product in 1846. If the numbers (just predictions, really) weren't exciting enough, the paper reported that digging for gold was not complicated. It involved simply collecting gravel in the bed of a stream and separating gold from the dirt by means of gravity and a little mercury. The arrival of the latest news and of gold itself sent a wave of excitement throughout the British colonial port. The following week the English brig *Richard and William* carried the first gold seekers from Hong Kong to California. They were not Chinese but Americans, including a former opium runner, a tavern owner, and a livery stable keeper.[2]

Chinese gold seekers were not far behind. Yuan Sheng, a business-man, left Hong Kong on May 6 on the English bark *Swallow,* along with two other passengers and a cargo of Chinese goods. Yuan Sheng was from the Zhongshan region of Guangdong province. He was born on Sanzao, one of the small islands off the coast, near Macao. Yuan had actually been to the United States before: he had traveled to New York in 1820, probably on one of the clipper ships of the early China trade, and from there he had gone to Charleston, South Carolina, where he became a merchant. While in the United States, Yuan Sheng became a Christian and a naturalized American citizen. It's not known when he returned to China, but in 1849 he decided to go back to America, this time to Califor-nia, most likely not to dig for gold but to find business opportunities in San Francisco, another kind of golden fortune. He already knew English and something of the ways of American life, notwithstanding the differ-ences between New York, South Carolina, and California.[3]

Yuan Sheng went by the Anglicized name of Norman Assing. His selection of this name is intriguing. His surname is a homophone for the Yuan Dynasty (1271–1368) that was founded by Kublai Khan, the son of Genghis Khan. He might have chosen *Norman* after the medieval Euro-peans, a contemporary analogue of the Yuan. The Normans and Mongols were formidable conquering forces of their time. *Sheng*, his given name, means "birth"; *Assing* is a rendering of "Ah-Sing," the familiar form of address of his name in Cantonese. *Yuan Sheng* means "born of the Yuan"; *Norman Assing* suggests "born of the Normans." His choice was a clever point of pride even if it remained opaque to his American acquaintances.[4]

An English-speaking merchant, Yuan Sheng was one of the few Chi-nese headed for California who were named in the ship's passenger manifest. We are not certain of those who ventured before him. Only seven Chinese arrived in San Francisco in 1848. When Yuan Sheng arrived in July 1849, there were barely fifty Chinese in California. Euro-Americans writing about exciting polyglot scenes on the streets of San Francisco in 1849 invariably commented on the Chinese they encountered, both high-cultured men in flowing silk robes and miners carrying bamboo poles strung with tools, straw hats, and gigantic boots.[5]

The first large group of Chinese to arrive in 1849 came under con-tract to an enterprising English merchant in Shanghai. That summer the Englishman contracted a Chinese firm, Tseang Sing (*xiang sheng*, or victory), which hired a ship and a number of Chinese mechanics and laborers, perhaps fifty or sixty men. Each man signed a printed bilin-gual contract, stating that he, "of [his] own free will, will put to sea . . . to proceed to *Ka-la-fo-ne-a*." The Englishman pledged to find employment for the men upon arrival; Tseang Sing advanced each man $125 passage money, which was to be paid back from future wages.[6]

The group arrived in San Francisco in mid-October. They traveled east to Stockton and down the San Joaquin River, whose many tributaries descending from the Sierra Nevada were already buzzing with activity. The company chose a spot on Woods Creek, south of the Stanislaus River, some fifty miles from Stockton. They set up camp on a high, wooded grade above the creek, near a group of Mexicans from Sonora, who called their camp Salvado. Not knowing anything about gold digging, the English-Chinese company hired a Sonoran to teach and supervise the crew. Other Chinese arrived around the same time in groups large and small, especially in Calaveras and Tuolumne counties. Soon there were five hundred Chinese in California, with miners making up two-thirds of the total. The Chinese dubbed "Ka-la-fo-ne-a" Jinshan (Gam Saam in Cantonese), or Gold Mountain (Figure 1).[7]

WE DO NOT usually think of the California gold rush as a Pacific-oriented event. But in its beginnings, before it became "national" (that is, Ameri-can) and "international" (that is, involving Europeans), it was very much a Pacific affair. John Sutter, at whose sawmill on the American River gold was discovered in January 1848, had arrived in Alta California in 1839 by way of Fort Vancouver, Honolulu, and Sitka, having attached himself to cargo clippers chartered by the Hudson's Bay and Russian-American companies. He obtained a land grant of 48,000 acres from the Mexican government, in exchange for which he nationalized as a Mexican citizen. He built a fort and started a small colony of settlers, named Helvetia for his native Switzerland, using indigenous and native Hawaiian labor, both willing and coerced. Sutter hired John Marshall, a veteran of the recent U.S.-Mexico war, to build a water-powered sawmill on the American River. Though Marshall claimed he was alone when he pulled a gold nugget out of the millrace, other accounts credited a worker named Indian Jim.[8]

As news spread of gold at Sutter's mill, people flocked to the rivers and streams of the Sierra Nevada. For nearly a year the gold rush was an exciting and energetic endeavor, albeit a local and regional one. The first gold diggers came from the existing population of about 165,000 people in Alta California, of which 150,000 were indigenous, with the balance more or less evenly divided between Californios, the descendants of the first Spanish settlers, and white Americans and Europeans. The U.S.-Mexico war had barely concluded at the time of the gold rush; the Treaty of Guadalupe Hidalgo was signed in February 1848, ceding California to the United States. Hundreds of American soldiers and sailors remained stationed in California under U.S. military command, but there was little to stop them from going AWOL for gold.[9]

By summer, Mexicans experienced in gold and silver mining were trekking along long-established routes from Sonora into Alta California. Then came gold seekers from Oregon, Hawaii, and Chile, arriving by trade routes along the Pacific coast that had been established in the 1830s. In the first year of the gold rush, half the people mining for gold in California were native American Indians, especially Maidu and Miwok in the north. Many Indians—perhaps half of those on the goldfields—worked in the placers on their own account, sometimes in family groups, and traded gold with whites for tools and blankets. But many others worked for Californios and white Euro-Americans, like Sutter, at low wages or for subsistence, replicating the system of Indian servitude of the Spanish-mission ranches.[10]

the traditional U.S.-China trade to Boston and New York via the Indian and Atlantic Oceans, had already begun to establish transpacific routes in the 1830s and '40s. They linked China to Hawaii and then to California, which was less a final destination than a transshipment point for goods headed to Acapulco, Valparaiso, or, via the Horn, New York. The gold rush represented a new opportunity for merchants in Hong Kong—both Euro-Americans and Chinese—to export diverse goods to California.[15]

Hong Kong was a British colony and a free port—that is, imported goods from one place could be unloaded and reloaded for export to another place without payment of customs duty—and as such it quickly became the premier Asian entrepôt for both goods and emigrants headed for the gold mountains. For the year 1849 alone, twenty-three vessels exported nearly five thousand tons of goods from Hong Kong to San Francisco, including sugar, rice, and tea; beer, coffee, cigars, and chocolate; hats and clothing; furniture and canvas; tools and implements; timber logs and planks, window frames, bricks, and marble slabs. In 1849 Chinese imported and erected some 75 to 100 buildings, modular designs of premade frames and constructed with interlocking camphor wood panels. Most of these were built in San Francisco—including John Frémont's home—but some were erected in the interior. One such "Chinese house" built in Double Springs, Calaveras County, was used as the county courthouse, then as the post office, and later as a chicken coop. In the early 1850s, Hong Kong merchants shipped thousands of blocks of granite, along with Chinese workers, for building the homes and businesses of San Francisco's new elites.[16]

The Chinese population of Hong Kong itself grew as nearly eight thousand people arrived in 1850, with many intending to produce goods for the California market, engage in the shipping trade, or otherwise work in the booming port. Chinese commercial firms in Hong Kong, although not as large or powerful as the venerable British house Jardine Matheson, or the American firm Russell and Company, nevertheless became important players in the California trade and in the economy of the diaspora. They entered the trade as shipowners and as cargo and passenger brokers and shipped "fancy Chinese goods" (silks, shawls, lacquerware, fans) that were popular among the forty-niners as exotic souvenirs, and rice, foodstuffs, herbal medicines, clothing, and opium for the growing overseas population of Chinese gold miners.[17]

THE *POLYNESIAN* also circulated to Sydney, Australia, via Pacific whaling ships, bringing news of California gold to the antipodes. Between April 1849 and May 1850, some eleven thousand people left Australia for California. Mostly they came from Sydney, a combination of fortune seekers and former convicts. White Americans on the goldfields disliked the Australians, considering them to be criminals of rough and immoral character, claim jumpers and "hardened thieves and robbers." The stereotype contained an element of truth in the predations of a San Francisco street gang known as the Sydney Ducks, so called for the convicts' bowed legs and peculiar gait that resulted from years of wearing leg irons. But most Australian gold seekers were not former convicts; the California census of 1852 showed that Sydney men were more likely to be married with children, working, and noncriminals than Americans.[18]

One such Australian gold seeker in California was Edward Hammond Hargraves, an adventurous spirit and a bit of a huckster. Hargraves, born in England, traveled in 1831 to Australia, where he tried his hand at gathering bêche-de-mer (sea cucumber) in Torres Strait, farming in Bathurst and Wollongong, and running a store on the Manning River. He married but left his wife and sold everything he owned to go to California in 1849. Hargraves did not strike it rich in California and returned to Australia two years later. But he was convinced by similarities in the topography of California and New South Wales that he would find gold in Australia. His return proved to be propitious because the colonial governor, Sir Charles FitzRoy, had just offered a ten-thousand-pound reward to the first person to come forward with payable gold.[19]

Colonists in New South Wales had noted the presence of gold since at least the 1840s, but authorities had not encouraged prospecting. In 1844 Governor FitzRoy quashed news of gold discoveries in the Blue Mountains west of Sydney, believing it would inflame rebellion and disorder among the large population of convicts and former convicts; in 1849 Charles LaTrobe, the superintendent of Port Phillip district, broke up a minirush near Melbourne on grounds of trespass on crown lands. But news of California gold convinced colonial leaders that Australia's future prosperity might lie in gold, not least to spur "a healthy emigration" of miners and workers to diminish the influence of convicts and paupers. FitzRoy appointed a geological surveyor in 1850 and announced his offer of a prize.[20]

Hargraves set out to find gold. "I knew I was in gold country for 70 miles," he wrote, before finding water to wash the earth at Auroya Goyong, near Bathurst, in February 1851. He enlisted three young men to help him, teaching them how to use a pan and build a rocker, skills he had learned in California. Hargraves claimed the reward (cutting out his three assistants), renamed the spot Ophir, and publicized his findings broadly. Within a few months there were several hundred people at the diggings, farmers and shepherds from the countryside and clerks and mechanics from Sydney.[21]

The Australian gold rush was on. Observers remarked that Sydney virtually emptied of people as carpenters dropped their tools, merchants shuttered their shops, and house servants fled their masters' homes. Not a few people from Port Phillip (Melbourne) trekked north up to Bathurst, but prospecting spread westward in earnest. In July 1851 the Port Phillip district of New South Wales separated and founded the new colony of Victoria. A month later gold seekers hit a rich strike north of Geelong. By mid-October upward of ten thousand people made their way to the central midlands of Victoria; many diggers were taking out an ounce of gold a day (£3). Most important, perhaps, Hargraves had introduced the "California rocker" to Australia, which enabled more efficient washing than tin pots and dishes. Over the next decade 170,000 colonial settlers (nearly half the entire nonnative population) moved to the goldfields, and another 573,000 gold seekers arrived from abroad, mainly from the British Isles, as well as continental Europe, California, and China. Chinese called Victoria Xinjinshan, or New Gold Mountain, and renamed California Jiujinshan, Old Gold Mountain. To this day Chinese call the city of San Francisco Jiujinshan (Figure 2).[22]

Melbourne in the fall of 1852 was a scene of merciless price gouging, cheating, theft, and chaos. With hotels and lodging houses bursting at the seams, many new arrivals slept on the wharf or in makeshift shelters in the scrub between beach and town. It took several months for the colonial government to establish sites for shanty "immigrants' homes" and a tent colony, the latter supporting seven thousand people paying five shillings a week for the privilege of staking a tent on swampy ground before it was shut down in 1853.

They made the trek to the diggings mostly on foot, as few could afford the cost of a horse and dray, across dirt tracks that were either knee deep in mud or dust, depending on the season. Historian Geoffrey Serle described it: "The first view of an established goldfield was fascinating—holes like gravel-pits and tents everywhere, an anthill swarming with frenzied activity, a steady roar as in an immense factory from hundreds of rocking cradles." The scene was not unlike California in the days of '49. But whereas California barely had a government in the early days of the rush, Victoria's colonial authorities urgently sent commissioners, police, and magistrates to the goldfields. They governed their districts with a heavy hand, issuing licenses and enforcing compliance; registering claims; guarding and exporting gold to Melbourne (from which the government took a cut); settling disputes; and keeping general order.[23]

As in California, the gold rush in Victoria boosted commerce and trade. As British colonials, Australians received most imports from England, but there was also an established intra-Asia trade between Australia, India, and China. In the late eighteenth and early nineteenth centuries, convict transport ships returned to England via China, where they picked up tea, or via Bombay, where they loaded cotton for the East India Company. In the early nineteenth century, colonial elites imported furniture and silks from Bengal and Guangzhou. During the gold rush, English exports to Victoria grew spectacularly, rising from £3 million in value in 1852 to £7 million in 1853. By 1857 Australia accounted for one-seventh of all British exports. Sailing traffic from Hong Kong and Xiamen to Victoria also increased, especially as Chinese gold seekers and merchants made their way to the new gold mountain. During the 1850s Australia became the fourth-largest importer of Chinese tea, consumed not just by Chinese emigrants but by British colonials as well. Americans joined the fray, shipping speculative cargoes from both New York and California. In 1853 George Francis Train described thirty to forty ships leaving New York bound for Melbourne, where upon arrival they found the bay crowded with six to seven hundred ships, a "complete forest of masts." Australian exports also dramatically increased, from £9 million in 1851 to £29 million in 1852 and nearly £45 million in 1857.[24]

BOTH VICTORIA AND CALIFORNIA bore the characteristic features of settler-colonial societies, located on the frontiers of metropolitan centers, claimed and settled with the ambition of territorial expansion, and achieved through native dispossession. The precontact indigenous population of Australia was estimated to be as high as 750,000, in over five hundred language groups. In Victoria, by 1850, the Aboriginal population declined by 90 percent, the result of death from European diseases (especially smallpox), violence, land encroachment and dispossession by pastoralists, and removal to reserves that the British called, without irony, "protectorates," although the project was given up for its failure to contain and assimilate.[25]

During the early years of the gold rush, Aboriginal peoples, especially Djadjawurrung and Wathawrrung, interacted with Europeans as guides, as provisioners of game, fish, and bark (for building huts), and in cultural exchanges. They also prospected for gold in an "independent and intermittent style," often quite successfully. If some Europeans benefited from Aboriginal knowledge and commerce, others disdained, distrusted, and violently attacked them. More generally, the arrival of some several hundred thousand nonindigenous migrants in Central Victoria in the span of a decade constituted nothing less than a massive dispossession: gold seekers overran Aboriginal lands, dug out mineral quarries, destroyed hunting and fishing grounds, and cut down forests. R. L. Milne, a contemporary critic, wrote that "the aboriginal inhabitants, with a title from Heaven . . . are plundered, dispossessed and slain. . . . Tell me not that the greater part of you are innocent, merely because ye have done the act with your own hands. Accessors, by social connexion, and participation of the spoil are . . . murderers as well as the actual perpetrators of the deed" (Figure 3).[26]

Later, in the 1870s, when gold mining opened in northern Queensland,

European and Chinese prospectors would confront larger numbers of indigenous people in the interior. Aboriginal people in the bush resisted European encroachment by burning villages, stealing livestock, and spearing settlers, but their spears were ultimately no match for the Europeans' rifles. Colonial patrols conducting official frontier "dispersals" and private settler violence committed more than sixty thousand Aboriginal killings in the latter half of the nineteenth century, a staggering index of the violence that enabled European settlement. Some Europeans worried over whether the Christian imperative to "multiply and replenish" the earth gave them the "moral right to take by forcible possession a Country inhabited by savages." But most were certain that "it is a question of forced occupation or none."[27]

In California, native peoples worked on the goldfields during the first year of the rush. But American gold seekers who came down from Oregon soon targeted them. With gold fever exacerbating racial suspicion, they attacked Indians on the diggings, raping women and killing men. Indians fought back against the Oregonians and then the forty-niners, who were soon overrunning traditional hunting and fishing grounds. Violence pervaded the mountains. During 1849 and 1850 Augustin Hale, who prospected north of Sacramento, filled his diary with entries about contact and skirmishes with Indians. At Beaver Valley, Hale wrote, "the Indians have their Sentinels out on the most commanding points of the high mountains & notify each other by shouts and signal fires of the white man's approach." He described passing "several Indian Ranches [villages] in flames, set by the preceding parties whose mules had been stolen" and whites who were "attacked in the night by a large number of Indians who fired some Guns and many Arrows & then rushed [in] with clubs." A party of men came down from the mountains after three months reporting they "found no Gold that would pay for working & fighting the Indians."[28]

Settlers' violence was relentless, and by 1850, the U.S. Army and then state and local militias joined them, committing even larger massacres. Miwok, Maidu, Pomo, Wappo, and other indigenous peoples retreated from the diggings to the mountains and then to sites still higher in the mountains, where they barely survived. State and federal lawmakers also refused to make treaties with California's Indians, which would have recognized a small portion of Indian lands as sovereign. As Peter Burnett, first governor of the California territory, promised, there would be nothing short of a complete "war of extermination . . . until the Indian race becomes extinct."[29]

Increasingly, whites both in the Australian colonies and in California believed that the extermination of indigenous peoples was a necessary condition for white settlement, by which they meant the replacement of native sovereignties with Euro-American possession and the reorganization of land and economic relations according to the laws of private property and the market. Victoria and California were also based on the principle of free labor. Victoria outlawed convict transportation and contract labor from its founding in 1851, when it split from New South Wales.[30]

During the first couple years of the California rush, unfree labor dotted the goldfields—enslaved African Americans brought by white southerners, California Indians held in servitude by Californios and Euro-Americans, *peones* brought by Chilean and Sonoran mining companies, and like those working at Woods Creek, Chinese brought under contract.[31]

But contracts were virtually impossible to enforce on the goldfields because people could simply walk away from their masters to seek their own fortunes in the hills. An English ship captain wrote in 1849, "Fifteen coolies I brought [to San Francisco] from China, and who were under a bond for two years with the party who engaged them, were no sooner ashore than they resisted their contract, and each turned his separate way." Ramón Gil Navarro, who headed a company from Chile, lost half his workers and even his manager within days of their arrival in San Francisco. Desertion was prevalent, and investors soon gave up the practice of contract labor.[32]

Desertion was also common among sailors, who in the nineteenth century worked in another mode of unfree labor. As early as March 1848, San Francisco merchants were complaining that desertions by ships crews threatened the promise of prosperity. The problem only got worse. The Hudson's Bay Company agent in San Francisco had trouble finding sailors, even at a promised wage of $200 for a short run to Honolulu. J. D. Borthwick, a Scottish observer, noted hundreds of ships lying idle in the bay in 1851, for want of sailing crews. Likewise, sailors in Port Phillip Bay at Melbourne left their ships in droves. In 1852 only three out of thirty-five foreign ships could muster a full crew. Some captains put their entire crew in jail until they were ready to sail out; others led their men to the diggings for a few weeks, where arduous conditions and doubtful returns cured most of them of gold fever.[33]

Victoria and California thus had many similarities as settler-colonial societies. In both locations the gold rushes accelerated native disposses-sion and mass in-migration, produced sudden wealth as well as financial loss, and introduced capitalist mining technologies. But they also dif-fered in important respects. Australia had already had decades of colonial governance, first over the penal colonies and then over a mixed popu-lation of convicts, former convicts, and free immigrants. The growing free population ranged from wealthy pastoralists, who set up enormous sheep runs and developed the wool trade, to the Irish poor, who came as assisted migrants, including many women for employment as household servants. Colonial Australia had a stronger presence of state authority in the 1850s than did California, which had just come into American pos-session in 1848. Victoria was nested in the British Empire's Asian orbit and was subject to the empire's laws, whereas the United States, while in many ways behaving like an empire, was a sovereign republic. Both gold rushes took place on land owned by the government, but only in Victo-ria did the government actually control the goldfields by means of police enforcement of myriad regulations, from taxation to sanitation. These differences would have important bearing on the development of the two societies, including Chinese-white race relations.

⁂

THE VAST MAJORITY OF Chinese gold diggers in California and Victoria hailed not from Shanghai but from southern China, especially the Siyi, or four counties, that lay on the western side of the Pearl River delta in Guang-dong province. Remarkably, the vast majority came from just one county, Xinning. Xinning was a poor place, owing to its rocky soil and hilly ter-rain, its cycles of drought and flood, and its relative isolation from the mar-ket. The land produced only enough rice to feed its people for half the year, so farmers grew sweet potatoes and peanuts on the hillsides to supplement their crops. Instability from British economic penetration and local political violence made conditions worse. Families sent sons and brothers to nearby cities for seasonal work as laborers, peddlers, and factory workers. No one knows who were the first Chinese from Xinning to venture to California, but they had probably already migrated from their home villages to Guangzhou or its environs. What is clear is that they established a classic pattern of chain migration to California and Victoria and, soon afterward, to the goldfields of Canada and New Zealand. Gold seekers from the Siyi founded the Chinese diaspora in North America and Australasia.[34]

They were not the first Chinese to emigrate beyond the seas. People from China's southeastern coastal regions had been trading and settling in the *nanyang* (southern seas, or Southeast Asia), from Thailand to Champa and Java, since at least the thirteenth century of the Common Era. But in the nineteenth century, mass Chinese emigration reached far beyond the *nanyang*, as greater numbers left in search of work abroad owing to difficult conditions at home. Southern China suffered from cycles of drought and flood, in addition to economic displacements caused by Western market intrusions and violent upheavals during the long Taiping Rebellion (1850–64), a messianic peasant movement that sought to overthrow the Qing. Two new streams of long-distance Chinese migration in the mid-nineteenth century arose from two different types of Euro-American colonialism: one involved indentured labor to plantation colonies in the Caribbean and South America, and the other comprised voluntary emigration to the frontier regions of Anglo-American settler colonies in North America and Australasia.[35]

Nearly a quarter-million indentured Chinese workers shipped to plantations in British Guyana, the British West Indies, Cuba, and Peru between the 1830s and '70s. Most of them worked on Cuban sugar fields alongside enslaved Africans and on the guano islands off the coast of Peru. Collectively they made up the so-called coolie trade, the notorious traffic of bound labor that snared the most destitute and dispossessed people of Asia for labor in New World colonies. The Chinese called the coolie trade in these unfortunate souls *mai zhuzai,* "selling piglets."[36]

The second stream of Chinese emigration started with the global rush for gold to the Anglo-American settler colonies of North America and Australasia, about 325,000 between 1850 and 1900. They went first to California, and then in the mid-1850s, as California became inhospitable to them, they went to the antipodes in increasing numbers. Of 15,000 Chinese people departing from Hong Kong in 1853, barely 3,000 were bound for California while more than 10,000 went to Victoria.[37]

Chinese who went to the two gold mountains were neither as poor nor as desperate as plantation indentures. They were farmers, rural workers, artisans, mechanics, and merchants who, in many respects, were just like other people from around the world who came seeking gold. Contemporary observers in Hong Kong routinely noted that unlike the contracted labor sent to the plantation colonies, Chinese emigration to California and Australia was "uniformly and actually free emigration." Also like Euro-American gold seekers, the Chinese were overwhelmingly men. The few women on the goldfields, whether American, Chilean, French, or Chinese, were wives of merchants, entertainers, barmaids, or sex workers. In time the sex ratio among Euro-Americans improved. But the Chinese population remained overwhelmingly male, in part because custom dictated that a wife should remain in the household of her husband's parents.[38]

MOST CHINESE GOLD SEEKERS paid for their own passage with family funds or borrowed from clan or district associations. Lee Chew recalled that his father gave him $100, half of which he spent on ship's passage to San Francisco. Lee's father was a middling farmer with ten acres near Guangzhou, who grew rice, sweet potatoes, peas, sugarcane, and bananas. Lee worked on his father's land until he was sixteen years old, when he became awestruck by the riches of a returned emigrant from California. With their fathers' support, Lee and five other boys from the village traveled together to Hong Kong and then to San Francisco.[39]

Families of lesser means pooled resources to send one or two young men. Those without much land or savings borrowed money. Loans and contracts were common throughout Qing China, including in rural areas, which were often connected to local and regional market networks. Especially in the first years of the gold rush, credit terms were high. In 1856 the Huang family of Xilong, Guangdong province, guaranteed a loan of 18 liang (about £20) from the Xilong Association to send their son, Huang Guanyi, to Gold Mountain, at an annual interest rate of 50 percent. If the loan was not paid back by the specified date, additional interest would accrue at the rate of 150 percent. The contract also gave the lenders the right to seize remittances Huang sent to his family in the event that debt payments were late or not paid. These steep terms were slightly mitigated by a clause that "unforeseen circumstance during his oceanic passage, or at Gold Mountain," would void the contract. The high cost of the loan suggests both the presence of a demand market and the emigrants' expectations that they would strike it rich on Gold Mountain.⁴⁰

That expectation was fueled by letters or return visits home by the first wave of emigrants, newspaper reports, and advertising. The British emigration officer in Hong Kong wrote in 1853, "Upwards of 800 Chinese have returned from California, . . . They appeared all of them to have plenty of money and stated their intention to returning to California. . . . The return of Chinese under such favorable circumstances must naturally stimulate emigration to that quarter." The first Chinese-language newspaper in Hong Kong, *Xia'er guanzhen* (China Serial, a missionary publication), carried articles on emigration as early as 1853 and practical information for people venturing abroad, as well as thoughtful commentaries about the spread of Chinese to different parts of the world. Emigration was further stimulated by shipping companies, which circulated advertisements boasting of the riches of the gold mountains. An emigration industry grew, operating between towns and villages in Guangdong, Hong Kong, and California and Australia, handling credit for passenger tickets as well as conveying letters and remittances from abroad back to the villages.⁴¹

THE GOLD RUSHES BROUGHT large numbers of Chinese and Euro-Americans into contact with each other on an unprecedented scale, far surpassing the limited experience of European colonial enclaves in Chinese port cities or the occasional Chinese visitors to the United States and England in the late eighteenth and early nineteenth centuries. The San Francisco Customs Office noted 325 arrivals from China in 1849 and 450 in 1850; in 1850 Chinese comprised only one percent of the California mining population. But 2,700 Chinese arrived in 1851 and 20,000 in 1852. Chinese comprised about 10 percent of the total population of California by the late 1850s, and upward of 25 percent in the mining districts. A similar pattern exists in Australia. By 1859 there were at 40,000 to 50,000 Chinese in Victoria, roughly 20 to 25 percent of the mining population. Historians of the Australian rush have remarked that many Britons had never "mixed so freely with foreigners, especially the Chinese."[42]

The English-Chinese-Sonoran mining party did not stay long at Woods Creek. Their efforts were reportedly successful, so it may have been competitive jealousy that prompted a group of whites to chase them off their claim. Violence and threats of violence were pervasive on the diggings, part of a hypercompetitive environment in which miners of all ethnic backgrounds quarreled and fought over claims. White Americans were especially aggressive toward foreigners, regardless of their national origin.

The Chinese gold diggers at Woods Creek relocated to the other side of the hillside, to a small mining encampment called Camp Washington. Soon other Chinese found their way there, although whites tended to pass the area by because the diggings were "dry"—that is, dirt had to be hauled to a water source in order to be washed. The site became known as Chinee, Chinee Diggings, and finally, Chinese Camp. The latter name became official when a post office for Chinese Camp, California, opened in the general store in April 1854.

Chapter 2

On the Diggings

By 1856 a thousand Chinese lived in Chinese Camp, with hundreds more on the placer flats to the north. At its peak, Chinese Camp and its surrounding area supported a population of five thousand Chinese. Chinese Camp grew into a thriving town because it was located where the main stage road from Stockton turned east toward Yosemite and hence was a good place for travelers to stop for supplies, rest, and information. A sizable white business section served both Chinese and whites, including the Wells Fargo office, a blacksmith, and an assayer, but Chinese comprised the majority of the population. Chinese businesses also served whites, especially washhouses and cafés. Ah Chi ran an eating house on Washington Street in a shack with a stove of creek stones covered by a sheet of iron. According to legend, he served forty-niners wild pigeon pie, grilled bear steak, and apple pie.[1]

Chinese shops and dwellings, simple wooden houses, crowded along rows concentrated on the west side of town. The vast majority of Chinese living in and around Chinese Camp were gold miners, but the town boasted a diverse population befitting a commercial and social hub: merchants, laundrymen, and prostitutes, as well as tailors, herbalists, bakers, butchers, gambling hall operators, and a musician. A Chinese vegetable garden and a fishpond lay at the edge of town, which meant that Chinese had access to fresh vegetables and fish, both especially prized elements of their diet, and even turtles, a delicacy. Two merchants, Ah Sam and Fin Lung, each held $500 in real estate and $2,000 in personal property. By the middle 1860s, Chinese merchant houses were reportedly earning from $50,000 to $100,000 a year. Chinese Camp had four native-place associations, called *huiguan* (literally, "meeting hall") and three "temples" that were large structures with luxurious gold-leaf carvings and images. The large halls may have been Buddhist or mixed-religion temples, or the meeting hall of the Zhigongdang (Chee Kong Tong, Universal Justice League), a secret brotherhood society with roots in the Tiandihui (Heaven and Earth Society) in southern China. The town also boasted several gambling halls, featuring fan-tan, the popular game of chance. The residents of Chinese Camp strived to make their surroundings beautiful. They planted persimmon trees, which bore fruit that they loved. At the lunar new year they planted narcissus bulbs, an early spring bloomer. And they planted "trees of heaven," a pungent variety of sumac native to China that was valued for the medicinal uses of its bark and leaves. Some said the tall shade trees reminded the Chinese of home.[2]

There were few women in Chinese Camp—seamstresses, prostitutes, and miners' and merchants' wives; only a few families were established. White Americans called a woman who raised fowl "Duck Mary" and the garden farmer "China Lena." A rare surviving marriage certificate shows that Ah Sam, age twenty-five, and Yo Sup, age twenty, wed on January 24, 1860, before J. Collingwedge, justice of the peace for Chinese Camp. Who was this young couple? The records yield little. Nine miners named Ah Sam are listed in the census records of Tuolumne County in 1860, and one woman is listed as "Ah Yow" (Yo Sup means "*née* Yo" in Siyi dialect) in Chinese Camp. She was one of seven women living at a saloon kept by Ah Sow. But they do not show up in later census records of Tuolumne or elsewhere in California. Perhaps Ah Sam took his wife, along with his gold earnings, back to China.[3]

Only a few other towns in the California interior had comparable concentrations of Chinese. Marysville, the gateway to the northern Sierra goldfields, included a large Chinese quarter along First Street, just above the Yuba River. Marysville was known among California Chinese as Sam Fow (Sanbu), or number-three city, after San Francisco (Dai Fow [Dabu], the big city) and Sacramento (Yi Fow [Erbu], number-two city). Marysville Chinese offered shops and services for Chinese in the vicinity. They built a temple in 1854 named Bok Kai Mui (*beiximiao*), or "temple of the north side of the stream," after its location on the Yuba River. It survives to the present day. Originally a Daoist temple, it evolved to include Buddhist and Confucian deities. The most popular god worshipped at the temple was Xuan Wu (mysterious warrior), the Taoist god of the elements. Xuan Wu controlled water, the gold digger's best friend.[4]

In 1860 Chinese in Oroville, north of Sacramento, numbered nearly one thousand, nearly 40 percent of the town's population. Half were miners or laborers employed in the construction of water flumes and ditches in the area, the latter perhaps men who had poor luck as prospectors. The other half comprised the usual occupations: merchants, butchers, herbalists, prostitutes, carpenters. The presence of a jeweler and a bookseller indicate wealth and literacy among the Chinese.[5]

Most Chinese gold seekers lived not in these large towns but in small settlements near their claims. In the early days, these were often just collections of tents. J. D. Borthwick, the Scottish traveler, observed Chinese miners on Weaver's Creek living in "a dozen or so small tents and brush houses," and, at a gulch near Angels Camp—the goldfields town later made famous by Bret Harte and Mark Twain—"about a hundred Chinese had here pitched their tents on a rocky eminence by the side of their diggings." Along the north fork of the Calaveras River, some two hundred Chinese worked alongside white Americans and a few French and Mexican miners but lived separately in an encampment that whites called Chinese Town.[6]

Chinese living on the diggings walked to the nearest town for provisions and amusements, either from white storekeepers or, if there was one, a Chinese merchant. One did not have to walk to a large town like Chinese Camp or Oroville; dozens of small goldfield towns in California had one or two Chinese merchants or a small Chinese quarter, a block or so long, with a few amenities and residents. The Chinese near Angels Camp had only a short distance to go to town, where there was a small Chinese section. Those working along the Calaveras River would have purchased basic supplies from Daniel Latimer, a rancher who ran a general store close to the diggings. Or they might have walked a short distance to Petersburg, the nearest town, which was infamously known as "Greasertown" for its large Mexican and Chilean population. There they would have found a greater variety of goods, a meal in a restaurant, or entertainment at a saloon. On occasion they would have walked farther, another five miles or so, to San Andreas, where there were a few Chinese merchants.[7]

The first Chinese stores were simple and rough, built with canvas, a stone chimney, and a dirt floor. These rude structures typified all construction in the early days of the rush, including stores and even "inns." Gradually they became replaced with "folk houses," simple one- or two-room structures made out of vertical boards with a gable roof and dirt floor. Chinese stores were slow to improve beyond this point, even as white businesses evolved with masonry fronts and iron fire doors and shutters. The Sun Sun Wo store in Coulterville, Mariposa County, is a rare sturdy construction. Built in 1851 with adobe walls and a dirt roof, it survived the fire of 1899 that razed the town. The store operated continually from 1851 until 1926; the structure remains standing today.[8]

Both Chinese and white merchants sold miners a range of goods—sugar, whiskey, and candles; canvas and cotton; rope, nails, sledges, and dynamite; ham, canned oysters, salmon, and eggs, the latter an expensive luxury in the hills. Americans often remarked on Chinese miners' willingness to pay good prices for quality food. A butcher in the southern mines commented, "I have sold in one day as high as fourteen hogs, averaging seventy-five pounds each. They will pay as high as a dollar a pound for nice dried sausage. They are very fond of fowls, and buy a great many. . . . I have sold a fat chicken at three dollars and a half, for a feast." Chinese merchants sold general merchandise and provisions as well as Chinese foodstuffs (black beans, salted fish, lichee), herbal medicines, opium, green tea, and ritual items used in ancestor and burial ceremonies. Both Chinese and white storekeepers sold on credit, settling accounts once a month without interest, the usual method of business across the goldfields. Chinese paid for their goods in cash, in gold dust, against wages, or in exchange for services, like washing clothes.[9]

✢

IN THESE WAYS Chinese carved out their own commercial niches while also participating in the larger goldfield economy. The same was true for the actual work of mining for gold. During the first years of the gold rushes, gold seekers sought their treasure in creeks and streams, where gold could be washed and sifted from river dirt, a type of mining called alluvial or placer mining. Chinese called it *xie jin* or "gold scrap" mining. The methods of alluvial mining were common to all gold seekers, with techniques that originated in different cultures but became adapted for universal use. Panning, for example, has its origins in the *batea*, the basket-woven bowl that dates to Spanish alluvial mining in Mesoamerica in the seventeenth century. Sonorans taught Europeans and Americans in California how to use it. To pan for gold, a person stood in a creek and washed dirt from the creekbed in a pan, swishing it around to separate gold from sand. Because gold is heavier than anything else found in the river beds, it remains after everything else has washed off.[10]

The next level of technology was the rocker, or cradle, a simple wooden device with a slanted, riffled board. Dirt was washed down the board, leaving gold in the riffles. A single person could operate a rocker, but it was more efficient when several partners divided tasks—hauling dirt, hauling water, cleaning gold from the ridges. Chinese mining on river placers favored the rocker, which was cheap, easy to build, and importantly for the Chinese, portable, in the event that they were chased from their claims (Figure 4).[11]

Edward Hargraves, the Australian who went to California and returned to claim the first discovery of alluvial gold in New South Wales, also brought back with him to Australia knowledge of the rocker. But even as they adopted it, Australians needed other means to break up the soil of Victoria's gullies, which was thick and heavy with clay. The puddling machine used human or horse power to pull a harrow around a circular trough filled with water, breaking the clay into clumps. The gold-bearing sludge could then be washed for gold. Chinese miners in

Victoria invested in puddling machines when they could, often pooling resources to purchase a horse.[12]

While Chinese used the same methods as Euro-Americans, they also brought and adapted water-management technologies from Guangdong agriculture, many of which were taken up and used by others. Chinese built sluices and dams and introduced the chain pump, an unwieldly contraption that used foot pedals, waterwheels, and gravity to pump and divert water. Borthwick considered the chain pump needlessly elaborate and inefficient, although it impressed others: "watch the miners on the river or study their water wheels and pumps from those of our celestial friends which John turns with his feet by a most industrious treadmill kind of operation to the most scientific arrangement." Borthwick admired the work of a Chinese company at Mississippi Bar, which built a two-hundred-yard-long wing-dam—a barrier that extends partly across a river, controlling the direction and speed of water—ingenuously applying mechanical power to handle the immense pine tree logs. Small Chinese companies in Victoria favored sluicing, a long wooden trough built down a hillside that operated on the same principle as the rocker. The *Bendigo Advertiser* reported in December 1878 that Chinese sluicing companies were working in three shifts, around the clock, using 3 million gallons of water per week.[13]

These various arrangements indicate that gold mining was most commonly taken up not by individuals working on their own, as the stereotype of the rugged, manly prospector suggests, but in partnerships and other group arrangements. Panning knee deep in creek water was cold, backbreaking, and time-consuming. Far better to work in groups. In California and Victoria placer mining, cooperative mining was the norm among all ethnic groups. Miners quickly learned that working in small groups enabled them to work more efficiently, to take turns at the more arduous tasks, and to share costs and rewards; hence the Australian historian Geoffrey Serle's observation that "in its early years the [Victorian gold] industry was almost exclusively worked by thousands of tiny cooperative groups." American forty-niners often traveled from home with partners and companies, and although many of them famously broke up upon arrival, they invariably found new partners on the diggings.[14]

Among Chinese gold seekers, partners were often close relatives or from the same village or clan lineage, indicating kinship as the medium of trust. Notwithstanding trust, Chinese miners sometimes formalized their partnerships by jointly registering their claims. In Calaveras County, California, for example, some two hundred Chinese worked along the north fork of the Calaveras River on its bars and in the riverbed. A rare surviving register of mining claims for Lower Log Cabin district includes sixty-one claims of Chinese miners from 1854 to 1857. Of these, parties of two or three accounted for twenty-seven claims (44 percent). In Tuolumne County, Chinese placer mining partners fared about as well as (or as poorly as) white partners working similar claims—earning about $75 per man per month on claims valued at $500 to $600.[15]

Victorian gold district registers of mining claims show the same patterns. For example, Ah Ping and Low Ying registered their claim of one hundred yards of Bendigo Creek, "commencing 50 yds from White Hills cemetery," in 1868. A map of the Golden Point section of Forest Creek in the Castlemaine district shows individual mining claims along the creek, with Chinese and Europeans working in close proximity to one another. The map shows claims belonging to Molloy, Lo Cheung, Murphy, Ah Cheung, A'Kut, and Burns arrayed cheek by jowl in the gully.[16]

American mining census reports reference Chinese mining companies with names such as the John China Placer Mining Company and the Hong Kong China Wing Dam Company. They are described as either owned or leased, with ten to twenty workers working with sluice boxes and races, wing dams, and waterwheels. In these companies a local merchant bought or leased the claim, furnished the equipment, and engaged the miners. The companies did not pay wages but operated on a share basis, in which the merchant-investor took a portion of the output and the miners divided the rest. Merchants also supplied the miners' provisions, which was convenient but may also have made the miners dependent upon them.[17]

Another common form of ownership was the egalitarian cooperative. These typically involved five to ten men working smaller claims with low-tech equipment, such as rockers. They also worked on the share system, but on the principle of equal shares for both profits and expenses. Local claims registers in El Dorado and Yuba counties also show that Chinese diggers often claimed rights by preemption. That is, they were the first nonnatives to lay claim to their sites, paying no money but registering ownership as squatters, which was the general custom among miners to take possession of unclaimed property, whether fresh or abandoned. The pattern is significant because it is belies the conventional understanding that Chinese worked only on depleted claims that whites abandoned or sold to them.[18]

The mining cooperatives practiced a strong ethos of egalitarianism. Ah Fock, one of seven partners mining in Sierra County, California, insisted that his group had no boss; he described himself as "merely the treasurer, the man who took charge of the [gold] dust as it come out. I don't claim any charge of the working there." In one story that circulated widely among Chinese, possibly apocryphal, a group chiseled a forty-pound nugget into small pieces so each man could have his share.[19]

The same cooperative arrangements existed in the Australian colonies. According to Rev. William Young's unofficial 1858 census of the Chinese population in the Victoria gold districts, more than half of the 2,200 Chinese miners in Bendigo worked in small companies. Three hundred men worked in companies with puddling machines, and around nine hundred worked in small companies—likely cooperatives—washing tailings (discarded rock debris, silt, and dirt from worked-over claims). Small groups also banded together to achieve economies of scale. According to Serle, the "most typical form" of work for Chinese was "paddocking," in which "gangs of one hundred or more lift and wash the soil of gullies from end to end, working either cooperatively or as companies of employees" (Figure 5).[20]

In Victoria claims registers, individually owned claims with substantial acreage or equipment indicate small companies, such as Ah Ling's sluicing claim of three acres at Old Race Course Spring, near Daylesford. Egalitarian cooperatives are evidenced in small claims with four to eight holders of equal shares. A cooperative located at Portuguese Flat near the town of Creswick comprised eight "mates," including at least two cousins. The miners slept in separate tents but ate breakfast together and divided chores such as cooking and collecting firewood. They held equal shares in the claim, each worth three to four pounds. One member, Ah

Yung, kept the group's gold and books and paid out weekly earnings of about thirty shillings to the members.[21]

Both companies and cooperatives were similar to mining organizations found in China and Southeast Asia. In southern China placer tin-mine operators sometimes hired local farmers during the slack season, but there were also small companies of full-time miners, often comprising landless and socially marginal types, who worked for shares under a manager-investor. These companies had minimal internal hierarchy and generous share division, reflecting the difficulty in holding labor. The practice of share division is also similar to the tradition of partnership arrangements from late Qing-era business organization.[22]

The cooperatives in California and Victoria bear a canny resemblance to the famous Chinese kongsi (company) of the West Kalimantan (West Borneo) gold mines of the eighteenth and early nineteenth centuries. These began as small, egalitarian share partnerships, as their names suggest—*shiwufen* (fifteen shares), *xinbafen* (new eight shares). As the mining industry developed, some of these cooperatives joined to create federations; a few became extremely powerful and acted as though they were sovereign states. The power of the West Kalimantan kongsi derived from the position of Chinese in between the native population and the Dutch colonizers. Those conditions, of course, did not exist in the United States or Australia, so Chinese cooperatives remained primitive. But their ethos of internal egalitarianism and solidarity carried over. Significantly, all these formations—mining companies in southern China, cooperatives in West Borneo, and their counterparts in California and Australia—were associated with the Tiandihui, the largest sworn-brotherhood network in southern China, which spread overseas as exiles fled the repressive aftermath of the Taiping Rebellion in the mid-nineteenth century.[23]

CHINESE MINERS ALSO WORKED for wages from white employers. Chinese from Guangdong province would not have been unfamiliar with wage labor. The Pearl River delta region had been substantially commercialized since at least the seventeenth century, and textile and metallurgic industries included work for wages or cash. In California's southern mines,

Chinese worked "shoulder to shoulder" with Cornish miners in John C. Frémont's mines at Mariposa. U.S. mining commissioner Rossiter W. Raymond reported "whole shifts of brawny pig tail wearers" working in deep mines in Mariposa, Merced, and Tuolumne counties from the late 1850s, in careers that ran as long as ten to fifteen years. By 1870, Chinese miners were earning between thirty-nine and fifty dollars per month, nearly the pay rate of white miners. Chinese also worked as unskilled laborers for sluicing companies and in the quartz mining mills, feeding the giant stamping machines that crushed the tons of rock dug up from the earth to release the gold from the veins within.[24]

A more extensive practice was the hiring of Chinese by hydraulic mining companies, which used high-pressure water hoses to blast the side of mountains to mine auriferous gravel from the ancient riverbeds deep within; and by water companies, which delivered water to the hydraulic mining systems from mountain lakes and reservoirs. These were California's first major capital-intensive mining endeavors, which sought to eliminate the unpredictability of rainfall and to mine gold in large quantities. The scale of these operations was staggering. By the late 1860s, California water companies had erected six thousand miles of flumes and water ditches at a capital cost of $200 million, delivering billions of cubic yards of water per year to mining companies. Chinese worked for wages in construction and in hydraulic mining operations. The Mariposa and Merced South Fork Canal hired as many as two thousand Chinese for ditch construction in 1857. California's largest hydraulic mining operation, the North Bloomfield Mining and Gravel Company in Nevada County, employed eight hundred Chinese and three hundred whites in its ditches. Beginning in the late 1860s, Chinese merchant-investors, who could not afford the initial capital cost of a hydraulic operation, bought or leased operations from white owners and ran them with technical expertise and good profit (Figures 6 and 7).[25]

Hydraulic mining was controversial because it dumped millions of tons of water, earth, and chemical waste into mountain streams and rivers. Sediment and silt clogged the rivers, causing floods that destroyed thousands of acres of farmland in the Sacramento Valley. Finally, in 1884 the federal court in San Francisco banned hydraulic mining, the first environmental court ruling in the United States. Judge Lorenzo Sawyer declared hydraulic mining was "a public and private nuisance" and forbade its operation in areas tributary to navigable streams and rivers. While hydraulic mining mostly ceased in California after Sawyer's decision, Chinese continued with the method. In some cases they flouted the law, and in other cases they conformed to it by constructing timber and rush dams to keep tailings from entering water streams.[26]

Chinese also performed work for whites for cash on an individual basis. For example, in Coloma, Hiram Hurlbet, his son Duane, and two other partners hired two or three Chinese, paying them $52.50 for twenty-one days of work. After paying the Chinese and accounting for supplies and board, each partner was left with $12 profit, not more than what they paid the Chinese laborers. Hiring out could also be reciprocal. H. B. Lansing, a young American miner working at San Andreas and Mokelumne Hill, sometimes hired Chinese (as well as German and French) miners to work on his claim, at times alongside him and at other times when he just wanted a break. Lansing also hired himself out, in one instance to prospect a claim for a group of Chinese and on other occasions for construction work on dams and flumes. Lansing's experience suggests that independent miners of all ethnic groups worked as day labor and for odd jobs according to need.[27]

In Victoria in the late 1860s and '70s, Chinese also found employment with quartz mining companies. A few of them were actually owned by Chinese, former miners who invested in quartz operations. William Young's 1868 census reported approximately seven hundred Chinese doing wage work for whites in the Ovens District. Smaller numbers were employed at European claims in Ballarat. Although some Chinese worked underground, more worked inside the mills, feeding and running the stamping machines. Others practiced "tributing"—not waged labor but a contract with a mining company to treat and stack tailings. Small companies or cooperatives likely made these contracts. For example, Ah Wah's company in Bendigo contracted to work fifty yards of creekbed between Short and Myrtle streets, to cart out tailings and wash them in a puddling machine nearby. According to a historian, tailings work was not "scrabbling around on rubble, but one stage in a complex and sophisticated set of processes" to which Chinese applied capital and expertise. Chinese also paid for the right to rewash tailings for gold—a low-yield proposition but remunerative with patient work.[28]

Chinese mining practices, then, were flexible and diverse and in many ways similar to the economic organization of Euro-American mining labor. As Serle noted, cooperation was common among all national and ethnic groups. White miners celebrated it as the quintessence of fraternity among free men but failed to recognize the practice among Chinese. But the Chinese cooperative practices endured. Built upon solidarities of native place and kinship, they might be considered a kind of refuge from—even resistance to—capitalist wage relations. Europeans and Americans did not have analogous cultural resources to sustain independent mining. Thus, when the quartz mining companies came to dominate the scene, Euro-Americans traded their autonomy for the relative security of a job—or quit mining altogether.

The diversity of Chinese mining practices also highlights the problem of thinking about labor in rigidly opposing categories of "free" and "unfree," common nineteenth-century distinctions that demarcated independent and wage-earning labor from slavery and servitude. The point is not to simply move Chinese miners from one column to the other. At a certain level, of course, Chinese miners were not "unfree." They were not held as chattels, unremunerated for their labor, or prohibited from quitting or moving—the normative conditions of bound labor. Miners who worked solo, with partners, or in egalitarian cooperatives had considerable if not complete autonomy, although the economic rewards of independent mining grew increasingly meager as the placers diminished. Working on proportional shares and for wages, whether for skilled underground work or in construction gangs, involved elements of both coercion and volition.[29]

⁂

CHINESE WHO DID WELL ENOUGH at mining in California often went into trading or bought a small store. Some moved to a city, to San Francisco, Sacramento, or Marysville, where life was easier than on the diggings. But many merchants remained on the goldfields, hiring others to work their claims while they ran a store or branched out into other lines of business, perhaps a restaurant or a washhouse. For example, Wong Kee started as a placer miner in California and later moved to American Canyon, Nevada. He was unusual in that he had immigrated with his wife, suggesting an intention to stay and build a life in the United States. At American Canyon he subleased his claims to other Chinese and hired others to build a ditch to bring water down from the mountain, which he sold by the bucket to miners to use with their rockers. He eventually owned all seven miles of water ditches in the area, which enabled full-scale placer mining of American Canyon.[30]

Men like Wong Kee became prosperous and influential among local Chinese miners and often served as representatives or liaisons with local white businessmen. But the most powerful Chinese merchants were located in the big cities, especially San Francisco. Yuan Sheng (Norman Assing), one of the first Chinese to come to San Francisco, opened a restaurant in San Francisco on Commercial Street, the Macao Wosung, and an eponymous trading company, Yuan Sheng Hao—two mainstays of commerce that nourished and supplied Chinese diasporic communities. Chan Lock (Chen Le), another early arrival, was also known by the name of his firm, Chy Lung (Ji Long), which in time was the largest and most famous Chinese business in town. In 1852 Chy Lung could import as much as $10,000 in Chinese goods at a time, sell it all in a few days, and return to China for another shipment. Chy Lung was a true transpacific merchant, whose San Francisco–based firm would establish branches in Hong Kong, Shanghai, and Yokohama. Some merchants purchased their own ships or became shipping agents. By 1852 there were some twenty stores kept by Chinese in San Francisco's budding Chinese quarter. The merchants owned their lots and erected their own buildings (Figure 8).[31]

Men like Yuan Sheng and Chy Lung were products of the gold rush, and San Francisco was the site of their wealth and power: from there they pivoted to China, where they bought, and to the interior, where they sold. Their social influence was situated in two networks: first, their connections to the American political and business leaders of the city (and by extension, to the state), and more important, their position at the top of the organization of the *huiguan*.

Chinese in San Francisco understood from the earliest days of their arrival that they needed to establish cordial relationships with Americans, not just with individuals but with the power structure. The first thing they needed was an adviser, an American who could serve as a culture broker. On November 19, 1849, a meeting of three hundred Chinese at the Canton Restaurant on Jackson Street resolved that, "strangers as we are, in a strange land, unacquainted with the language and customs of this, our adopted country, to have some recognized counselor and advisor . . . in the event of any unforseen [sic] difficulties arising, wherein we should be at a loss as to what course of action might be necessary to pursue."[32]

They chose as their adviser Selim E. Woodworth, a New Yorker and a former naval officer who in the 1830s and '40s had traveled the world from Madagascar to the Mediterranean to the Pacific and had served in Monterey, California, during the Mexican War. Woodworth was elected to the legislature of territorial government in 1849 and was partner in a merchant-commission business. We don't know how the Chinese came to know him, but it may have been through business dealings in the China trade. Perhaps Woodworth's abolitionist background encouraged him to befriend San Francisco's most visible racial minority.[33]

A few days later the Chinese held a celebration to honor their new counselor with speeches, toasts, and singing. Mayor John W. Geary, former port official Edward Harrison, and other notables also attended. Newspaper accounts of these gatherings do not mention Yuan Sheng, but then he was fairly new to the city, having just arrived a month earlier. Nevertheless he quickly established a presence as a leader and culture broker, no doubt because he spoke English and understood American politics and social norms. In October 1850 he led a contingent of fifty Chinese in the parade celebrating California's admission to the Union. "Arrayed in their richest stuffs," reported the *Daily Alta California*, they carried a banner of "crimson satin, on which were some Chinese characters and the inscription 'China Boys.'"[34]

More central to Yuan Sheng's social standing was his position as a founding member and the first president of the Yeong Wo Association (Yanghe Huiguan), formed in 1852. Yeong Wo represented emigrants from present-day Zhongshan county, east of the lower Pearl River and its entrance to the sea. Although Siyi people comprised the largest group from Guangdong province in California, many early emigrants came from the Zhongshan region, which was close to Macao, Canton, and Hong Kong. By the early 1860s, Yeong Wo boasted over twenty thousand members in California.[35]

The *huiguan* were Chinese versions of the mutual aid organizations that virtually all immigrant groups formed on the basis of a common regional origin, known among eastern Europeans as *Landsmannschaften* and among Mexicans as *mutualistas*. In China *huiguan* dated at least to the Ming Dynasty, when traders and sojourners in big cities formed hostels and guilds where they could commune among people from their home districts, speaking their own dialect. Chinese formed native-place *huiguan* wherever they emigrated abroad, including North America and Australasia.[36]

Chinese in America translated *huiguan* as "company," not in the narrow sense of a business but more generally as a corporate entity. The first *huiguan* to organize in California were the Siyi (Sze Yup) Company and the Canton Company or Sanyi (Sam Yup) Huiguan, both in 1851. The Siyi people were the most numerous, but the Sanyi Huiguan's concentration of cosmopolitan merchants from Guangzhou and its three surrounding counties gave it disproportionate influence. In the 1882 the California *huiguan* formed a coordinating body called Zhonghua Huiguan, formally translated as Chinese Consolidated Benevolent Association but familiarly known as the Six Chinese Companies. In Victoria, Siyi and Sanyi people also formed *huiguan*, as well as associations for people from Xiamen in Fujian province (Figure 9).[37]

Huiguan served as organizations of both solidarity and social control. A new immigrant arriving at San Francisco or Melbourne would find a representative from his home district at the dock, who would take him to the *huiguan*'s headquarters in the Chinese quarter. There he would find a place to sleep, a hot meal, information about mining and other job prospects, and where he might find his cousins and village friends. The individual merchants who financed credit-tickets that covered emigrants' passage collected debt payments through *huiguan*. The associations adjudicated disputes among members, cared for members who were sick or indigent, buried those unlucky enough to die in America, and at a later date, sent their bones back home. Some *huiguan* provided translators and paid legal fees for members who ran afoul of the law.

Huiguan leaders represented the community to white society in public discourse, in formal meetings, and in bringing civil rights lawsuits. The larger and wealthier *huiguan* bought land and erected buildings in San Francisco and Melbourne for their headquarters. Their offices boasted full-time officers and staff, including a secretary, a treasurer, clerks, a translator, cooks, servants, and altar-keepers. They often had representatives in the goldfield towns wherever there was a concentration of Chinese.[38]

Merchants traditionally ranked at the bottom of the Confucian social hierarchy, below farmers, workers, and soldiers. But through their leadership roles in emigrant communities, Chinese merchants found prestige and power. Their social status would filter back to China as well. But Euro-Americans imagined that *huiguan* were despotic organizations that brokered slave labor and exercised total control over their members. White Americans and Australians who were actually familiar with the Chinese community understood that *huiguan* were mutual aid associations similar to those organized by other immigrant groups. Chinese themselves considered their membership in *huiguan* not as enslavement but as integral to the networks of trust forged through native-place and clan lineage. They also considered the repayment of debts a matter of honor, and most Chinese cleared their debts fairly quickly, in less than a year in Australia.[39]

Nevertheless, merchant leaders disciplined ordinary workers through *huiguan*. In California they ensured collection of debt by issuing "debt clearance tickets" to emigrants returning to China, which they were required to show to a ship officer before departure. This was not a legal requirement but a custom that shipping officials agreed to in order to maintain good relations with the merchants. Chinese sometimes bristled at the dues they had to pay to remain in good standing or at the harsh disciplinary measures meted out by *huiguan* leaders in the settlement of disputes. Some accused *huiguan* leaders of corruption, signaling their use as vehicles of social power for the Chinese merchant elite. Europeans focused on and exaggerated these aspects of *huiguan* and failed to see their similarity to the social organizations of other immigrant groups.

Their inclination to caricature *huiguan* as despotic was part of a more general Western view that Chinese civilization was backward.[40]

Distinct from *huiguan* were secret brotherhood societies, which were fictive kinship groups that organized without regard to clan lineage or native place. Throughout the diaspora as in China, they embraced socially marginal men who were orphaned, estranged from their families, or otherwise cut off from the villages of their birth. In China they were internally egalitarian and sources of mutual support, but they could also be predatory, engaging in thievery among the general population. In the mid-nineteenth century, during the Taiping Rebellion, the largest society in southern China, Tiandihui (Heaven and Earth Society), assumed an anti-Manchu political cast and spread across the diaspora as militants fled political repression. The far-flung, decentralized network was known in Southeast Asia, North America, and Australasia by various names: Zhigongdang, Hongmen (Hungmen, Vast Family), or Yixing (Yee Hing, Righteous Prosperity). They were all based on the same secret book of oaths, codes, verse, and rituals. The book itself was the medium by which the network spread because possession of the book authorized one to establish a chapter. Secret societies served similar functions as *huiguan,* providing mutual aid and burial rites for their members.[41]

They also adjudicated conflicts between members. Hearings tended to concern relatively minor cases involving disputes, such as theft. There were rules for calling witnesses and for all parties to "cut a rooster and swear to clarify their innocence," as dictated by the Bendigo Yixing. The same rules applied in California. At times, cases were handled long distance. For example, Ah Tre (probably of San Francisco) sent a telegram to Ah Yu Dick in Sierra City: "Ah Chee send a dispatch to me saying that you snatched his money Give it all back to him and not make any trouble answer." For more serious matters, however, such as property disputes or in cases involving a claim against a *huiguan* leader, Chinese resorted to the civil courts.[42]

In California the Zhigongdang and other "tongs" controlled the vice trades (gambling, opium, prostitution). But in Australia the Yixing strived for respectability and competed directly with the Sanyi and Siyi Huiguans to claim leadership of the community. The Yixing arguably became the most prominent Chinese organization in Australia, describing itself to whites as a Masonic society. In the 1870s a British observer described *huiguan* as mere "tea-shops," having lost their benevolent character, while the Yixing continued to exercise "wide and wise influence over all classes of society."[43]

The Yixing acquired legendary status among Australian Chinese. According to one story, Huang Deci, the Southern Conquering King of the Taiping Rebellion, fled Qing repression with his comrades in small boats and arrived on the northern coast of Australia, at present-day Darwin, then walked to the goldfields. It's an unlikely tale, since even if they had successfully navigated the South China Sea, they would have had to walk over two thousand miles through tropical jungle and outback desert to get from Darwin to the Victoria goldfields. But the myth informed a proud Chinese Australian identity well into the twentieth century. Writing in 1933, Vivian Chow credited the Yixing with sending "great expeditions" of Chinese, a "marshalling of the entire Chinese population in order to make the offensive irresistible." These fanciful descriptions exaggerated a core truth that the Yixing and its leading merchant members in Australia facilitated the migration of the first cohorts of Chinese gold seekers.[44]

In addition to *huiguan* and brotherhood societies, Chinese living abroad also established institutions and networks to facilitate the sending of remittances. These networks also built upon clan and native-place ties, but they were distinctive in form and function. In the early years of the gold rushes, Chinese gold miners sent their families a portion of their earnings by entrusting their gold dust with a relative or village acquaintance who was returning home after having made his "pile" or for a temporary visit, or perhaps with a trusted merchant on a business run.[45]

The Australian colonies imposed a gold-export duty, but not all gold remittance was reported. For example, in 1857, seventeen Chinese miners boarded the *Ethereal* in Sydney, bound for Hong Kong, carrying £9,480 in gold dust on behalf of 370 Chinese. One of the returning emigrants, Sang Hyo, carried a pouch with 175 ounces of gold, divided into small packages and wrapped in "large strips of linen," for himself and seventy-one other people, mostly from his home village. Others wrapped their gold dust in handkerchiefs, which they hid under their clothes.[46]

During an eighteen-month period at the high point of the gold rush, Victoria customs reported that Chinese sent nearly 216,000 ounces of gold through the Port of Melbourne to Hong Kong, worth about £830,000 (over $4 million). The data do not distinguish between individual remittances and merchant transactions, but Melbourne merchant Lowe Kong Meng estimated that during this time, Chinese in Victoria sent £8 to £30 a year to their families in China, where the cost of living was £10 a year (about 30 taels). By the late 1870s, however, customs houses estimated that Chinese remitted £50,000 a year, or barely more than one pound per person, reflecting the demise of gold mining but also the probability that gold continued to be carried home unreported. During the 1870s Chinese laborers in California typically sent thirty dollars a year in remittances, the equivalent of 18 to 25 taels of silver, enough to buy a year's worth of rice and other necessities for a small family. If only a quarter of the 148,000 Chinese living in California in 1878 sent that amount, the total would have been about a million dollars a year.[47]

Remittances supported a transnational culture that sustained emigrant family ties. Sending monies home fulfilled familial obligations and raised the standard of living and social status of emigrants' families in towns and villages. Remittances built houses for families as well as buildings and infrastructure for communities—schoolhouses, libraries, hospitals, and roads, even railroads. The people of Kaiping, Guangdong, lined the roads leading into their county with fortified watchtowers to repulse bandits who were attracted to the wealth of remittance families.[48]

The volume of overseas remittances spawned a large industry, with Hong Kong serving as the central node connecting Chinese sojourners abroad to their home villages in southern China. In Hong Kong, *jinshanzhuang*, "gold mountain firms," originally established to facilitate the overseas Chinese import-export businesses, added the service of directing correspondence and remittance. Emigrants could send their *yinxin*, "silver letters," with the firms' agents, who made regular trips to Hong Kong. There, gold was converted to silver and sent to the villages in China by hired runners, called variously "feet," "water guests," and "horses patrolling the city." Remittance agencies profited from fees (which were fairly modest) by operating on volume, and by manipulating exchange rates. Some firms also sold transoceanic passage on credit and facilitated labor recruitment. By the early twentieth century, emigrants could wire money directly to China through banks and post offices, although some agencies persisted.[49]

⚜

LOWE KONG MENG (Liu Guangming) was a leader of the Yixing and the most powerful Chinese man in Victoria. Unlike Chy Lung and other Chinese merchants in San Francisco, whose trade ran bilaterally between California and Hong Kong, Lowe Kong Meng's interests nested in broader overlapping networks of Chinese and British commerce in Asia. Lowe was born to a Cantonese merchant on Penang Island, in the British Straits Settlements (Malaysia), which made him a British subject. The Lowe family had been doing business there for over a hundred years, having settled there before the arrival of the British in the late eighteenth century. By the time Lowe Kong Meng came of age, his family was deeply embedded in colonial connections between China, Southeast Asia, and the Indian Ocean. As a boy, Lowe went to the Penang Free School, the first English school in Southeast Asia, and studied English, French, and Malay. When he was in his midteens, he went to Mauritius—the former French island colony in the Indian Ocean that was taken by the British in 1810—to extend the family's business connections. In 1853 Lowe traveled from Mauritius to Victoria. After a few months of unsuccessful prospecting, he went to Calcutta and brought back to Melbourne a shipment of goods. He founded Kong Meng and Co., an import firm; soon he'd own a half-dozen shipping vessels (Figure 10).[50]

Lowe imported mainly from Calcutta and Penang/Singapore in wholesale trade in rice, tea, opium, sugar, and other foodstuffs. A single shipment of his in 1857 was worth over ten thousand pounds. The Melbourne *Argus* said he traded on a "gigantic scale." Although Lowe said he sold only to Chinese because his volume was "not largely [*sic*] enough to sell to Europeans," his investments in the Australian Chinese diaspora were extensive and broader than trade in rice and tea. He was a major agent of credit-tickets, the main way Chinese financed their passage to Australia. Some emigrants sailed in Lowe's ships from Hong Kong along with his merchandise. Like other labor agents, Lowe engaged headmen to act as group leaders for migrants on the sea voyage and to the goldfields, to supervise their work, and to collect debt payments. Headmen usually came from the same districts of the Siyi and commanded respect owing to local reputation, age, or knowledge of English. Although there are no surviving records of Lowe's business in credit-tickets, it was undoubtedly substantial because Chinese rarely defaulted on their debts. Lowe was both a leading member of the Yixing and of the Sanyi Huiguan. He underwrote the construction of the Sanyi headquarters building on Little Bourke Street in Melbourne's Chinese district.[51]

Finally, Lowe Kong Meng was an investor and founding director of at least a half-dozen companies, including a distillery and several gold and silver mining companies. Kong Meng Gold Mining Company, a deep lead operation south of Marysborough, was reputedly one of the most successful mines in the region. Lowe also engaged in finance, having shares in insurance companies and banks; in some cases he was a co-founder with prominent British Australian capitalists. For example, he was a founding shareholder and board member in the Commercial Bank of Australia in 1866, a position that signaled the bank's intention to attract Chinese depositors. The bank issued bilingual notes, which facilitated their use by Chinese on the goldfields. Eventually Lowe's business network extended to mining and mercantile ventures in New South Wales, Queensland, the Northern Territory, and New Zealand.[52]

Lowe's business dealings reveal an important distinction in the opportunities Chinese faced in California and Victoria. Although California banks, notably Wells Fargo and Company, also did business with Chinese, and although Chinese merchants sat on San Francisco's Merchant Exchange, no American corporation welcomed Chinese capital. Such a relationship between American and Chinese capitalists was unthinkable. In contrast, Lowe Kong Meng was part of a Southeast Asian Chinese elite that was confident in their identity of belonging within both the British Empire and the Chinese diaspora. They believed their status as British subjects entitled them to equal political and economic rights (even if these were not always forthcoming); although they were formally subjects of the Qing empire, their Chinese identity was more cultural than political.

Like the biggest Chinese merchants in San Francisco, Lowe Kong

Meng did not live on the goldfields. He lived with his wife, Annie, an English Australian woman, and their family in the wealthy white suburbs of Melbourne—another marker of the social possibilities for wealthy Chinese in Australia that were nearly impossible to attain in California. Of course, Kong Meng Company, Lowe's principal business, was located in Melbourne's Chinese district on Little Bourke Street. Another prominent Chinese merchant in Melbourne, Louis Ah Mouy (Lei Yamei), was also a co-founder and director of the Australian Commercial Bank. Unlike his colleague Lowe Kong Meng, Louis Ah Mouy had come to Australia directly from the Siyi in the early 1850s. He started as a carpenter in Melbourne and then went to the diggings. He succeeded at gold mining, which enabled him to become a merchant. Louis brokered credit-tickets, built a rice mill in Melbourne, and owned several gold mining companies in Victoria (some in partnership with Lowe Kong Meng), in addition to his bank interest. And like Lowe, Louis married a white woman, a young Irish woman named Mary Rogers, with whom he had two children (Figure 11).[53]

By 1856 Little Bourke Street boasted some twenty to thirty merchant businesses and lodging houses and a population of about two hundred, although this number included many transients, people who came down from the diggings and were waiting for an outbound ship to China. As in California, most Chinese miners lived on or near the diggings at some distance from the main towns. In 1857, for example, only 360 Chinese lived in the municipality of Ballarat, but there were 7,532 in the district. The exception was the town of Bendigo (Sandhurst), where nearly two thousand Chinese, two-thirds of the district's Chinese population, resided.[54] The vast majority of the Bendigo's Chinese population were gold miners. Others worked as shopkeepers, doctors, tailors, and barbers; butchers, market-gardeners, and fish-hawkers; carpenters and blacksmiths; booksellers and scribes; and prostitutes. A good number also worked for Europeans as seasonal harvesters and sheep shearers.[55]

Chinese across the goldfields tended to live in villages with members of their home counties. At Bendigo, Siyi people, who predominated the overall population, concentrated at Ironbark, and Sanyi people at Jackass Flat. Xiamen people lived at Little Bendigo and at Golden Point, Ballarat.

At Beechworth, the Siyi and Hakka kept separate villages. A number of Victoria Chinese villages were quite large, some comprising over a thousand residents, with tents organized along a grid of lanes and with their own shops and entertainments, not just gambling houses but also theatrical companies and, reportedly, even a circus (Figures 12–14).[56]

Many villages began as "protectorates," segregated encampments mandated by the colonial government in 1853 ostensibly to reduce racial conflict between Europeans and Chinese. Ultimately the protectorates proved a failure, as many Chinese simply refused to live in them and even those who did often refused to pay the protection tax levied against them. But some of the protection villages continued as thriving communities. Ironbark Village, outside Bendigo, for example, boasted shops, cookhouses, butchers, bars, and gambling rooms in wooden buildings that lined well-swept central streets, as well as a large public meeting hall built by the Yixing. A British visitor in 1877 described scrolls hung along the entryway that read "Light is rendered by sun and moon; Life reproduced by earth and heaven." The central hall was used for meetings and ritual exercises. A chamber on one side of the main hall featured an altar for paying respect to ancestors; a room on the other side served as a kind of mortuary, where the bodies of the deceased were washed and prepared for burial.[57]

Over 750 Chinese lived in Creswick, about ten miles north of Ballarat, making up 16 percent of the town's population in the late 1850s. Most Chinese lived at Black Lead village, just outside the town. The village consisted entirely of wooden houses, described in official rate books as "tenements." The *Argus* described Black Lead as "large, miserable [and] ricketty [sic]." Like Ironbark, Black Lead included dwellings, workshops, stores, saloons, and lodging houses. In addition to miners, the village population included blacksmiths, cooks, a goldsmith, a barber, a tailor, doctors, chemists, and herbalists; opium dealers; and a fruit and fish dealer. Numerous market gardens surrounded the village. If the village appeared "miserable" to observers, it was not for residents' lack of effort to improve its condition. They repeatedly called upon the town of Creswick—to which they paid property taxes—to build and repair roads and footpaths, clear contaminated water and sludge that came from nearby mines, and extend the town's water supply to the village, though to little avail.[58]

Creswick's most famous Chinese denizen was Ping Que (Mei Zhen), who arrived in Victoria in 1854 from Hong Kong at the age of seventeen. Ping Que joined the rush to Creswick, where the discovery of rich alluvial fields that year attracted twenty thousand miners, including some four thousand Chinese. He was a successful prospector, who turned his profits into larger mining operations. He became a tributer, who leased land from a European company and hired Chinese to work the claim. By the 1870s he was managing Chinese working both on alluvial flats and in drift mines for the Key Gold Mining Company. He had also acquired property and tenements in Black Lead, paid eighteen shillings a year in taxes, and was naturalized in 1873. But Ping Que made his real fortune when he left Victoria for the Northern Territory in 1875, where he was one of the region's first gold mining entrepreneurs. Working initially as a tributer and then on his own account, he pioneered gold mining in the Pine Creek region (which continues to produce gold to this day) with hundreds of Chinese workers whom he brought from Guangdong and Singapore on two-year contracts. As his interests grew, he had European co-investors and Chinese mining supervisors, on whom he increasingly relied while he focused his attention on running a store on the Union Reef and a hotel in Pine Creek. He was a respected civic figure in the early days of Port Darwin.[59]

Although Chinese diggers in Victoria suffered from discriminatory taxes and violence from whites, the colonial government enforced the same basic rights and duties upon both Chinese and European gold diggers, which afforded Chinese some basic protections and privileges. Chinese were subject to purchase the same miner's right (license); they entered their claims in the same goldfield registries; they had access to the magistrate's court. They enjoyed the same entitlement to land adjoining their claims, where they could build a house and plant a provision garden. Men like Ping Que and James Ni Gan owned real property and entered their names in the ratepayers rolls. Many Chinese on the goldfields became market gardeners, not only because they came from farming backgrounds but because they had easier access to land.[60] Ping Que was exceptionally successful in large part because he was one of the first to open gold mining on the frontiers of the Northern Territory. Without precise data it is not possible to compare Chinese mining capitalists in Australia to those in North America, but the nature and scale of independent Chinese mining operations in Victoria (to say nothing of the Northern Territory) suggest that Chinese enjoyed more favorable legal and social conditions in the Australian colonies than they did in California.

Nor did Victoria prohibit marriage between Chinese and whites. However, only a few gold miners married European women, indicating the general practice of diasporic Chinese men to keep a conjugal household in China. Young's 1868 census of Chinese on the goldfields counted just fifty-six Chinese-white marriages, with 130 children. Those who married European women tended to have come as single young men who then decided, at some point, to settle on the new gold mountain. Many started as gold diggers but became, disproportionately, merchants, ratepayers, and mine company owners. Though numerically small, they formed an important social stratum that bridged Chinese and white communities. They were not necessarily the big merchants of Melbourne like Lowe Keng Meng and Louis Ah Mouy. More typically they were like James Ni Gan, who was born in Guangzhou and came to Bendigo, probably in the 1850s or early '60s, when he was in his twenties. He married Mary Ann Mooney of Dundee and then was baptized and naturalized. He was a butcher at Ironbark and with his wife ran the Emu Point Hotel; in the late 1870s he employed Chinese in a sluicing operation at White Hills. He also organized the Chinese community's participation in Bendigo's annual Easter Fair. He is among the few Chinese in the Victoria mining claims registers with white partners. Ping Que was cut from similar cloth, but he did not take a wife in Australia. He returned to China for extended stays in the 1870s and perhaps married a Chinese woman while there, which made him more typical of male emigrants. Regardless, not having a European wife in Victoria freed him to relocate to the Northern Territory.[61]

AUSTRALIAN WHITE SOCIETY respected Chinese merchants who married white women because their unions bespoke a European bourgeois sensibility about proper gender and family relations. Most of these Chinese also became Christians, a nod to their interest in assimilation that further cemented their standing in white society. In California, however, antimiscegenation laws forbade mixed-race marriages. Marriage among Chinese Christians might have been considered respectable, but this was touchy because the wife was typically a former prostitute, who had been rescued by, or run away to, the Christian missionaries. Although whites praised these conversions and marriages, the stigma of the woman's former status could never be fully erased. The merchants, who were the most likely to bring wives with them from China, also did not pass the test for respectability because their wives usually had bound feet and rarely left the home, their domesticity mistaken for enslavement. In goldfield towns like Oroville and Chinese Camp, the first generation of Chinese couples also lacked respectability because the wives worked, often alongside their husbands, in a tailoring shop or a market garden. These women violated another middle-class norm: that married women should not work outside the home. They sometimes earned a grudging respect for being rugged and hardworking, but these were obvious masculine traits and also bended gender norms.[62]

White Americans also feminized Chinese men as they came to dominate occupations such as cooking, laundering, and domestic service when white women were scarce on the diggings and domestic jobs perhaps seemed less risky for Chinese than gold mining. Men of all ethnic groups outnumbered women: European and Latin American women on the goldfields were barmaids, entertainers, and prostitutes. Occasionally they were merchants' wives. Lucy Bryson was a rare case of a woman who went west to start a new life after a divorce; she supported herself by baking pies for the miners. But if a homosocial culture pervaded the diggings, Euro-American men viewed their own condition to be a predicament of the rush, exceptional and temporary, even if they worried that doing their own cooking and washing damaged their masculinity. To the Chinese, however, they ascribed a normative "queerness," not in terms of same-sex relations but in the sense that they were a kind of "third sex," neither male nor female. White men actually had no understanding of real Chinese people; they imagined and projected these stereotypes onto Chinese in order to stiffen their own resolve to be manly in the social upheavals of the gold rush era.[63]

Euro-Americans had at best a dim understanding of Chinese family structure and gender relations. Many Western observers (including sympathetic ones) considered the Confucian patrilineal family and its central imperative of filial piety (ancestor worship) to be central to Chinese feudal despotism, especially its oppression of women. Just as Westerners imagined Chinese men who were sold into the coolie trade as "slaves," they also considered the practices of concubinage and of selling daughters into servitude as "slavery." They imagined coolies and women to be the chief victims of "oriental despotism."

In fact, Chinese family relations harbored a tension between property interest and bonds of affection. Within status constraints, both men and women in subordinate positions—second and third sons, wives and concubines—acted in their own interests. During the late Qing Dynasty, the patriarchal family came under various pressures, including demographic imbalance (shortage of women), extreme poverty among the peasantry (leading some families to sell daughters into servitude or prostitution), and among elites, contact with Western missionaries (including schooling for girls). Gender relations were not as rigid and static as Confucian stereotypes suggested.[64]

Still, the institution of the family remained central to Chinese society; hence the strong ties of clan lineage, anchored in native place, which provided support and solidarity to emigrants seeking gold abroad. Hence also the attraction of fictive kin associations, like the secret brotherhood societies. During the late Qing, fictive kinship and other all-male living and working arrangements, using survival strategies like pooled resources, solidarity, and sexual relations, enabled marginalized men to make their way in a society that otherwise gave short shrift to untethered individuals. Although there is no evidence of the existence or prevalence of same-sex relations among Chinese gold diggers and members of secret brotherhoods in California and Australia, such relationships are entirely possible. Regardless, the brotherhoods were bulwarks of companionship and care among men on the goldfields, not just a cooperative economic form.[65]

※

THE INTERNAL SOLIDARITIES of the brotherhood societies did not necessarily extend to nonmembers, however. Both in China and abroad, the brotherhoods could be predatory toward outsiders, whether by stealing from locals or, in some overseas communities, by controlling the sale of opium, prostitution, and gambling. Violence did not just take place between whites and Chinese. Just as whites fought with each other, so did Chinese. Sporadic eruptions of conflict between factions of the brotherhood societies—the so-called tong wars—were usually jurisdictional fights within the vice trades. And as in all communities, individual Chinese fought disputes over matters both petty and large.

In California, when one Chinese assaulted or killed another, it usually merited only brief mention in the newspaper. A perfunctory trial might be held, where the accused would be quickly convicted and sentenced. Chinese in criminal trials rarely received justice. Prosecutors did not closely examine witnesses, a result of both a lack of concern and their own prejudices—most notably the claim that they could not distinguish one Chinese person from another. Even sincere efforts on the part of prosecutors and judges were hampered by the problem of translation. Most Chinese emigrants did not speak English, most Euro-Americans did not speak Chinese, and competent interpreters were few. Thus was born the idea of "the Chinaman's chance" in California's courts of law, especially when Chinese were accused of committing a crime against a white person, but also in cases of intraethnic conflict.

One such case concerned an unemployed Chinese gold digger, Ah Jake, who stood trial for the murder of Wah Chuck, another gold digger, in Sierra County, California, in 1887. The two men had met on the main stage road on the way to Downieville, the county seat. They argued over an unpaid loan of twenty dollars. In the ensuing argument and altercation, Ah Jake fatally shot Wah Chuck. Ah Jake fled the scene and managed to hide out for two days in the attic of a cabin of Chinese miners near Forest City, some ten miles away, before he was apprehended. His subsequent murder trial reveals some unexpected dynamics about the Chinaman's chance and, more broadly, about Chinese-white relations.[66]

Chapter 3

*

Talking to White People

A t the hearing before the county magistrate judge on whether to bring the charge of murder against Ah Jake, the court swore in Lo Kay, a Downieville grocer, as interpreter.

It was common practice, in small towns and cities in the California interior, for court officials to call upon a local bilingual Chinese merchant to help with criminal proceedings. In Ah Jake's case, Lo Kay assisted with the district attorney's examination of a man named Ah Ting. A traveling companion of the victim, Ah Ting was the only witness to the alleged murder.[1] Lo Kay's knowledge of English and his contact with the local power structure likely derived from his customer base among white residents. However, Lo Kay did not speak English well; instead, he spoke pidgin, or Chinglish, a rough contact language spoken between Chinese and whites in the gold districts. Even more interesting, the district attorney and judge also spoke in pidgin when addressing the witness and interpreter. A rare surviving court transcript includes the following exchange:

Q: (Smith, the district attorney): When Ah Jake shoot Wah Chuck, what Wah Chuck do?

A: (Lo Kay, translating for the witness, Ah Ting): You mean Ah Jake shoot, what Wah Chuck do?

Q: Yes.

A: No say anything at all.

Q: What he do after he get shot? After he get shot what he do?

A: You mean Wah Chuck?

Q: Yes.

A: He say he fell down; no do nothing; no do anything.

Q: He bleed any? . . . Did he got back to where Wah Chuck was?

A: No. . . .

Q. Did he see him dead afterwards?

A. He see him down here, no see him dead that place. . . . He say he see him Funk Kee store; outside door; take him down buggy; see him that time.

Defendant. He no see him dead; he lie.[2]

Ah Jake had already interrupted Ah Ting's testimony twice, interjecting in Chinese (Lo Kay: "He say he don't know what he say") before resorting to Chinglish to challenge the witness, but the judge ordered Lo Kay and Ah Ting to ignore him. However, because Ah Jake did not have legal counsel, the judge, F. D. Soward, accorded him the opportunity to cross-examine the witness:

Court. To Defendant. Q. You want to ask him some questions?

Defendant. Me askum him.

Court. You want to ask him some questions?

Defendant. He lie; he lie too much.

Court. You don't want to ask him any questions?

Defendant. Wah Chuck give him my money—

Court. You don't want to ask him any questions? You like to ask him some questions this man. You don't want to ask any question this man.

Mr. Smith. That is all I want to question this witness.

Defendant. He talk lie.[3]

Ah Jake did conduct a spirited cross-examination of the next witness, S. C. Stewart, the sheriff, and put forth his own case that he shot Wah

Chuck in self-defense. He spoke directly to the court in pidgin rather than risk having his words mediated by the interpreter, whom he seemed to believe was complicit with Ah Ting's lie telling.

Defendant: You see up here hole me fall? You see hole that stage road?

Stewart: I see two places.

Defendant: One place down river; one place down river; up road; two places, one place down river me fall down; you no see that time; you see up here two time?

Stewart: There were two places; two marks in the road—

Defendant (illustrating on floor): He lay me down that way; he hold my queue that way; me tell him let me up; he no let me up. (Witness lays on floor making motion, etc., many of his remarks being unintelligible) . . .

Stewart: All I know about it there were two marks in the road there.

Defendant: One mark in the road down side river; one mark down side; one mark up side—I catch him that side; he catch me that side. He shoot me I no know—I burn my coat—I no see him; he fight me back side; he catch my queue that way . . . he make me scare—I no kill him, he kill me; he strong me. . . .

Court: You want to ask him some question. . . . You got any witness. You want some man swear?

Defendant: I no got man swear. Everybody help him. He talk lie (pointing to Ah Ting). He talk lie; he no say take my queue; put on floor; he no talk. . . . He no hold my foot I no fall down at all; first time he take my bag money; catch my money put him pocket . . . he [Wah Chuck] say he kill me; I get scare. . . . He no rob my money I no shoot him. . . . He say killum me; make me scare. . . . I think make him scare let me up; he say "You shoot me I no care G—d—s—b—."⁴

We may safely assume that Ah Jake and Wah Chuck spoke to each other in their native Chinese, in this case, in Siyi, a subdialect of Cantonese. An interesting question arises as to whether Wah Chuck uttered "You shoot me I no care G—d—s—b" just as it appears in the transcript—that is, in Chinglish—or if he spoke in Chinese but swore "G—d—s—b" in English (what linguists call code-switching), or if he spoke entirely in Chinese and Ah Jake translated his Chinese swearing into the common American English epithet. Each possibility suggests a different kind of language translation or hybridization, in which speakers mixed Chinese with English phrases or translated idioms not literally but through cultural common knowledge.

It is tempting to read the judge and district attorney's use of pidgin as an infantilization of their speech, a condescension toward Ah Jake and Lo Kay. Did Ah Jake understand "Have you got lawyer man?" but not "Do you have a lawyer?" It is possible that the court's officers believed Ah Jake's ignorance of English indexed a general condition of ignorance, a common presumption held by Americans about those of non-European and non-English-speaking origins. This analysis of the transcript follows our experience with pidgin on the printed page, used by white writers to represent the speech of racialized subjects. The modern reader cringes when presented with dialogue written in dialect. But the courtroom is an arena of the spoken word, which functions in real time. In that context the judge and district attorney's use of pidgin appears less as mocking and more as a sincere effort to communicate with the defendant. They reached for the language they used when they engaged with local Chinese, a house servant, perhaps, or the garden farmer.

In any case, pidgin was the lingua franca of the proceeding. This pidgin derived from Chinese English Pidgin (also called Canton Jargon by contemporaries), the contact language of Guangzhou, Macao, and Hong Kong that developed during the colonial China trade. *Pidgin* is a corruption of the word *business* (itself shortened from *pidginess*): *pidgin English* means "business English." Chinese Pidgin English is characterized by reduced grammatical structure (lack of copulas, plurals, verb tenses, definite articles, etc.) and certain phonological inventions (replacement of [r] with [l], e.g., *tomollow*; and insertion of vowels [i] or [u] to word endings, e.g., *lookee*). Its vocabulary draws from English, Portuguese, Hindi, and Cantonese: the word *mandarin,* for a government official, comes from the Portuguese verb *mandar,* "to command"; *joss* derives from *deös. Lac* is from the Hindi number for one hundred thousand. A *chop,* from the Hindi *chhap,* for "seal" or "stamp," is a document of any kind—an invoice, an imperial edict, a receipt, a bill of lading (the latter a *chop boat*). A servant sent on an urgent errand is told to go *chop chop*—a clever combination that uses the likely object of the errand (fetching or delivering a document) with the Chinese syntax of repetition, recalling *kuai kuai*, "fast fast" or "hurry." Chinese Pidgin English, in service of European-Chinese business in the exchange of tea, silks, opium, hemp, and silver that was the stuff of the early colonial China trade, was linguistically creative and vigorous.[5]

Outside the trading house, however, pidgin had limited uses. It was spoken in colonial households with servants but did not carry over to judicial or diplomatic venues, where precision and nuance in language carried a high premium. Under the colonial convention of extraterritoriality, Europeans living in China's treaty ports were not subject to Chinese law, but when they had occasion to appear in a Chinese court as plaintiffs or as witnesses, interpreters were used. In diplomacy and treaty writing, the British were scrupulous about controlling language. Their diplomats spoke only through their own interpreters, and they wrote into the Treaty of Tianjin (1858, following the second Opium War) a provision that the English-language version, and not the Chinese, would determine the final meaning of official communications.[6]

The pidgin spoken by Chinese migrants in California was similar to that used in Guangzhou and Hong Kong, but there were important differences. While the syntax was similar, not surprisingly Chinese American pidgin was shaped by American English and American social practices. It included local word forms and importations from other vernaculars, like *askum* and *sarvie* (savvy). More important, nineteenth-century American Chinese pidgin was much less robust than its colonial antecedent. It did not evolve from sustained interactions between Chinese and whites, as it had in China, but was mainly the product of Chinese migrants' efforts to engage with their new environment, by learning, as one observer described, the "few necessary words and sentences, to assist in mining, traveling, bartering, marketing, and procuring various kinds of employment."[7]

White Americans who engaged with Chinese occasionally but not regularly or in a sustained way, as in China's treaty ports, may have acquired just a passing familiarity with pidgin. At Ah Jake's trial, the judge and the D.A. spoke pidgin awkwardly. They mimicked imperfectly its syntax and resorted to clumsy repetition: "You don't want to ask him any questions? You like to ask him some questions this man. You don't want to ask any question this man." Arguably they were not speaking pidgin at all. Linguists contend that pidgin, like any language, must be learned and "cannot be produced by an ad-hoc simplification of his or her own language."[8]

The pidgin of late nineteenth-century Sierra County denotes the social location of Chinese as a group of ethnic outsiders with regular but limited contact with the mainstream of society. It is a contact language at the very margins of society and not, as in Guangzhou and Hong Kong, a central dynamic in a vibrant market where parties met, if not as equals, as contenders. The limitations of Chinese American pidgin English are manifest in the California courtroom: it simply did not have the depth to express complex ideas or to address the contingencies of a trial-court examination. At Ah Jake's hearing, linguistic confusion and misunderstanding at times overwhelmed the parties' ability to communicate. If the British deemed pidgin inadequate for legal proceedings in China, its appearance in a Sierra County court of law suggests the extreme marginality of its Chinese residents.

Insofar as the court did provide an interpreter—the pidgin-speaking Lo Kay—the transcript does not record the primary testimonies given orally in Chinese, only the interpreter's translation into pidgin. Those voices are forever lost, unavailable to an appeals court and beyond, to history. Unlike translations of printed text, which can be checked and verified, in oral interpreting the translation usurps the authority of the original utterance. No wonder, then, that the non-English-speaking migrant often feels him- or herself to be at the mercy of the court interpreter.[9]

Ah Jake, whose English/Chinglish was comparable to Lo Kay's, realized that he would gain nothing from Lo Kay's interpreting, so he spoke for himself. But Ah Jake's limited knowledge of English was compounded by his lack of proficiency in yet another language: law, the language of the court. He attempted to show how Wah Chuck and Ah Ting assaulted and robbed him, but he did not know how to make his case through the conventions of a criminal proceeding. He declined the opportunity to cross-examine Ah Ting, dismissing him as a liar, without understanding the necessity of revealing his lying through cross-examination.

Perhaps because of Lo Kay's linguistic limitations as well as the gravity of the charge against Ah Jake, the court hired the services of a professional interpreter for the trial. The interpreter was Jerome Millard, a Euro-American who worked for the criminal court in San Francisco. Millard had come to California during the gold rush, traveling from Michigan by oxcart on the "early road." He befriended and worked with Chinese miners, favoring them over whites, he said, because they did not drink alcohol, and he learned Chinese. In the 1860s he supervised the first Chinese labor gangs hired by Charles Crocker and Company to build the transcontinental railroad. By the 1880s he was working full time as a translator for the criminal court in San Francisco. But the goldfield towns in the interior of the state lacked translators of Millard's capability. Millard welcomed occasional assignments to "the country" to translate for "important case[s]."[10]

Millard, who was nearly six feet tall and wore a large handlebar mustache, must have cut an imposing figure in the courtroom. Witnesses who testified through him are heard to speak in standard English, and possibly they assumed some of his bodily authority. Ah Jake appears to be a different person than the Chinglish speaker in the previous examination transcript: "I have worked at cooking for whites whenever I could get work, and other times I have worked at mining." "He pulled me down by the cue [sic] on the ground, as I have here shown [showing] and struck me again. I then got up and he struck me again and it hurt me and I fell in the road. . . . I was then very mad and says I: 'You got my money and won't pay me and strike me' and he says: 'I like to strike you.' "[11]

Ah Jake also had legal representation: two lawyers, A. J. Howe, a local retired judge, appointed by the court, and Bert Schlessinger, a young attorney new to Downieville, hired by Ah Jake's clan association. They contended that the defendant—overwhelmed, assaulted, and robbed by two men—had acted in self-defense. Unfortunately, the only eyewitness to the event, Ah Ting, did not support that account. The prosecution argued that Ah Jake robbed and killed Wah Chuck and then returned to the scene of the crime, where he created marks in the road to give the appearance that a scuffle had taken place. As evidence for this theory, the district attorney produced two white witnesses, who testified that they had seen Ah Jake shortly after the incident and that he did not have dust on his clothes or in his hair or face and also that he was pretending to cry.[12]

The jury convicted Ah Jake of murder in the first degree, apparently finding the testimony of the defendant unpersuasive in light of contradicting testimony by Ah Ting and the two white witnesses. The jurors also seem to have heeded the judge's instructions that the "will, deliberation and premeditation" required for a first-degree conviction applied even if only a few seconds lapsed between thought and action. The court sentenced Ah Jake to death by hanging; a motion for a new trial was denied. It would appear that Ah Jake fared no better with the aid of professional translation and legal counsel than he had while representing himself in pidgin. The conviction and sentence strike us as an unsurprising outcome of a trial in which Ah Jake had only a "Chinaman's chance."[13]

⁂

THE PROBLEM OF TRANSLATION shaped Chinese interactions with Euro-Americans from their very arrival at the two gold mountains. Among the earliest emigrants, those who were bilingual had usually acquired their linguistic skills in China or Southeast Asia. The San Francisco merchant Yuan Sheng went to a missionary school in Macao, and the Australian impresario Lowe Kong Meng attended an English private school in Penang; both men had experience in business dealings with Europeans and Americans before arriving on the goldfields. The first Euro-American missionaries in California and Victoria had previously served in China or Southeast Asia.[14]

Chinese who went to the goldfields in groups often included one person who spoke English. Headmen accompanying Chinese emigrants to Australia all knew enough English to navigate their groups' travel to and settlement on the goldfields. The same pattern existed in California. For example, the American miner Timothy Osborn wrote in his diary that a group of Chinese miners who were camped near him included a friendly English speaker, who wrote down various Chinese words and their translations for the curious American. Few Americans went so far as to learn Chinese. Jerome Millard was a rare exception.[15]

Many Chinese merchants learned enough English to conduct business with local whites, or they employed a young clerk who learned enough to do so. Most were barely proficient in English, learning key words and phrases but rarely grammar. Often they inserted English words into Cantonese sentence structure. For example, Jung Ah Sing, a gold digger in Victoria, wrote a journal while imprisoned after a knife fight. Because the journal was actually a brief attesting to his innocence, he wrote in English: "My buy that hatchet that day months of January 1867 Cochran Diggings Chinamen gone away sell the my, my buy that hatchet that time my been Chinamen tent go home." ("I bought that hatchet in January 1867 from Chinamen at Cochran Diggings. They were moving away and sold it to me. Then I left the Chinamen's tent and went home.")[16]

Missionaries in California offered English classes to bring Chinese to Christianity, a strategy that attracted many students but few converts. The Rev. William Speer conceded that the young men who came for English classes stayed long enough to learn a few words and phrases. It would be fairer to say that, apart from well-educated men like Yuan Sheng and Lowe Kong Meng, most Chinese communicated with Euro-Americans not really in English but in pidgin. The limits of pidgin were most clearly displayed when Chinese tried to express themselves in the courtroom and in other legal matters, usually to sad outcomes.[17]

It was necessary, therefore, to use interpreters when there was important business to conduct. The larger *huiguan* had "linguists" on their staffs to assist individual members as well as to represent the association to mainstream society. San Francisco's police courts employed on an ad hoc basis not only Chinese but also French, German, Russian, and Spanish interpreters, reflecting the city's international population. But even in San Francisco, few Chinese could speak English well enough to meet the needs of the police and the courts; the situation did not improve until a second generation of Chinese Americans came of age in the 1870s.[18]

During the 1850s and '60s, the city's interpreters included Euro-American missionaries and educated Chinese merchants. Yuan Sheng frequently appeared in court when Chinese faced criminal charges and acted as both interpreter and as advocate. In one case of larceny, for example, Yuan successfully persuaded the judge to discharge A-He, who was accused of stealing ten dollars, on grounds that he was a "crazy man." Yuan promised to send him back to China.[19]

In Australia the goldfield commissioners in each district hired Chinese interpreters and "scribes" to support the heavy work of issuing mining licenses and compliance with goldfield regulations. Two brothers, Ho A Low (He Yale) and Ho A Mei (He Yamei), were typical of the first Chinese interpreters in Victoria. They had been educated at the Anglo-Chinese school at the London Missionary Society station at Malacca. Ho A Low first came to Victoria as a missionary worker in 1857 and was fast recruited to work as an interpreter by the Beechworth resident warden. Both brothers held positions as interpreters, but neither stuck with the job. At one level, they found they could make more money by investing in gold mining companies or in Melbourne as merchants and shipping agents. Their superiors also criticized them for lacking impartiality. Ho A Mei was fired from his position in Ararat in 1860 for acting as "counsel" to the accused, although that did not prevent him from obtaining another position in Ballarat in 1866. Both brothers eventually returned to China, Ho A Low to Shantou (Swatow), a treaty port, where he worked for the Chinese Maritime Custom Service; and Ho A Mei to Hong Kong, where he became an influential leader in Chinese business and politics. But if the first generation of Chinese interpreters on the goldfields included skilled linguists like the Ho brothers, by the late 1860s and '70s many interpreters spoke English poorly. Observers reported that at times they even resorted to pantomime to communicate with magistrates. The Rev. William Young remarked, "Almost any Chinese who has a smattering of English thinks himself to occupy the post of interpreter."[20]

Not only were there more profitable opportunities for an educated bilingual man, but just as important, a person with other options might not wish to be the vexed position of a government employee. Interpreters occupied a position in between colonial officials and the mass of Chinese, and as such both sides questioned their loyalties. Among the Chinese population, many distrusted the interpreters' alignment with government authority; moreover, some abused their positions by extorting phony taxes from the Chinese or by demanding "protection" fees from gambling houses. At the same time, authorities often suspected that interpreters withheld information or translated selectively in order to protect Chinese in police matters. Ho A Mei was not unusual in this regard. The Melbourne *Argus* complained, "We are absolutely at the mercy" of Chinese officials.[21]

⚛

CHINESE GOLD DIGGERS and merchants who lacked recourse to an interpreter could turn to any of the Chinese-English phrase books that circulated in both California and Victoria. In 1875 Wells Fargo and Company published *An English-Chinese Phrase Book, Together with Vocabulary of Trade, Law, etc.*, compiled by "Wong Sam and Assistants." Wong Sam was Wells Fargo's chief Chinese interpreter. He supervised a staff of Chinese clerks, who made sure to deliver letters and packages sent between San Francisco and the interior that were addressed in Chinese. The phrase book anticipated situations in which Chinese would need to explain themselves to white people. In business, as both buyers and sellers:

"I want to get a pair of your best pants."
"Have you any other kind better than these?"
"Will you sell on credit?"
"Well sir, it costs us $10, and besides we have to pay very heavy duty on our best goods."
"Don't fear I am cheating you."
"Why don't you buy them?"

In restaurants, as proprietors and customers:

"Please take a seat."
"Which do you desire?"
"Will you have something more?"
"Your food is very nice."
"You also have a good cook."

And for situations of conflict:

"I struck him accidentally."
"I have made an apology, but still he wants to strike me."
"He assaulted me without provocation."
"He insulted me first."
"The men are striking for wages."
"The house was set on fire by an incendiary."
"He claimed my mine."
"He squatted on my lot."
"I will expel him if he don't leave the place"
"He perjured himself in Court."[22]

A phrase book compiled by Zhu Rui-sheng for use in Australia contains many similar phrases. A second book added a list of towns in the Victoria and California goldfields, which raises the possibility that Chinese traveled between the two places. Alternatively, the book may have been published in China for use on both gold mountains.[23]

The Australian phrase book is more sophisticated than the Wells Fargo book. The latter simply pairs Cantonese vernacular with the English phrase. The Australian version includes three lines of Chinese for each English phrase, one a translation of the English in a mixture of vernacular and classical Chinese; and two in transliterations of the English using Cantonese and Siyi dialect, respectively. This enabled a person who could not read English to sound out the English phrase using Chinese phonetics. Meanwhile one could learn rudimentary English from chapters with the alphabet, vocabulary words (colors, days of the week, etc.), and writing exercises.

The Australian book includes phrases for business, employment, and law:

"Can you employ me?"
"He is skillful."
"How many people are in the new diggings?"

"How much do you charge?"

"I want a cup of tea."

"I will go to take tiffin" (lunch).

"He has done wrong."

"Help me catch a thief."

"He impels me to run away."

"He owes me a great deal of money."

"Why do you abuse me?"

"I have four pegs marked on [my claim]."

"Who saw him take your claim?"

"My mates saw him take it."

"Why did you strike me?"

One page presents four sentences that, when spoken consecutively, guide the user through a conflict:

"If you touch me a little bit first . . ."

"You may see whether I strike you or not."

"If I cannot overcome you by fighting . . ."

"I will go to accuse you."

There are phrases for use by women, likely for prostitutes:

"Put a tortoise comb in my hair."

"Is my cosmetic well applied?"

"Have you any perfumery for me?"

The book also includes phrases that are conversational:

"How old are you?"

"They are wise."

"I have not seen you in a long time."

"Come to dine with me today."

"What your heart wishes may your hand obtain."

These last phrases suggest that Chinese on the goldfields viewed exchanges with their white neighbors not simply in transactional terms but also in hopes of comity with them. They seem to have had limited success in this regard. Race relations were not always hostile or violent, and in many communities whites and Chinese got along, conducted business, and even acted kindly toward one another. But only in rare instances did they become friends or, in fewer instances still, lovers. Most whites complained that language was a barrier to learning anything about the Chinese. At one level this was true, but few whites made any effort to understand the Chinese and even less to learn *their* language. The claim of linguistic difference was as much an alibi for distrust and, worse, for producing negative stereotypes that justified discriminatory and violent treatment.

Chapter 4

Bigler's Gambit

John Bigler was not a gold miner, but he was part of the forty-niner generation. He was one of many Americans who went to California during the rush to make a fortune by doing business with gold miners. In that sense he was also a gold seeker.

Bigler was born in 1805 in Carlisle, Pennsylvania, to German immigrants. He entered the printing trade at an early age. In 1831 he and his brother bought the *Centre Democrat*, a newspaper affiliated with Andrew Jackson, but within a few years he sold it and decided to study law. He then settled in Illinois and married. In mid-1848, when news of gold reached the eastern United States, he decided to go to California. He was forty-three, no longer young, but he had always been somewhat restless; in California he smelled opportunity. The Biglers traveled west by ox train on the overland road.

When they arrived in Sacramento in 1849, there were no law positions. Bigler chopped wood and unloaded freight at river docks—he couldn't be choosy, as he had a wife to support—and then decided to try his hand at politics. Why not? Everything was new, wide open. His background in law was an asset at a time when the territorial government was just getting organized. But he also was burly and gruff, which fed his persona as a man of the people, especially the rough-and-ready forty-niners. Bigler

Population of Chinese Miners, California, 1860

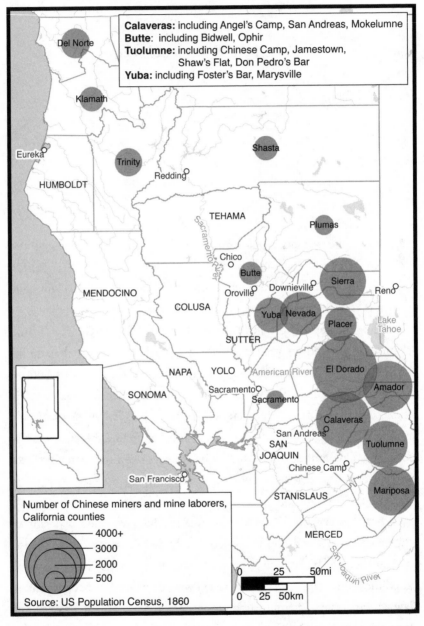

Calaveras: including Angel's Camp, San Andreas, Mokelumne
Butte: including Bidwell, Ophir
Tuolumne: including Chinese Camp, Jamestown,
Shaw's Flat, Don Pedro's Bar
Yuba: including Foster's Bar, Marysville

Number of Chinese miners and mine laborers,
California counties

4000+
3000
2000
500

Source: US Population Census, 1860

Map by Dan Miller

ran as a Democrat for state assembly in California Territory's first general election and won. He rose quickly in the assembly, becoming speaker in 1850, and in 1851 he received his party's nomination for governor and won that election. He was the first governor of the new state of California.[1]

When Bigler took office in January 1852, California was swirling with debate over how to best harness the energies of the gold rush and develop the state's economy. By this time, gold that could be easily sifted from the gravel of riverbeds had declined to near exhaustion. From the Trinity River to the San Joaquin, a region six hundred miles long and thirty miles wide, the country was "dug over in all its ravines, gulches and streams, at many of its flats, and some of its hills." Still, it was known that gold also existed in veins of underground rock, and mining entrepreneurs were digging deeper into the hills and experimenting with ways to extract gold from hard quartz.[2]

In addition to their continued faith in gold, many believed California was unrivaled in its agricultural potential, given estimates that the state had no less than 20 million acres of arable land. Bigler stoked the promises of prosperity that boosters had been crowing about since the discovery of gold. California's salubrious climate would reward efforts of individual labor, and the "vast, safe, and beautiful Bay of San Francisco" destined the city "ere long to become the manufacturing metropolis, and commercial emporium of Western America." Some imagined that California would anchor a Pacific coast empire, even one that would stretch from "Alaska to Chili."[3]

One such booster was William Gwin, who was one of California's first U.S. senators, along with John Frémont. Gwin, a physician from Tennessee, had migrated to Mississippi, where he had been a congressman, and then to California. Like Bigler, Gwin was not interested in standing in a river stream with a bent back, panning for gold. Still, he had an interest in gold: in 1851 he acquired property in Calaveras County that soon became a highly profitable quartz mine. But Gwin's real love was politics. He participated in the state constitutional convention and was elected to the U.S. Senate in 1850. Gwin was a big advocate for developing the Pacific coast. California entered the union as a free state, but Gwin, a southern Democrat, remained committed to slavery. As the sectional

crisis worsened and southern secession appeared on the horizon of possibility, Gwin promoted the idea of another secession, the formation of an
independent Pacific Republic, from the Rockies to the coast, with labor
provided by black and native Hawaiian slaves.[4]

Others envisioned the use of Chinese labor. The proposals to develop
the Pacific coast with Chinese varied in concept. The Presbyterian Rev.
William Speer, a former China missionary who established the first Christian mission in San Francisco's budding Chinese quarter, imagined Chinese labor in California as part of a grand vision of Sino-American unity.
Speer promoted a mutual embrace between China and the United States,
one that would be based on friendship, commerce, and cultural exchange.
In *The Oldest and the Newest Empire,* Speer sought to correct Americans'
misconceptions about China and Chinese. In a chapter on Chinese labor,
he refuted the idea that "Chinese are a class who work for wages not sufficient to maintain laboring men comfortably, and who subsist upon cheap
and refuse food." Speer explained that Chinese workers were willing, honorable, and industrious. Moreover, they knew how to cultivate cotton, silk,
and tea, which Speer believed could be planted in California profitably.[5]

Others advocated for indentured labor. In February 1852, two "cooley
bills" were introduced into the state legislature, one sponsored in the senate by George Tingley, a Whig from Ohio, and the other in the assembly by Archibald Peachy, from Virginia, who like Gwin was a pro-slavery
Democrat. Both bills envisioned importing foreign labor under contracts
that would be, in principle, voluntary; Peachy's would have restricted
contracts to Chinese and Hawaiians and explicitly denied them to free
blacks. Tingley and Peachy were no doubt aware of the "coolie trade"
that was supplying indentured contract workers from China and India
to Caribbean plantation colonies in the wake of the abolition of slavery.
Plantation coolie labor was hotly debated in the United States across the
deepening sectional divide: Was it a new kind of slavery? Or was it based
on voluntary contract and hence free labor?[6]

Now that the gold rush had opened transpacific trade, Chinese were also
going to Hawaii as contracted sugar plantation workers, a development
that encouraged the ambitions of men like Gwin, Tingley, and Peachy.

The coolie bills proposed that the state guarantee labor contracts made abroad between American citizens or companies and foreign workers for work in the United States. Peachy's bill set a minimum contract at five years and Tingley's at ten years, which exceeded anything in the Caribbean or elsewhere, and a minimum wage of fifty dollars a year, a pathetically low amount. Workers who broke their contracts could be punished with imprisonment and fines, penal sanctions that recalled the master-servant laws that had been a dead letter among white Americans since the 1820s.[7]

Tingley and Peachy were not interested in contracting labor for gold mining. Peachy explicitly excluded mining from his bill; Tingley represented burgeoning agricultural districts in Contra Costa and Santa Clara, where large landowners were crying for labor. In December 1851, an enterprising Yankee ship captain, Leslie Bryson, left San Francisco on the *Robert Browne,* armed with foreknowledge that the coolie bills would be introduced in the legislature after the new year. Bryson planned to go to China and return in six months with "Chinese under contract to serve five years in California. About 150 of them I have already engaged among the Farmers and Government officials at San Jose," he wrote to a friend before leaving San Francisco.[8]

Initially the coolie bills received support from both Whigs and Democrats, and the assembly passed the Peachy bill on March 20. But opposition to the senate bill gathered force from Free Soilers, who outmaneuvered Tingley there. He made a last-ditch attempt to save it with a strange speech, in which he said that because California had insisted on welcoming all foreigners (a policy that he had opposed), foreign labor in the state was unavoidable. The question now, he claimed, was whether American or foreign companies should profit from their labor. Tingley's appeal to nativism backfired, perhaps because it suggested the coming of large companies to exploit quartz mining, a prospect that many forty-niners dreaded as a threat to their independence. On April 13 the state senate soundly defeated the bill, 16 to 2. Without a senate bill, the assembly bill died on the vine.[9]

Captain Leslie Bryson's plan to import indentured Chinese for California agriculture was not to be, but not because the coolie bills failed. In

March 1852, Bryson had indeed taken on board the *Robert Browne* some
four hundred Chinese at Xiamen, but ten days after she sailed, the Chinese rose up in mutiny, in response to unsanitary ship conditions, sick-
ness and death, and rumors that they were headed not to Gold Mountain
but to the guano islands of Peru. Bryson, his first and second officers,
and four crewmen were killed during the uprising. Americans regained
control of the ship, but it went aground during a storm near Ishigaki, a
small island in the Ryukyu chain (Okinawa), and there the crew stranded
most of the Chinese mutineers before the *Robert Browne* limped back to
Xiamen. A yearlong investigation involving American, Qing, Japanese,
and British officials ensued to rescue (or seize) the Chinese on Ishigaki
and return them to China. In the end, the Qing court determined that
the coolies had not mutinied but rather had resisted the illegal *mai zhuzai,* "selling of piglets," as Chinese called the coolie trade.[10]

OPPONENTS OF THE California coolie bills were not necessarily against
Chinese immigration in general. The *Daily Alta California* supported
free immigration, which in principle it believed applied to all, regardless of origin. According to the *Alta,* gold had brought to California an
international population, and that populace, in time, would take up a
range of occupations and develop the state. It noted that Chinese had
already acquired, with the assistance of their American agent, Woodworth, a large tract of agricultural land on the Mokelumne River, where
they "have commenced cultivating, and are fast settling." The newspaper lauded the Chinese for being "among the most industrious, quiet,
patient people among us," who "live under our laws as if born and bred
under them." The *Alta* optimistically predicted that California's immigrants would assimilate and "vote at the same polls, study at the same
schools and bow to the same Altar as our own countrymen"—including
the "China Boys," the "Don from Santa Fe and the Kanaker [*sic*] from
Hawaii."[11]

The *Alta*'s liberality bespoke the Free Soil politics that came from the
antebellum North and that in this case assumed a multiracial Pacific per-

spective. By the same token, the *Alta* opposed bringing any system of servitude to California, and therefore it opposed the coolie bills before the
legislature. Recent experience with the "labor contract system in the English
Colonies" (Jamaica, Guyana, Mauritius, etc.), it warned, showed that the
work "in which these menials engage, though voluntary, is hard and sometimes cruel." It reminded readers, "Already this physical bondage is classed
by the press of the country as slavery, of the most iniquitous species."[12]

The distinction made by the *Alta* between free and indentured Chinese emigrants quickly blurred. Bigler himself was largely to blame for
the obfuscation. Although the coolie bills were dead—"at last dead—very
dead, indeed," according to the *Alta*—the governor could not help but
give the issue another kick. On April 23 Bigler issued a "special message" to the legislature, his last address before the close of the session.
Its sole subject was the Chinese Question. Bigler raised alarm over the
"present wholesale importation to this country of immigrants from the
Asiatic quarter of the globe," in particular that "class of Asiatics known
as "Coolies." He said over twenty thousand Chinese were currently leaving China for California and warned there would soon be one hundred
thousand in the state. He declared that nearly all were being hired by
"Chinese masters" to mine for gold at pitiable wages, while their families
in China were held hostage for the faithful performance of their contracts. The Chinese, Bigler alleged, dug up gold and removed it from the
country; they had no interest in becoming citizens, caring not to "avail
themselves of the blessings of free government"; and they were a menace
to public safety. Worst of all, perhaps, was the prospect that the contracts
binding Chinese workers to their Chinese bosses might be considered
valid and enforceable in American courts. Bigler called upon the legislature to impose heavy taxes on the Chinese to "check the present system
of indiscriminate and unlimited Asiatic immigration," and for a law barring Chinese contract labor from California mines.[13]

Bigler's address was an incendiary mix of vagueness ("there is no
information" about the nature of mining contracts or about whether
Chinese were in "voluntary or involuntary servitude"), mundane facts
(names of sailing vessels arriving at San Francisco and the number of

Chinese on each), and wild, unsubstantiated charges (families held hostage and wages of three to four dollars a month). What was his intention? The coolie bills were dead. Chinese in California were neither contracted nor indentured labor. But Bigler knew that whites were uneasy about the growing Chinese population, which had nearly doubled during 1851, from 4,180 to 7,520, and might double again in 1852.[14] Bigler, who had come far in life by seizing opportunities, saw political potential in the Chinese Question. He had won his first election in 1851 by fewer than five hundred votes. His reelection in 1853 was uncertain, especially with the state Democratic Party dividing between pro- and antislavery factions, mirroring national political trends. Bigler used the Chinese Question to excite the populous mining districts to his side. The forty-niners were restive, as the placers were rapidly giving out and a diligent miner could now make only five dollars a day. Many were already working at wages for others, earning about the same.[15]

By tarring all Chinese miners as "coolies," Bigler found a racial trope that compared Chinese to black slaves, the antithesis of free labor, and thereby cast them as a threat to white miners' independence. In fact, the specter of Chinese coolies was of a piece with racist policy toward African Americans. The legislature passed a law in 1852 that declared all African Americans who had entered the state *before* 1850—including free blacks—to be fugitive slaves, liable for arrest and return to their former owners. This was an outrageous position considering California's entrance into the Union as a free state. It betrayed the Democratic Party's belief that all "colored" races were inherently unfree.[16]

Bigler's message was published in full in the *Alta*; the governor also had it printed on "small sheets of paper and sent everywhere through the mines." A senate committee issued a report echoing the same charges and circulated it as a pamphlet throughout the interior. As he had intended, Bigler roused the white mining population. Miners gathered in local assemblies and passed resolutions banning Chinese from mining in their districts. In May, at a meeting held in Columbia, Tuolumne County, miners echoed Bigler's charges. They railed against those who would "flood the state with degraded Asiatics, and fasten, without sanction of law, the system of peonage on our social organization," and they voted to exclude Chinese from mining in their district. Other meetings offered no reasons but simply bade the Chinese to leave, or to "vamose the ranche [*sic*]." Sometimes they used violence to push Chinese off their claims.[17]

Bigler would be the first politician to ride the Chinese Question to elected office. He won reelection in September 1853, defeating the Whig reform candidate, William Waldo, with barely 51 percent of the vote. The Chinese Question enabled Bigler to carry the mining counties with substantial majorities. His reelection surprised some observers, who had considered him politically toxic after a string of corruption scandals, including a failed scheme with land speculators in San Francisco. But the election announced the consolidation of Democratic power in the state, built on tactics that critics averred resembled those of Tammany Hall—party strong-arming, ballot stuffing, and demagoguery. The Chinese or "coolie" question was a core element of "Biglerism" and became a bedrock principle of the Democratic Party in California.[18]

Bigler's success in tarring the Chinese as a "coolie race" gave California politicians a convenient trope that could be trotted out whenever conditions called for a racial scapegoat. But more than a political tool, anticoolieism became a kind of protean racism among whites on the Pacific coast. In time it would be embellished with more elaborate theories, in particular by the political economist Henry George, who cut his first ideas about monopoly and labor on the Chinese Question.

Henry George arrived on the goldfields in 1857 at the age of eighteen. He was a restless young man, having several years earlier left his parents' home in Philadelphia and sailed to India and South America before landing in Oregon. When he traveled from San Francisco to British Columbia during the Fraser River rush, he later recalled, "I had never intently thought upon any social problem." But, he continued, the miners on deck of the schooner

> got talking about the Chinese, and I ventured to ask what harm they were doing here, if, as these miners said, they were only working the cheap diggings? "No harm now," said an old miner, "but wages will not always be as high as they are today in California. As the country

grows, as people come in, wages will go down, and some day or other white men will be glad to get those diggings that the Chinamen are now working." And I remember well how it impressed me, the idea that as the country grew in all that we are hoping that it might grow, the condition of those who had to work for their living must become, not better, but worse.[19]

George did not pursue gold mining but found work as a typesetter at the *San Francisco Times*. He would go on to become a reporter and in the 1870s the publisher of the *Oakland Daily Transcript*. He would become one of the leading political economists of the late nineteenth century, writing prolifically about labor, land, and monopoly. When he heard the miners' conversation on the deck of the schooner, he was still a dozen years from writing about Chinese labor and farther still from his most famous work, *Progress and Poverty* (1879). But many of his ideas grew from the soil of commonplace racial stereotypes that he encountered on the goldfields.

Bigler's gambit would continue to pay off well into the twentieth century. The leader of the American Federation of Labor, Samuel Gompers, who published *Meat vs. Rice: American Manhood Against Asiatic Coolieism, Which Shall Survive?* in 1902, theorized the Chinese Question in terms of race, class, and gender in one fell swoop and yoked the notion of free labor to anticoolieism.

⁜

YUAN SHENG AND TONG K. ACHICK (Tang Tinggui) were not afraid of John Bigler. Like Bigler and other white elites, they were not miners but businessmen and political leaders. The two men were leaders of the Yeong Wo Association (Yanghe Huiguan), which represented a sizable population of the Chinese in California. In addition to their leadership of the Yeong Wo, Yuan and Tong were educated men and fluent in English. They were well positioned to push back against the governor's message.

Yuan Sheng and Tong K. Achick hailed from the same region in what is now Zhongshan county in Guangdong. Both attended school in Macao. Tong studied at the prestigious English-language school established by the first Protestant missionary in China, Robert Morrison. His classmates at the Morrison school included Lee Kan (Li Gan), who would become the Chinese editor of the *Oriental*, published by missionaries in San Francisco, and Yung Wing (Rong Hong), the first Chinese to graduate from an American university (Yale College, class of 1854) and founder of the Chinese Educational Mission, which sent over one hundred Chinese adolescent boys to study at Hartford and New Haven in the late nineteenth century. As we know, Yuan was one of the first Chinese to travel to San Francisco in 1849. Tong probably came to California in 1850. He quickly established himself in San Francisco as a successful merchant, heading Ton Wo and Company, one of the city's largest Chinese firms. He became the second president of the Yeong Wo in 1854, after Yuan became ill and returned to China.[20]

Within days of Bigler's special message, Tong K. Achick wrote a letter to the governor. He signed it along with Hab Wa, a merchant with the Sam Wo and Company who was also a ship chartering agent. Hab Wa had recently arrived on the *Challenge*, one of the largest American clipper ships of the day that had been built expressly for the transpacific trade between China (Shanghai and Hong Kong) and San Francisco. In their letter to the governor, Tong Achick and Hab Wa attested that, contrary to Bigler's claims, none of the five hundred Chinese passengers on the *Challenge* were coolies.[21]

The letter opens, "The Chinamen have learned with sorrow that you have published a message against them. Although we are Asiatics, some of us have been educated in American schools and have learned your language, which has enabled us to read your message in the newspapers for ourselves and to explain it to the rest of our countrymen. . . . We have determined to write you as decent and respectful a letter as we could, pointing out to your Excellency some of the errors you have fallen into about us." The letter was indeed written in a "decent and respectful" tone, although one can sense anger and defiance just beneath the surface. It explained that Chinese in California included laborers as well as tradesmen, mechanics, gentry, and teachers; "none are 'Coolies' if by that word you mean bound men or contract slaves." It stated emphatically, "The poor Chinaman does not come here as a slave. He comes because of his desire for independence."

Hab Wa and Tong Achick dismissed as absurd Bigler's claims that Chinese came to America to labor for three to four dollars a month, less than they earned in China. "It is foolish to believe they will leave [their families] for trifling inducements," they wrote. As to Bigler's charge that Chinese were a menace to society, they pointed out that "there are no Chinese drunkards in your streets, nor convicts in your prisons, madmen in your hospitals, or others who are a charge to your State. . . . In the important matters we are good men; we honor our parents; we take care of our children; we are industrious and peaceable; we trade much; we are trusted for small and large sums; we pay our debts and are honest; and of course we tell the truth."

In addition to defending the integrity of Chinese emigrants, Hab Wa and Tong Achick astutely argued that there was a positive relationship between migration and trade. The circulation of people and things was linked. Migration begat commerce, which contributed to the "general wealth of the world." Whereas Bigler saw only hundreds of coolies disembarking from the *Challenge* and other ships, Hab Wa and Tong Achick saw both people and freight. Bigler might not have been aware how great the U.S.-China trade was, they allowed, "how rapidly it is increasing and how many are now returning to California as merchants who came over originally as miners." San Francisco's Chinese merchants sold not only Chinese goods—rice, silks, tea—but also a "great quantity of American goods, especially boots, of which every Chinaman buys one or more pairs immediately on landing. And then there are the American stores dealing in Chinese articles on a very large scale, and some with the most remarkable success." Chinese emigration was "attended with the opening of this Chinese trade, which . . . will yet be the pride and riches of this city and State."

Knowing that "your country wishes [to trade] with China," they argued that trade "cannot all be on one side. . . . The gold we have been allowed to dig in your mines is what has made the China trade grow up so fast, like everything else in this country. If you want to check immigration from Asia, you will have to do it by checking Asiatic commerce."

Hab Wa and Tong Achick spoke of what all reasonable observers knew: that migration and trade were mutually supporting elements of foreign contact and exchange. American and European businesses in California who were interested in foreign trade had resisted nativist calls to restrict immigration. It was one of the key reasons the California legislature had defeated proposals to limit gold mining to American citizens. California businessmen spoke highly of Chinese, not because they were docile coolie laborers but because Chinese merchants were good businessmen, known for honest dealing. Writing in response to Bigler's message, a group of eleven prominent businessmen predicted that the entire U.S.-China trade would soon "pass through the golden gate of San Francisco, and the golden hills of California, enriching this State to an extent unconceived [sic] now." They implored the legislature to not "check or damage this system, just now in its infancy, by establishing ignorant or hasty laws and restrictions [lest] we may injure ourselves," perhaps irreparably.[22]

The *New York Times* expressed the same sentiment. It chastised Bigler's racism that had endangered the "California process," which was achieving what all commercial nations aspired to: "commercial intercourse, free and unrestricted trade" with China. Indeed, over the course of the next several decades, anti-Chinese nativists would come up against opposition from diplomatic and commercial interests in the China trade. It would be their challenge to solve the Chinese Question by tearing asunder the ties that connected the movement of people and things, to restrict immigration while preserving trade.[23]

Yuan Sheng also spoke out against Bigler's message. In early May he wrote, under the name Norman Assing, to the governor and sent a copy to the *Alta*. He announced himself as "a Chinaman, a republican, and a lover of free institutions; [and] much attached to the principles of the Government of the United States." The letter was angry and direct: the "effects of your late message has been thus far to prejudice the public mind against my people, to enable those who wait the opportunity to hunt them down, and rob them of the rewards of their toil." Like Hab Wa and Tong Achick, Yuan challenged the logic of Bigler's notion that "by excluding population from this State you enhance its wealth. I always have considered that population was wealth; particularly a population of producers."[24]

Yuan pointedly reminded Bigler of his own immigrant heritage and mentioned that America's "immigration made *you what you are*—your nation what it is. . . . I am sure your Excellency cannot, if you would, prevent your being called the descendant of an immigrant, for I am sure you do not boast of being a descendant of the red men," which got to the heart of American historical amnesia. He considered Bigler's assertion that the Constitution "admits of no asylum to any other than the pale face" to be "false" and even "reprehensible." He acknowledged that "you have degraded the negro because of your holding him in involuntary servitude, and because for the sake of union in some of your states such is tolerated"; more to the point, Yuan wrote, "amongst this class you would endeavor to place us; and no doubt it would be pleasing to some would-be freemen to mark the brand of servitude upon us." He insisted, "We are not the degraded race you would make us. We came amongst you as mechanics or traders, and following every honorable business of life. . . . As far as regards the color and complexion of our race, we are perfectly aware that our population have been a little more tanned than yours. Your Excellency will discover, however, that we are as much allied to the African race or the red man as you are yourself, and that as far as the aristocracy of skin is concerned, ours might compare with many of the European races."[25]

Yuan challenged not so much the American racial hierarchy as the place of Chinese within it, on grounds of both status (free, not enslaved) and color (closer to white than black or red). His stubborn insistence that the United States welcomed and treated equally all people, not just whites, was a bit confused, but his confusion was understandable because policy and practice at the time were inconsistent. The Naturalization Act of 1790 limited citizenship to "free white men of good moral character," but during much of the nineteenth century some Chinese did naturalize, among them Yung Wing (Yale '54) and Yuan himself. Free blacks could vote in northern states until the 1820s; the Supreme Court's ruling in *Dred Scott*, which denied that any black person, whether free or enslaved, was or could ever be a citizen, was still five years away. Not until 1882 were Chinese expressly excluded from citizenship.

Yuan Sheng used his own case as a naturalized citizen to refute Bigler's claim that no Chinese had ever made the United States his domicile or applied for naturalization. Hab Wa and Tong Achick similarly argued that "if the privileges of your laws are open to us, some of us will doubtless acquire your habits, your language, your ideas, your feelings, your morals, your forms, and become citizens of your country; many have already adopted your religion [as] their own;—and we will be good citizens. There are very good Chinamen now in the country; and a better class will, if allowed, come hereafter—men of learning and of wealth, bringing their families with them."

The publication of these letters in the San Francisco newspapers prompted sympathetic whites to encourage the Chinese to continue to press their case, especially in light of reports that white miners were attacking Chinese in the mountains. The Chinese leaders sent Tong Achick to Sacramento to meet personally with Governor Bigler, hoping to "soften his heart towards us" and to appeal to him to persuade white miners to abide by the law. Tong was also prepared to say that Chinese were willing to pay a foreign miners tax.

In Sacramento, Tong Achick was "very honorably entertained" by the governor and his "colonels and captains." Bigler asked him to write another letter, which he said he would answer, and that he would then print and circulate the two statements together to the American people. Believing that their "sorrows were nearly at an end," the Chinese wrote and sent another letter, but Bigler rejected it. The governor sent by messenger a substitute letter for them to sign. The presumption outraged the Chinese leaders. They protested that "the words are not our words, and that we cannot say them with the truth of honest men, and that they contradict what we have already said." They proceeded to publish their own letter, along with Bigler's address, their first letter, and a supportive memorial from California businessmen, as a pamphlet with the title, "An Analysis of the Chinese Question." It was printed and distributed by the San Francisco newspaper, the *Herald*.[26]

The second letter, signed by Tong Achick and Chun Aching (a leader of the Canton Company, or the Sanyi Huiguan), was filled with pain. "Many evils which we were then fearful of, have fallen upon our countrymen in the mines," they wrote. "At many places they have been driven away from their work and deprived of their claims . . . some of which they had bought from Americans at a high price." They specifically named the Middle Yuba River, Deer Creek, Foster's Bar, the north and south forks of the American River, and Weaver's Creek as places where whites had driven out Chinese miners. At Weaver's Creek, men had used long ropes to sweep down and drag off the tents of the Chinese. They turned away Chinese traders coming with provisions. "Many hundreds of Chinamen have thus been reduced to misery, and are now wandering about the mountains," Tong and Chun wrote. Some were "suffering even for want of food and . . . have fallen into utter despair. We are informed that grown men may sometimes be seen, sitting down alone in the wildest places, weeping like children."[27]

The Chinese driven from their claims and camps included recent emigrants who had just arrived on the goldfields. They had invested all their funds on provisions and equipment—shovels, picks, pans, and boots—and sustained heavy losses, not to mention humiliation. They promptly returned to San Francisco and departed on the next ship out. Tong Achick predicted that upon their return to China, they would tell of their suffering and dissuade new emigration. In fact, the Chinese leaders had already written home to report that Chinese should stop coming to America until they were again welcome. Nonetheless, they knew that many, if not most, of the Chinese living in California would remain. In fact, only some five thousand returned to China in the wake of Bigler's speech and the instigation of violence and expulsions in the gold districts. Tong and Chun beseeched Bigler to protect the Chinese remaining in the state. He hoped that the governor would want to "save our people," that he was "too humane to desire that we shall be murdered, or starved, or beggared in the mountains, by violent people who make use of your name when they are doing us wrong and think they please you by their acts."[28]

In their letter to the governor, Tong and Chun pledged that the Chinese would "cheerfully" and "without complaint" pay the foreign miner's tax of three dollars a month, which the legislature had just imposed at Bigler's urging. Formally the tax was a license to mine, a requirement made of all noncitizens. Tong understood that a license, even more explicitly than a tax, embodied a commitment on the part of the government that "when we have bought this right [to mine] we shall enjoy it." They asked, "Will you bid [the tax collector] to tell all the people that we are then under your protection, and that they must not disturb us?"[29]

THE FOREIGN MINERS TAX of 1852 was California's second such tax. The first, passed in May 1850, was set at twenty dollars a month, an exorbitant amount that, for many, exceeded a month's earnings. It aimed to punish foreign miners, especially Mexicans and Chileans, who were among the most skilled and hence the most competitive, as well as Europeans. (Chinese were not then the focus, as few had yet arrived on the goldfields.) The tax aroused angry opposition. In the town of Sonora in the San Joaquin valley, four thousand foreign miners—Mexican, Chilean, Peruvian, French, German, and English—confronted the tax collectors en masse and vowed they would not pay. There were violent clashes between foreign miners and sheriffs. Thousands of foreigners quit the mines, returning home or, in some cases, taking up new endeavors in towns and cities. Merchants in Sonora, suffering from the loss of business caused by the mass exodus, challenged the legality of the tax in the state supreme court. They lost the case, but continued unrest led the territorial governor, Peter Burnett, to lower the tax to five dollars a month. In March 1851 the legislature repealed it. But by then the tax had already driven twenty thousand foreign miners from the goldfields.[30]

Although many Californians believed the first foreign miners tax was a disaster, the legislature again used its power to tax to attack the Chinese. The new foreign miners tax was set at three dollars a month, about the same amount that Bigler believed Chinese coolies earned, and thus aimed to drive the Chinese out by making mining unremunerative. Although the new tax law did not specify any particular group, it was understood in the legislature that "the bill is directed especially at Chinamen, South Sea Islanders [Hawaiians], etc. and is not intended to apply to Europeans."[31]

Although Chinese miners dutifully paid the tax, harassment and violence against them continued. At least some whites, it seemed, were not satisfied with punishing Chinese with an onerous tax but wanted their wholesale removal and exclusion from the goldfields and from the state. Bigler had unleashed a powerful racist politics, based on theories of "slavery" and "cheap labor" that provided easy rationales for nativism, particularly among those miners who were anxious about their own future. Placer mining was rapidly depleting, and many worried about the coming of heavily capitalized companies that threatened to transform the industry—ditch companies that would bring water but at high prices, and quartz mining companies that might reduce independent prospectors to wage workers. When the next session of the legislature opened in January 1853, several bills were introduced seeking to amend the foreign miners tax law. Proposals ranged from increasing the tax to four dollars a month and giving greater powers to the tax collectors to the exclusion of Chinese from mining.[32]

Leaders of the Chinese community followed these developments closely. Their white American legal advisers likely had connections in the state capitol, and bilingual Chinese like Yuan Sheng and Tong Achick undoubtedly read the newspapers. They took the proactive step to advocate directly for their cause, asking for a meeting with the legislature's Committee on Mines and Mining Interests that was tasked with considering amendments to the law. Committee members traveled to San Francisco in February to meet with the leaders of the four Chinese native-place associations that had been established in California. Tong Achick, one of the Yeong Wo Huiguan's representatives, served as spokesman and interpreter for the group.[33]

When they met, the legislators did not approach the Chinese as their social equals, but neither were they unfriendly or disrespectful. Most of the committee members opposed the radical politics of racial exclusion, instead favoring the interests of the trade between China and California and the United States. They sought a solution that would allow for the development of trade by accepting a "place" for Chinese in America, especially for the merchants with whom they did business and, for the rest, a place at the margins, where miners could scratch at worked-over claims and pose no economic or social threat to whites. They were confident that Euro-Americans, being a "superior race," would not be contaminated or degraded by the presence of inferior Asiatics but might (over time) uplift the latter.[34]

On their part, the Chinese leaders presented their grievances to the committee, namely, that they continued to suffer from harassment and molestation despite their payment of the tax, that the state did not protect them, and that they had been prevented from testifying in court against whites on account of the color of their skin. At the same time, the Chinese leaders sought to ease the minds of the legislators that Chinese were free emigrants, not "coolies." They explained that whereas some Chinese had come to California under contract to Chinese or Euro-American capitalists in the early days of the gold rush, those arrangements had proved to be unprofitable and were abandoned. The overwhelming number of Chinese emigrants now came on their own account. Others, they said, paid for their passage on credit, using family property as collateral. The Chinese also took the opportunity to describe to the legislators the role of the *huiguan* as mutual aid associations. They explained that as leaders of these organizations, they had influence, but not control, over their people.[35]

The meeting went on to discuss practical proposals regarding the operation of the foreign miners tax. Both sides agreed that it should be better enforced. The Chinese suggested that the state employ a Chinese interpreter who would accompany the tax collectors in order to assist in the collection. The legislators demurred. The committee wanted the *huiguan* to bear responsibility for the full collection and payment of the tax. Tong Achick replied that the Chinese leaders would do their best to encourage compliance, but the associations could not assume so large a burden of liability for individuals whom they did not, after all, control. Although the proposals regarding collection fell flat, the Chinese offered a proposal for distributing the tax revenue that the legislators viewed positively. Tong Achick suggested that the revenue be shared between the state and the various counties where it was collected. Such an arrangement, he explained, might provide an incentive for local communities to tolerate and accept the Chinese. Possibly, over time, they might become friends. In fact, the Chinese would be willing to pay a higher tax to offset reduced funds to the state.[36]

Tong Achick and his fellow *huiguan* leaders displayed a sophisticated grasp of the stakes in the foreign miners tax. Their eagerness to embrace the tax, even an increased one, and their willingness to assist in its collection, was not a capitulation to racism. They understood that racist fever against Chinese still ran high, and they sought to counter it by appealing to the economic interests of local communities in the form of shared revenue. The Chinese had already invested as much as $2 million in businesses and property in California.[37] If the Chinese could prevent wholesale exclusion, if they could establish and hold some ground, even if marginal, they could survive and persist, and perhaps eventually prosper, on Gold Mountain. Theirs was a calculated view that considered the long game.

The upshot of the negotiation is evident in the amendments to the foreign miners tax passed by the legislature in 1853. The license fee increased to four dollars per month. The law stipulated that tax collectors be bonded, presumably to ensure honest and just interactions with the Chinese; but also gave collectors power to pursue scofflaws and to seize their property and sell it at auction. It also designated half of the revenue to go to the county where it was collected, as the Chinese merchants had suggested. The revenue generated by the foreign miners tax was considerable: $100,000 to the state and $85,000 to the major mining counties in 1854 and as high as $185,000 to the state and nearly as much to the counties in 1856.[38]

AS TONG ACHICK PREDICTED, the income from the foreign miners tax underwrote a grudging toleration of the Chinese on the goldfields. As well, many Chinese who had been chased away simply returned to their claims, and white miners did not have the energy to be constantly fighting them. It bears noting, too, that whites did business with Chinese, selling them claims they no longer wanted and, in the little towns, buying goods and services from Chinese laundries, restaurants, and vegetable peddlers. This is not to say that that harassment and violence ended. Unscrupulous whites posed as tax collectors to take money from Chinese;

one group of "rascals" swindled Chinese of $40,000 under the guise that they could purchase influence in the state legislature to reduce the tax. In 1861 Chinese merchant leaders reported that during the 1850s whites had murdered at least eighty-eight Chinese, including eleven killed by tax collectors; only two were convicted and hanged. More subtly, the tone in mainstream newspapers became less generous. The *Daily Alta* in 1850 and 1851 had written about Chinese arrivals as novel curiosities, dubbing them the "China Boys," which, although patronizing, was not hostile. By the mid-1850s, newspapers no longer ran curiosity stories, and "China Boys" were replaced with "Chinamen," the latter term carrying no affection.[39]

Still, an uneasy coexistence settled on the goldfields, marked in general by both suspicion and transaction, and by both occasional violence and occasional cooperation. In Yuba County, for example, white miners were not successful at eliminating the Chinese from their river claims. At Foster's Bar, a white miners' assembly passed a resolution in May 1852 requiring Chinese to leave in four days, but some two hundred Chinese were back by July, working on both sides of the Yuba River. Independent Chinese miners continued to mine along the Yuba, Middle Yuba, and North Yuba Rivers into the 1860s. Several hundred Chinese could still be found at Foster's Bar in 1860, some working quite profitably, with assets of $100 to $900. Chinese paid whites as much as much as $700 for a claim, sometimes throwing tools and equipment into the deal; others continued the practice of claiming first rights by preemption. The Chinese section of Marysville continued to provide goods and services to the miners working the rivers. By 1860 nineteen were engaged in garden farming, and there were cooks, servants, and a number of laundries, including a few operated by women and located in white neighborhoods, signaling that Chinese were doing business with whites.[40]

Chinese also persisted, after the crisis of 1852, in the southern mines. Although the mining district of Columbia, in Tuolumne County, was the first in the state to write a mining code that excluded Chinese, no other mining district in the county passed such a rule. Chinese continued to work in placer mining in the county. On Woods Creek, near Chinese Camp, Chinese were averaging eight to sixteen dollars a day at the time of Bigler's message. Whites attributed their success to diligence and luck; there is no record of expulsion. In general, whites did not bother Chinese in this little corner of gold country, tucked into the side of Rocky Hill, likely because diggings there were "dry," meaning there was no proximate water supply to sluice out the gold. The Chinese hauled gold-bearing dirt to nearby creeks at Sim's Ranch and Six Bit Gulch, with impressive results. By the time white miners caught on, too many Chinese had established themselves on the diggings to be driven out. As whites moved in, they worked alongside the Chinese, apparently without hostility, and cooperated to dig ditches that brought water down from Woods Creek. But white miners worked their claims "lightly once over, with precision and dispatch," and then moved on.[41]

The idea that whites sold worked-over and "worthless" claims to Chinese, who were content to scratch out a dollar or two a day, has long endured in California gold rush history. But through experience, Chinese became wiser in their dealings with white miners. H. B. Lansing, who mined around San Andreas and Mokelumne Hill in Calaveras County, frequently sold, or tried to sell, his claims to Chinese. In 1855 he lamented in his diary, "Tried to sell a claim to some Chinese but could not come it. They are getting entirely too sharp for soft snaps." Chinese gold diggers could obtain good yields through their knowledge of water engineering and by working cooperatively. Understandably they underreported, or failed to report at all, their earnings to mining and population census takers. In the year 1861 alone, when there were about thirty thousand Chinese miners in the state, Chinese paid an estimated $1.3 million buying claims. They also paid over $2 million in taxes and licenses, suggesting the likelihood that on average they made a decent living, if not a fabulous one.[42]

During the late 1850s and '60s, as the placer mines became exhausted, many Chinese moved from river mining to wage work, building ditches and flumes for water and hydraulic mining companies and working in deep mines. Beginning in June 1869, the white miners league staged a twenty-month-long strike against the underground quartz mining companies and included the expulsion of Chinese from the deep mines as part of their strike demands. Mining companies had lowered wages for underground miners in 1869 as part of a general trend of declining wages on the goldfields. The miners league wanted their wages restored as well as equal pay for underground and aboveground work, although the former involved greater skill as well as greater danger. Rumors held that Chinese would be brought in along with "giant powder" (dynamite) and single-handed drills, cost-saving devices that were gradually being introduced into the mines. In fact, Chinese in large numbers had been working in deep mines in the Mariposa, Josephine, and Pine-Tree mining companies for ten or more years, proving themselves able and garnering wages nearly equal to those of whites. In the end, the miners league lost the strike, losing on all their demands save for the expulsion of the Chinese.[43]

The shift to capitalized mining and the general decline in wages and income across the goldfields led many gold miners to leave the California diggings in the mid- and late 1860s, both whites and Chinese. Chinese were now working as farmers and as farm laborers, reclaiming the San Joaquin River delta and clearing the valleys of Butte County of brush for agriculture. The huge workforce of twenty thousand Chinese who built the western portion of the transcontinental railroad included many former gold miners, in addition to those recruited in China. And they went to San Francisco where they worked in woolen mills and cigar and shoe factories.[44]

But they had started in gold, and many stayed in gold. In 1861, 60 percent of the Chinese in the state remained in mining. Some moved to newer goldfields in Oregon, British Columbia, and Nevada. But many remained on the California goldfields, like Ah Jake of Goodyears Bar in Sierra County, who eked out a living from their river claims and took on other work, like cooking for white people, to subsist. Others bought or leased old hydraulic and drift claims from whites, some of which turned a steady profit for years.[45]

One remarkable stroke of luck and canny entrepreneurship exploited a new goldfield that was discovered a few miles south of Oroville in Butte County in 1872. After a young white man named Kline found placers in the area, local ranchers offered small parcels of land to Chinese to buy or rent. For whites, it seemed to bring a more certain profit than digging for gold; for Chinese, who were forbidden to locate first claims on their own, it was a way in. Soon there were hundreds of Chinese, then thousands, at the site, known first as the Modoc claims, after the indigenous people of the area, and then as the Lava Beds, after the famous Modoc hideout and fort in northern California.[46]

The gold was plentiful, but the terrain of the Lava Beds was not hilly enough to support hydraulic mining or sluicing. Rather, the miners sank a shaft twelve to eighteen feet deep, excavated gold-bearing gravel with a windlass, which they washed with a rocker, using water also from derived the shaft. These rough methods dated to the early days of the gold rush, but Chinese who made money from the Lava Beds also invested in capital equipment like steam pumps, for draining water from the shafts. Most of the work on the Lava Beds followed the model of the small Chinese mining company, led by a merchant-investor and employing ten to sixty men who worked in gangs. During the 1872–73 season, Chinese reportedly made ten and twenty dollars a day, an amount not seen since the early days of the gold rush. Chinese continued to arrive; new stages were added to the Marysville-Oroville line to meet demand, including a special stop, "China station," near the diggings. By November 1873 as many as eight thousand Chinese were working the Lava Beds. The minirush drove up the price of a claim, which had started at $400 and rose to $2,000 or more within the year. To purchase their claims, Chinese relied on the services of Euro-American brokers and lawyers and a Chinese banker, Sin Yet, who ran through the streets of Oroville with sacks of twenty-dollar gold pieces.[47]

The Lava Beds sustained more or less continuous gold mining until 1878, despite an outbreak of a deadly fever that killed seven hundred people in the spring of 1874. A local newspaper estimated that the Chinese mines had produced $720,000 a year, much of which was spent on provisions and amenities (benefiting local merchants, both white and Chinese); the balance was sold to gold houses in Oroville. At times Wells Fargo transported as much as $20,000 a week in gold from Oroville to San Francisco. A number of Chinese settlements sprang up; the main encampment built within months of the rush laid out parallel lanes and accommodated 150 dwellings—mostly roughly built shanties—a dozen canvas tents, and a brick store. Soon a temple was added, then a Chinese theater, and more stores.[48]

ANTI-CHINESE AGITATORS CLAIMED that Chinese contributed nothing to California but took all their gold back to China, and that whatever they spent in the United States went to Chinese businesses. In fact Chinese poured millions into the California economy: in 1861, for example, in addition to paying the foreign miners tax, they contributed $14 million, which included customs duties on imports; the purchase of American products; payment of steamboat and stage passenger fares and freight charges; and water charges and buying claims.[49]

Some Chinese emigrants who did well at gold mining poured their profits into other endeavors, typically becoming merchants or investing in larger mining operations. Others did send gold back home—just as all miners did, whether they were American or came from Europe, Australia, or Chile. The amount of "treasure" (gold and silver bullion) shipped from the port of San Francisco to China in 1874, for example, totaled $6.2 million, nearly one-third of a total export of $21.5 million. (The largest share, more than half, went to New York.) But this figure includes more than gold directly derived from mining, because businessmen (both Chinese and non-Chinese) shipped gold and silver as payment for commercial and banking transactions. At the same time, a fair amount of gold was likely shipped overseas without being recorded, as people carried gold dust in the hidden bottoms of their satchels and in the linings of their coats.[50]

RACE RELATIONS BETWEEN Chinese and whites in the mining districts were not always marked by conflict or violence. Some relationships were cordial, even friendly, especially in the context of ongoing transactions in the small towns of the gold country. Various points of engagement developed and persisted among these "longtime Californ'," both Chinese and white: selling vegetables, buying grub, changing gold dust to coin, cooking and performing domestic service, doing missionary work. Such

contact did not (and could not) produce among the white people an inti-
mate knowledge of the Chinese around them, but neither did whites view
Chinese indiscriminately as anonymous Chinamen.

That approach bitterly disappointed the ardent restrictionists, who
decried the failure of white people to forgo immediate economic gain for
the general interest of the white race. "It has been proposed that the people of California shall take the settlement of the Chinese question into
their own hands, by refusing to employ them in any way, or to deal with
those who employ them," opined the *Sacramento Daily Union*. "More than
one attempt has been made to put it in practice," it continued, but "everyone knows that there are thousands of people who care more about money
than for principle."[51] But if it was true that some whites profited from Chinese labor, it was also true that economic motives were not the whole of it.

Let us return to the case of Ah Jake, who was convicted of murder and
condemned to hang in Sierra County. Ah Jake did not die by the hangman's
noose. Intervention from prominent white citizens of Downieville saved
him from the gallows. Leading townspeople appealed to Governor Robert Waterman to commute the sentence to life imprisonment. Jerome A.
Vaughn, editor of the *Mountain Messenger* and a county supervisor, and
Charles Kirkbride, a Methodist minister, wrote letters; and some fifty others signed two petitions, citing "grave doubt" as to the guilt of Ah Jake.
Among the signatories were merchants, lawyers, the superintendent of
schools, a notary, miners, a cabinetmaker, a jeweler, a surveyor, the telegraph and express agent, and the court reporter. Six of the jurors, including the foreman, asked that the sentence be commuted. Two local citizens
who had been at the crime scene shortly after the incident and testified at
trial as witnesses for the prosecution wrote the governor to say that they
believed a scuffle between Ah Jake and Wah Chuck had taken place there.[52]

Of greatest consequence was an affidavit submitted by Sheriff S. C.
Stewart, a longtime resident of Goodyears Bar and a former lumberman
at the sawmill there. He testified at trial that he had known Ah Jake for
some number of years. He may have regretted that his testimony about
the track marks on the Downieville stage road was not fully elaborated
when, after the conviction and sentencing, the judge issued a death war-

rant that "command[ed] and require[d] you [Stewart] to execute the said Judgment . . . by hanging the said Ah Jake by the neck until he is dead." Only four people had ever been officially executed in the history of Sierra County—three in the 1850s (including an Indian named Pijo who had killed two Chinese miners) and the last in 1885, James O'Neill, as punishment for murdering his employer. As sheriff, Stewart was committed to enforcing the law, and he had in fact hanged O'Neill. But Ah Jake's case seemed different: Stewart knew Ah Jake, and he knew Ah Jake was not guilty of first-degree murder. Perhaps the prospect of hanging him was chilling. Stewart brought his concerns to Judge Soward and to Jerome Vaughn, editor of the *Messenger*.[53]

Stewart's affidavit offered a detailed explanation of his examination of the crime scene and his opinion that the marks in the road showed not only that there had been a fight but also that Ah Jake's footprints (he had been barefoot after his assailants took his boots) did not track back to the scene of the crime. Judge Soward wrote a letter in support of the sheriff and stated that Ah Jake's lawyers had not mounted a proper defense, as they had not elicited a full testimony from the sheriff at trial and, moreover, had argued with each other in open court.[54]

No doubt some white residents of Downieville supported Ah Jake because they knew him; he had worked as an occasional cook for white people, including Vaughn, the newspaperman. His relations with white people seemed to be friendly. For example, Victor Bouther, a farmer at Goodyears Bar, had met Ah Jake on the way into town on that fateful day. He gave Ah Jake a ride in his wagon and offered to carry his provisions back to Goodyears Bar. But whereas at least some local white citizens considered Ah Jake to be a good man and spoke in the language of clemency on his behalf, no white people described the dead man, Wah Chuck, as a good man, and none demanded justice for him. Wah Chuck was even more marginal to white society than was Ah Jake. Unlike Ah Jake, he did not work for white people. He lived farther out of town, at a small Chinese mining encampment at China Flat, along the South Yuba River, about halfway between Downieville and Sierra City. He came into Downieville occasionally to buy provisions for his "company" and to visit the Chinese gambling house. His patronage there may have prompted the *Mountain Messenger* to declare that "Ah Jake bore an excellent character, whereas that of the deceased was notoriously bad."[55]

Wah Chuck did have powerful Chinese advocates: handsome rewards were offered for Ah Jake's arrest and, later, for his conviction. Local whites said that Wah Chuck belonged to a bigger and more powerful native-place association than did Ah Jake, but in fact they both were members of the Hop Wo Company (Hehe Huiguan), one of the *huiguan* from the Siyi region. They even may have been from the same lineage, with "Jake" and "Chuck" being transliterations of the same surname. But Wah Chuck also may have been affiliated with the sworn brotherhood society, the Zhigongdang. He belonged to a small mining cooperative, which were commonly associated with the brotherhood. Plus, he was an inveterate gambler and would have been a frequent visitor to the Zhigongdang's lodge in Downieville.[56]

In November Governor Waterman commuted Ah Jake's sentence to life in prison. Citing evidence not adduced at trial, a lack of competent counsel, and petitions from prominent citizens, the governor concluded that Ah Jake had acted "to a certain element in self-defense" and that there was a "reasonable doubt" as to whether he had committed murder in the first degree. On November 28 Ah Jake was committed to Folsom Prison.[57]

About a year later Lo Kay, the occasional interpreter, told Sheriff Stewart that Ah Ting, the deceased Wah Chuck's traveling companion (who had since returned to China), had given him a different version of the killing than the story he told at the trial. Rumors also circulated in Downieville that Lo Kay had been promised a large sum of money for Ah Jake's conviction. In light of this information, Judge Soward asked the governor to grant Ah Jake a full pardon.[58]

Ah Jake also wrote to the governor directly. His letters were written in formal English in a neat hand, perhaps by a prison scribe or minister. "I was sent to Folsom Prison for defending my Life and Property for life," he wrote. And: "My friend Mr. Spaulding writting [sic] from Downieville tells me that all of my papers are in your hands and Dear Sir I do hope

that you will let me go as I have borne with as much fortitude my punishment one possible could do." He added that he was in poor health and
submitted a letter from the warden attesting to his good behavior.[59]

Finally, on December 30, 1890, Ah Jake received a full pardon. In his
statement, Waterman said that he was "convinced that Ah Jake is an innocent man and should be restored to his liberty." On January 1, 1891, Ah
Jake walked out of prison a free man. He returned to Goodyears Bar,
where he lived out his days. He continued to mine for gold, scratching out
a bare living, going to Downieville once a month to sell what little gold dust
he accumulated.[60]

AH JAKE WAS NOT the only Chinese person in nineteenth-century California to receive an executive pardon. At least fifteen Chinese prisoners
in the state received pardons between 1854 and 1885. Chinese prisoners received pardons for good behavior, for serious illness, and, most frequently, as in Ah Jake's case, when conviction was deemed to have been
based on insufficient evidence or perjured testimony. Prosecutors often
had little evidence to bring a conviction, and white people in general
professed difficulty distinguishing one Chinese person from another,
especially when trying to recall the details of a crowded scene. Contemporaries routinely cited language and cultural barriers as the main problems in trying criminal cases involving Chinese.[61]

Some local prosecutors dismissed charges against Chinese for want of evidence, while others were determined to "round up the usual suspects" and
press for a conviction even when evidence was weak and witnesses lacked
credibility. In granting pardons, the governor often referred to "doubt as to
his guilt," "a conspiracy on part of Chinese witnesses," "circumstances [that]
have come to light which tend to establish his innocence," and the like.[62]

The practice of granting pardons to convicted Chinese on grounds of
perjured testimony is an ironic outcome of broader contemporary judicial
opinion that Chinese could not be counted on to tell the truth. During
the nineteenth century, a body of law evolved in western territories and
states that restricted or excluded testimony from Chinese witnesses and
defendants in both criminal and civil cases. In California, *People v. Hall*

(1854) established testimonial exclusion on simple grounds of racial inferiority—like blacks and Indians, Chinese victims and witnesses could not testify against white defendants.[63]

Courts also justified testimonial exclusion, more generally, even when defendant and victim were of the same ethno-racial group, on grounds that Chinese did not understand the sanctity of the Christian oath. Some courts disallowed Chinese testimony because the court could not properly swear in Chinese witnesses. On occasion, judges conceded that Christians were not the only people who valued "truth" and allowed non-Christians to be sworn in according to their own cultural precepts regarding truth telling and lying. But more often, a proclivity toward lying was deemed to be a racial trait of the Chinese, a critical index of their alleged barbarism. In California, the inability to testify in court exposed Chinese to violence and murder "at the hands of lawless wretches," as Pun Chi, a young merchant, wrote in an appeal to Congress. He continued, "Yet though there be Chinese witnesses of the crime, their testimony is rejected. The result is our utter abandonment to be murdered and that our business to be ruined. How hard for the spirit to sustain such trials!"[64]

In nineteenth-century California and other western jurisdictions, testimonial exclusion was a pillar of racism against Chinese and Native American Indians in the criminal justice system.[65] That this widespread racist belief should come full circle to vindicate Chinese wrongly convicted for capital crimes is a small wonder of history's unintended consequences.

Chapter 5

The Limits of Protection

The young Chinese gold digger blushed when he stepped forward to speak at the mass meeting in Castlemaine on Monday, August 10, 1857. Pon Sa was nervous speaking before the large, agitated crowd of thirteen hundred of his countrymen who had gathered on Mechanic's Hill to protest the latest tax imposed on Chinese residents of Victoria. But once Pon Sa started speaking, he could not stop. In a "fluent harangue," Pon Sa decried Englishmen's treatment of Chinese on the goldfields. Englishmen drove Chinese away from any claims that paid well. Chinese diggers obtained so little gold, sometimes as little as ten shillings' worth a month, that many could barely afford to eat or buy tools, let alone send anything home to their wives and families. Those who were unable to pay the taxes already imposed on them were jailed and fined, and many would have languished and died in jail if not for the collections that their fellow Chinese made to help pay their fines. The latest tax proposal—a steep one pound per month—promised to push Chinese into abject poverty and starvation, said Pon Sa. Chinese wished to follow the Englishmen's laws, but the tax was onerous, wicked, and unjust. The audience frequently interrupted Pon Sa with calls and murmurs of agreement.

Virtually the entire Chinese population on the Mount Alexander diggings went to Castlemaine that day. Throughout the morning they pro-

Population of Chinese Miners, Victoria, 1857

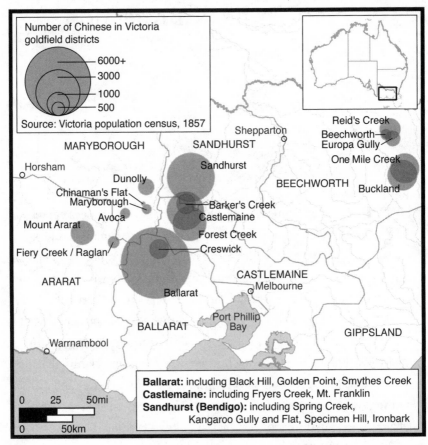

Number of Chinese in Victoria
goldfield districts

- 6000+
- 3000
- 1000
- 500

Source: Victoria population census, 1857

Reid's Creek
Shepparton
Beechworth
Europa Gully
One Mile Creek

MARYBOROUGH
SANDHURST
Horsham
Sandhurst
BEECHWORTH
Buckland
Dunolly
Chinaman's Flat
Maryborough
Barker's Creek
Castlemaine
Avoca
Mount Ararat
Forest Creek
Fiery Creek / Raglan
Creswick

ARARAT
CASTLEMAINE
Melbourne
Ballarat

Port Phillip
Bay
BALLARAT
GIPPSLAND
Warrnambool

Ballarat: including Black Hill, Golden Point, Smythes Creek
Castlemaine: including Fryers Creek, Mt. Franklin
Sandhurst (Bendigo): including Spring Creek,
    Kangaroo Gully and Flat, Specimen Hill, Ironbark

0   25   50mi

0   50km

Map by Dan Miller

ceeded to the missionary Chu-a-Luk's chapel, where they signed petitions protesting the tax. They then "paraded" about the streets until Chu-a-Luk opened the meeting on the hill at two o'clock. After Chu-a-Luk and Pon Sa spoke, the petitions were read and cheered. The meeting determined to raise funds in order to support the "movement" and to hire counsel to plead their case before the "English governors." The audience then cheered the King and adjourned.[1]

The residency tax was not the first suffered by the Chinese in Victoria. They also had to pay landing fees and a "protection" tax, as well as the standard mining license. Like the foreign miners tax in California, the Victorian race taxes were aimed to discourage Chinese immigration, impoverish those who came anyway in the hope of driving them out, and marginalize those who insisted on remaining, while at the same time enriching the government's coffers. Tong K. Achick and other California *huiguan* leaders accepted the foreign miners tax in exchange for the state's protection, a reasonable expectation but one that was honored only in the breach. But unlike their California counterparts, Victoria's Chinese merchants and miners protested the colony's unjust taxes with mass meetings, petitions, delegations, noncompliance, and civil disobedience.

As in California, Victoria's policies toward Chinese on the goldfields responded to white opinion that Chinese were a potential menace to society. But whereas anti-Chinese sentiment in California congealed quickly into a theory of anticoolieism, racism in Victoria was more inchoate. No overarching theory about Chinese as a "coolie race" emerged on the goldfields. Europeans in Australia viewed Chinese with suspicion and prejudice against, variously, their heathenism, alleged uncleanliness and immorality, and general unintelligibility. If Australian racism and race policy had a recurrent and dominant theme, it was fear that their tiny outpost on the fringes of the British Empire would be overrun by the proximate millions from China. The Chinese Question in Australia emerged in context of a perceived clash between two empires in Asia: British and Chinese.

THE FIRST CHINESE WHO arrived in the Australian colonies in the late 1840s were, in fact, indentured workers, contracted to work on the huge sheep runs of New South Wales. As convict transportation declined and, with it, the use of "assigning" convicts for shepherding and other rural work, the pastoralists—Australia's first big capitalists—turned to indentured Asian labor from India and China. In the late 1830s and early '40s, pastoralists imported several hundred contract laborers from West Bengal; between 1847 and 1853, Australians brought another 500 Indians and 3,608 Chinese, the latter recruited overwhelmingly from Xiamen on the South China coast of Fujian province. Australians likely recruited in Xiamen because that port was a major source of Chinese labor emigration to Singapore, another British colony. Indentured Chinese went to Australia to work as shepherds, hut-keepers, farmhands, and domestic servants under contracts of four to five years. They earned about ten pounds a year (less than half the average European wage) and were subject to the colonies' masters and servants laws, which imposed penal sanctions for absconding or disobedience.[2]

From the outset, Australian colonists were skeptical about the use of Asian indentured labor. Many believed free British emigrants should settle Australia and not unfree labor, whether convicts or coolies. They feared that Australia would come to resemble the British plantation colonies of the Caribbean, where the use of indentured Indians as a replacement for enslaved Africans seemed to barely diminish the evils of slavery. In 1843 four thousand people in New South Wales, self-described working people, signed a petition declaring that the importation of "coloured workers" would be a "grave injustice to freemen who had come to better their condition." A contemporary warned that British emigrants, even the poorest Irish laborers and servants who came on government assistance, would find their wages reduced to 20 rupees a year or be "trampled into beggary and ruin." The antitransportation movement, modeled on the British antislavery societies, deemed the importation of indentured coolies even worse than that of convicts, whom they considered at least potentially redeemable. But the Colonial Office in London conceded, "The supply of really eligible Emigrants, that is, of those of the proper age, and possessing the requisite health and knowledge of some useful description of labor, is limited. . . . [It] is doubtful whether the requisite number will be obtainable."[3]

The sheep ranchers were defensive about using indentured workers but adamant that they had no other recourse to labor. As on other settler frontiers, indigenous people resisted working for Europeans. A Port Phillip pastoralist, Charles Nicholson, declared, "The fact is that we must have labour in some shape or other—free labour if we can get it; if not, prison labour; and failing either, coolie labour." The *Melbourne Age* echoed that rationale with the view that importing Asians was the "*dernier* resort."[4]

By the early 1850s the opponents of indentured labor had largely prevailed, owing to the association of coolies with convict labor and the penal origins of the colonies, beyond which proper settlers wished to progress. Many settlers argued that replacing convict labor with indentured Asians would create vast inequalities and thus would make democracy impossible. A critic of the wool capitalists asserted, "Chinese laborers were the offspring of that morbid craving for cheap convict labor, which cannot be appeased while hope remains that it may be supplied. Chinese emigration is merely an extension of the slave trade." When the Port Phillip District separated from New South Wales as the new colony of Victoria in 1851, it founded as a free colony and banned all indentured labor, regardless of origin. In New South Wales, where the pastoralists wielded considerable political clout, the use of indentured Chinese continued, albeit modestly and not without public criticism.[5]

But the onset of the gold rush in the early 1850s shifted the framework for how white Australians imagined the Chinese question. The gold rush was an unexpected answer to Australians' prayers for free labor, and much more. It promised a level of prosperity previously unimaginable and brought tens of thousands of people to Australia. In general, they were free emigrants of diverse social background who hailed mostly from the British Isles but also from continental Europe (especially Germany), the United States, and China.[6]

Chinese arrived on the Victorian goldfields in 1853, about a year and a half after the initial rush. By 1854 there were ten thousand Chinese in the colony, a relatively small number, but their presence sparked controversy. Historians have recounted the animosity of Europeans toward the Chinese, and some have compared it to the racism on the California goldfields. But the Chinese Question in Australia began quite differently than it did in California.[7]

Many Europeans on the Victorian diggings believed the Chinese were an "annoyance," in particular because they considered the Chinese method of alluvial mining to waste or spoil water. Henry Melville, a shopkeeper in Castlemaine, explained that that was the Europeans' "great complaint; they [Chinese] take the water out of one hole, and let their 'tailings' [detritus] fall into another one, and so destroy the water of two holes." According to William Hopkins, a miner in Sandhurst, "they destroy our water; they cannot talk with us, and we cannot reason with them."[8]

Aside from the water question, conflicts sometimes erupted over the right to mining claims. It was common for Chinese to work on old claims that Europeans had abandoned, perhaps because it was easier than having to prospect new areas, even though washing tailings was a low-yield endeavor. But Europeans, who left their claims when they heard of new leads, often returned after those leads disappointed or were exhausted. In their minds, they had not abandoned their earlier diggings but were holding them in "reserve," although one could legally hold only one claim at a time. Europeans drew ugly images to justify chasing Chinese from their claims, as in the politician William Westgarth's description of Chinese as "devouring locusts" who "follow on the heels of others, rewashing and gleaning up everything."[9]

Racial tension and conflict dotted the goldfields but were not ubiquitous. Chinese and whites often worked alongside each other in the gullies; they got along and they quarreled, like all gold diggers in the competitive environment of the rush. Nor was European opinion about the Chinese of one mind: some considered the Chinese to be "a most quiet, inoffensive class of persons" and "perfectly harmless," not "insolent," and even "elevated physically and intellectually." But others called them a "set of thieves" and "notorious gamblers."[10]

As the population of Chinese in Victoria grew—to 2,000 in 1854 and 42,000 by 1859, nearly 20 percent of all adult males—the increase itself became the focus of concern among Europeans, who now imagined a heathen race flooding the colonies. Conflict over mining practicalities assumed the contours, albeit vague, of a racial discourse, which served as a kind of feedback loop and inflamed racial tension on the diggings. In Bendigo, where three thousand Chinese had settled by 1854, a "monster meeting" of over a thousand European diggers resolved to forcibly drive the Chinese from the goldfields. The gold commissioner, John Panton, averted mob violence by sending for police reinforcements and promising the Europeans an investigation into their grievances.[11]

The arguments against Chinese gold seekers differed from those in California or in Victoria itself during the indentured labor debates. Victorians did not allege that Chinese diggers were coolies or otherwise unfree; precisely the fact that Chinese were free migrants disturbed whites, because free migration was theoretically unlimited and uncontrollable. British settler colonials understood—and dared not challenge—a cardinal principle of English liberalism, that of free immigration and settlement, which principle extended throughout the empire. But they began to argue that such freedoms ought not apply to Chinese because they threatened to overrun the country like "locusts"; that they were not assimilable; and that they brought "neither a moral, physical, nor political gain" to Australia. One newspaper opined, "It would be absurd to suppose that because English soil is free to all the world, that the Government and people of England would suffer overwhelming hordes of inferior races to settle down upon the land, and effect the degeneracy of the nation." "Home-Stayer" wrote similarly to the *Empire*, "The law of Britain grew up on British soil suited to the circumstances of the British Islands. There was not that wide difference of races. . . . We stand in a position no people, perhaps, ever did before—a nation with liberal and enlightened institutions, with open door at the threshold of the great Pagan world."[12]

The arguments for a Chinese exception to liberal principle centered on religious difference. That difference appeared to be an unbridgeable chasm, was presumed to be irreconcilable, and hence ruled out the possibility that Chinese could ever be proper settlers. Notwithstanding the work of Christian missionaries on the goldfields, most Europeans, even those who considered Chinese to be inoffensive and harmless, believed, "We cannot instruct them."[13]

Heathenism was not just a lack of Christian faith; it meant a lack of Christian morals. This lack was the root source of all that appeared suspicious about the Chinese, from their method of using water to their alleged criminality to, most important, the absence of women and families. Europeans believed that only Christians valued the nuclear bourgeois family, and that the family, in turn, was the cornerstone of an ordered and moral society. Without stable families, society was in danger of moral degeneracy. Indeed, the large population of single male European gold seekers also disturbed many observers, although common belief held that they would eventually marry and settle down. From another angle, some critics worried that the lack of Chinese women in the colony would lead Chinese men to marry European women, creating a degenerate "piebald breed."[14]

There were some references to Chinese "slavery" in the public debate, much of it hyperbole. A typical statement claimed, "It would be far better . . . to receive two thousand convicts from the parent country than five hundred of these yellow slaves from a land of lies, infanticide, and heathenism." The governor of Victoria, Sir Charles Hotham, privately expressed the view that financing passage from China on credit was "something very closely approaching a traffic in slaves." Hotham read a theory about "oriental despotism" into the phenomenon of immigration credit, even though virtually all nationality and ethnic groups in the nineteenth and early twentieth centuries used credit to enable long-distance migration. Corrupt officials in Sydney used the same stereotype to justify the seizure of £9,480 of gold from Chinese on an outbound ship in 1856: "The Chinese are sulky," said John De Courcey Bremer, the customs officer. "The gold will just go to their rich masters to pay their debts."[15]

In general, though, Australians did not use the term *slavery* promiscuously. The success of the coolie trope in California depended on proximity to African slavery in the American South. No ready racialized comparison existed in Australia, where the history of unfreedom was not racial slavery but convict transportation, convict-labor assignment, and more recently, Asian indenture. Rather, the foremost fear among Australians was that the Chinese might "overrun" them, an exaggerated view but one that had purchase in context of Australia's small white population (about 400,000 in 1850) relative to its Asian neighbors. The *Argus* explained that "geographically, we are nearer the pent up millions of China than any other large tract of country occupied by the white man. . . . We are but still a handful of men and women and children" (Figure 17).[16]

The alarm over the "Chinese invasion" was ubiquitous and often hysterical in tone. An official government report wrote that the *"great number"* of Chinese was "already almost *incredible*, . . . yet appears to be still *fast increasing.*" Victoria faced an "unpleasant possibility . . . that a comparative handful of colonists may be buried in a *countless throng* of Chinamen." The goldfield commissioner at Eureka spoke of "Chinamen" who *"swarmed* about [Europeans] like *devouring locusts.*" Speakers at anti-Chinese monster meetings raised the specter of "dark-complexion Mongols" outnumbering whites ten to one. Some predicted that *"one or two millions"* were coming. Newspaper editorials and letters railed against an "abhorrent *mass of foreign* Paganism" and the "great social question arising out of a *vast influx* of an inferior race, having no sympathies in common with the people whose soil they inhabit, and drawing after them *countless hordes* from a *population practically inexhaustible.*"[17]

Some Victorians took notice of recent conflicts between China and Britain at Guangzhou, that is, the Opium Wars; others commented on disturbances involving Chinese in Singapore and Java. Australian colonials could not escape the greater geopolitical stakes of the British Empire in Asia. Indeed, gold rush emigration from China inverted the dream of an earlier generation of British colonials in Australia that they, not China, would be the force of expansion throughout the Pacific. The call to restrict Chinese emigration was, at some level, a crisis of confidence, an admission that colonials were unable to engage the Chinese on a free and equal basis.[18]

‡

OPPOSITION TO CHINESE on the goldfields took place in context of growing discontent against the colonial government. Although some whites blamed

Chinese for "taking" their abandoned diggings, most did not scapegoat Chinese for their own difficulties or misfortunes. The main target of the diggers' ire was the colonial government, specifically its licensing requirement for mining on crown land and its heavy-handed methods of enforcement. The license was expensive, initially thirty shillings a month, and limited claims to eight square feet per individual. Gold commissioners, responsible for licensing in the districts, were part of a veritable army of commissioners, collectors, inspectors, magistrates, and constables that policed the goldfields. Victoria contrasted sharply with California, where authorities did nothing to stop miners from digging up and squatting on federal land.

Popular resentment of and protest against the licensing requirement grew steadily. Opposition to the tax and the arbitrary nature of governance on the goldfields generated broader political demands for the franchise and land reform, all perceived as the constitutional rights of British subjects. Centering in Bendigo and spreading throughout the colony, miners wore red ribbons, swore nonpayment of the tax, held mass meetings, and organized petitions. The legislature made one reduction in 1853, to about thirteen shillings monthly (£8 a year), still quite costly.

By the fall of 1854, the government's response to continued widespread evasion of the tax was to conduct twice-weekly license inspections on the goldfields, which inflamed greater resentment and resistance and culminated in the Eureka Uprising at Ballarat in December. After months of popular protest, which included the burning of the Eureka hotel, an armed group of several hundred British and European gold diggers built a stockade and called for rebellion against the colonial government. They were violently crushed by the militia, resulting in hundreds of arrests and some thirty miners killed. The crisis prompted Governor Charles Hotham to convene a Goldfield Commission of Enquiry, which generally found legitimacy in the miners' grievances against tyrannical and corrupt goldfield administration. The legislature passed several reforms, including replacement of the license by a "miner's right" of one pound a year; local governance of goldfield districts; goldfield representation on an enlarged legislative council; and a gold export tax.[19]

The same commission made recommendations for dealing with the

Chinese Question. The commission explicitly did not recommend "absolute exclusion" of Chinese, but it believed "some step is here necessary, if not to prohibit, at least to check and diminish this influx." It proposed that vessels sailing from British ports (Hong Kong and Singapore) restrict the number of Chinese they took on, perhaps fifteen to thirty per ship, and pay a hefty fine for each additional passenger. The legislature duly responded later that year with a law that restricted the number of Chinese passengers on each ship to one person per ten tons of tonnage; and it further imposed a landing fee of ten pounds on every immigrant arriving in Victoria. The law also authorized the governor to make "rules and regulations" for the "management and good government" of the Chinese, under which authority he imposed a one-pound annual "protection" tax. Eighteen months later the legislature imposed a monthly residence tax of one pound on all Chinese. These added up to a substantial burden, especially since Chinese also had to pay the standard miner's right.[20]

The Chinese responded with a sustained resistance that combined active protest and noncompliance, bearing marked resemblance to the European antilicensing movement, although few Europeans acknowledged the similarities at the time. A "humble petition" signed by 5,168 Chinese merchants, miners, and others residing at Bendigo protested the ten-pound landing fee. The Chinese called it a head tax and as such "unjust in principle, a violation of a fundamental law of the British Constitution, and degrading to your Petitioners." The collection of over five thousand signatures represented a substantial portion of Chinese population in the Bendigo area, suggesting a high level of organization. It would have operated through the Siyi Huiguan and the Yixing brotherhood, through their clubhouses in the villages, and by word of mouth across the diggings. A second petition from "Chinese in Victoria," which was perhaps organized with the assistance of the Ballarat Chinese protector, William Henry Foster, boasted 3,089 signatures.[21]

Considerable organization also underwrote a massive evasion of the landing tax. Ships coming from Hong Kong and Xiamen avoided Port Phillip (Melbourne) and traveled an additional three hundred miles to land at Port Robe in Guichen Bay, in the neighboring colony of South Australia, which had no landing fee. Some arrived with headmen who spoke English and dressed as Englishmen. From Port Robe the Chinese walked 220 miles overland to the Victorian goldfields, a journey that took them through difficult terrain and dangerous bush, including mountains, swamp, and desert. They walked, sometimes guided by compass, and showed up by the hundreds in Avoca, Ballarat, even Melbourne. An estimated fourteen thousand Chinese arrived at Port Robe during the first half of 1857, turning the little wool-exporting town (population 200) into a bustling port town. Europeans, who quickly trebled the population, profited from selling food, supplies, information, and guide services to arriving Chinese gold seekers.[22]

The walking parties sometimes numbered as many as six hundred Chinese men, whose line stretched for two miles. Each man carried a bamboo pole with two baskets, and each group was accompanied by several wagons carrying provisions and those who fell sick along the way. They covered twenty miles a day. En route they dug wells for fresh water, bought sheep for fresh meat, and left messages in towns for those who would follow. As a hedge against unscrupulous guides, they carved the barks of trees to mark the trail.[23]

The Victorian government pleaded with its neighbors to legislate similar landing fees in order to halt the overland migration of Chinese to the goldfields. South Australia complied in 1857. But Chinese migration to the goldfields continued as ships diverted to New South Wales. Twelve thousand Chinese landed at Sydney in 1858, of which nine thousand crossed the Murray River into Victoria. The legislature added a four-pound overland-entry tax to discourage crossings from neighboring colonies, although it was almost impossible for isolated land border guards to collect, as the Chinese muttered "no savvee" while walking by them.[24]

The one-pound-per-month residency tax imposed in 1857 generated a new round of petitioning. The mass protest at Castlemaine took place just weeks after the legislature passed the tax, again displaying a high level of organization. The missionary Chu-a-Luk, who organized the petition and meeting, was also the official Chinese interpreter in Castlemaine. In that capacity he was connected to Chinese throughout the district and their social networks comprising the *huiguan* and brotherhood societies. Though he was working for the colonial goldfield bureaucracy, Chu-a-Luk's loyalties lay squarely with his people. The same was true for headmen employed by the resident wardens, whose jobs, ironically, were to assist in the collection of license and protection tickets. The headman A-Luo reported to the Castlemaine meeting that he would communicate with the Chinese in other districts in order to build the "movement."

Thousands of Chinese across the Victorian goldfields signed at least nine petitions and submitted them to the colonial government in 1856 and 1857. In addition to the large number of signatures, the petitions are noteworthy for their arguments and justifications. Petitioners cited inability to pay, their poverty owing to previous taxation, and losing their mines to jealous Europeans; invidious discrimination at odds with British constitutional principles of equality; and the economic contributions made by Chinese who patronized local merchants and worked abandoned mines. They often wrote in the language of rights, drawing upon the tradition of English constitutional liberty. "Taxation without representation is 'tyranny,' says JOHN. And who shall gainsay him?" wrote the Melbourne *Argus*. Echoing the logic of Chinese merchants in California, the Bendigo petitioners also pointed out benefits of migration to trade and commerce, that "the presence of such a numerous body as your Petitioners on this, and other goldfields, gives a great impulse to trade, and yields very considerable profits to the mercantile community of the Colony."[25]

Petitioners also rebutted the common complaints and stereotypes made against them, especially the charge that they were undesirable as settlers because they brought no women. Several petitions noted cultural and practical reasons for leaving wives at home. Pon Sa, who spoke before the mass meeting in Castlemaine, made a special point to address the question, stating that "Chinamen's wives would not be safe [in Australia]. Sometimes Chinese ladies had been stopped on the roads and disgraced, and they were afraid that if they came here they would be insulted." Others explained that the future in Victoria was too uncertain for Chinese to make any long-term commitments. Lowe Kong Meng testified to colonial authorities that Chinese would settle in Australia and bring their families if they were welcome and if there were clear laws, as in Singapore and

Penang. In a sense the Chinese were saying that Europeans, not Chinese, were responsible for the latter's reluctance to settle in Australia.[26]

In November 1857 the legislature passed a revised law that reduced the residency tax by half, to six pounds a year. Although the penal clause was removed, the law stipulated that anyone without a residence license forfeited the right to bring suit against anyone who seized their claims. A new petition from fourteen hundred Chinese in Ballarat protested that this provision made "outlaws" of those unable to "meet this sudden imposition" by depriving them of their legal rights to ownership already held in the miner's license. Claim jumping by Europeans was increasingly consequential, as many Chinese had moved beyond shallow alluvial mining to working deep leads, which required greater investment in purchase and equipment. Just a few hundred Chinese paid the six-pound tax, and only a few thousand were taking out the miner's right and protection tickets, out of a Chinese mining population of over forty thousand. There was also a growing chorus of European criticism of Chinese policy from missionaries, defenders of Aboriginal people's rights, and others with clearer commitments to English traditions of equality and humanitarianism. The Melbourne Chamber of Commerce twice passed resolutions, citing the "spirit of the age," that opposed passage of "any law peculiarly applicable to the prevention of the Chinese from landing in this colony."[27]

The government amended legislation again in February 1859, further reducing the residence tax to four pounds a year and including in it the miner's right and protection tickets, expressing the hope that it would be "less harassing to the Chinese" and a "more effective system of causing them to contribute to the revenue." In fact, the government was not moved by any humanitarian impulse; in effect, it was negotiating with the Chinese over a price they would finally be willing to pay. (The Chinese said they would pay two pounds a year.) The revised law also added penal sanctions (stiff fines, imprisonment, and labor on public works) and was accompanied by new administrative regulations requiring Chinese to carry their tax receipt on their person at all times and to receive written permission to move from the district.[28]

Protest moved to another level that spring when the government determined to crack down on collection and inspection, jailing those who failed to produce a residence license. In May seven hundred Chinese at Bendigo resisted tax collectors and the policemen accompanying them, and rescued from the police several Chinese who had been arrested for refusal to pay. Mounted police charged and dispersed the crowd. Chinese continued to refuse and gave themselves up for arrest, filling the jails in a manner that Gandhi and Martin Luther King, Jr., later would make famous. Four thousand Bendigo Chinese signed a petition denouncing the actions of police, which arrested those without tickets and "marched [them] through the public streets . . . like common felons" and put on prison labor gangs, "with the most abandoned criminals to sweep pathways and other similar degrading occupations, with policemen standing sentry over them with fixed bayonets."[29]

Chinese clashed with police at Beechworth after police arrested the local headman, Pig Mon, for distributing "seditious" placards advocating non-payment of taxes. Three thousand met in Castlemaine, marched to the resident warden's camp, where they said they could pay no more than two pounds per annum, and then gave "themselves up to be dealt with according to law" should their offer be refused. A group called the United Confederacy of Chinese, comprising Chinese at Bendigo, Castlemaine, Ballarat, and the Ovens district called upon "all diggers and puddlers to suspend operations, and upon all storekeepers to close their place of business and have no dealings with Europeans." They also proclaimed that in the event that police attempted to enforce a tax collection, the Chinese would proceed to the resident warden's headquarters and hold "indignation meetings."[30]

Lowe Kong Meng and other Chinese merchants in Melbourne also opposed the residence tax. In May 1859 Lowe, together with two other merchant leaders, John A. Luk and A. Kim, met with the colonial governor's office to discuss the tax. They were accompanied by prominent Europeans: James Grant, a member of the legislative assembly; Mark King, a merchant; and the Rev. William Young, the missionary on the goldfields. The merchants pleaded only their own case, that is, that a tax aimed at miners was being improperly applied to merchants in the city. They also pointed out that they paid the ten-pound landing fee every time they came with a shipment of goods from abroad, whether from China or elsewhere. The merchants further distanced themselves from the miners' acts of civil disobedience and expressed shock when John O'Shanassy, the governor's chief secretary, informed them that the United Confederacy was fomenting violence. Lowe Keng Meng and 150 other merchants went to the Treasury two days later and duly paid their taxes.[31]

The Melbourne merchants' unwillingness to stand by the miners undermined the general strike and civil disobedience. The government continued its crackdown; by 1860, some four thousand had been fined and two thousand were imprisoned for nonpayment. The movement lost momentum, and although there were no more mass demonstrations, only a minority of Chinese paid the residency tax: 12,000 in 1859, 8,000 in 1860, and 5,000 in 1861.[32]

In many ways the Chinese resistance was similar to the Eureka Uprising, which white Australians consider one of the wellsprings of their democracy. Chinese wrote petitions in similar language to that of Europeans, invoking British constitutionalism and equality, and they staged their mass meetings with British political symbols, such as flying the British flag and ending with three cheers to the king. At the same time, the Chinese resistance operated from a logic that stressed fairness and the obligation of rulers to act with benevolence, rather than the Anglo-American association of taxation with political representation. It is worth noting that by important measures, the Chinese resistance exceeded the scope of the Eureka Uprising: it involved more people in more places and took place over a longer period of time. Historian Geoffrey Serle wrote that it "might have shamed any old digger with a tender conscience."[33]

IN ADDITION TO THEIR sustained campaign against unjust race taxes, Chinese gold diggers resisted the colonial government's efforts to force them to live in segregated villages under the banner of "protection." Chinese simply refused to live in these ghettos and refused, as well, to pay for the privilege of living (or not living) there. Their resistance ultimately led the government to abandon the project.

The idea for the Chinese protectorate aimed to reduce conflict between Europeans and Chinese by separating the races. In 1854 the gold commissioner of Bendigo, John Panton, suggested to Governor Hotham that appointing special Chinese "protectors" and locating Chinese in camps separate from the European population would ensure their safety and promote racial order. Panton, a former military officer, also ought to deter European agitators from using the Chinese Question to foment dissent against the colonial government.[34]

Panton's proposal recalled a similar strategy of government "protection" of Aboriginal peoples from European settler violence in the 1830s and '40s. As Aboriginal peoples resisted Europeans' encroachments by killing or stealing cattle and sheep, Europeans self-righteously and violently defended their property. The colonial governments of New South Wales and South Australia encouraged settlement but opposed violent assaults and murders against Aboriginal peoples. The Port Phillip Aboriginal Protectorate was established in 1838 to guard indigenous peoples from "acts of Cruelty, oppression or injustice" and the "evils of settlement" and to "compensate for those evils by imparting to them the truths of Christianity and the arts of civilized life." The policy invited Aboriginal people to live at European "stations," where they would be safely harbored, clothed, and fed in exchange for "a little work." Few Aboriginal people took the government up on the deal; nor did the protectors discern any change in the "social condition" of indigenous people. The colonists' conceit that they would attract the indigenous to European norms rather quickly gave way to the belief that Aboriginal peoples would become extinct, that their primitive, childlike nature would cause them to collapse and die before the advance of European civilization. "Protection" was thus seen as a temporary measure that gave a gloss of civility to elimination.[35]

If the colonial government suggested that Chinese, like Aboriginal peoples, needed protection from European violence, the Chinese protectorates were in fact quite different from the indigenous precedents. The Chinese protectorates drew their main inspiration from strategies of racial management in European colonies in Southeast Asia. Colonial Victorians cited practices in the Philippines, Java, and Malaya as models for the Australian case. In May 1855 a special deputation from the Melbourne Chamber of Commerce visited Hotham to urge special regulations for the Chinese. In Singapore, they told Hotham, the colonial government "chose two of the oldest and wealthiest Chinese traders in the settlement, representing different classes [clans], to act as Magistrates and settle disputes among the Chinese." They cited the use of headmen in Batavia who were responsible for the "collection of Taxes and good behavior of the Chinese" and special police regulations for Chinese in Hong Kong. The British also levied taxes in Singapore on pork and opium, items consumed by Chinese.[36]

Panton and Hotham agreed to organize the protectorates with "the Chinese under an authority of their own," which authority was conceived to reside in "headmen." But although colonial officials wanted to coopt local leaders as headmen in order to collect revenues and adjudicate disputes among the Chinese, they did not go so far as to institute a system of plural governance such as existed in the Straits Settlements, which operated with British, Chinese, and Malay (Muslim) law.[37]

The use of headmen had to be adapted to the fact that the British colonies in Australia were settler colonies. Whereas Europeans were a small minority in the Southeast Asian colonies, in Australia they aimed to be the majority. The Aboriginal population was assumed to be in terminal decline, and the Chinese had not established themselves as a prosperous and influential ethnic group. Paradoxically, Chinese emigrants in the Australian settler colonies provoked among whites the desire for an even greater measure of control than existed over Chinese in the Southeast Asian colonies. In the *nanyang*, neither Chinese nor natives were forcibly confined to "protectorates."

Victorian officials had only a dim understanding of the Chinese population and its social organization, but they did know that among the Chinese there were men of high standing who could potentially give them access to the mining populace. Robert Rede, the commissioner at Ballarat, believed Chinese miners would respect only a headman who was a "Mandarin or a man of importance in their own country," if possible one appointed directly by the emperor of China, although "unfortunately there is no Chinaman in this District of any importance." In fact,

Chinese social organization was sophisticated, but it was not easy for Hotham and Panton to fathom, let alone utilize.[38]

Initially the Chinese themselves were not averse to the idea of colonial protection. Those on the diggings were in constant conflict with Europeans over mining claims and water usage. Chinese often argued that mining on worked-over claims was noncompetitive with Europeans and socially useful because they found ore that otherwise would not have been dug up. To lose even these seemed patently unjust. When in early 1855 Panton toured the mining districts on Hotham's behalf to elicit the cooperation of the "leading men of the four great clans" for the protectorate, he reported that they were generally supportive of the proposal, especially if it would protect them from "unjust and jealous Europeans."[39]

The Chinese also wanted to have their own courts and policemen, as in other Southeast Asian colonies. But Hotham was unwilling to concede such a degree of self-governance. The misalignment of Chinese and European interests made it difficult for colonial officials to enlist Chinese headmen to their project. Notably, Chinese *huiguan* rules required their headmen to collect fees for the associations, not for the miner's license. Under the protectorate, the headman's role looked like that of a subordinate, if not a lackey, to the British. Those who were not already leaders among the Chinese understood that taking a position as a headman was risky. For example, when officials in Bendigo wished to appoint as headman O Cheong, who worked as the interpreter for the district commissioner, O Cheong demurred. He claimed he did not have the standing among the Chinese to warrant such an appointment and noted, with some apprehension, the influence of the secret societies. In fact, O Cheong appears to have been something of an outsider among the local Chinese; he had learned English during a ten-year sojourn in London, where he trained for the Christian ministry. He would not have been a member of the Yixing and was probably not a Siyi man.[40]

In May 1855 a pilot protectorate was established at Bendigo, with Captain Frederick Standish appointed as Chinese protector and the Chinese population organized into seven "villages." In October Hotham formalized and expanded the system, appointing Chinese protectors at Ballarat,

Avoca, and Castlemaine, and a process of moving the Chinese into "villages" began. In time protectors were appointed for Maryborough and Beechworth. The legislative council issued regulations for erecting Chinese camps; appointing headmen; settling disputes; and prohibiting the use of water "specially reserved" for purposes of washing auriferous earth. It also allowed for (but did not require) relief for Chinese who became destitute because of illness.[41]

"Protection" was rapidly, if not immediately, eclipsed by the restrictive and regulatory impulse. Whereas the Victorian protectors for Aboriginal peoples had been missionaries and teachers, three of the first four Chinese protectors were former military or police officials. The protectors adjudicated disputes that arose between Chinese and Europeans but spent most of their time issuing and checking on licenses and protection tickets. The work journal of William Foster, the protector for Ballarat, showed that in two weeks in February 1856, he spent nine days visiting Chinese camps, where he searched for Chinese without protection tickets and settled disputes among Chinese miners, and an entire day on the bench hearing a case between Chinese and English miners (which he settled in favor of the English). While on the diggings, he also searched for a Chinese murder suspect who had escaped from the Avoca jail. He spent the remainder of his time filling in for the magistrate and in his office.[42]

The Chinese protectorate was a considerable bureaucracy unto itself, with a protector, clerks, interpreters, a scribe, headmen, and police constables. But Chinese leaders, as noted above, were often unwilling to serve the colonial government as headmen; Frederick Standish, the protector at Bendigo, reported that Chinese found the job of headman "rather an annoyance than an assistance to the administration of the Gold Fields." Remuneration was less than what a successful Chinese merchant or miner earned, making the job even less desirable, he added. By December 1855 no headmen had yet been appointed in Avoca, and six months after the protectorate was established in Ballarat, there were only three headmen covering nearly four thousand Chinese living in a dozen camps.[43]

Those Chinese who accepted appointments as headmen often carried out their duties selectively. The protector at Castlemaine, John Hamilton, complained to his superior that headmen were incompetent or that they simply "refused to interfere in any matter which would render them obnoxious to their fellow countrymen." Frederick Standish similarly "found the Chiefs [headmen] of the different villages utterly useless. . . . They feel little or no interest in their position, and with one single exception, they utterly disregard the instructions which I occasionally transmit for their guidance."[44]

Without reliable headmen, the protectors had trouble collecting fees. Frederick Standish reported in July 1856 that "since the first issue of Miner's Rights on this gold field, very few of the Chinese have taken them out." Standish issued notices translated into Chinese to inform them of the regulations, including the penalties they risked by their "unauthorized occupation of Crown Lands. . . . I am of opinion that without some stringent measures, both those fees [miner's right and protection tickets] will be evaded by the great majority of the Chinese." Through the 1850s the protectors issued protection tickets to only half the Chinese under their jurisdiction. Still, revenues more than paid for the protectorate's budget. In 1856 the colony collected £12,242 in Chinese landing and protection fees but expended just £9,481 on Chinese affairs. Income from Chinese was actually greater because they had to pay all manner of additional fees, including those for medical inspection of their camps, special duties on food imports, even a two-pound fee to lodge a complaint against a European miner with the protector.[45]

If staffing and collection problems plagued the Chinese protectorate, they paled before the basic question of organizing and keeping the Chinese population in the protection villages designated for them. Initially, protectors declared existing Chinese camps to be the official villages but made important modifications. They replaced the winding lanes of the camps with a grid of straight streets and issued new sanitary regulations, displacing the existing rules of the Chinese *huiguan*, which were quite adequate. In the Bendigo district, the protector insisted that Chinese could not leave their villages without written authorization and patrolled the area to send back "strays" and "escapees." These actions made the villages appear like a military or prison camp.

Just as important, residency in the villages interfered with many Chinese miners' work. Chinese who usually camped near their claims now had to carry their equipment—implements, tubs, cradles, even the cumbersome horse-powered puddling machines—to and from the village every night or leave them unattended and risk theft. Individuals working on distant claims or living among Europeans were also expected to relocate, on pain of a five-pound fine or two months' imprisonment.[46]

Noncompliance frustrated the protectors from the start. Standish wrote to the colonial secretary that he found it "impossible" to prevent many Chinese from residing outside the villages. His two constables were engaged daily with removing the obstinates and pulling down their tents, but to no avail, "as they are put up again as soon as the Police have left." Graham Webster, the protector at Avoca, conceded that requiring Chinese to live in the villages was "not at all times advisable and the strict carrying out of the regulations falls heavily on those who wish to live near their claims and where the nature of the ground does not admit to many living together."[47]

Bernhard Smith, the protector at Castlemaine, wrote to the resident warden in October 1855 that "owing to the scattered and migrating nature of the Population . . . it frequently happened that a Camp which had taken me some days to complete is abandoned for some other locality within a very short time." Nine months later Smith concluded, "I do not think any advantage arises from locating the Chinese in particular localities and their operating as miners are thereby often impeded." He noted that Chinese tended to self-segregate and advised that they should be allowed to form their own camps, providing they posed no inconvenience to others, and he further stated that he had not interfered with those Chinese who lived among Europeans and acculturated to their habits.[48]

By 1858 fully half the Chinese in the Bendigo area were living outside the villages with the acquiescence of two successive resident wardens. The warden advised the chief secretary that with a diminution of racial tensions, the villages had become unnecessary. Indeed, he continued, they were counterproductive, destroying the Chinese miners' self-respect, imposing on them undue hardships, and encouraging defiance of the authorities. They also allowed Chinese without legal papers to hide among the mass and prevented the Chinese from learning the English language and customs. He advised that the system be abolished. Yet the policy continued, in large part because colonial officials believed the protectorates were necessary to justify the imposition and collection of fees.[49]

Despite increasingly harsh regulations promulgated from Melbourne, the Chinese protectorate system was falling apart. Local protectors routinely sanctioned Chinese living out of camp, and after the government discharged the Chinese headmen and most interpreters and reassigned the protectorates' constables, collection became impossible. Government income from Chinese licenses fell from £55,442 in 1859 to £20,452 in 1861 and to a mere £2,743 in 1862, although by then the Chinese population was also falling. Through passive and active resistance on the part of the Chinese, a weak will to enforcement by local protectors, and legislative backpedaling, the protectorate became a dead letter. In 1862 and 1863 new laws abolished the Chinese landing and residence taxes and officially ended the protectorate.[50]

A DECADE LATER a minority of Chinese on the Victorian goldfields still lived in villages that had formerly been organized under the protectorate. Although Chinese mining communities were not prosperous, they were vibrant ethnic enclaves organized around mining, market gardening, mutual aid, and homosocial entertainments. Chinese associations like the Siyi Huiguan and the Yixing arguably operated more freely once they were no longer encumbered by the ill-fitting overlay of the protectorate structure. Chinese associational leaders resumed their role as spokesmen to Victorian authorities.[51]

Victorian policy was not really about protection but rather about containment and regulation, and ultimately about justifying state fiscal policy. "Protection" was spoken in the language of paternalism, but it was a legal fiction based on a logic that racial conflict could be avoided only if Chinese were removed from the general population. By this logic, it was the Chinese who had to be policed, not whites.

THE FAILURE OF THE Chinese protectorate marked the limit as to how far settler colonials were willing to go to contain the Chinese. Although colonial authorities, both in Melbourne and in the gold districts, viewed the Chinese as a racial problem, they had neither the political will nor the resources to enforce the protectorate policy; to achieve that end, they would have had to use sustained violence against the Chinese. Such measures would have drawn certain criticism from London and perhaps from sectors of Australian society as well.

The failure of the Chinese protectorate was also a piece of the broader Victorian political trajectory from interventionist colonial rule to laissez-faire and democratic government. If that trend was motored by popular sentiment and mobilization, it was no less true for the Chinese, even though democracy benefited them little. Chinese on the Victorian diggings exhibited the same qualities of ascendant liberal ideology that historian David Goodman used to describe European miners: "self-seeking, self-regulating, morally and emotionally autonomous, transnational." Certainly, Chinese miners displayed many of the characteristics lauded by Anglo-Celts and Australian-born democrats seeking greater self-government, as they organized themselves into self-governing communities, resisted the strong arm of the state, and mobilized against injustice. But, the racialist justification of the protectorate—that Chinese were not able to self-govern and were unassimilable to the norms of colonial settlement—persisted in the imagination of white Australia and continued to cast Chinese as undesirable outsiders.[52]

"Protection" did not prevent the ongoing harassment of Chinese by Europeans. In 1857 a series of disturbances in the Ovens district in northeastern Victoria unfolded over the course of several months, culminating in the Buckland River Riot on July 4, the largest race riot committed against Chinese gold diggers in the colony's history. Early in the year Chinese were arriving in large numbers from Guichen Bay via the overland route, but at that time mining in Victoria was depressed. News of Chinese protests against Europeans in Singapore and Sarawak also inflamed anti-Chinese anxieties in Australia. In May a party of Chinese, en route from Port Robe to Bendigo, discovered gold near Ararat—soon dubbed the Canton Lead—that proved to be one of the richest of Victoria's shallow alluvial deposits. Europeans rushed to Ararat, but the Chinese were there first, nearly 2,500 of them, far outnumbering the five hundred European latecomers and holding the best claims. Fighting between Chinese and Europeans broke out across the diggings. In May a group of Europeans disguised in blackface attacked a small camp of about thirty Chinese miners who had begun sinking on "good ground." The whites tore down the Chinese huts, pelted the Chinese with stones, and set the camp on fire.[53]

In June a group of Europeans forced Chinese from their claims at Ararat, burning their tents and four stores. The storekeeper A Tai stated that five men came into his store, "smacked me down and cut my belt with a knife," taking eighty pounds from the belt. "After robbing me they drove me out of the store and then set fire to it," he continued, destroying its contents—rice, oil, sugar, tea, and opium that he estimated to be worth £230. Ah Wing, another storekeeper, lost his store—a Calico tent, sixteen by twenty-five feet, erected on a wooden platform—after Europeans set it on fire with a burning branch. The store and its contents burned all night.[54]

Less than a month later, these acts were repeated on a large scale at the goldfields in the Buckland River district, near Beechworth. On July 4 some eighty Europeans held a meeting at Tanswell's Hotel and resolved to expel the Chinese from the district because they were "robbing us of our gold fields" and because of their "gross and beastly practices." After the meeting a gang of Europeans accosted the Chinese, ordering them to leave. The single constable at the scene tried to stop them, unsuccessfully. Soon a hundred white miners, armed with picks and ax handles, systematically moved down both sides of the river. They drove the Chinese eight miles downstream, burning their tents and robbing their stores and temple before setting them on fire. They beat anyone who dared to resist, including Europeans who came to the aid of the Chinese. The *Argus* reported "the most frightful scenes on the road up; Chinamen worn out with hunger and exposure, dying on the road. One poor fellow was found lying near a fire in the bush, with his foot burnt off, others in a dying state from starvation, many were rushed into the river . . . and it is believed that some were drowned." Several others died from their injuries or from exposure.[55]

Colonial authorities in Beechworth sent police reinforcements and arrested several Europeans. The warden estimated that over 750 tents, thirty stores, and the temple, "a large building the best one of the description in the district," had been destroyed. The accused pleaded not guilty. White diggers in the Ovens district supported them—with caveats deploring violence—and at trial few were willing to testify against them. The jury acquitted them of serious charges and found only three men guilty of unlawful assembly and riot.[56]

Colonial police promised to protect Chinese who returned to the Buckland diggings, and some did return, but within weeks whites forced most of them out of the district. The government compensated Chinese storekeepers for their losses, paying out £1,347 to four Chinese storekeepers in Ararat, whose shops were burned in June, and £11,032 to twenty store owners and the proprietor of a tea parlor at the Chinese camps on the Buckland for losses incurred during the July 4 riot. The accounting listed property destroyed, "money taken away," and "gold missing." In submitting their affidavits, the storekeepers emphasized their good standing, noting that they held duly issued licenses to conduct business and, without irony, protection tickets.[57]

THE CHINESE QUESTION had emerged during the gold rushes in California and Victoria as a response to the first mass contacts between Chinese and whites, but with distinctive racial idioms grounded in local place. Over the course of the next decades, the Chinese Question would spread beyond the goldfields, morphing and adapting along the way. By the last quarter of the nineteenth century, the debates in the United States and Australia sounded increasingly alike, as though anticoolie and invasion rhetorics merged into a single theory of racial danger. In both places the Chinese Question culminated in national exclusion laws—although once again, the political roads to national exclusion legislation differed. In the United States, debates over the Chinese Question took place in the context of post–Civil War Reconstruction politics. In Australia, the Chinese Question revealed a schism within the British Empire between local settler-colonial interests and imperial diplomatic and commercial interests with China. The Chinese Question would prove to be both robust and malleable enough to serve both causes.

PART II

MAKING WHITE MEN'S COUNTRIES

Today is not yet the Age of Great Unity;
We only compete in cleverness and power.
The land of the red man is vast and remote;
I know you are eager to settle and open it.
The American eagle strides the heavens soaring,
With half of the globe clutched in his claw.
Although the Chinese arrived later,
Couldn't you leave them a little space?

—HUANG ZUNXIAN,
"EXPULSION OF THE IMMIGRANTS"

Figure 1. A sluicing company hired both Chinese and whites at Auburn
Ravine, north of Sacramento, California, 1852.

Figure 2. Chinese gold seekers loaded on a coach, heading for Castlemaine, Victoria, 1853.

Figure 3. On Djadjawurrung land, indigenous people prospected for gold and interacted with European gold seekers as guides and provisioners. But the gold rush accelerated native dispossession. Mount Alexander from Saw Pit Gully, Victoria, 1856.

Figure 4. The rocker was the favored method for alluvial mining among Chinese gold miners in the American West and Australasia. It was inexpensive, easy to build, and portable. California, c. 1875.

Figure 5. Chinese miners worked cooperatively, sometimes joining in groups to turn and wash dirt along the entire length of a gully. Mount Alexander diggings, Victoria, c. 1861. Photograph by Richard Daintree.

Figure 6. The North Bloomfield Gravel Mining Co. in Nevada County, California, hired eight hundred Chinese and three hundred whites in the 1870s. A federal court banned hydraulic mining in 1884 because of the environmental damage it caused.

Figure 7. Chinese in California built the flumes that carried water from the mountaintops for hydraulic mining companies. Magenta Flume, Nevada County, California, 1870s. Photograph by Carleton Watkins.

Figures 10–11. Two leading Chinese merchants and civil rights leaders in Victoria in the late nineteenth century: Lowe Kong Meng (top) came from a merchant family in Penang; Louis Ah Mouy (bottom) came as a carpenter from Guangzhou.

Figure 12. The Chinese quarter, Ballarat, Victoria, 1868.

Chapter 6

✳

The Roar of the Sandlot

California governor John Bigler's gambit to weaponize the Chinese Question not only paid off in his reelection in 1853, it also set down the enduring myth that Chinese labor in California was unfree. That kind of "big lie" would persist throughout the rest of the nineteenth century and well into the twentieth. As governor, Bigler continued his efforts to rid California of Chinese, signing into law several foreign miner tax laws, each steeper than the last. At the height of his popularity in 1854, the state assembly named a mountain lake in northeastern California in his honor.

In 1855 Bigler was defeated for a third term, after which he led a peripatetic political career. He served briefly as U.S. ambassador to Chile, then lost a bid for Congress in 1863, during the Civil War. By this time the former Free Soiler was an open sympathizer of the Confederacy. In 1862 Unionist mapmakers in California changed the name of Lake Bigler to Lake Tahoe, after a local Indian tribe, but the name remained disputed for decades. In 1867 Bigler was appointed railroad commissioner for the Central Pacific Railroad, a federal patronage position. At that time the Central Pacific employed ten thousand Chinese workers—both former gold miners and fresh recruits from Guangdong—for the massive project to build the transcontinental line across the Sierra Nevada. If Bigler was skeptical about it, he kept his mouth shut.[1]

✢

NOTWITHSTANDING Bigler's fall into obscurity, the Chinese Question in California gave the mining districts—and the state Democratic Party more broadly—a racial political position that combined manifest destiny, free labor, and economic scapegoating. It was a neat package based on a single theory (coolieism) aimed at a single target (Chinese laborers). But during the 1850s, even as California enacted racist laws against Chinese and other people of color, Democrats' fortunes in California suffered. Not only was the state party in disrepute on account of its notorious corruption; it also fractured in tandem with the national sectional crisis. Although there were proslavery elements in the state party (most famously the former U.S. senator, William Gwin), most California Democrats identified with the Jacksonian or "workingmen's" Democracy of northern cities like New York and Philadelphia. Throughout the 1850s Bigler had associated with that trend. During the Civil War, notwithstanding Bigler's newly found sympathies for the South, California remained firmly on the side of the Union. Whigs were now Republicans, and Democrats renamed themselves Union Democrats to signal their loyalty to the nation. Leland Stanford, a Republican, was elected governor in 1861, and Republicans gained majorities in both houses of the legislature.[2]

For a short period of time, the dynamics of the Chinese Question shifted. Republicans used their control over the state legislature to reintroduce the idea that the China trade and Chinese labor held the keys to California's economic development, especially in manufacturing, agriculture, and viticulture. A joint select committee of the legislature reported in 1862 that there was "no system of slavery or coolieism amongst the Chinese in this State." It praised Chinese merchant leaders in San Francisco as "men of intelligence, ability and cultivation" and the Chinese in general as "peaceful, industrious and useful." The report warned that additional oppressive legislation against the Chinese would damage California's economic prospects.[3]

Meanwhile, during the 1860s, the situation in the mining districts was changing. There were fewer violent conflicts between Chinese and whites largely because both groups looked beyond the goldfields for employment. Whites were particularly discouraged by the depletion of the placers and by the new reality of class inequality that came into focus. Large-scale capital investment and ownership came to dominate the scene, controlling water companies; ditch digging, tunneling, and hydraulic mining operations; and underground quartz mining. While not a few whites and some Chinese worked for wages for these companies, many more left the goldfields, seeking other opportunities. Some Euro-Americans flocked to the Comstock Lode, the massive silver and gold deposit discovered in Nevada in 1859, while others went to towns and cities. Many unemployed Chinese miners found work on the construction of the transcontinental railroad.[4]

During the late 1850s and through the Civil War, California enjoyed economic growth, especially in agriculture and manufacturing. Isolated from eastern markets and distant from the ravages of the war, California wages and prices remained high. But the postwar recession reached the West in 1867 and, with it, substantial unemployment, especially in San Francisco. In the context of economic transition and recession, a new anti-coolie movement emerged in the city, led by white craft workers—ship carpenters, masons, metalworkers, and other skilled workers. These workers faced no competition from Chinese labor, but they stoked the fears of white laborers, especially unskilled Irishmen. Only in one industry, cigar making, had mass manufacture with Chinese labor displaced the white craft guilds. But San Francisco's artisans took it as an omen, and their anxiety spread throughout the white laboring class. They found in the Chinese Question a racial scapegoat and a racial theory ready at hand.[5]

In February 1867 a gang of four hundred whites, mostly young Irishmen, attacked Chinese working on the Potrero Street railway with stones and bricks, inflicting serious injuries. They burned the Chinese workers' barracks and then roamed the city, burning shanties and threatening the ropewalk and the Mission woolen mill, which both employed Chinese. The police put down the mob and arrested the leaders; ten men were convicted and sentenced to jail. Under pressure from mass meetings of the trade unions, the board of supervisors voted to appeal the convictions. Two months later the state supreme court released all ten men on grounds of "technical errors." The affair led to the establishment of a permanent, statewide "anti-coolie association" and established anticoolieism as a "working class" political force to be reckoned with. It also signaled that whites, even riotous mobs, would suffer little consequence for violent attacks against Chinese.[6]

The rhetoric of the late 1860s was similar to that of 1852. A joint memorial and resolution made by the state legislature in 1868 returned to the old chestnuts: "The Chinese in our midst are Pagans. . . . It is utterly impossible that they should ever become citizens. . . . Our entire Chinese population is composed of slaves and their masters, or agents of their masters." But a new argument also came into focus, linking coolieism to the interests of monopoly. The central state council of the Anti-Coolie Association declared "that whatever present benefit may be derived from the employment of Chinese as a cheap system of labor, is chiefly confined to a few capitalists—any real advantage in the State being neutralized by the system of peonage under which they are introduced; . . . the number of desirable citizens they displace, and the number of free immigrants who would become citizens that they keep from our shores."[7]

THE PHILOSOPHER and political economist Henry George elaborated on these ideas, giving them theoretical heft and bringing them to national attention. George had come west in 1857 as a young gold seeker, but he found his vocation as a journalist in the San Francisco Bay Area. He was thirty years old in 1869 when he developed his theory of wages through a consideration of the Chinese Question; he had not yet written *Progress and Poverty* (1879), in which he famously advocated a single tax on land as the key to unlocking the power of monopoly. In a lengthy essay "The Chinese in California," published in Horace Greeley's *New York Tribune*, George sought to explain why Chinese competition must necessarily reduce wages and why a reduction in wages was in the interest of capital and opposed to the interest of labor.

Although the proposition seemed obvious to some, it was by no means universally embraced. Proponents of Chinese immigration had various defenses, and George carefully rebutted them, each in turn, albeit somewhat simplistically. To the idea that lower wages resulted in lower prices, George pointed out there were always more consumers than workers, so the worker's gain in lower prices would be less than his loss in wages. To the widely held belief that Chinese labor would, by its cheapness, support rapid economic development and create higher-paying jobs for whites as skilled workers and managers, George responded that the number of these jobs would be far fewer than the number of whites displaced by Chinese.[8]

George contended that the only certain outcome of lowering wages was an increase in profits. "Plainly," he wrote, "if we speak of a reduction in wages in any general and permanent sense, we mean this, if we mean anything, that in the division of the joint production of labor and capital, the share of labor is to be smaller, that of capital greater." Furthermore, even if the use of Chinese labor resulted in a greater aggregate of production, he argued, the social and political cost of such prosperity was too great: "the utter subversion of Republicanism upon the Pacific, perhaps the continent."

George's analysis distinguished Chinese from other immigrant labor, which also tended to be cheaper than that of native-born white Americans. He assumed European immigrants would sooner or later assimilate into the American working class, that their current cheapness was a temporary phenomenon. George believed that the employment of Chinese would cause a reduction in wages in a "general and permanent sense." That view was based on the racist premise that Chinese could never be assimilated. He rehearsed the common stereotypes about Chinese: that they were filthy, treacherous, completely ignorant of Christian values and American political institutions, and came on a "contract system" enforced by the Chinese Six Companies, which was akin to slavery. Moreover, Chinese workers did not form trade unions or agitate for "rights." These characteristics, argued George, made Chinese the ideal labor force for the big capitalists. He invoked the specter of slavery by comparing the employers of Chinese to the recently defeated Confederacy and its vision of a racially stratified society, "where the laboring class are of one race, the ruling and employing class of another."

Finally, George warned that China's vast population of 500 million constituted a limitless labor supply and that, without government restrictions, Chinese emigrants would not only flood the Pacific coast but spread across the entire country, transforming America into a place more like British India than New England.

The *Tribune* article received widespread attention. California papers reprinted it, and the Anti-Coolie Association memorialized it. To generate more publicity, George sent his piece to the British political economist John Stuart Mill. But Mill sent George a letter that politely suggested that George's views were illiberal. Mill wrote that the Chinese Question involved "two of the most difficult and embarrassing questions of political morality—the extent and limits of the right of those who have taken first possession [*sic*] of the unoccupied portion of the earth's surface to exclude the remainder of mankind from inhabiting it, and the means which can be legitimately used by the more improved branches of the human species to protect themselves from being hurtfully encroached upon by those of a lower grade in civilization."

Mill conceded that from a strictly economic standpoint, immigrant labor lowered the wages of the native-born. But like George, he viewed that phenomenon as temporary. Mill considered immigration to be a correction to the unequal distribution of population (and hence wealth) in the world. Cutting to the chase, he questioned George's assumption that the Chinese were unassimilable: "There is much also to be said on the other side. Is it justifiable to assume that the character and habits of the Chinese are insusceptible of improvement?" He suggested that "compulsory education" and other democratic institutions might "raise the level" of the Chinese population to that of Americans. Mill absolutely opposed indentures that bound laborers to particular employers, but he distinguished between indentured and voluntary emigration. He argued from a classic liberal standpoint—that is, he considered Chinese to be free individuals with the same rights as any other persons.[9]

George, who was now editor of the *Oakland Daily Transcript*, published Mill's letter along with an editorial reply. He lavished the "great Englishman" with fulsome praise and asserted that Mill supported Chinese exclusion. He coopted Mill's qualification about indentured labor with the claim that nine-tenths of the Chinese were "contract laborers," anticoolieism's central fiction. In this way he gave himself the authority of Mill's imprimatur, but on false grounds, and gained political notice in California politics.[10]

More than twenty years later George wrote that the ideas he expressed in 1869 were "crude," but he was referring to his ideas on political economy, not to his racism. To be sure, George's claim that labor and capital were locked in a zero-sum game would give way to his view that monopoly, not capital per se, was the problem, and his single-tax theory proposed a cooperation, if not a harmony, of classes. That would be his legacy, not his views on Chinese immigration. But Henry George's analysis of the Chinese Question had both immediate and lasting impact. He made a theoretical link between coolieism and monopoly, which empowered exclusionists with an outlook that justified racism and nativism in the name of working-class interest. He made it commonsensical that labor's response to cheap immigrant labor should be to exclude the latter, rather than to advocate for equal wages, thereby cleaving the working class along lines of race and nationality, which lines he presumed were natural. This view was deeply problematic as a "class" position because it placed racial and national interest above that of class. George ignored the fact that Chinese labor did in fact often demand higher wages in the mines, on the railroads, and elsewhere, although they did not always win. George himself would continue to give lectures and write essays on the Chinese Question through the 1870s and '80s. As his stature as an antimonopoly thinker and reformer grew, so did the credibility of anti-Chinese nativism.[11]

THE ANTI-CHINESE MOVEMENT in California crested again in the mid-1870s, in response to changes wrought by the completion of the transcontinental railroad in 1869. That national connection brought many migrants from the east coast to San Francisco, and as well as manufactured goods from eastern factories to the west coast, creating pressure on the high prices and high wages that had previously flourished in a market of scarcity. Far from delivering untold wealth and development to the Pacific coast, the railroad brought joblessness and poverty—the long tail of the national depression of 1873–77. By 1876 there were reportedly fifteen thousand unemployed workmen in San Francisco, nearly one-quarter of the workforce.[12]

Again, the urban craft unions representing the aristocracy of labor and the small-producer guilds led the movement. The anticoolie clubs used boycotts to put economic muscle behind their demand to expel Chinese from manufacturing jobs. These boycotts were the first to use brand identification as a tactic: consumers were urged to purchase, for example, only those cigars and boots that came in boxes with a label declaring them "made by white labor." The white label was the ignominious precursor to the union label.[13]

The clubs composed ditties that were sung at protest meetings. This verse, from a lengthy song written to the tune of "Glory Hallelujah," connected anticoolieism with manly patriotism:

> *We have no place among us for the Coolie or the slave.*
> *But only for the manly, the enlightened and the brave.*
> *Cheap labor to the freeman is the pest-house and the grave,*
> *As our flag goes marching on.*
> *Chorus—Glory, etc.*[14]

Violence against Chinese became commonplace. The clubs held sand-lot rallies at which speakers railed against the depraved and immoral coolie class. These speeches excited crowds, prompting them to roam the streets, assaulting any Chinese person they came across; breaking windows, and burning places of Chinese residence or work. Chinese "wash-houses" (laundries) all over town were vulnerable to attack from gangs of "hoodlums." Chinese were "promiscuously stoned and outraged" on the streets of San Francisco. Rev. Ira Condit of the Presbyterian church assailed the persecution of the Chinese: "They have been stoned, spit upon, beaten, mobbed, their property destroyed, and they themselves unjustly imprisoned and murdered."[15]

Not all Californians were seduced by the siren of racial nativism. A considerable swath of Euro-American society opposed the anticoolie movement's demands for exclusion, including businessmen, professionals, and missionaries. Merchants, manufacturers, agriculturalists, shippers, and other commercial men testified in government hearings about the virtues of the Chinese both as workers and as businessmen. William Babcock, direc-tor of the San Francisco commercial house Parrott and Company, described Chinese factory workers so: "If you will look at their hands and feet and neck you will see them as clean and neat-looking people as you ever saw in the world. They are different from the lower white classes." Richard Sneath of the Merchants Exchange praised Chinese merchants for their honesty and reliability. "I have never had a single one of them to fail to live up to his contracts," which, he said, was more than he would say for the white race.[16]

Other businessmen disputed the charge that Chinese were enslaved to Chinese headmen; some went further and credited them for defending their own interests. George Roberts of the Tidewater Reclamation Company testified, "There is nothing of that kind [coolie contracts] at all. I find my Chinamen entirely independent of the [Chinese] bosses. When the bosses do not pay them they come to me. If the boss does not pay them any wages they tie him up and call on us. . . . I find that each man has his account, and he holds the boss accountable." These practices pointed to the possibilities of assimilation via free labor. Some businessmen pointed to the progress made in Christianizing the Negroes in the South. James Rusling predicted that American schools and churches would "receive and absorb . . . Sambo and John" and "fashion even these into keen American citizens."[17]

The Christian missionaries' stance on the Chinese question dovetailed with that of the business class, but it also reflected particular interests. Early on, the missionaries understood the links between transpacific commerce, immigration, and evangelical work. They knew that restric-tions on Chinese immigration would fuel Chinese resentment against Euro-Americans and make conversions more difficult. As early as the 1850s, Rev. William Speer advocated for Chinese immigration in terms of both political economy and Christian morality. During the 1870s mis-sionaries such as the Methodist Rev. Otis Gibson and the Presbyterian Revs. Augustus Loomis and Ira Condit actively defended the Chinese, giving speeches and writing pamphlets that aimed to dispel negative stereotypes, especially the specters of coolieism and unlimited immi-gration. Gibson cited not only Christian teachings but the Fourteenth Amendment as well; he called for a "True China Policy" that would be "broad, statesmanlike," based on fundamental principles of "open doors and equal rights for all . . . a view that understands the value of the commerce of Asia to us as a nation."[18]

Yet the missionaries were no more advocates for assimilation than the exclusionists were. Indeed, assimilation was counterproductive to the missionaries' goal of recruiting native (i.e., Chinese) Christians for evangelical work in China. Reverend Gibson explained, "The missionaries, who understand their business rather better than newspaper writers do, know that true religion requires a change of heart rather than a change in the cut of the hair." He added, "A number of Chinese who are very far from being Christians have also changed their dress and discarded the cue [sic]" for reasons that were "exceedingly material and practical." The missionaries were not cultural relativists: they believed in the superiority of Western civilization and that as long as Chinese were "heathen," they were not civilized. But they targeted idolatry and superstition, not clothing and hairstyle.[19]

A generation of Reconstruction-era civic leaders, lawyers, and diplomats also weighed in on the Chinese Question. Samuel Wells Williams, an old missionary hand in China and former member of the American Legation in Beijing, pointed out the asymmetry of power and justice in American policy: "One cannot but feel indignant and mortified at the contrast between the way in which the Chinese have treated us in their country into which we have forced ourselves, and the way we have treated them in this country, into which we have invited them. . . . Is not our Christian civilization strong enough to do right by them?"[20]

Other civic leaders who opposed the anti-Chinese movement included Daniel Cleveland, an attorney who spent some time in San Francisco before moving to San Diego, where he was one of that city's leading citizens; and J. Ross Browne, a peripatetic writer who worked in various roles for the federal government as a surveyor of western mineral resources, official reporter of the California constitutional convention, and investigator for the Land Office, before becoming the American representative to China in 1869. These men took the Chinese Question seriously and argued in support of American democratic principles (the Declaration of Independence, the Fourteenth Amendment), treaty obligations, and the benefits of trade.[21] An 1871 Thomas Nast cartoon in *Harper's Weekly*, titled "The Chinese Question," summarized the Reconstruction-era debate, showing Columbia defending an abject Chinaman from racial hostility and an Irish mob (Figure 15).

Chinese continued to defend themselves from the ideological and physical assaults of anticoolieism. In the 1870s *huiguan* and merchant leaders testified before government hearings reiterating what they had been saying since the 1850s, that they were not slaves, that they contributed to the economy, that they were peaceable. On occasion they invoked the Declaration of Independence and principles of fairness, equality, and justice that marked America as a democratic and Christian nation. Wong Ar Chong, a merchant, wrote a letter (in English) to William Lloyd Garrison. The aging abolitionist had recently taken to task James Blaine, a U.S senator from Maine, whose campaign for president included a call for Chinese exclusion. Wong praised Garrison, noting, "In your Declaration of Independence it is asserted that all men are born free and equal, and it is understood by the civilized world that the United States of America is a free country, but I fear there is a backward step being taken by the government."[22]

IN 1877 the trade unions and anticoolie clubs formed the Workingmen's Party to promote their antimonopoly, anticoolie program. Its chief slogan was "The Chinese must go!" The party was led by Denis Kearney, a recently naturalized Irish drayman famous for his incendiary sandlot speeches. Mass meetings, street rallies, petitions—backed by boycotts and made edgier by violence—established the movement as a formidable power in city and state politics. The Workingmen's Party won nearly 40 percent of delegate seats to the state's 1880 constitutional convention, which wrote into the California constitution a section condemning Chinese as dangerous to the welfare of the state. The party did not last, as its leaders were shortly coopted by the Democrats. The state Republicans soon also embraced the demand for Chinese exclusion, notwithstanding the party's business constituents in the China trade. But support for Chinese immigration among the industrial class waned as manufacturers were able replace Chinese workers with white labor, of which there was no longer a shortage, thanks to new migrants from the eastern United States. Anticoolieism achieved bipartisan consensus in California.

With increased vigor, the anti-Chinese movement in California pressured the U.S. Congress to pass legislation banning Chinese immigration. Members of Congress had no special attachment to Chinese immigrants, but in the aftermath of the Civil War, explicitly race-based discrimination was difficult to justify. Congress also subordinated the Pacific coast's regional political interests to American diplomatic and trade relations with China. Most important, the 1868 Burlingame Treaty between the United States and China included a provision that recognized the "mutual advantage of the free migration and emigration of their citizens and subjects."

The treaty was an unusual document, the product of American antislavery and Reconstruction politics. It was negotiated by Anson Burlingame, a Free Soiler and congressman from Massachusetts whom Lincoln had appointed as American envoy to China in 1860. Burlingame abhorred the British attitude toward China, which was to "take them by the throat," and sought to reform Sino-European relations away from gunboat diplomacy and unequal treaties and toward cooperation and equal relations, and to "awaken an enlightened interest among the Western nations . . . something which will react upon the Chinese heart and mind to make them . . . feel that there is Christianity in the world." His energetic lobbying among European diplomats in the foreign legation and his respect for Chinese ministers led the Qing government to appoint him—an American—as envoy extraordinary and minister plenipotentiary to the Western powers. Wenxiang, the Manchu reformer of the Zongli Yamen, the foreign ministry, told Burlingame, "You must be our friend in foreign lands, where we are so misunderstood."[23]

In 1867–68, Burlingame led a mission to Washington that included British, French, and Qing representatives. The eponymous treaty negotiated with U.S. secretary of state William Seward explicitly guaranteed China's sovereignty and its control over inland navigation and internal improvements. It defined most rights as reciprocal, including the stationing of consuls in each country, the right of each country's nationals to immigrate to the other (albeit not to naturalize), and prohibition of religious discrimination in both countries. Although the Burlingame Treaty did not eliminate inequality in U.S.-Sino relations—notably, Americans continued to enjoy extraterritorial rights in China—it nonetheless represented an advance from the imperialistic style of taking them "by the throat." It was signed on July 28, 1868, coincidentally the same day the Fourteenth Amendment was ratified.[24]

The Burlingame Treaty stalled the drive for national exclusion legislation during the 1870s, but that drive was relentless. The national councils of organized labor embraced opposition to Chinese immigration, and both Democrats and Republicans identified Chinese immigration as a problem in their national platforms of 1876. For the Republican Party, Chinese restriction was a retreat from the principles of racial equality that it, the party of Lincoln, had espoused. It was no coincidence that national bipartisan support for Chinese exclusion occurred at the same time as the Compromise of 1877, which famously settled the contested presidential election in favor of the Republican, Rutherford Hayes, in exchange for a withdrawal of federal troops from the South. The compromise effectively ended Reconstruction, paving the way for the disenfranchisement of black freedmen and the return of the planter class to power. And just as the end of Reconstruction reflected the demise in influence of abolitionism—which demanded antislavery and equal rights based on religious and moral principle—Christian missionaries also found themselves marginalized in the debate over the Chinese question.[25]

Congress passed the first Chinese exclusion law in 1875. Known as the Page Act, it sought to exclude most Chinese by specifically banning criminals, contract laborers, and "Mongolian" prostitutes from immigration. Taking aim at unfree "coolies" and "slave girls," the Page Act did not contravene the Burlingame Treaty's provision for "free migration." Under the Page Act, Chinese female immigration dropped precipitously—not because all Chinese women were prostitutes but because they were interrogated and inspected as though they were, and few were willing to subject themselves to the degrading treatment. However, the law did not stop the immigration of Chinese men, because they were not, in fact, indentured.

Undeterred, the anti-Chinese movement ramped up its political campaign. The California state senate held hearings on the "social, moral, and political effect" of Chinese immigration in 1876, and the U.S. Congress held similar hearings in 1877. Scores of witnesses testified as to the condition of Chinese in California and their impact on American society. Witnesses came from diverse backgrounds and interests—local elected leaders, customs officials, former diplomats, businessmen, labor leaders, missionaries, police, academics, and Chinese themselves. Their testimonies reflected the range of opinion that characterized the Chinese Question over the previous three decades. Those who charged that the Chinese were unfree "coolies" offered little in the way of empirical evidence other than a loose association between "cheap labor" and "slavery." As in past hearings, businessmen, missionaries, former diplomats, and Chinese leaders testified that Chinese were free men and voluntary emigrants and not slaves. Despite the diversity of views on offer, the hearings had a negative impact, no doubt because the political winds for exclusion were already blowing strong.[26]

In 1880, under bipartisan pressure for Chinese exclusion, President Chester Arthur directed a revision of the Burlingame Treaty to allow for a ban on immigration between the United States and China. The Qing conceded, allowing for a "temporary suspension" of emigration of Chinese laborers. With the treaty removed as an obstacle, exclusionists pressed to get a bill passed through Congress. It was not a foregone conclusion that they would succeed when, in March 1882, an exclusion bill was introduced into the Congress. Members of Congress from the Midwest and Northeast questioned whether Chinese really cheapened white labor, compared Chinese to Irish and German immigrants, and worried about violating the treaties that promoted commercial relations with China. Some went so far as to declare the bill racist and contrary to American ideals. The exclusionists, led by the California delegation and with solid support from the South, rehearsed Pacific coast claims that the "cooly system is a system of slavery"; that it was preposterous to compare the "unassimilable" Chinese to European immigrants; and that Chinese exclusion was a matter of national self-defense and self-preservation.[27]

Meanwhile, the Qing Foreign Ministry met with American diplomats in Beijing. The Qing had already agreed to a modification of the Burlingame Treaty; now they tried to stanch the reach of the bill. They sought to exclude artisans from the category of laborer and to limit exclusion of laborers to those employed by U.S. citizens—without success. But they persuaded President Arthur that a suspension of immigration for twenty years—nearly a generation—violated the intent of the treaty. Arthur vetoed the bill on April 4 and sent it back to the Senate, which debated for another month.[28]

WHILE CONGRESS DEBATED the Chinese exclusion bill in Washington, Huang Zunxian arrived in San Francisco to assume his post as Qing consul general at San Francisco. He sailed directly from Yokohama, where he had been secretary to the Chinese legation in Japan, and arrived just as the debates over the bill were unfolding. A local reporter, reporting on his arrival on March 26, described him as a young man (he was thirty-three) who projected intelligence, confidence, good manners, and experience. Most important, the reporter noted that Huang "authoritatively" stated that the Chinese exclusion bill had the Chinese government's "approval." The reporter's choice of language may have exaggerated Huang's meaning—the Qing had acquiesced to modifying the Burlingame Treaty, but it was also objecting to the terms of the current bill as it was being crafted. Huang was no doubt already familiar with the discussion over the Chinese Question in the U.S. Congress. The Qing government and Chinese press had been long following the American debates. For example, *Xinbao* and *Wanguo gongbao,* both influential newspapers in Shanghai, had translated and reprinted the *Daily Alta California*'s coverage of the hearings held in 1877, including excerpts from testimonies. *Xinbao* expressly hoped that the translation of American viewpoints might assist future Qing diplomatic efforts (Figure 19).[29]

Huang was not the first Qing official to be posted at San Francisco; the imperial consulate had been established in the city in 1878. The consulate operated under the direction of the Chinese legation (embassy) in Washington. Its establishment was a remarkable acknowledgement of the need to protect the interests of Chinese living abroad at a time when the Qing still formally banned emigration and officially did not recognize Chinese who settled outside its domain. In fact, Chinese had been demanding consular protections abroad for some time. The Hong Kong newspaper *Qiri bao* opined in 1871, "The emperor should protect his people as his priority.... Should we let [Chinese people] scatter around all over the world and offer no assistance for them to seek for protection?... Although they have traveled outside [China's] map, they are still our brethren. We should not say that they should be abandoned since they have lived in foreign countries."[30]

As Huang was settling in and following the debate in Washington, an eruption of racial violence in northern California grabbed his attention. A riot took place in Martinez, a small fishing town on the Carquinez Strait, which feeds into the eastern part of San Francisco Bay. On April 27 a mob of whites, claiming resentment against Chinese employed in a local fish cannery, gathered outside a Chinese lodging house and demanded that the Chinese residents leave. When the Chinese refused, the mob rushed into the house and assaulted them, threw several people out of a second-story window, and set the house on fire. The mob then attacked Chinese laundries in town. The Chinese reportedly resisted, some with firearms—since the days of the gold rush, Chinese carried guns to defend themselves—but they were outnumbered and overcome. Many Chinese men were wounded, some critically, one fatally.[31]

Reaction in the press followed partisan lines. The *Sacramento Daily Union* reported that most residents of Martinez "denounce the horribly cruel and cowardly outrage committed ... by a band of irresponsible and lawless white savages.... We want to exclude the Chinese but not to mangle and murder them." Newspapers allied with the Democratic Party weaponized the Martinez riot to push for passage of the exclusion bill. An article in the *Sonoma Democrat* was typical of the approach: "The citizens of Martinez tired of waiting for relief by the shambling acts of a Republican Congress and Administration on the Chinese Question took the matter in their own hands the other day and drove the Mongolians by force from their midst.... Our people have been long suffering and there are those who think forbearance has ceased to be a virtue." The *Los Angeles Herald* opined that the failure of the Republican Congress and the president to "handle the Chinese curse with vigor" was responsible for the Martinez riot and warned, "We expect to witness a good many riots in the United States."[32]

The Martinez riot made clear to Huang that the Chinese Question in America was a symbiosis of elite and popular racisms that played out both in legislatures and on the streets. He wrote immediately to the Qing ambassador in Washington, Zheng Yuxuan, who in turn lodged a diplomatic protest with the U.S. State Department, along with a demand for $20,000 in damages for the Martinez Chinese. The State Department referred the matter to the governor of California, who in turn referred it to the district attorney of Contra Costa County, where it trickled down to Martinez. A few white men were arrested, then acquitted in local court. Despite the disappointing outcome, Huang's diplomatic efforts signaled a new level of involvement for the Qing's representatives abroad. In fact, Huang Zunxian's work was just beginning.[33]

ON MAY 6, 1882, after some fifteen years of agitation from the Pacific coast, President Chester Arthur signed the law suspending the immigration of Chinese laborers for ten years. Merchants, diplomats, students, treaty traders, and ministers were exempt from exclusion, as were Chinese laborers already living in the United States. They would be permitted to leave the United States for a short time with a "return certificate" and allowed to enter upon return.[34]

It was the first immigration law to name a specific group for exclusion on grounds of its alleged racial unassimilability. Although the law was to be in effect for ten years and exempted nonlaborers, it was absolute in its racial logic. It applied to all Chinese, regardless of their country of origin, whether China, Hong Kong (a British colony), or Cuba; and it barred all Chinese, regardless of class, from the privilege of naturalized citizenship. The exemptions were attuned to American commercial and missionary interests and the conventions of diplomatic reciprocity. But the bureaucrats in charge of enforcing the exclusion laws would use administrative means to restrict and deny entry to those of the exempt classes, as well as laborers and even those with U.S. citizenship, ensuring ongoing conflict over Chinese exclusion.[35]

The anti-Chinese movement on the Pacific coast exulted in the passage of the exclusion law. "Victory at last!" declared the front-page headline of the *Daily Alta*, with a lengthy kicker that praised the "Indefatigable Exertions of our Representatives." Chinese, of course, were dismayed, bitter, and frightened.[36]

When the exclusion law went into effect on August 4, Huang met each arriving ship at the wharf and observed customs officials as they inspected disembarking passengers from China. He brought with him a member of his consular staff, Frederick Bee, a Euro-American entrepreneur who, since his earliest days during the gold rush in Hangtown, California, had advocated for the rights of Chinese. Bee adjudicated conflicts between whites and Chinese on the goldfields and later represented the interests of the Chinese Six Companies during the 1877 congressional hearings on Chinese immigration. He became a consultant to the Qing when it opened its first consulate in San Francisco in 1878 and assisted Huang when he arrived in 1882. Huang called Bee "my comrade" and memorialized him in a poem as a man whose "guts are bigger than his body, his spirit is naturally heroic and fearless. . . . Even in smiling, he always carried a boot dagger."[37]

Huang was right to distrust customs officials implementing the new exclusion law. On August 8, just days after the law took effect, Chinese crewmen on the American steamship *City of Sydney* were refused landing and detained on board after it returned from a four-month round trip to Australia: Ah Sing, Ah Tie, and others, all longtime residents of California, had been hired at San Francisco on the outbound journey as ship kitchen workers and cabin waiters. In another case, Low Yam Chow, a merchant from Panama, arrived in San Francisco to purchase goods for his Central American business. Customs officials refused to land him on grounds that he lacked the so-called Section 6 certificate that vouched for his identity as a merchant and hence exempt from the exclusion law.[38]

Huang Zunxian and Frederick Bee threw themselves into the work of advocating for Chinese who were barred from entry upon their arrival. They retained lawyers to file writs of habeas corpus in order to bring their cases before the federal court and succeeded in winning the cases of the ship crewmen and the merchant. In two cases involving the crewmen on the *City of Sydney*, the court ruled that prior residence in California exempted them from the exclusion law and that their employment aboard an American ship meant that they remained within the jurisdiction of the United States during their entire journey. In the case of merchant Low, the court interpreted Section 6 of the exclusion law to apply to merchants in China and not to those traveling from other parts of the world. It would be "unjust and absurd" to require someone in Panama to travel to China in order to get a certificate to enter the United States, said the court.[39]

Huang attended the hearings. The courtroom atmosphere was charged; heated exchanges took place between the district attorney, lawyers, and judges. Merchant Low's case was heard before a large and noisy group of spectators. Notably, Justice Stephen Field, an associate justice of the U.S. Supreme Court, presided at the cases in the circuit court, indicating the high stakes involved in the interpretation of the exclusion act. Field made a strong impression on Huang. The consul wrote to the Qing ambassador in Washington that he considered Justice Field to be "upright and tough." He added, "During the debate, he [Field] said the U.S. is broad and populated, why couldn't they tolerate a small group of Chinese! He is fair and never avoids speaking the truth in front of the public. I really appreciate his courage." Field would write as much in his decision in *Case of the Chinese Cabin Waiter,* "The object of the act of congress was . . . not to expel [Chinese] already here. . . . [I]t was not thought that the few thousands (of Chinese) now here . . . would sensibly disturb our peace or affect our civilization."[40]

In the case of the merchant Low Yam Chow, Field recalled the Burlingame Treaty (and its 1880 revision) to defend the rights of Chinese merchants to "go and come of their own free will and accord." The treaty prohibited "excluding Chinese merchants, or putting unnecessary and embarrassing restrictions upon their coming," which would interfere "with the commercial relations between China and this country. Commerce with China is of the greatest value, and is constantly increasing."[41]

Over the course of the next few months, with the Low Yam Chow ruling serving as precedent, Huang succeeded in landing some thirty merchants who had initially been refused entry upon arrival, including those from Peru, Chile, and Panama. He considered distributing Section 6 certificates to merchants arriving from places other than China, under his authority as consul for the Qing government, but customs officials demurred. The cases resolved by late October, and Huang dropped the idea.[42]

These early cases gave Huang hope that the exclusion law would not be applied unjustly or absurdly. He knew that public opinion was divided

on the Chinese Question and was particularly encouraged that Justice
Field expressed support for the U.S.-China trade, Sino-American treaty
relations, and the fair exercise of the law. But Huang was not entirely correct in his assessment of Field. Justice Field harbored no special animus
toward Chinese, but he was also no special friend. He saw in the Chinese
cases occasion to extend the reach of federal power, especially in the regulation of commercial and economic matters. His influence would be most
famously felt a few years later, in *Yick Wo v. Hopkins* (1886). That case
involved a San Francisco fire ordinance that required all laundries to be
built from brick. The law exempted existing laundries in wooden buildings, as long as the owner obtained a certificate from the city. Authorities
gave exemptions to over two hundred white laundry owners but none to
Chinese. Huang Zunxian and his lawyers organized a test case to challenge the ruling, arranging for the owner of the Yick Wo laundry to be
arrested for violating the ordinance and using habeas to force a court hearing. The Supreme Court ruled that a law that is race neutral on its face
but is administered in a prejudicial manner violates the equal protection
clause of the Fourteenth Amendment. *Yick Wo v. Hopkins* is a landmark
ruling in the history of constitutional law because it extended the protection of the Fourteenth Amendment to economic activity and affirmed protection of equal rights and due process to all persons, not just citizens.[43]

Huang Zunxian left San Francisco in September 1885, before the
Supreme Court ruled on *Yick Wo*. He had spent his three-year rotation in
California working tirelessly on behalf of the overseas Chinese community. He had bid San Francisco's family and district associations to formally
unite under a consolidated structure, to provide better social services, and
to be more transparent in reporting their financial accounts to their members. In addition to his legal work in the immigration cases and *Yick Wo*,
he provided legal assistance to overturn the exclusion of Chinese children
from San Francisco's public schools. When he learned that his mother had
passed away in China, he applied for a leave—for the standard period of
mourning during which his government service would be suspended—
but his superiors denied his request. That extraordinary decision reflected
the Qing's awareness of the racial volatility in the United States. When

Huang finally left in 1885, he was exhausted. He sailed on the SS *City of Peking*, along with a thousand Chinese in steerage and a heavy cargo of wheat flour, ginseng, cheese, silver bullion, gold coin, and gold dust. His Pacific crossing coincided with the Chinese midautumn festival. He spent a sleepless night on deck at the ship's railing, looking at the moon and thinking about the sufferings of the Chinese laborers in steerage below and the vast chasm that separated Chinese and Western cultures.[44]

WHEN HUANG LEFT CALIFORNIA, the Chinese Question was by no means settled. To the contrary, the mid-1880s would be perhaps the darkest time for Chinese in the American West. It was as though the exclusion law had affirmed the racist logic of the Chinese Question and authorized further violence against Chinese. Theft, assault, murder, and arson had followed Chinese since their first arrival during the gold rush, but during the mid-1880s a new wave of violence swept up and down the Pacific coast. The "driving out" campaigns signaled that the slogan "The Chinese must go!" was not just for exclusion but also for removal. Historian Beth Lew-Williams has accounted for 439 cases of expulsion or attempted expulsion of Chinese from towns in western states between 1885 and 1887. The methods included harassment, bombing, arson, assault, roundups, murder, and lynching. At least eighty-seven Chinese died in these events.[45]

Many expulsions resulted from sustained campaigns. In September 1885 in Tacoma, Washington, an expulsion movement led by the Knights of Labor and city officials passed a resolution giving Chinese residents until November 1 to leave. Declaring that the expulsion would be orderly and nonviolent, they backed up the demand with mass meetings and parades, but also with threatening door-to-door visits. Chinese residents resisted the expulsion until armed vigilantes compelled a forced march of eight miles under heavy rain; two men died from exposure. The vigilantes then set the Chinese quarter on fire.[46]

Other attacks were like spontaneous combustions that exploded from long-simmering animosities. At Hells Canyon on the Snake River in Oregon, white farmers and schoolboys went on a rampage, robbing and murdering thirty-four Chinese miners and then throwing their bodies into the river. Perhaps the most famous riot took place in September 1885 at Rock Springs, Wyoming Territory, at a large coal mine owned by the Union Pacific Railroad. Chinese and white miners earned the same wages, but racism against Chinese ran deep among whites, dating to the Union Pacific's use of Chinese as strikebreakers in 1875. Ten years later, when Chinese refused to support a strike called by the Knights of Labor, whites vowed to drive out the Chinese. An armed mob of 150 white workers attacked the Chinese quarter in town, setting fire to some eighty houses and firing upon fleeing residents. The mob rampaged through the mining camps, driving out four hundred Chinese miners. Some Chinese died from gunfire, others perished in their burning homes, and still others died from exposure after they fled to nearby hills. The Union Pacific transported refugees to relative safety and called upon the federal government to send troops to escort them back to Rock Springs. But the use of police or troops to protect Chinese was rare. Most officials—including those in Wyoming Territory—did nothing to stop the violence or to seek justice for Chinese killed, injured, or robbed of their property (Figure 16).[47]

Qing ambassador Zheng Yuxuan directed consuls Huang Shi Chen of New York and Frederick Bee of San Francisco to proceed to Rock Springs for a direct investigation. The consuls produced three documents that provide rare detail from the Chinese perspective. The first was a chilling account signed by 559 Chinese survivors of Rock Springs. The memorial described two days of terror. It read in part:

> Some of the Chinese were killed at the bank of Bitter Creek, some near the railroad bridge, and some in "Chinatown." After having been killed, the dead bodies of some were carried to the burning buildings and thrown into the flames. Some of the Chinese who had hid themselves in the houses were killed and their bodies burned; some, who on account of sickness could not run, were burned alive in the houses. One Chinese was killed in "Whitemen's Town" in a laundry house, and his house demolished. The whole number of Chinese killed was twenty-eight and those wounded fifteen.

The memorial also revealed that white women and children joined in the mob, including women who had taught English classes to Chinese residents.[48]

The second report by Consul Huang gave a listing of the twenty-eight dead men: their names, the manner of their death, and whether they had family in China. By naming each victim, Huang humanized each one. For example,

3.   The dead body of Yii See Yen was found near the creek. The left temple was shot by a bullet, and the skull broken. The age of the deceased was thirty-six years. He had a mother living at home [in China]. . . .

7.   A portion of the dead body of Leo Lung Hong was found in a pile of ashes in a hut adjoining Camp No. 27. It consisted of the head, neck, and breast. The two hands, together with rest of body below the waist, were burned off completely. I also ascertained that deceased was forty-five years old, and had a wife and three sons living at home.[49]

The third report by Consul Bee was based on interviews with white residents, including the postmaster, a railroad employee, and local merchants, who testified to the peaceable and law-abiding character of the Chinese and that the unprovoked attack was carried out by Irish, Cornish, and Scandinavian miners in broad daylight. Bee called it "one of the most murderous, cruel, and uncalled-for outrages ever perpetrated in any Christian country." Rock Springs authorities made no attempt to quell the riot. Afterward the coroner held inquests but called no witnesses; the coroner was also the same official who granted a "paltry bail" and quick release to a few men who were arrested for murder and arson. The grand jury refused to bring any indictments. The whole thing struck Bee as "burlesque." Bee concluded, "not one of these criminals who murdered the Chinese, burned and robbed them at Rock Springs, will or can ever be brought to punishment by the so-called Territorial or local authorities."[50]

AMBASSADOR ZHENG LODGED a lengthy, official protest with Secretary of State Thomas Bayard—one of many that he wrote during this time—

attaching Bee's report and a half-dozen affidavits from white residents of Rock Springs. The ambassador requested "that the persons who have been guilty of this murder, robbery, and arson, be brought to punishment; that the Chinese subjects be fully indemnified for all the losses and injuries they have sustained by this lawlessness; and that suitable measures be adopted to protect the Chinese residents of Wyoming Territory and elsewhere in the United States from similar attacks." He submitted a bill for $147,748.74, estimating the value of Chinese residents' property destroyed or stolen during the riot. Zheng also reminded Bayard of the treaty obligations that existed between the two nations to protect the nationals of each country residing in the other, and precedents (there were many) where the Chinese government had paid the United States for losses incurred by Americans in China.[51]

Secretary Bayard responded that the incident at Rock Springs, while regrettable, was the action of private individuals and that the U.S. government was therefore not liable. But American diplomats in China reported great "excitement" in Guangzhou over the Rock Springs massacre. Reports in the Hong Kong press and telegrams received from Chinese Americans, posted around the city, fueled public outrage. The American ambassador to China, Charles Denby, worried that the "troublesome" Cantonese would attack American businessmen and missionaries in China. Denby went so far as to order a second American gunboat to Guangzhou.[52]

Alarmed at the prospect of retaliatory violence in China, Congress passed legislation that appropriated $147,758 for reparations for Rock Springs and an additional $130,000 for "all other losses and injuries sustained by Chinese subjects within the United States at the hands of residents thereof." Congress later made additional payouts for damages incurred by Chinese during race riots in Tacoma and Seattle, Washington, and in Redding, California, for a total of $424,367. The reparations went directly to the Chinese government; it is unknown whether any of the money went to individual victims or their families.[53]

ANTICOOLIEISM IN CALIFORNIA and the United States sustained a core argument that Chinese were an unfree race. But it was a protean ideology capable of adjusting its tilt to fit the trajectory of state and national politics. In the 1850s it had depicted Chinese as "coolies" and "slaves" to associate them with enslaved African Americans and thus a threat to free labor. After the Civil War and the passage of the Thirteenth Amendment, which outlawed slavery and all forms of servitude, the anticoolieist argument shifted to allegations of "debt bondage" imposed upon Chinese laborers by the "credit ticket system" and the trafficking of "slave girls" as prostitutes. This line of thinking had the added benefit of placing the entire blame on the Chinese for being both slaves and slave masters. The Fourteenth Amendment's principle of equal rights posed another challenge for exclusionists. Writing in 1869, Henry George reconciled the contradiction between liberal inclusion and illiberal exclusion by way of nationalism and racial exception. By introducing the problem of monopoly into the equation, he gave the racial argument an alibi of class interest, which interest became increasingly central in the latter decades of the nineteenth century. With Reconstruction's demise and the rise of Jim Crow, anticoolieism no longer had to answer to abolitionism.

So much was clear in an 1893 exchange of letters between Henry George and William Lloyd Garrison, Jr., the son of the great antislavery activist. Garrison, a Boston businessman, criticized the single-taxers for supporting the Geary Act, which extended Chinese exclusion for another ten years and required domiciled Chinese to carry an identity card at all times, on pain of removal. Garrison stood by the principle of equal rights. George responded to him, "That the right to the use of the earth is not confined to the inhabitants of the United States, I most cordially assent. But . . . that the humblest Chinaman has as much natural right to use the earth of California as yourself . . . I must emphatically deny. Are men merely individuals? Is there no such thing as family, nation, race?" George recast the stakes of the Civil War to defend Chinese exclusion. "Your parallel between those who supported slavery and those who oppose Chinese immigration is not a true one," he wrote. "The first of the evils wrought by African slavery in the United States was the bringing hither of large numbers of the blacks, an evil which still remains a source of weakness and danger, though slavery is gone. Let me ask you: If to-day there was the same possibility of a great coming of African negroes to this country as there would be of Chinamen if all restrictions were removed, would you consider it a wise thing to permit under present conditions?"[54]

George was not the only one to compare Chinese and African Americans; it was common to use analogies between the two groups to justify the treatment of one or the other. And just as the Supreme Court reckoned with the meaning of equality for African Americans in the last decades of the nineteenth century, culminating with the "separate but equal" doctrine enshrined in *Plessy v. Ferguson* (1896), it also introduced justifications for Chinese exclusion that would have far-reaching consequences. Federal regulation of immigration had, after the Civil War, been understood as a matter of commerce. But Chinese exclusion occasioned the Court to shift to sovereignty, that is, to national security, as the rationale for federal regulation of immigration.[55]

That grounding enabled Congress to act with plenary, or absolute, power in matters of immigration. In the *Chinese Exclusion Case* (1889), the Court considered Chinese emigrants to be agents of a foreign power and therefore excludable as a matter of national security, even if there were no "actual hostilities" taking place. It also ruled that legislation superseded treaties, thus making regulation of immigration a unilateral affair. Between 1882 and 1901, Congress would pass successively harsh exclusion laws while rebuffing Qing efforts to modify exclusion through treaty negotiation.

In 1893 the Court extended the principle of national security to matters of deportation, declaring that aliens may "be and remain in this country, except by the license, permission, and sufferance of Congress." By declaring that regulation of immigration was part of the Congress's conduct of foreign relations, along with declaring war and making treaties, the Supreme Court ruled that aliens have no constitutional rights in matters of entry and removal. The principle that immigration is a matter of national security continues to underwrite American immigration law to this day.[56]

Chapter 7

The Yellow Agony

Both Chinese and whites in Australia closely followed the course of events in the United States. Beginning in the late 1870s, the Australian press gave considerable attention to California politics. Newspapers reported on the progress of American exclusion legislation and the oratory of the sandlot king, Denis Kearney. The California theory of coolieism crossed the Pacific into Australian popular discourse. For example, the *Bulletin,* a nationalist Sydney weekly, rehearsed the major components of California coolieism: "He imports his fellows here and keeps them in a condition of slavery. . . . He imports Chinese women sometimes and sells them. . . . There is an authority enforceable by his own tribunals." An illustration spread across two pages depicted a hideous Chinese man as an octopus, its tentacles labeled with vices of "cheap labor" "small pox," "fan tan," "opium," and "immorality" (implying sexual unions with white women). Australia, added the *Bulletin,* should learn from the experience of Chinese immigration in California and exclude Chinese from the colonies (Figure 18).[1]

Victoria's venerable Chinese merchants and advocates, Lowe Kong Meng and Louis Ah Mouy, watched these developments unfold with alarm. They too were knowledgeable about the exclusion movement in the United States and sought to take their own lessons from the resistance of Chinese

Americans. Lowe and Louis, together with the young Chinese Christian reformer and Melbourne merchant Cheok Hong Cheong (Zhang Zhuo-xiong), published a pamphlet in 1879, titled *The Chinese Question in Austra-lia*. It referenced U.S. congressional investigations, missionary statements on the positive qualities of the Chinese, and the writings of San Francisco's *huiguan* leaders, to underscore common themes, such as the symbiosis of trade and migration. They also pointed to international law and treaty obli-gations, in this case, the Anglo-Chinese Peking Convention of 1860, which granted Chinese the right to travel to and work in British territories.[2]

"If you wish to shut out the Chinese from this part of the British empire," they wrote, "you are bound, by every obligation of law and jus-tice, to do so in a just and legal manner," that is, by "asking for a repeal of the existing treaty. You cannot say to [the Chinese emperor], 'You must admit British subjects to trade and settle in any part of China; but we will not suffer Chinese subjects to trade and settle in any part of the British empire.'" Such a position "stooped" to the conduct of barbarians, heed-less of international law and the principle of reciprocity in treaties.[3]

IF THE CHINESE QUESTION in Australia looked more and more like its American cousin, it came to that point along a different path. During the 1850s Victorian gold rush, anti-Chinese racism was more inchoate than in California and did not advance a general theory of "coolieism." Legal restriction also followed a different route. Victoria, New South Wales, and South Australia had imposed various measures aimed at restricting Chi-nese emigration to the goldfields—a tonnage requirement on ships, land-ing and protection fees, and the residency tax. These impositions, while onerous and subject to evasion and conflict, avoided explicit restriction or exclusion, in deference to British imperial policies of free migration and its diplomatic relations with China. Victoria and New South Wales even repealed some of their restrictions in the 1860s, as the gold rush waned and the Chinese population in those colonies declined by 40 per-cent, which pleased the Colonial Office in London.[4]

But by the late 1870s, white Australians were increasingly demanding an explicit policy of exclusion, increasing tensions between the colonies and

Great Britain. For the latter, the Chinese Question primarily concerned the empire's formal relations with China and, more generally, its commercial and geopolitical stakes in Asia. *The Times* of London considered the problem of Chinese immigration in Australia to be one in a series of the empire's "direct contests" in Asia, along with the second Opium War in China (1856–60) and the Indian uprising (1857). Britain's imperial interests seemed to be at odds, or at least in tension with, white settler-colonial interests in Australia.[5]

The revival of the Chinese Question in Australia began not on the old goldfields of Victoria but in white anxiety over a growing population of Chinese in the Northern Territory and northern Queensland. The so-called Top End—some two thousand miles north of Melbourne—lay in an entirely different ecosystem that was tropical and dotted with rain forests. It was still predominantly populated by indigenous peoples. These conditions deterred European development. Chinese settlement in the far north—both transplants from Victoria and new emigrants from southern China—helped open the area to mining, agriculture, maritime industries, and commerce. These new migrations brought into focus a tension in the nature of Australian colonialism itself: Europeans conceived of New South Wales, Victoria, and South Australia as temperate zones of white settlement based on free labor and democratic government. In contrast, the tropical north offered lucrative economic potential from sugar and fruit plantations, gold and tin mining, and maritime pearl shelling, all of which sought the use of cheap and indentured colored labor. Australia posed an unusual case, where white settler colonies were contiguous to plantation colonies. The abutting areas with different political economies generated anew the specter of a Chinese "invasion" and opposition to "cheap" colored labor more generally.

ONE OF THE FIRST Chinese to settle the Northern Territory was Ping Que, who moved there in 1875. Over the course of the previous twenty years, he had built a successful career as a mining entrepreneur in Creswick, Victoria. He had begun as a prospector and then owned several small gold mining companies; in 1873 he became a naturalized British subject. One of the first mining entrepreneurs of any ethnic background on the Top End, Ping Que would make a fortune in gold mining and other ventures and become a leading citizen of Port Darwin and the Pine Creek region.

Ping Que and other gold seekers of the 1870s were not the first outsiders to arrive at the Top End. A regional trading network in the eastern Indonesian archipelago, including the northern Australian coast and islands, had existed before European contact, since at least the early seventeenth century. Indonesian seafarers called the area Marege, "wild place" in Malay. By the early eighteenth century, a robust annual trade had developed in trepang (bêche-de-mer, or sea cucumber), fished and cured by Aboriginal people in Marege and shipped by Macassan ships through Sulawesi (Celebes) to China, where the delicacy was (and remains) a staple course of the Chinese banquet.[6]

Although Chinese merchant-shippers were part of the early modern trepang trade, it was the opening of Arnham Land for gold prospecting in 1872 that spurred the Chinese presence in the Northern Territory in the late nineteenth century. Ping Que began on the Union Reefs, arriving on horseback with a half-dozen Chinese workers (who walked) via the 110-mile bush track from Palmerston (Darwin). He began as a tributer, meaning he paid a percentage of his earnings to the claim's owner. His workers were among the 173 Chinese brought from Singapore by the colonial government on contracts in 1874 for distribution to various gold mining employers and for work on the telegraph line; thousands more would be recruited in the 1880s to build the Pine Creek–Darwin railroad. Ping Que increased his tributing operations and then acquired claims of his own, some of them in joint ventures with whites. By 1877 he was crushing quartz rock that consistently produced over an ounce of gold per ton or more, and he began directly importing Chinese workers from Hong Kong and Singapore. Adam Johns, another early mining magnate on the reefs, called Ping Que "the whitest man in the Territory."[7]

The scale of Ping Que's operations was far greater than Chinese-owned gold mining in Victoria or, for that matter, California. Ping Que played multiple roles in a closed system, as mine owner or lessee, merchant, and labor contractor. His holdings were so vast that he tributed leases to smaller Chinese merchants. He expanded into other areas as well, building sheep pens and slaughtering yards for cattle and purchasing a hotel in Pine Creek. He was also a model citizen who gave generously to hospital construction and other charities, and he was elected to the Mining Board under the Northern Territory Mining Act of 1873.[8]

Contemporaries called the Chinese who emigrated to the Northern Territory "coolies." The first Chinese imported by the government likely came under contracts; when Ping Que directly recruited workers from Hong Kong and Singapore, he underwrote their passage for repayment after arrival. It does not appear that he held them with long-term indentures or that he treated his workers poorly (at least no records of complaints over abuse exist). As in other gold mining frontiers, laborers could easily desert their contracts if they were dissatisfied with their condition. Ping Que was the largest employer of Chinese in the territory, but the goldfields also supported numerous small Chinese merchant share companies and cooperatives, which might have offered alternative means of employment.[9]

Nonindigenous people comprised less than a quarter of the population in the Northern Territory, with Chinese accounting for nearly 80 percent of the settler population in 1888. Darwin was predominantly Chinese, with as many as thirteen hundred residents and an additional itinerant population of several thousand railroad workers, miners, and servants. Still, the numbers were small: the government counted 6,122 Chinese and barely two thousand Europeans in the territory that year. The demographics indicated the slow pace of white settlement and Europeans' dependence upon Chinese for labor, food production, and services. The Northern Territory resembled a plantation colony, with a thin layer of elite white managers and officials and a large number of non-Europeans, including Chinese workers and settlers and a diverse Aboriginal and Asian maritime workforce employed in the trepang and pearl-shelling industries.[10]

While dependent upon Asians, white Australians were also anxious about the growth of the nonwhite population and ethnic mixing between Aboriginal and Asian peoples. In 1881 South Australia, which administered the Northern Territory, drew an imaginary line two hundred miles south of Darwin and announced that Chinese would have to pay a fee in order to migrate beyond it. Western Australia barred Asians from pearling and boat licenses; Queensland and South Australia decided Asians could be pearling workers but not owners. During the 1890s the colonies removed Aboriginal peoples from pearling labor and from the townships in order to segregate and "protect" them from Chinese and Malays. Aboriginal and Asian peoples in the far north, who had had a long history of contact, mixing, and mobility, now became partitioned and isolated from each other under an increasingly rigid racial regime.[11]

IN CONTRAST TO the Northern Territory, Europeans arrived in greater numbers and with greater aggression in Queensland. Brisbane on Moreton Bay, six hundred miles north of Sydney, began as a penal colony and opened to white settlement only in the 1840s. From there, pastoralists, agriculturalists, and miners pushed relentlessly up the coast and into the interior. In the process they faced considerable resistance from Aboriginal peoples. Settlers and a paramilitary force called Native Police killed as many as 65,000 native people during a "never ceasing war" through the end of the nineteenth century, making Aboriginal dispossession bloodier in Queensland than in any other Australian colony. As Chinese gold seekers, merchants, and farmers moved into Queensland, they became implicated in the war between natives and settlers. Because Europeans relegated Chinese to camps and villages on the fringes of white settlement, the Chinese were often the first to encounter Aboriginal resistance. Unlike the Northern Territory, Queensland was not a good place for mixing and sharing.[12]

Colonists' exploration of the Queensland interior in the 1850s and '60s resulted in the discovery of gold and a few small rushes. Kong Shing Yung was one of the early Chinese settlers, moving to Queensland in 1865 following the discovery of gold at Peak Downs. He was a merchant whose store in Victoria was destroyed during the Buckland River Riot in 1857; he relocated to Bendigo and then to New South Wales where, he said, "the Europeans . . . were very bad" on account of their convict background. Tired of robbery and harassment by bushrangers and highwaymen, he moved again. Northern Queensland was yet undeveloped, with far more sheep than people. Kong Shing Yung shared in the British dream that Queensland would, in time, become "one of the great emporiums of the world, as the country contains in itself the germs of national greatness," with mineral and timber resources, boundless pasture, and both tropical and temperate climes that could support the production of rice, coffee, tea, sugar, tobacco, cotton, and oil.[13]

The biggest and most consequential gold rush in Queensland took place at the Palmer River, twelve hundred miles north of Brisbane, beginning in 1873. The Palmer rush drew both Europeans and Chinese from the older goldfields of Victoria and New South Wales, as well as from the Northern Territory. It was a huge goldfield, some six hundred square kilometers in area; its rich alluvial deposits prompted tales about gullies where one could "literally shovel the gold out." The nuggets were "lovely to look at, all water worn and of the most fantastic shapes." Some weighed nearly a pound. But it was a remote, tropical environment, riddled with fever and under constant attack from Aboriginal peoples resisting foreign encroachment. Dead bodies were said to litter the bush tracks. "If Australian miners have fallen by the scores, Chinese must have fallen by the hundred," wrote J. Dundas Crawford, a contemporary British observer. Wild rumors abounded about blacks wielding ten-foot-long poison-barbed spears. But as always, the promise of gold outweighed the dangers of the frontier.[14]

The Chinese population in Queensland, only 540 in 1861, rose to 3,300 by 1871 and increased dramatically thereafter with the Palmer rush. In 1875 steamer service connected Hong Kong and Cooktown, the main port in northern Queensland, whereupon greater numbers came directly from southern China, mostly from Zhongshan, in Guangdong province. By 1876 there were over twenty thousand Chinese in and around Cooktown and overwhelming the European population on the Palmer diggings.[15]

Observers noted patterns that were similar to those among voluntary emigrants in Victoria. On the Palmer diggings, Chinese miners used well-tested methods emphasizing cooperation, thoroughness, and physical mobility; they worked with rockers, with a group of ten working in pairs, digging, carrying water, washing dirt, and packing gold and gold dust.[16]

Chinese market gardeners and storekeepers did business in small towns across the region. As in Victoria (and California), they were often former gold miners. In the town of Mayfield, the administrative center of the Palmer gold district, Chinese owned most of the shops, saloons, and services; they also built forge sites, a temple, and a cemetery. Chinese built their dwellings according to feng shui principles and with floors made from flagstone and flanked by terraced vegetable gardens.[17]

Europeans resented the arrival of so many Chinese on the Palmer; as goldfields warden William Hill complained, "Only for the influx of Chinamen the Palmer would have given profitable employment to thousands of Europeans." In 1877 white miners formed an anti-Chinese association, and ugly threats surfaced—"Any Chinaman found higher up this creek will be seized and hanged until he is dead," read a note posted on a tree—but the sheer numerical superiority of the Chinese militated against white violence. The mining wardens on the Palmer limited the size of Chinese claims and discouraged them from quartz mining in order to avoid jealousy from Europeans.[18]

Opinion in northern Queensland was not entirely against the Chinese, who, as in Darwin, provided farm produce and services in and around the new port towns on the northern coast, Cooktown and Port Douglas. In remote areas they supplied goods for Chinese, whites, and Aboriginal people; the latter also sometimes worked as guides for Chinese shops. Chinese settlers also helped establish the first sugar plantation in Queensland and opened the Cairns district to corn, rice, and fruit production, especially bananas. The largest Chinese agriculturalists imported their own contract workers from southern China; and Chinese businessmen maintained commercial ties to Singapore and Hong Kong and across Southeast Asia. The prevalence of Chinese in northern Queensland signaled the region's proximity to China as well as the European belief that the tropics were ill suited for white settlement or labor.[19]

As Europeans abandoned the Palmer, they appealed to the colonial government to enact restrictions on Chinese. The Queensland legislature proposed raising the cost of mining and business licenses for African and Asian aliens and new regulations on ships from Hong Kong landing at Cooktown in 1876. But Governor Cairns tabled it, concerned that it might violate Anglo-Chinese treaties and jeopardize the rights of Chinese from Singapore and Hong Kong, who were British subjects. A later bill passed in 1878 addressed imperial concerns by excluding Asian aliens (not British subjects) from "new" goldfields, which in effect limited Asians to mining areas that were already worked out.[20]

Increasingly, whites looked with alarm upon the growing population of not just Chinese but all Asians and Pacific Islanders in northern Queensland. The use of labor from the Melanesian islands of the southwestern Pacific (whom whites derisively called "Kanakas") on sugar and cotton plantations stirred particular controversy. Anti-Asian petitioners in the Mackay area declared that "for every Islander introduced a European labourer is driven away," while planters asserted their "rights as British subjects" to import labor under contracts, citing agreements with India and general laissez-faire theory. Although the Queensland legislature passed regulations over labor importation, "blackbirding" (kidnapping) and horrific work conditions persisted.[21]

Of more general concern was the prospect of permanent settlement, competition in the free labor market and in petty commerce, and population accretion, all of which seemed to doom the future of white society. "Townsville carries off the palm," wrote a white resident of the far northern coastal city, "for want, misery, and prostitution. Chinese, Kanakas, Javanese, Cingalese, Japanese, and all the other leprous races under the sun have found their way to Townsville." The *Telegraph* asked, "Can it be expected that [white workingmen] will stand quietly by and see these black-fellows wheeling perambulators; driving buggy horses; doing up gardens; peeling potatoes, scrubbing floors; and washing up dishes, whilst they themselves, or their young-lady daughters, are desirous of doing the same work, according to fitness of sex or strength, for less wages?. . . . It is clear that [Pacific Islanders] like the country from the fact of their remaining in it after the term of their engagement has expired." The Kanaka Question and Chinese Question merged into the "black and yellow agony."[22]

AT THE SAME TIME that the Chinese Question stoked controversy in Queensland, it resurfaced in the southern colonies, not on the goldfields but in Melbourne and Sydney. In fact, the urban Chinese population was numerically small and concentrated in a few niche occupations—market gardening, hawking, and furniture making. Chinese competed with white craftsmen only in the latter trade. In the late 1870s, a trade association of manufacturers and employees in Victoria formed to "maintain the furniture trade in the hands of the Europeans by every legitimate means." It attained an agreement with the commissioners for the upcoming Melbourne International Exhibition to purchase chairs only from Victorian manufacturers who employed no Chinese. But the agreement was canceled, perhaps owing to pressure from colonial officials mindful of Anglo-Chinese relations. The chair makers appealed to the white labor in other trades, warning that the "fleabite" of evil done to them was but the opening of a full-scale Chinese invasion of the colony. Thousands turned out at "monster meetings" (mass demonstrations), an Anti-Chinese League formed, and middle-class and small business interests in the city and in the suburbs joined the fray—all key elements of an emerging pattern of cross-class political agitation on the Chinese Question.[23]

Around the same time in Sydney, the Australian seamen's union took on the Australian Steam Navigation Company (ASN) for its decision to replace Europeans with Chinese crewmen on its Fiji and New Caledonia trade routes. Since the 1860s the hiring of Chinese in Singapore and Hong Kong to work on Asia-Pacific steamship lines—including transpacific routes to California—had become increasingly common. The ASN's move in 1878 aimed to stave competition from companies based in Hong Kong. The seamen's union waged a year-long mass campaign for legislation restricting the use of Chinese on Australian-owned ships, but the NSW assembly and the colonial secretary, Michael Fitzpatrick, demurred, citing imperial obligations. The union responded with a militant strike, which won support from the trades council and the general public. The Queensland government threatened to cancel its mail subsidy to the ASN if it continued to employ Chinese. When it was reported that the ASN was importing Chinese strikebreakers from Hong Kong, ten thousand people protested in Sydney's Hyde Park. The racial stakes of the Pacific could not have been clearer.[24]

The strike sparked a political crisis, for although there was considerable support for Chinese restriction in the NSW legislature, the Chamber of Commerce and the premier, Henry Farnell—although not necessarily unsympathetic—refused to let the trade unions set colonial policy. In the event, Farnell's ministry collapsed in December 1878; Sir Henry Parkes, a radical liberal with a long history in NSW politics, formed a new coalition government on the promise to introduce legislation to restrict Chinese immigration. That would take longer to achieve, but in January 1879 the strike settled with an agreement that the company would reduce the number of Chinese in its employ.[25]

As in Melbourne, the seamen's union and the Sydney Trades and Labour Council won support from the middle class, small producers, and reformers, who were exercised over the alleged lack of morals and sanitation among the city's Chinese. Though relatively few in number—960 Chinese, mostly males, lived in Sydney in 1878—nearly a third were paired with white women, with whom they had 586 children. The trend might have been considered evidence of settlement and assimilation, but whites viewed it as racial contamination and "moral pestilence."[26]

The local contours of anti-Chinese opposition in the different colonies thus converged in a general discourse of Australian nationalism, which had at its center the imperative for a "White Australia." Queensland critics of indentured colored labor modified the racial theory of climate, suggesting that whites could work in the tropics if adequately compensated. The *Brisbane Courier* intoned, "We aim at making Queensland from south to north a British colony, and some day to be, portion of an Anglo-Australian nation. . . . We want no servile race amongst us with which ours will not amalgamate."[27]

Moreover, the problem of Chinese and other Asians in the Northern Territory and Queensland appeared to be directly consequential to whites in New South Wales and Victoria, who imagined hordes of coolies in the north migrating southward into the temperate regions. John Parsons, the government resident at Port Darwin, warned of a "powerful syndicate" of merchants in southern China, who were ready to "pour Chinese" into Darwin. "Once landed in the centre of Australia," he said, they would "spread all over the Colonies." New South Wales premier Henry Parkes wrote that the Qing were plotting to establish a Chinese "colony" in Australia.[28]

The fear of Chinese invasion, which originated in the gold rush era, thus resurfaced with a vengeance. During the 1850s, Europeans had feared that

Chinese threatened their tenuous grip on the continent; by the late 1880s, they believed they had built a maturing, if not mature, prosperous society based on free labor and democracy, values they believed were beyond the grasp of Chinese. In fact, since the gold rush era, Chinese in Australia had demonstrated an embrace of modern values, as entrepreneurs, as ratepayers, and as wage earners. As for invasion, the Chinese population in the colonies remained small—from less than 1 percent in Victoria to barely 5 percent in Queensland in 1891. But politicians found in the Chinese a racial "other" against which a nationalist vision could be constructed.[29]

⚜

LOWE KONG MENG, Louis Ah Mouy, and Cheok Hong Cheong pushed back against the efforts to further restrict Chinese immigration. Their 1879 pamphlet, *The Chinese Question in Australia,* ran the gamut of familiar arguments: respect for international law and treaties between Britain and China; the positive contributions made by Chinese to Australian society; the long history of abuse and violence suffered by Chinese; the appeal to justice. The text is noteworthy for two innovations. First, echoing John Stuart Mill's rebuke to Henry George on the problem of cheap Asiatic labor, Lowe, Mouy, and Cheong compared Chinese to the Irish immigrants in Australia, who had earned as little as four shillings a week in Ireland but once in Victoria refused to accept wages less than other farmhands. They wrote:

> Human nature is human nature all the world over; and the Chinaman is just as fond of money, and just as eager to earn as much as he can, as the most grasping of his competitors. . . . And so it will be, after a very little time, with our own countrymen here. Living among people who have invented thousands of artificial wants, and thousands of means of gratifying them, the expenditure of the Asiatic will soon rise to the European level, because his habits and his mode of living will approximate to those of his neighbors.[30]

They added that the diet of the Chinese in Victoria grew "more costly and generous in proportion to the improvement of their circumstances."

Moreover, the settled Chinese "conform to British methods of house-keeping" and were "not less liberal and hospitable" than Europeans.[31]

Lowe, Mouy, and Cheong refuted the myth that the Asiatic standard of living was a natural—that is, a racial—condition. In fact, in addition to changing Chinese consumer habits, Chinese wages were in some cases nearing the level of whites, especially in areas of labor scarcity. Writing from northern Queensland in the mid-1860s, Kong Shing Yung observed that Chinese shepherds earned good wages. Chinese "battery hands" working in Queensland mines demanded white men's wages. White cabinetmakers waged an ongoing campaign against Chinese "cheap labor" and "rice eating slaves," but average wages for European and Chinese cabinetmakers were actually on par.[32]

AS ANTI-CHINESE AGITATION GREW in the late 1880s, colonial officials, as well as the press, called on the Foreign Office in London to negotiate a new treaty with China to allow for immigration restriction, citing the American model. The Australians' request recognized imperial authority in diplomacy, asking only that Britain's foreign policy should protect the colonies. At the same time, they threatened to take local action if Her Majesty's government failed them.

But Britain received pressure from the other direction as well, that is, from the Qing government. The Qing were receiving complaints from Chinese living and working abroad, not only from Australia but also from Canada, the United States, and Latin America, and were increasingly sensitive to the mistreatment of Chinese overseas, believing it to be yet another marker of its national humiliation by Western imperialists. China had started to establish diplomatic missions abroad in the 1860s, originally to learn directly about the West and to establish direct channels of communication, but increasingly Qing consuls became involved with the problem of discrimination against Chinese abroad.

It made a difference if Chinese emigrants could appeal directly to a representative of the Chinese government. When Huang Zunxian was stationed as the Qing consul in San Francisco during the early 1880s, he assisted many emigrants. Chinese ambassadors in the United States negotiated reparations for the Rock Springs massacre and other riots. Zhang Deyi, as a member of the Chinese legation in London in the late 1870s, also assisted Chinese who came for help. In one case, for example, seven Chinese sailors from Guangdong and Fujian who were employed on a British merchant ship came to the legation office to complain that the captain was a bully and a tyrant and had refused to pay them when they asked to transfer to a different ship. Zhang and his colleagues intervened on their behalf.[33]

Qing diplomatic efforts on broader policy questions yielded uneven results. Official commissions sent to Cuba and Peru in 1876 to investigate the treatment of indentured Chinese laborers led the Qing to shut down the coolie trade to both locations. In 1880 the Qing agreed to renegotiate the Burlingame Treaty with the United States, which led directly to the Chinese Exclusion Act and, in its aftermath, a fresh wave of racial violence. But if the Qing government blinked in the American case, it was not about to make the same mistake with the British.[34]

During the 1880s the Chinese legation in London lodged numerous diplomatic protests with the British Foreign Office over mistreatment of Chinese in Canada and Australia, citing violations of treaty provisions for mutual respect and reciprocal privileges. The Qing understood there was a general pattern of abuse. In January 1887, Marquis Tseng (Zeng Jize), recently the Qing ambassador to Great Britain and now back in Beijing as an official of the Zongli Yamen, published an article, "China—The Sleep and the Awakening," in *Asiatic Quarterly Review,* a London publication; it was subsequently reprinted in the influential *Chinese Recorder and Missionary Journal,* among other journals. Marquis Tseng forcefully argued that the West must recognize China's equal standing in the family of nations—equality of sovereignty, racial equality—and its regional sphere of influence, that is, its status as an imperial power. He denounced the unequal treaties that violated China's sovereignty and vowed, too, that China would "denounce these treaties on the expiry of their present decennial period." By racial equality, the Marquis meant that Chinese living in European colonies in Asia and the Pacific should be treated the same as other immigrants in those societies. He considered the treatment of Chinese abroad to be "outrageous." He decried legislation passed in countries that made Chinese a "scourge" and where "justice and international comity exist for everybody, bond and free, except the men of Han." As suggested by the title, Tseng's essay put the West on notice that China had woken from its supposed historical torpor and would no longer countenance unequal treatment.[35]

In May 1887, shortly after publication of Tseng's essay, the Zongli Yamen sent two imperial commissioners to investigate the conditions of the Chinese in the Australian colonies. The commissioners, Wang Ronghe and Yu Qiong, the latter formerly the Qing consul in Japan, arrived in Australia as part of a tour of a half-dozen Southeast Asian colonies. Their Australian visit lasted three weeks, comprising stops in Melbourne, Sydney, Brisbane, Cooktown, and Port Darwin. In Melbourne, Chinese merchant leaders presented the commissioners a long petition, signed by Lowe Keng Meng, Louis Ah Mouy, Cheok Hong Cheong, and forty-four others. The petitioners asserted their loyalty to the Qing emperor as grounds for seeking his protection. They detailed the many indignities they suffered in Australia, first among them the Chinese poll tax and the requirement for permission to travel from one colony to another, in addition to a transit tax. They complained that "larrikins" (hoodlums) assaulted "tea and vegetable vendors" on the streets of Melbourne. They further aired their grievances at meetings with the commissioners. Lowe Keng Meng personally knew commissioner Wang, as they had been classmates at the English school in Penang, so their meeting may have had a poignant character. One wonders if the two cosmopolitans discussed their respective trajectories that crisscrossed two empires, the British and the Qing.[36]

Throughout their visit, the commissioners repeatedly raised their objection to the "obnoxious tax" levied on the Chinese, both in meetings with colonial officials and in public, through interviews with the press. Wang explained to the Melbourne *Argus*, "We should never think of objecting to any laws that were general in application. Our objection is to laws which deprive us of the liberties enjoyed by other people."[37]

Victorian officials treated the imperial commissioners with deference and accommodation, a proper performance of diplomatic respect. The commissioners lunched with Sir Henry Loch, the premier of Victoria, and Lady Loch; toured the city's sights; visited factories and a winery; attended the opening of Parliament as official guests; and enjoyed a lavish banquet thrown by the governor in their honor. The Melbourne press, impressed by the stature of the Mandarin officials, reported on their every step.[38]

But tension ran just beneath the surface. At the banquet, Victoria's chief justice, George Higinbotham, raised his glass to the Qing emperor, the "Good Ally of Our Beloved Queen," and also welcomed the commissioners with a toast, though he could not help but add, "It might be necessary for the Parliament of Victoria to prevent an undue flow of immigrants into the colony." He assured them, however, that Victoria "would always act with the strictest justice towards those whom they deemed proper to residence here." To speak in this manner to foreign dignitaries who were guests of honor at an official banquet was a rude violation of diplomatic courtesy. Higinbotham's assurances, of course, were insincere.[39]

The commissioners' report to the Zongli Yamen detailed the discriminations suffered by Chinese in the Australian colonies. It also recommended that a Chinese consul be stationed in Australia. The Zongli Yamen sent the report to the Chinese ambassador in London, Liu Ruifen, who in turn lodged an official protest over the discrimination against Chinese in Australia with the Foreign Office. In response, the British prime minister asked the Colonial Office to make inquiries into the matter. This was the standard procedure by which Chinese-Australian affairs were conducted through Beijing and London. And of course, nothing came of it, not least because the British government was caught between two increasingly irreconcilable forces, the demands of the settler colonies and the demands of imperial relations and commercial interests with China.[40]

THE CONFLICT IN AUSTRALIA reached a climax in 1888 when officials in Melbourne and then Sydney, backed by public agitation, refused to allow 268 Chinese passengers arriving from Hong Kong on the *Afghan* to disembark, including some sixty Chinese who held British naturalization papers. The crisis paralyzed British officials in London, while hysteria that the *Afghan* represented the leading edge of a new "invasion" swept Melbourne, Sydney, and Brisbane. Cheok Hong Cheong led a committee of Chinese merchants to protest the agitation surrounding the *Afghan* affair, which tried to meet with Victorian premier Duncan Gillies but was continually rebuffed.[41]

Cheong went on to deliver a public address and publish it. He rebuked Australia for waging a shameless campaign rooted in "the selfishness, the prejudices, and the shams, which form the warp and woof of the present agitation." He asked, "Is it possible that common human rights, accorded to other civilized peoples, are to be denied to us? That it is to be a crime, punishable by imprisonment with hard labor, if man or woman of the Chinese race travels over the line separating any of the colonies without a permit?"[42]

Cheong and his colleagues were constructing a rhetoric about China and Chinese rights on the world stage that mirrored the perspective articulated by Qing diplomats. Cheong echoed Marquis Tseng's assertion of China's awakening: "That such a time may come, nay, probably will come sooner than is supposed, when the presence and power of China as a great nation will be felt in these seas, and it lies with you to say, as wise men or otherwise, if this is to be for good or evil."[43]

Victoria placed the *Afghan* in quarantine and declared the passengers' travel documents to be fraudulent, barring their entry. The ship then ventured to Sydney, where authorities also refused to land the Chinese, goaded by a crowd of five thousand demonstrators shouting "Out with the Chinamen" in front of the New South Wales Parliament. South Australia pledged that it would also refuse the ship. With three colonies vowing to refuse admission of the Chinese aboard the *Afghan,* the Chinese Question took center stage in intercolonial politics.[44]

Taking advantage of the crisis, Premier Parkes rushed legislation through the NSW assembly that exponentially increased poll taxes and residence fees on Chinese and declared that NSW would no longer recognize naturalization papers, including those previously issued by NSW. He backdated the law so it applied to the passengers on the *Afghan.* It was not a full victory, however, because the courts heard the habeas cases of naturalized Chinese and ordered their disembarkment. The *Afghan* then returned to Hong Kong with the remaining passengers.[45]

The *Afghan* affair raised disturbing questions. When the Chinese passengers aboard the ship obstructed the unloading of cargo, they threw open the idea that Australia could refuse people while welcoming goods. From a simple business calculus, Hong Kong shippers considered the Australian trade finished, as passenger fees had kept cargo rates down. In London, officials struggled over how to sever migration from trade, that is, how it might possibly accommodate Australians' demands for immigration restriction while protecting its broader commercial interests in Asia.[46]

The *Afghan* crisis also accelerated the movement to federation. Parkes had long been a proponent of federation, a strategy to strengthen Australia's position in Asia and within the British Empire. The Chinese Question provided a racial urgency that rallied the masses and brought divergent colonial interests into closer alignment. In June 1888 an intercolonial conference in Sydney discussed the need for the uniform restrictions on Chinese immigration. Much was riding on the outcome. The southern colonies hoped to bring the tropical colonies firmly to the side of restriction and to present a united front to London. The Colonial Office hoped that the conference would produce an agenda reasonable enough—or at least not as obnoxious as standing colonial policies—to take to the Qing as the basis for a new treaty. London asked the colonies to behave as responsible imperial partners, expressing to them the hope that the "Conference will endeavour to conciliate the susceptibilities of [the] Chinese Government as far as practicable."[47]

The conference agreed that immigration restriction should be secured simultaneously through imperial diplomacy and by uniform colonial legislation. But it could not get unanimous support for all its resolutions. Tasmania and Western Australia abstained on a general statement in support of exclusion and on specific legislative models, which included the continued criminalization of unauthorized intercolonial travel and stricter shipping regulations. Tasmania balked at the blatant disregard for the home (British) government's authority and discrimination against Chinese who were British subjects. Western Australia's reticence lay in the territory's use of Asian labor in the northern maritime industries, although in 1886 it had banned Chinese from work on the huge goldfields discovered at Kalgoorie. South Australia agreed to all points in the interests of intercolonial unity, but it insisted that restrictions should apply only to Chinese and not to Indians or Pacific Islanders, who continued to work in the Northern Territory, which South Australia administered. Although unanimity eluded the conference, the basis was laid for further negotiations toward a full White Australia policy.[48]

In 1891 the Privy Council, the official advisory body to Queen Victoria, conceded broader discretion to the colonies over Asiatic restrictions, ruling that foreign aliens had no legal right to enter British territories. Although the rule did not cover Chinese in Hong Kong or Singapore, who were British subjects, it confirmed the colonies' use of local legislation to restrict Chinese immigration.[49]

MEANWHILE, the demand for White Australia remained insistent, even irrational. European labor refused overtures from the Chinese workers' union who wished to join the Melbourne trades council; and white cabinetmakers made striking shearers return donations made in solidarity by the Chinese union. Although nonwhites comprised only 5 percent of the Queensland population, the *Worker* warned that "Queensland Capitalism" was determined "to make Queensland and Australia as much like Fiji and Hindostan as possible." Victoria introduced a minimum wage law in 1896, the first in the world, in response to the evils of sweated labor; proponents of the law had argued in the language of "protection," not just protection of labor from capital but protection from Chinese immigrant workers as well. Labor's strength in Australian politics would long rest on the appeal to its economic betters that they shared a common racial interest. It would serve as an exemplary model for pro-labor/anti-immigration statism for labor in other British settler colonies for decades to come.[50]

In the late 1890s, as negotiations among the colonies for federation proceeded, the Chinese Question was not prominent. White Australians assumed that a consensus had already been reached. And when federation came into existence in 1901, there was little open talk about Chinese exclusion. It was, of course, implicit in the invocations of Australian nationalism, but public celebrations spoke not of race but of "one flag, one hope, and one destiny," a sentimental nationalist vision. Local Chinese were invited to participate in welcoming federation, and as many as twenty thousand Chinese did, marching in parades and processions and erecting celebration arches in their communities. Not all Chinese were so sanguine. The *Chinese Australian Herald* of Sydney, for example, wrote, "This paper wants to know why on earth Chinese should hold celebrations in honor of the British crown when . . . the crown has already given its assent to restrict immigration." Historian John Fitzgerald suggests that Chinese Australians may have identified more with the imperial aspect of federation than with its nationalist aspect—after all, it was the Anglo-Chinese treaties that protected Chinese in Australia—or, more profoundly, that Chinese Australians were claiming their place in a nation that was being founded on the principle of equality.[51]

When the new Parliament got down to business, it became clear that Australian equality did not include racial equality. The Immigration Restriction Act of 1901 continued restrictive colonies policies against Chinese and added new ones that aimed at excluding Asians and nonwhites, by adding a fifty-word dictation test in a European language. Some Chinese interpreted the dictation test to be a ban on Chinese labor. "Most of the Chinese workers who go abroad to make a living . . . definitely cannot be a scholar. Now we know how foreigners despise and abhor us Chinese workers!" wrote "Huagong Nanzuo," a pseudonym meaning "difficult to be a Chinese worker," to a newspaper in Hangzhou.[52]

But the policy was meant to be broadly exclusive, targeting not just workers but all Chinese. Luo Zhongyao, the Chinese consul in Singapore who was responsible for Australia, reported that the "new regulations now are nothing but adding fuel to an already burning fire," noting that the inability to travel back and forth between China and Australia would doom Chinese business in Australia. He remarked that the Chinese population of Darwin had dropped by 75 percent and in Queensland and New South Wales by more than half.[53]

On the heels of the immigration act, Parliament passed the Pacific Islander Labour Act, which ordered a mass deportation of colored labor from the far north; and the Australian Franchise Act, which gave the vote to all white women but excluded from the franchise Aboriginal peoples (save for Victoria and New South Wales, where it had been previously established) and denied political rights to "natives of Asia, Africa, or the Islands of the

Pacific, except for New Zealand." Social welfare and labor legislation, argu-ably the most progressive in the world, excluded "Asiatics" not born in Aus-tralia and "Aboriginal natives" of Australia, Africa, and the Pacific Islands.[54]

Just as passage of the exclusion law in the United States actually encouraged more racist attacks against Chinese, the Australian feder-ation's Immigration Restriction Act did not end harassment. After it passed, white Australians continued to agitate against the "yellow agony." Complaints arose in the following years that Chinese, "slippery as eels," were landing in Western Australia and the Northern Territory in vio-lation of the act. There were calls to exclude Chinese and other Asians from working in the northern pearling industry. The Labor Council and the Anti-Chinese and Asiatic League in Sydney and white agricultural-ists in Western Australia agitated against Chinese in the furniture trade and market gardening. Anti-Chinese demands ranged from branding Chinese products to forbidding Chinese to work on Sunday to prohibit-ing Chinese from working in any trade or business.[55]

Police raids and arrests for gambling and unsanitary vegetable shops took place from Sydney to Perth. Chinese sometimes physically resisted during police raids and convened mass meetings, where they vowed to protest laws that aimed to "cut our throats." Zhong Hongjie, owner of a furniture factory and a Christian leader among the Chinese in Perth, Western Australia, defended Chinese people's contributions to Australia, noting that they cleared forests and dug irrigation channels to establish plantations. He urged Chinese to unite against the attempts to bar them from work and trade. He remained hopeful, perhaps naïvely, that the White Australia policy would be hard to maintain, because "all countries in the world now have free transportation and peaceful trade."[56]

The most extreme proposals to forbid all Chinese labor and businesses failed to pass. But Chinese Australians continued to feel beleaguered by ongoing efforts to discriminate and exclude them. They lobbied for a con-sul to be stationed in Australia and finally received one in 1909, but at least three consuls to Australia quit their posts in the first three years, despair-ing over the treatment of Chinese. In 1905 the commonwealth Parliament amended the Immigration Restriction Act to make it even more restrictive, replacing the requirement that the dictation test be given in a European language to "any prescribed language" and canceled a clause that allowed Asian Australians to immigrate their wives.[57]

WHITE AUSTRALIA WAS part of a larger trend among Great Britain's white settler colonies to hold dearly to their racial prerogatives. The dominions also imagined a kinship with the United States (especially the American West), another white settler colony with Anglo roots (indeed, Britain's first), another white man's country. These affinities were not new; in 1868 the Anglo-Saxon triumphalist Charles Dilke had embraced America in his notion of a Greater Britain. Historian James Belich describes a "broader Anglo collective identity, racist but also transnational, inclusive as well as exclusive. It lacked a consistent folk label—'real white men' may have come closest."[58]

Both in the United States and in the British dominions, anticoolieism was foundational to identities of class, nation, and empire. The American and Australian working classes created identities and interests bounded by race, boundaries sharpened on the knife edge of anticoolieism. That in turn gave them a stake in their respective national identities, with their broader domestic agendas of racial management and their positioning as white men's countries in the Pacific world.

PART III

THE ASIATIC DANGER
IN THE COLONIES

Thus, a thousand mouths keep up their clamor,

Ten thousand eyes, glare, burning with hate.

Signing names . . . Begging their rulers to reconsider.

Suddenly the order of exile comes down,

Though I fear this breaks our treaties.

—HUANG ZUNXIAN,
"EXPULSION OF THE IMMIGRANTS"

Southern Africa, c. 1905

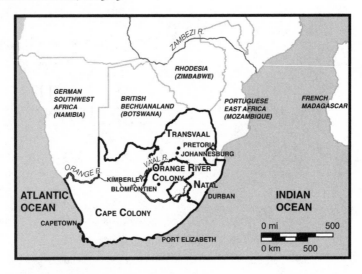

Transvaal and the Witwatersrand

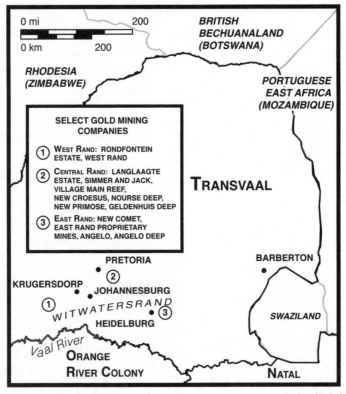

Maps by Cailin Hong

Chapter 8

✳

The Richest Spot on Earth

I t was three a.m., in the middle of a winter's night, on June 18, 1904, when the SS *Tweeddale* pulled into Durban. She had traveled twelve thousand miles from Hong Kong with 1,049 Chinese men, who were contracted to work in the Witwatersrand gold mines in the British colony Transvaal. The captain reported there had been no bad weather during the monthlong voyage, but forty of the passengers had fallen ill en route with beriberi—a debilitating disease caused by vitamin B deficiency—and three died while at sea. Upon arrival, the authorities arranged to repatriate the sick and shuttled the rest to a nearby depot called Jacob's Camp, a former British concentration camp used during the recent South African War. Over the course of the next three days, officials from the Transvaal Foreign Labor Department registered, inspected, photographed, and fingerprinted the laborers at the depot. Each worker received a brass tag with a number. A gaggle of sightseers and newspaper reporters crowded outside the compound gate, hoping to get a glimpse of South Africa's latest labor experiment.[1]

The men left Durban in three groups, traveling by train in locked third-class carriages. They rode sixty to a car. Each man received a blanket, a can of tea, and three light meals during the journey to the Transvaal, which took twenty-seven hours traveling at "ordinary mail speed." Upon arrival on the

Rand, the train pulled up directly alongside the property of the New Comet Mining Company, east of Johannesburg, and the workers disembarked.[2]

In addition to New Comet managers and staff, a number of notable figures were likely on hand to welcome the Chinese: William Evans, superintendent of the Foreign Labor Department; Sir George Farrar, head of East Rand Proprietary Mines (ERPM), New Comet's parent company, and chairman of the Transvaal Chamber of Mines; and William Honnold, an American mining engineer. Evans had twenty years of experience as a civil servant in the British Straits Settlements (Malaysia). His job in South Africa was to oversee the recruitment, distribution, and treatment of Chinese mine laborers.[3]

Farrar was among the first mining capitalists on the Rand and one of its biggest magnates, controlling about one-quarter of the Rand's total output. He had been knighted for his service in the South African War and was a political leader of the mining interest. The assignment of Chinese workers from the *Tweeddale* to Farrar's company was his reward for having led a difficult, year-long political campaign to establish the indentured labor program.[4]

Honnold was consultant to the Transvaal Chamber of Mines. He had arranged for a major portion of the recruitment of Chinese workers for the Rand, in collaboration with his longtime colleague and fellow engineer Herbert Hoover—the future president of the United States—who had mining and financial connections in Tianjin, London, and the Transvaal.[5]

Also likely to be on hand was Xie Zixiu, Chinese adviser for ERPM and the former secretary of the Johannesburg Cantonese Club, the *huiguan* that served the town's small Chinese merchant community. Xie was born in Sydney to a wealthy Cantonese merchant and moved to Hong Kong in 1887, perhaps in response to the rise of anti-Chinese hostility in Australia. In Hong Kong he worked as a piano tuner. Along with his father and brother, Xie was active in Hong Kong's anti-Qing activities as allies of Sun Yatsen; he and his brother participated in the failed uprising of 1902, with which Sun had hoped to take Guangdong province.

Xie moved in 1903 to South Africa, a Chinese emigrant outpost at the western edge of the Indian Ocean–Southeast Asia trade networks that the Chinese Australian Lowe Kong Meng's family had plied. He arrived in Johannesburg in October. Upon hearing about the Chinese labor program, Xie offered his services to the colonial government as a translator and liaison. Farrar quickly hired him to work for ERPM as Chinese adviser and then as Chinese controller at New Comet, the latter a managerial position usually held by Europeans.[6]

Over the next several years, from their different vantage points, these men would wrestle with myriad challenges and conflicts that accompanied the Chinese labor experiment on the Rand. The *Tweeddale* was the first of thirty-four ships that brought a total of 63,296 Chinese laborers to South Africa between 1904 and 1907. They worked under state-sponsored contracts at fifty-five gold mines, including the largest companies on the Rand, mostly in deep underground shafts and tunnels. It was a bold experiment undertaken by the Chamber of Mines in order to get the gold mines back to prewar levels of production and to expand the industry to new, even deeper reefs.

The program proved extraordinarily difficult to execute logistically and politically. Despite Evans's optimistic first report—that the men at New Comet found that "the work was hard, but they could manage it"—the Chinese labor program stirred constant controversy and conflict: between the workers and their overseers, between mine managers and the Foreign Labor Department, between the Foreign Labor Department and the Colonial Office in London, between local Afrikaners and the British colonial government, between the Conservative and Liberal parties in Britain, and between Qing diplomats and the British Foreign Office. It provoked sensational coverage in the press locally and in China, Britain, Australia, and New Zealand. The conflicts all turned, in one way or another, on the latest iteration of the Chinese Question: what was the appropriate role and treatment of Chinese labor in the white settler colonies of the British Empire?[7]

The Chinese Question on the Rand may be measured in terms of human and political costs: 3,192 Chinese laborers died while on the Rand from illness and work-related conditions, and 19,530 displayed their dissatisfaction by refusing to work, rioting, staging work actions, and deserting the compounds. Forty-five were sentenced to jail terms of ten years or more, executed, or shot dead during disturbances.[8]

There were electoral upheavals in both metropole and colony, where the
Chinese Question dramatically served partisan purposes. In Britain, the
Liberal Party ended twenty years of nearly unbroken Conservative rule in
1906 by stoking working and middle-class opposition to "Chinese slavery"
on the Rand. In the Transvaal, the Chinese Question emerged as an incendiary issue during the first elections for responsible (self-)government in
1907, used most effectively by the victorious Afrikaner-nationalist Het
Volk party led by the former Boer commandos Louis Botha and Jan Smuts.
The new Parliament promptly terminated the Chinese labor program and
moved to impose discriminatory restrictions on all Asiatics in the colony.

THE WITWATERSRAND RISES FROM the high veld of northeastern South Africa
to six thousand feet above sea level. Many waterfalls descend along its northern face; its name in Afrikaans means "rocky ridge of white waters." It runs
sixty miles east to west, forming a watershed on the subcontinent between
the Atlantic and Indian oceans. Tswana speakers claim it as a place of origin.
Dutch-descended farmers from the eastern Cape Colony settled there beginning in the 1840s, clashing with indigenous people as they pushed eastward
and plundered Africans' land and livestock. In 1852–54 the British, who
were also making territorial claims in the interior, recognized the right of
self-government of settlers north of the Vaal and Orange rivers. The Dutch
Afrikaners (or Boers, the Dutch word for farmers) proclaimed two independent republics, the South African Republic (Zuid-Afrikaanse Republiek,
ZAR, informally the Transvaal) and the Orange Free State. By turns war-
ring against Africans and taking advantage of divisions among them, they
continued to seize land and to exact rent and labor from African peasants.
Notwithstanding its hostility to the British, the ZAR benefited from British
military defeat of the Pedi and the Zulu in neighboring Natal in 1879.[9]

The dynamics in the ZAR/Transvaal were part of a complex of political
transformations taking place in the region in the second half of the nineteenth century. Before federation as the Union of South Africa in 1910,
"South Africa" was not a single political identity or state. The subcontinent
comprised diverse African territories and ethnicities, British colonies, and

Boer republics. The nature and growth of the European settler states varied, depending on the process and pace of conquest of indigenous peoples and the appropriation of their land and labor. The native population included large kingdoms, smaller polities, and Africans displaced by Europeans as well as by other Africans. The question of "race"—as theory, as identity, and as policy—was evolving and pertained to intra-European difference as well as to relations among whites, blacks, "coloureds" (mixed-race), and Indians, the last having been brought as indentured sugar plantation workers to Natal in the late nineteenth century.[10]

The discovery of diamonds in the northern Cape in 1867 and then gold in the ZAR in the 1870s and '80s spurred industrialization, urbanization, and immigration. The "mineral revolution" generated fabulous wealth and political power to a new class of mining capitalists, such as Cecil Rhodes and George Farrar, and the growth of a wage-earning class, both white and African. It accelerated efforts by British imperialism to integrate the region under its control. But neither process nor outcome was preordained. If Europeans aspired to make South Africa a "white man's country," as in Australia, that was more complicated in South Africa. Whites were not only divided by various interests but were also vastly outnumbered by Africans. The Native Question—the problem of how whites could control and exploit the Black majority—informed all South African politics, including the Chinese Question.

THE FIRST GOLD RUSH in the ZAR took place in 1873, at Barberton in the eastern Transvaal. It drew about a thousand diggers from the Cape and Natal, as well as Britain, California, and Australia. Gold seekers found gold in virtually every stream in the valleys and gorges of the countryside. But the alluvial deposits quickly declined.[11]

Prospectors had long noted gold in outcrops —underground rock exposed above the surface—on the Witwatersrand, about two hundred miles west of Barberton, although the main reef line was not identified until 1886. But there were obstacles to extracting it. The gold was embedded in conglomerate rock, a mass of pebbles bound together by sediment made of silica, called banket, after a Dutch candy. Australians called it

cement rock. A mining engineer examined an outcrop at the request of
Cecil Rhodes, the diamond magnate, who was considering gold mining on
the Rand. The engineer was unenthusiastic. "If I rode over those reefs in
America I would not get off my horse to look at them. In my opinion they
are not worth Hell room," he reported. Nevertheless, Rhodes, Alfred Beit,
and other Kimberley diamond capitalists began investing on the Rand.
A few hundred people clustered around Ignatius Ferreira's wagon on the
diggings. Within a year there were three thousand people at Ferreira's
Camp, which grew quickly into the town of Johannesburg. It was here that
a number of Chinese, erstwhile gold seekers whom the ZAR refused mining licenses, found a living selling provisions. Rhodes, Beit, and others of
the mining capital vanguard worked the outcrops profitably. A speculative
rush brought gold mining capitalization to nearly £25 million in 1889.[12]

The riches of the Rand gold reef lay not only in its enormous size.
Whereas gold mining in its placer and quartz modes was famously risky,
the consistency and predictability of South African gold promised that
enterprise would be based on "normal economic categories"; that is to
say, it was "an industry rather than a gamble." But mining it required
capital investment on an unprecedented scale, especially as mining magnates looked beyond the outcrops on the Central Rand, which were showing signs of depletion even in the mid-1890s, to the long-term potential
of deep-level mining on the East Rand. At about 180 feet down, the
banket gave way to pyrite, an iron-based rock. Pyrite does not yield gold
according to the standard mercury-based method used in quartz mining.
Fortunately, two Scottish brothers had recently discovered that cyanide
attracted gold. A second and greater capital expense was required to reach
the reef, which was extremely thin and long and ran steeply to thousands
of feet below the surface. The solution was to sink a deep vertical shaft
and to run horizontal tunnels at different depths to reach the reef.[13]

Moreover, the amount of gold in the pyrite was very small and difficult to
locate. One writer described it as amounting to the commas on a single page
in a telephone directory, which page is crumpled and torn, and the book
itself broken into parts. Pyrite gold was also of much lower grade than gold
in the outcrop and in Australia and California; the deeper the ore, the lower

the grade and the higher the cost of extraction. Finally, the price of gold was fixed on the world market, so that higher capital and production costs could not be recouped in higher prices. The only way to profitably mine gold was to excavate massive quantities of ore using cheap labor. American engineering consultants like William Honnold and Herbert Hoover made their careers from designing the requirements—both technical and with regard to the cost and organization of labor—to make deep-level low-grade gold mining into a profitable and "scientific" industry. The three major ingredients necessary to develop the industry were met thusly: capital from local (Kimberley), British and Continental sources; scientific mining expertise, especially from the United States; and labor supplied by Africans.[14]

On the eve of the South African War in 1899, the Rand gold mines employed 107,482 African workers, with half recruited from Portuguese East Africa (Mozambique), and 12,530 whites (managers, engineers, miners, and skilled workers). Prewar production from a total of seventy-seven mines peaked in 1898 at 4.3 million fine ounces, valued at £15 million, making the Witwatersrand the single largest producer of gold, accounting for 27 percent of world output.[15]

THE MINING OF Witwatersrand gold had both global and regional effects. At the level of world trade and finance, the economic historian Jean-Jacques Van Helten argues that expansion of international trade in the 1880s and '90s required an enlargement of the overall money stock and hence the world supply of gold. The gold standard was not yet universal, but since the 1870s it had become the basis of international payments among the leading industrial countries. Witwatersrand gold, along with gold discoveries in the 1890s in Western Australia and Canada, increased the global supply of gold and strengthened the position of Britain, which was already the center of the international financial market.[16]

Van Helten presents the late-century gold discoveries as a fortuitous meeting of a demand, but it also might be considered a *stimulus*, a new phase of capital accumulation, that powered the expansion of trade and foreign investment. Although this accumulation built on previous decades of gold discoveries in North America and Australasia, South African gold helped inaugurate a new period of capitalist development, the so-called New Imperialism, in which monopoly and finance capital came to the fore; when the great powers scrambled to carve up Africa, the last continent to fall to European colonialism; and Germany and the United States nipped at Britain's heels for position at the top of the world economic order.[17]

The supremacy of the pound sterling (i.e., gold) in international finance and trade lay at the heart of Great Britain's strategy to maintain global dominance. The City of London reaped handsome profits from international investment and trade, both within the empire and without: the British compensated for desultory investment in domestic industries by exporting "old" English manufactures to sheltered markets within the empire. The colonies were induced to buy these products (often at artificially high prices) while they in turn sold primary products to the rest of the world (wool from Australia, cotton from India). These enabled Great Britain, in turn, to offset its trade deficits from importing wheat from the United States and Argentina for domestic consumption.[18]

In southern Africa, labor patterns that had been established on the diamond fields carried over to the Rand. The rapid capitalization of diamond mining had reduced independent diggers to wage workers while the industry relied increasingly on African migrant laborers contracted on meager wages and confined to compounds. White miners adopted an aggressive racism to police the color line in order to protect their superior position and wages.[19]

The mining of gold also shifted the center of economic power from the Cape Colony to the heretofore isolated and undeveloped Transvaal. Lord Selborne, who served as undersecretary to Colonial Secretary Joseph Chamberlain, considered the Transvaal "the richest spot on earth," the key to South Africa's future. "It is going to be the natural capital state and centre of South African commercial, social and political life," he wrote in 1896.[20]

By then, Johannesburg had grown to a cosmopolitan city of 100,000, with a large population of uitlanders (foreigners), British and other Europeans, who were aggrieved over political exclusions (fourteen years residency for naturalization and the franchise) and high taxes. Mine owners agitated against high railway tariffs and inflated prices set by state monopolies over essential resources (especially dynamite). More broadly for the British Empire, political instability in the Transvaal threatened to unravel the assumptions of its superior position in southern Africa based on commercial and financial domination, British immigration, and geopolitical power. After the failed Jameson raid of 1895 (a botched coup d'état backed by Cecil Rhodes and other leading mine magnates), ZAR president Paul Kruger stiffened his resolve. The British did not want the vote, he said. They wanted his state.[21]

Indeed, if Chamberlain adopted a hard line on *uitlander* rights in order mobilize British public opinion, he never lost sight of the larger stakes. As Selborne had famously warned, South Africa must not be allowed to develop as another United States, outside the empire; rather, it must develop as another Canada, within it. South Africa held strategic importance to the empire as protection of the sea route to India and East Asia, as a counter to the other European powers in Africa (especially Germany), and as a repository of immense mineral resources, not least gold, the key to its financial supremacy.[22]

On the whole, Britain's imperial interest was something greater than the sum of these parts. Alfred, Viscount Milner, appointed Cape governor and high commissioner for all of southern Africa in 1897, was, like Chamberlain and Selborne, a Liberal Unionist and social imperialist who believed in state intervention, efficiency, and planning at home and abroad. Chamberlain and Milner stoked confrontation with Kruger on the *uitlander* franchise and dynamite monopoly. They were willing to resort to war if necessary because they thought it would be a swift gentlemen's war. But the British armed forces were ill prepared for the tenacity of the Afrikaners. The British deployed 180,000 troops, an imperial force as large as the entire white citizenry of the Boer republics, to secure a conventional military victory in June 1900. The Boers then switched to guerrilla war; it took another two years for the British to end it, which they did by burning farms to the ground, rounding up women and children into concentration camps, and crisscrossing the terrain with barbed-wire fences and blockhouses.[23]

AFTER THE WAR LORD MILNER assumed the governorship of the former Afrikaner republics, now the British crown colonies of Transvaal and Orange

River. He pursued a vigorous reconstruction strategy aimed at integrating South Africa into a single political economy with a modern state capable of providing the material and political infrastructure for capitalist development and social reproduction. Milner advocated greater British emigration (to balance the influence of the larger Afrikaner population), linguistic Anglicization, and the development of mining, railroads, and commercial agriculture. He had said in 1897 that he envisioned South Africa as "a self-governing white community . . . supported by a well-treated and justly governed black labour force from Cape Town to the Zambezi."[24]

But a severe shortage of African labor for the gold mines presented one of the greatest challenges to British South Africa's reconstruction and progress. The shortage resulted in part from population displacement caused by the war and disruptions to the East African labor supply. The mines also had to compete for labor with other industries, both urban and agricultural. The Transvaal Labour Commission, convened in July 1903 to study the problem, took the paternalistic view that Africans were "nomadic or pastoral" people who lacked experience with the requirements of industrial capitalism. In fact, Boer farmers clung mightily to their African tenants, and as long as Africans still had access to land for farming and herding, they resisted capitalist wage relations.[25]

Whites understood that only landlessness would produce a proletariat, and many put suggestions before the commission toward speeding that process: modify the system of land tenure, abolish tribal reserves, modify or destroy native social structures, impose heavy taxes on peasants, and the like. But in 1903 colonial authorities were not yet ready to take those steps, in no small measure because such solutions were "fraught with . . . danger to the white population," that is, to the Afrikaner farmers.[26]

Moreover, African workers, who had disliked mine work before the war, saw even fewer reasons to return to the mines afterward. Conditions were arguably worse. Employers slashed native wage rates by nearly half, from the prewar rate of 52 shillings a week to 30 shillings. In 1903 a group of Transkei natives deserted the mines over wage disputes. Supervisors "hurried" workers with leather prods, and compound police carried *sjamboks* (heavy whips). African workers resisted the introduction of handheld drills, which required arduous work at narrower stopes. A new pass law was promulgated; another banned sale and consumption of liquor. Illness and death, whether from accident, foul air, scurvy, silicosis, or pneumonia, were widespread. The mortality rate was between 50 and 100 per 1,000, which Milner recognized was unacceptably high, "the weakest point in our armor." For all these reasons, Africans shunned the mines after the war. The labor shortage meant stagnant output and falling rates of profit. Investors on the London money market began to shy away from Transvaal gold.[27]

THE RANDLORDS CAST ABOUT for an alternative source of labor to get the mines running again. They rejected using unskilled white labor (whether local or imported from southern and eastern Europe) as too costly. They considered importing African Americans from the United States, but Honnold believed that introducing them would be "the very worst thing." Those workers were also too dear, and, moreover, they would "tend to awake a spirit of insubordination among the ordinary natives." The mine owners also considered India as a source, but the Indian government rejected proposals that imposed strict limits on mobility and a requirement for repatriation at term.[28]

The Randlords turned to China as a last resort. In some respects, it was a fantastic proposal, given the numbers, distance, and expense involved; moreover, it cut against the prevailing view that South Africa should be developed as a "white man's country." But over the ensuing months, advocates for Chinese labor strengthened their position, in part because there appeared to be no credible alternative for solving the unskilled labor shortage. Using Chinese labor became part of the chamber's larger strategy, which also included efforts to rationalize African labor recruitment and to discipline costs with industry-wide wage rates. Mine owners believed Chinese labor at the "right price" would keep a check on the native wage rate. In fact, indentured Chinese labor promised a measure of control and coercion that had been, to date, impossible to impose directly upon African workers.[29]

In February 1903 the chamber sent a representative, Harry Ross Skinner, on a lengthy tour to investigate the possibilities for employing Asian workers in the gold mines. Skinner, a thirty-six-year-old Scottish engineer, had started in Kimberley diamonds and then worked on the Rand, where he became manager of Durban Roodepoort Deep. He briefly visited California and British Columbia; Singapore and the Malay states; and Japan and Korea. His main focus was China, where he spent several months on coastal tour from south to north. The Chamber of Mines framed the trip as an investigation to determine the suitability of Chinese labor for South African gold mining and to compare Chinese labor practices in different locales. But it was already making preparations. Skinner was contacting labor brokers in Guangdong, Shanghai, Beijing, and Tianjin. Meanwhile the Chamber of Mines began drafting a legal ordinance to govern a Chinese labor program.[30]

Skinner reported that Chinese labor was suitable for mining and available in sufficient numbers to meet the needs of the Witwatersrand mines. Unlike African workers, he said, Chinese miners would "go underground without much trouble." He was careful to point out that Chinese miners in California were free men and skilled workers and that Chinese mine workers in the Malay states also were free labor. But he believed the Transvaal could successfully use unskilled and indentured "raw Chinese coolies." Skinner asserted that Chinese "are docile, law abiding and industrious people, and will carry out whatever contracts they enter into and perform the tasks assigned to them." In addition, Skinner expected the Chinese government to respond "passively" toward the South Africans' project.[31]

Most important, Skinner believed strict requirements were necessary to make a Chinese labor program work. Racial conflict in California, he said, resulted from the Americans' prohibition on indentured labor and hence their inability to control the physical and social mobility of Chinese emigrants. Unless the Chinese were strictly controlled, they would always undercut the wages of white workers and the prices of white businesses. The United States had finally had no choice but to exclude them, he said, in order to protect its white citizens. Skinner advised that any program importing Chinese labor must be designed to confine them to certain jobs and places of abode; to prohibit them from engaging in trade or acquiring property; and to compel them to return at the end of their contracts.[32]

THE IDEA OF RECRUITING Chinese to South Africa was not entirely novel. During the nineteenth century, nearly sixty thousand Chinese indentured workers labored on French plantation island colonies off the east African coast and in German, British, and French colonies on the continent. The Chinese presence in South Africa dates to the eighteenth century, when the Dutch East India Company shipped Malay and Chinese convicts from Batavia to the Cape Colony. During the 1870s and '80s a few hundred Chinese artisans and workers arrived in the Cape Colony and Natal, along with greater numbers of Indians, contracted for infrastructure construction after the opening of the diamond fields. Voluntary merchant emigrants from southern China followed in their path. By 1904 there were 2,398 Chinese in all of British South Africa, more than half of them living in the Cape Colony. Chinese in the Cape worked mostly as small traders and also as cooks, carpenters, basket weavers, fish sellers, and wagon drivers.[33]

There were hardly any Chinese in the former Afrikaner republics. The Orange Free State excluded Chinese from settlement altogether. The ZAR excluded from citizenship "any of the native races of Asia, including 'Coolies' [Indians and Chinese], Arabs, Malays and Mohammedan subjects of the Turkish Dominion." It forbade Asiatics from walking on footpaths and pavements; from driving public carriages; from riding in first- and second-class railway compartments; and from buying or possessing liquor. The anti-Chinese laws of the former Afrikaner republics remained in place when power transferred to the British after the South African War.[34]

Notwithstanding these restrictions and discriminations, Chinese carved out small niches in Johannesburg. By 1890 there were more than a hundred Chinese in the town, shopkeepers, laundrymen, and market gardeners; by 1904 the Chinese population of the Transvaal was about nine hundred. Chinese often did business in poorer white districts. Unlike white-owned shops, the Chinese sold at low prices, in small quantities, and on credit.[35]

The Chinese in Johannesburg at the turn of the century followed the same patterns of social organization Chinese practiced across the diaspora. In the 1890s, they formed a *huiguan* called the Kwong Hok Tong (*guanghetang*) or Cantonese Club. It built a "clubhouse" on leased land in Ferreirastown, the original settlement of Johannesburg, which now lay at the city's fringe. The house had several reception rooms, six bedrooms, a kitchen, and a latrine. Membership cost five pounds for initiation and dues according to one's occupation. The club rented rooms at two pounds a month; kept a library of books and periodicals; and held social events and meetings that drew as many as 150 people. Yeung Ku Wan (Yang Feihong), a collaborator of Sun Yatsen who arrived in South Africa in 1896, formed a second group, the Xingzhonghui (Revive China Society). Photographs of members of both groups show educated men dressed in Western-style clothing.[36]

Thus in 1903, when the idea of importing Chinese labor for the gold mines circulated, there was already a history of Chinese migration to South Africa and a small but established Chinese community in Johannesburg. These served as both precedent and warning—for both Chinese and whites.

White South Africans perceived indentured Chinese labor in context of the history of mass migration from India, which had morphed from indentured labor on plantations and railroads into a growing community of artisans, traders, and shopkeepers. Indians had been agitating against legal restrictions imposed upon them, and in 1893 a young lawyer in Pretoria named M. K. Gandhi joined their cause in earnest. To whites, South Africa's experience with Indians was an object lesson in how a solution to a labor problem would beget a greater race problem and threaten the entire project of building South Africa as a white country. Because of these larger stakes, debate over whether to import Chinese labor for gold mining reached beyond the Transvaal. Residents of numerous towns in the Cape Colony sent resolutions to the governor, which typically called importation of "Asiatics" a "wrong . . . inflict[ed] upon the whole South African community." The Cape Colony government passed a Chinese Exclusion Act in 1904, conceived as a prophylactic measure against the threat that Chinese mine labor in the Transvaal might overrun the Cape, which was over eight hundred miles distant.[37]

Farrar understood the dangers of bringing Asians into South Africa. "I have seen the evil of the Indians holding land and trading in competition with white people, and on no account whatever would I be a party to any legislation that permitted this," he said. But he considered it "absolutely absurd . . . that [the gold mines] should be crippled for the want of labor. Surely, common sense says that if you cannot get labour in Africa, you must get it elsewhere and get to work."[38]

To secure political support in South Africa and in London, Farrar and the Chamber of Mines vigorously lobbied Lord Milner, convincing him of the necessity for Chinese labor, with strict precautions that Chinese did not "flood us in other industries and trades." While carefully maintaining a "public attitude of neutrality," Milner worked behind the scenes to "leave nothing in my power undone to secure it." He arranged for Chamberlain to meet mining engineers when he visited the Transvaal in 1903; lobbied the Colonial Office in London; and helped secure political support from the other South African colonies. He assigned Farrar as the Transvaal representative to the intercolonial conference in Bloemfontein in March 1903, where he lobbied aggressively—and successfully—for a resolution recognizing the need for "new sources of labor . . . for all of the South African states."[39]

Milner appointed a special commission to investigate the labor needs of the Transvaal, in order to document the mining industry's needs in the public record and to win an official report in favor of importing Chinese labor. The Chamber of Mines testified that the mines were currently employing less than half of the 130,000 unskilled workers they needed and projected that in five years they would require nearly three times as many. The chamber presented dramatic extrapolations as factual certainties, when its calculations were really based upon assumptions that were contingent and political: the desire for maximum profitability in the short term; a preference for using vast quantities of cheap unskilled labor instead of investing in more advanced technologies; and a belief that white men would never do the work of Africans or work alongside them. Two members of the thirteen-person commission submitted a minority report with a different perspective, J. Quinn, a baker, and Peter Whiteside, an Australian who was president of the Witwatersrand Trades and Labour Council. They advocated modest increases in the native labor force, mechanization, and employing whites in unskilled jobs. The commission's majority concluded that its best options lay in China.[40]

A war for public opinion unfolded. The Trades and Labor Council in the Transvaal and the South Africa Trade Union organized against the use of Chinese labor. Notably, like Whiteside, many white trade unionists were Australian immigrants to South Africa, who brought with them the politics of the White Australia movement. As in Australia, the arguments against Chinese labor raised the bogey of Asiatic economic competition and the ideology of white settlerism. "Is this what we spilled our blood for?" read a banner at a demonstration. "We want to be governed here, not 6,000 miles away," read another. In April 1903 the White League, an organization committed to "fight all forms of colour and to win the Transvaal for the white man and the white man alone," drew five thousand people to a meeting at Wanderers Hall in Johannesburg.[41]

The prospect of Chinese labor immigration also drew out the Afrikaner population, which had generally kept a low profile in the immediate years after the war. In July former Boer commando generals organized a mass meeting in Heidelberg that endorsed a resolution, written by Jan Smuts, that Asiatic labor would "largely contribute to the closing of the Transvaal for white immigration." Smuts also organized a petition to the British Parliament to show that there "burns in the Boer mind a fierce indignation against this sacrilege of Chinese importation."[42]

The Chamber of Mines fought back by arguing that Chinese labor was not just for Randlord profits but key to reversing depressed conditions in the Transvaal. Development of the mining industry would create more prosperity for the entire colony, including more jobs for whites not only in the mines but also in other trades and in the towns. The chamber's greatest ally was the Imperial South Africa Association (ISSA), which held close ties to the Tory party, Milner, and the mine magnates. ISSA had formed in 1896 to promote the "English-speaking empire into a more consolidated and cohesive unit" in order to meet the challenges of "military rivalry and cutthroat economic competition." After the South African War, it focused on importing Chinese labor as the best strategy for South Africa's development. ISSA fielded dozens of agents and speakers, addressing over five hundred meetings and distributing some 4 million pamphlets.[43]

Between July and October, public meetings along the reef passed resolutions supporting the importation of Asiatic labor, as did local municipal-ities and chambers of commerce and various professional and technical associations representing engineers, geologists, surveyors, and the like. The Chamber of Mines Labor Importation Agency garnered petitions from virtually every mine on the Rand in support of Chinese labor.[44]

⚜

IN DECEMBER 1903 George Farrar introduced into the Transvaal Legislative Council a bill authorizing the importation of Chinese labor. On December 30 the council voted overwhelmingly to approve it; the Colonial Office gave its assent on January 16, 1904. At the Chamber of Mines' annual meeting in February, Farrar reported, "We have now a pure and sympathetic government. . . . The government, instead of looking upon us with jealous eyes, fully recognize that our industry is the pioneer of the prosperous development of the country."[45]

Ordinance no. 17, "To regulate the introduction into the Transvaal of Unskilled Non-European laborers," defined the terms of importation, contract, control of laborers, and repatriation. Sensitive to the various political contexts, it included provisions to ensure that Chinese entered the contracts voluntarily and with the right to quit and return at any time (at their own expense). In its main thrust, though, Ordinance no. 17 provided for strict controls over the importation of unskilled non-European laborers. It stipulated that such laborers might not enter the Transvaal except under contract of service by a licensed importer (i.e., a mine company). Contracts were set at three years and were renewable once, constituting a much longer term than local and Mozambique contracts (six months and one year respectively).[46]

The ordinance restricted laborers to unskilled work and excluded them from fifty-five skilled occupations, from Amalgamator to Woodworking Machinist. It further forbade laborers from acquiring any trading license or hawking; any house, land, building, or fixed property; any mining claim or "any right whatever to minerals or precious stones." It required laborers to reside in mine company compounds and allowed them to leave only with a pass. Lastly, it ensured repatriation by imposing bonds on importers and by imprisoning and deporting any laborers who were reluctant to depart. Notably, the ordinance left it to the attorney general to write specific regulations concerning the wage structure, hours, days off, medical care, and diet. Writing these as separate regulations gave the Foreign Labor Department (FLD) greater flexibility and denied Chinese workers statutory protections over their immediate working conditions.[47]

DESPITE ANOTHER ROUND of protest—including a trade union rally of eighty thousand in London's Hyde Park—the Chamber of Mines and the Transvaal government moved with dispatch to set up a program. Transvaal agents, who had already laid the groundwork for recruiting in China, went into high gear. In fact, recruitment in Yantai (Chefoo) in Shandong province had started in January, before the ordinance was finally approved.[48]

But there was just one problem: China had not approved the program. The lapse violated long-standing diplomatic protocols, established in 1860, regarding the recruitment of Chinese labor to territories within the British Empire. The Foreign Office did not show Ordinance no. 17 to the Chinese ambassador in London, Zhang Deyi, until mid-February. Zhang promptly intervened via the Foreign Affairs Department in Beijing (Waiwubu, the successor to the Zongli Yamen). Everything ground to a halt while Zhang Deyi and the Foreign Office commenced negotiations in London in March. The Transvaal Chamber of Mines called the delay "quite unexpected" and "much to be regretted."[49]

When Harry Ross Skinner had recommended importing Chinese indentured labor for the gold mines, he had predicted that China would respond "passively" to such a project. The Foreign Office should have known better. Zhang Deyi was no naïf—he was a seasoned diplomat with forty years of experience in the Qing foreign service. His appointment as Qing ambassador to the Court of St. James's in 1902 was his eighth assignment abroad. He had begun his career as a young translator on the Qing's first overseas mission in 1866 and in the Burlingame delegation in 1868; he had then served in various capacities in Chinese embassies, mostly in Europe. Zhang was also one of China's most prolific diplomat-diarists, who wrote and published eight books chronicling his trips (Figure 20).[50]

Nor was Zhang a stranger to South African affairs. From 1896 to

1900, he had served as councilor in the Qing legation in London, and from there he closely followed the South African War. As ambassador, Zhang was well aware of the debates taking place in South Africa over proposals to import Chinese labor. He worried that the mining companies would abuse Chinese workers in the manner that had made Peru and Cuba the most notorious destinations of the nineteenth-century coolie trade. He further worried that ill treatment of indentured Chinese in South Africa would have negative effects on overseas Chinese communities throughout Africa, from Mauritius to Tanganyika to the Cape Colony. He knew indentured Chinese labor emigrants were vulnerable to the "three harms"—low wages, tight controls, and poor benefits. As early as February 1903—nearly a year before the Transvaal passed Ordinance no. 17—Zhang reported to Beijing that South Africa was likely to recruit Chinese labor. He wrote repeatedly throughout the year that China should forbid labor from going to South Africa without a convention with Great Britain. He was furious when he learned that recruitment was already taking place in Yantai before China had agreed to the program.[51]

On May 13, after three months of negotiation in London, Foreign Secretary Lord Lansdowne and Ambassador Zhang Deyi signed the Emigration Convention of Great Britain and China of 1904. The convention underscored the distance traveled from the mid-nineteenth-century heyday of the coolie trade. It stipulated a minimum age of twenty for emigrants and inspection to ensure that laborers were of sound body and mind. Contracts were to be written in Chinese and English and specify wages, hours, and rations; free passage and return; and the right to free medical care and medicine. It required witness from both Chinese and British officials. It gave China the right to station a consul or vice-consul in the colony and gave Chinese workers "free access to the Courts of Justice to obtain the redress for injuries to his person and property" as well as access to postal facilities for sending letters and remittances to their families.[52]

Zhang pressed hard for a prohibition on corporal punishment, but he was unable to insert an outright ban into the agreement because, the Foreign Office informed him, Transvaal law provided for corporal punishment for certain offenses for "everybody, including whites." The British assured Zhang that floggings would be administered only by order of a magistrate or judge after trial and conviction, and only with government-approved instruments, and that it would not exceed twenty-four lashes. Although the agreement showed improvement in China's ability to negotiate protections for its emigrant workers, enforcement of the terms of the ordinance would be determined on the ground.[53]

※

THE CHAMBER OF Mines Labor Importation Agency (CMLIA) began recruitment in China in May, as soon as the ink on the convention was dry. It opened four offices in China and sent its own staff to manage the operation. The lead emigration agents were British civil servants and officers with experience in Asia, holding positions as consul-delegates. The original plan was to recruit both in southern China, the historical center of labor emigration to Southeast Asia and beyond, and in northern China, in order to recruit as many workers as possible in the shortest time possible. The northern provinces of Shandong and Hebei held particular promise for labor emigration: North China was still recovering from drought, famine, and the Boxer Rebellion; and unemployment was exacerbated when the Russo-Japanese War, which broke out in February 1904, closed Manchuria to seasonal labor migration. In Shandong the CMLIA contracted with firms that had experience recruiting for Russian enterprises in Vladivostok; in Hebei it worked with a company established by Herbert Hoover, operating out of the Kaiping Mining Company in Tianjin, where he had a major interest.[54]

The first two shipments of about two thousand workers, on the *Tweeddale* and the *Ikbar*, which arrived a week later, brought workers from Guangdong province through Hong Kong. But southern China soon collapsed as a labor market for the Transvaal mines. Bad publicity about South Africa and the mining program had been circulating in the Hong Kong and Guangzhou press for nearly a year. Chinese merchants in Johannesburg had sent articles and letters to China warning that Chinese suffered "tyrannical" ill-treatment in South Africa, including racial restrictions, special taxes, and segregation. They painted a grim picture of work in the

Witwatersrand gold mines and warned Chinese not to sign on for work in "a living hell." They wrote, "It is not uncommon to see poor negroes while working in the cave . . . blown to death" by the mine explosives, "some losing their arms and feet and some with heads scalded and burnt." Black miners worked with their feet immersed in water in the mine tunnels for "nights and days. . . . Such hardships are unbearable even by oxen and horses. How is it possible for the Chinese to endure it? . . . We, living in Africa ourselves, cannot bear to see the tragedy done to our race."[55]

After recruitment and shipment of laborers commenced in the spring of 1904, there was ongoing coverage in Chinese newspapers and journals, including *Waijiao bao* (Diplomatic Review) and *Dongfang zazhi* (Eastern Miscellany). The reform journal *Xinmin congbao* (New Citizen) published a long commentary, "An Account of the Miserable Condition of the Overseas Chinese in South Africa," which detailed the history of discrimination against Chinese in South Africa from the late eighteenth century. The discussion of gold mining was disapproving on several accounts. First, it reported on the trend of declining wages for both white and African labor. The Chinese starting wage, set at one shilling a day, was even less than the African wage. More disturbingly, the commentary described Africans as pitiable savages, barely clad and eating goat's head and corn mixed with crude implements made from twigs. It asked, "The savage lives in a cave, can the Chinese laborer do that?" While not unsympathetic to the plight of Africans, the journal expressed an emerging Chinese nationalism influenced by a Social Darwinist view of the world. The commentary carried an implicit warning that the mine owners were using Chinese in a racial gambit and that paying Chinese even less than Africans would surely drag Chinese down to the level of savages and slaves.[56]

In the spring of 1904, a poster campaign against the South African program went up in Guangzhou and Xiamen. In June the viceroy of Liangguang (Guangdong and Guangxi provinces), Cen Chunxuan, long an opponent of indentured-labor emigration, declared recruiting for South Africa to be illegal and halted the shipping of laborers from Guangzhou to Hong Kong. The following month the magistrate of Xinning—the county of origin of tens of thousands of Chinese emigrants to North America and Australia—arrested agents working for the British recruiting firm Butterfield and Swire. In October *Xinmin congbao* acknowledged the efforts of Guangdong officials but feared that, with the agreement between the British and the Qing Foreign Relations Department, the program would be difficult to stop. It considered the per capita fees paid by the CMLIA to the Chinese government to be a payment for selling people into slavery and called for the establishment of a special government bureau to protect emigrant workers.[57]

Recruitment was thus crippled by a combination of negative publicity, the actions of provincial and local authorities, and news about outbreaks of beriberi in the first shipments. More generally, long-distance indentured Chinese emigration from southern China was declining. A British intelligence report acknowledged the real reasons for the "absolute failure" of South African recruitment from the region: "For many years already the Kuangtung [*sic*] Chinaman has been emigrating to the Straits Settlements, to the Malay States, to Burma, the Dutch Indies, Borneo and British North America," where he is "bound down by few or no restrictions." It was no surprise, then, that "Cantonese laborers exhibit no eagerness to bind themselves down by indentures to proceed to a country where all their movements are strictly controlled, where they are obliged to live in a compound, where they are restricted to unskilled labour in the mines." And it was not only the South African project that experienced difficulty. French efforts to recruit indentured labor for building the Yunnan Railroad were "at a standstill," and labor for a German project in North Borneo could not be negotiated. In fact, by the turn of the century, the era of the coolie trade was on the wane. The worst abusers of the practice, Cuba and Peru, had by then abolished it; the few iterations that remained were plagued with difficulty, not least owing to the reluctance of Chinese labor.[58]

IN DECEMBER the CMLIA suspended recruitment in southern China and shifted all its efforts to the northern provinces of Hebei and Shandong, where it had already begun work. There, it rationalized, men were "of an altogether larger and heavier build" than southern men, although northerners were "reported to be duller in intellect." In the end, fully 98 percent of the Chinese laborers sent to the Transvaal mines came from the north.[59]

Northern provincial Chinese officials agreed to cooperate, in light of high unemployment in the region, though they worried about reports of low pay and "suffocating" conditions in South Africa. Perhaps learning from the troubles it encountered in Guangdong, the CMLIA mounted a positive advertising and propaganda campaign in the north. It published an illustrated booklet in Chinese, for use by recruiters in the field, that described the emigration program in great detail, from the sea voyage to the reception depot in Durban to the mine compounds, using Simmer and Jack, the largest employer of Chinese on the Rand, as the prototype. Predictably, it presented a rosy picture of work in the gold mines, with high wages and good food. It included the names of 1,155 workers at fourteen mining companies, listing each man's hometown, the job he performed on the mines, and his monthly earnings, which made the whole affair seem real. Perhaps the CMLIA thought that a prospective emigrant might recognize the name of an acquaintance and feel encouraged to sign up.[60]

The first two shipments from north China were almost entirely recruited from the industrial port city of Tianjin. By March 1905, however, more than half of the men shipping out of Tianjin were "working men, small farmers and agricultural labourers, drawn from districts in the interior." The Foreign Labor Department described them as mostly "peasants fresh from the plough or petty traders." In fact, the CMLIA preferred labor from the countryside from the outset. Skinner, in his 1903 report, had noted the importance of avoiding the "weeds" and "unfits" in the cities and of recruiting "good stout laborers" from "round the coast and even inland."[61]

The recruitment process involved a number of steps. First, local agents of the brokering companies recruited men in towns and villages and brought them to a receiving depot, where they received a medical examination and an explanation of the contract by Chinese clerks and a Transvaal agent. Xie Zixiu and other contemporaries believed deception with false or no information was common in Tianjin, especially with regard to underground work. Those who were accepted were then transferred to the CMLIA's depots at the ports of Qinhuangdao in Hebei and Yantai in Shandong. Each depot comprised two repurposed sheds with concrete floors and wooden bunks and could house five hundred men.[62]

After more interviews and inspections, a final medical examination took place on embarkation day. Only at this point was the medical certificate signed and the CMLIA paid the broker the fee—a practice that avoided paying fees for workers who did not in the end ship out. In fact, "wastage" was considerable. In March 1905, for example, nearly half of the 2,700 men recruited at Tianjin were rejected during the preliminary medical examination. Among those who were accepted, another half either deserted en route to the CMLIA depot at Qinhuangdao, some 150 miles up the coast, or failed the second medical examination there. The reasons for so many desertions, even before departure, may be that recruits were treated so badly at the depots that they had second thoughts about making the trip. A Chinese interpreter who worked on the transport ships wrote in the *Shandong Daily*, "The men are treated with the greatest brutality. Whilst they are in Chefoo (Yantai) the headmen at the emigration office are constantly beating them. . . . [In South Africa] some die from disease and some are foully murdered . . . Truly they are living in a hell upon earth; the foreigners are fierce and evil as the Devil himself."[63]

Still, the lure of gold prevailed upon most. Upon passing the final medical check, the emigrant bathed in a "disinfection tank." He received a towel, a straw hat, a padded coat and trousers, a money belt, shoes, and socks. After dressing, he picked up a passport, a numbered identification tag, and a ticket for drawing a cash advance, to be deducted from future wages. He then appeared once more before the Transvaal emigration agent and again affirmed his willingness to go to South Africa. He signed his contract with a fingerprint and received a copy. At this point, said an observer, "the coolie is transformed into an indentured laborer."[64]

The workers traveled to South Africa on chartered British-owned freighters, which were retrofitted to meet conditions governed by the Emigration Convention of 1904 and the Hong Kong Passenger Acts. The ships stopped at Hong Kong and Singapore for food and fuel, then proceeded through the Malacca Strait to the Indian Ocean. At the Seychelles Islands they turned southwest for Durban. The journey took thirty days at an average speed of ten to eleven knots.[65]

During the long journey to South Africa, the CMLIA strictly enforced health and sanitary regimens. It used the time on board to train "boss coolies," or headmen, who had been selected just prior to embarkation. Disciplinary measures were meted out against gambling, fighting, theft, opium smoking, and violations of sanitary rules, measures that included "deprivation of food, . . . being tied or locked up for a period, with or without full diet, or a number of strokes with the bamboo." At a certain level, however, it was impossible to maintain discipline. The men had cash to spend on purchases from hawkers at Hong Kong and Singapore and on gambling on board. Gambling rackets quickly emerged on the voyages and would continue to be a source of trouble on the mines.[66]

Upon arrival at Durban, the men received a medical inspection while still on board and then disembarked. They then transferred by rail to the Foreign Labor Department's depot at Jacob's Camp, which was large enough to house four thousand men, or two shiploads, at a time. The camp comprised over sixty bunkhouses, latrines, bathing houses, and kitchens, in addition to offices used by FLD officers and clerks. Outside the main gate there was a hospital, quarters for FLD staff, and a police station. The laborers ate rice, meat or fish, and vegetables for breakfast and dinner, and rice congee at noon. A small shop on the premises sold cigarettes, cakes, and the like and reportedly did a brisk business.[67]

During the processing of the first group of laborers from the *Tweeddale,* three of the men who had arrived suffering from beriberi died at Jacob's Camp. The CMLIA repatriated forty others, but it is not known how many survived the return trip home. Of the 1,006 men who left Jacob's Camp for the Witwatersrand, forty-eight more would be stricken with beriberi after their arrival at the New Comet Mine. Within a month most of them had recovered and were able to go into the mines.[68]

Chapter 9

Coolies on the Rand

Xie Zixiu, the Cantonese from Sydney who moved to Johannesburg by way of Hong Kong in 1903, was eager to make his mark in South Africa. He was in his early thirties and seems to have rather easily become the secretary of the Cantonese Club, though it was probably not a paying position. But the position, as well as his bilingualism, gave him some standing among both Chinese and whites. In other words, he was a culture broker. People in this position facilitate exchange between two groups that otherwise cannot communicate or do business with each other; they derive power from their monopoly over information or goods. But that monopoly can lead both sides of the exchange to mistrust the person in the middle. Chinese interpreters and labor agents could do an immigrant a favor—say, by tweaking their translations to help them before a judge or by putting in a good word with an employer—but they could also demand money for such favors. Xie Zixiu does not appear to have been corrupt. He considered himself a "progressive," believing that Chinese in South Africa, whether merchants in town or indentured laborers on the mines, should be treated fairly, and he put his skills and talents to the task. If he was also status conscious and a bit proud, these were minor flaws.

When Xie arrived in Johannesburg in October 1903, the public debate over whether to import Chinese mine labor was well under way. The men at the Cantonese Club undoubtedly discussed and speculated about it. At the end of the year, when the legislature was preparing Ordinance no. 17, Xie took a job with the newly established Foreign Labor Department. He might have just shown up and offered his services. The FLD was responsible for overseeing the importation and operation of the program: issuing licenses and passports (both revenue-generating); overseeing the arrival, reception, distribution, and repatriation of labor; keeping data on illnesses, deaths, arrests, and convictions; and monitoring the mining companies' compliance with the terms of the programs. There was a lot of work to get the program set up. Being in the office, Xie had access to valuable information about the program.

Sir George Farrar probably met Xie when he stopped by the department to observe its operations. Xie—introducing himself as Thomas Ah Sze—would have impressed him with his command of English such that Farrar offered him a job as a "Chinese adviser" for the East Rand Proprietary Mines (ERPM). This promised to be much more interesting than bureaucratic work in the FLD's office. Xie's job at ERPM was to visit the company's mines, talk to the workers, and convey their complaints to the company. No doubt Farrar's goal was to maintain a smoothly operating program; Xie's interest was to protect the laborers from mistreatment. At New Comet, Xie reported on the poor quality of the food served to Chinese laborers and the manager's use of the mine's infirmary to lock up workers who refused to work.[1]

Although New Comet initially addressed some of the workers' complaints, Xie came to believe that he had "no say in matters." The ERPM's general superintendent told him not to encourage the laborers to make complaints. When he visited another ERPM mine, the Angelo, the superintendent warned him against "influencing" the Chinese interpreters and coolies there. Xie resented the insinuation, "as if I was putting them up to it."[2]

Both frustrated and offended, Xie quit his position in March 1905, after just six months on the job. When he submitted his resignation, company officials pressured him to sign a report stating that he found conditions at the mines satisfactory. He refused and, forfeiting a month's salary, left for England to bring a complaint directly to the London office of Farrar Brothers and to the Chinese legation. He was also carrying a petition for the Qing ambassador from Chinese merchants in Port Elizabeth, who were protesting new requirements of registration and identification passes newly imposed upon them by the Cape Colony government. Xie was thwarted, however, by a telegram from ERPM officials to Farrar's London office, which warned that Thomas Ah Sze was a "somewhat dangerous man," liable to agitate and blackmail. Farrar's people also tipped off a British staffer at the Chinese legation, who blocked Xie from meeting with Qing ambassador Zhang Deyi.[3]

From London Xie wrote to his former employer, defending his qualifications to speak on the subject of the "Chinese Labour question" given the knowledge he gained in "government service, and your company. . . . There is no need for me to exaggerate matters in the least, what I shall have to say, will be the truth and nothing but the truth." He added, "I must say that as a Chinese Progressive, I have a duty to perform, [first] for myself, and [second] for my Country and Countrymen and no one can blame me for taking the steps I have adopted."[4]

Mining and colonial officials went to great lengths to deter Xie Zixiu. They also tried to diminish him by scoffing at his claim that he was a British subject—which he was, having been born in Australia—while also alleging that he could not read Chinese, challenging his authenticity. Xie Zixiu was precisely the kind of proud Chinese who mining and colonial officials feared would expose the problems in the labor importation program that had quickly emerged on the Rand.

Xie returned to Port Elizabeth and wrote *South Africa Travel Journal*, a lengthy essay of ten thousand characters in classical Chinese. He completed it in July and sent it as a gift to Zhao Erxun, a high-ranking scholar-official, who had held various provincial posts before being appointed secretary of revenue at Beijing.[5]

The gift was fortuitous; although it does not appear to have circulated among Qing officials or to have influenced policy, it became known to reformers, who referred to it in their brief on the Qing's failure to protect Chinese laborers abroad. It is valuable to historians because it is one of a very few documents extant that describe firsthand and from a Chinese perspective the common violations of the labor ordinance and the hard

realities of Chinese mining labor. Although its contents are not necessarily indisputable, it enables us to check or counter claims made in the
British and South African sources.

☗

THE SOURCE OF the tensions surrounding Xie Zixiu's brief tenure at ERPM
lay in the high hopes for the Chinese labor program held by colonial and
mining officials. The stakes of the program are evident in one of the first
communiqués sent by Lord Milner to Colonial Secretary Lyttelton, a month
after the first group of Chinese laborers arrived at the New Comet Mine. Milner reported that the Chinese were over the worst of the beriberi outbreak.
He was also pleased to report that labor efficiency was showing constant
improvement. On July 7 (barely two weeks after starting work), 440 laborers drilled 542 feet and 2 inches, an average of 15.6 inches per man. Twenty
men drilled 2.5 feet each and nine drilled 3 feet each. There was little that
could dampen the governor's enthusiasm. He dismissed rumors of desertions from the mines that were already circulating in British newspapers.
It was difficult to keep track of everyone, he explained, because the ERPM
covered three miles, and no permit was necessary while on mine premises.[6]

Milner's concise telegraphic message to London captured the main
issues that would preoccupy South African colonial authorities and mine
owners over the coming months and years. The central question, of
course, was how much ore they could get out of the ground. This pertained not only to how many inches each man drilled but also to "wastage" that resulted from illness or walking off the mines. The question
of desertion demanded attention to discipline and surveillance. Politics
lurked constantly in the background, criticizing the program, variously,
as a menace to white interests or as subjecting Chinese to conditions that
amounted to "slavery." Although Chinese wages were theoretically on par
with native African wages, considerable expense had been committed to
import tens of thousands of workers from China. The owners hoped that,
over the course of each man's three-year contract, the workers' accumu-
lating experience would yield ever-greater rates of productivity, enabling
them to recoup the cost of recruitment. With labor accounting for the

single greatest cost variable in the industry, the mine owners counted on the Chinese workers to reverse the crisis of labor shortage and falling rate of profit that they faced in 1903.

Notwithstanding Lord Milner's sanguine outlook, beriberi continued to plague the workforce. In October the FLD repatriated another eighty workers suffering from the debilitating disease; some were so weak they could not walk, and fourteen died at sea before arriving home. The Chinese workers did become more adept at drilling, but they resisted ongoing pressure to drill ever more per day, despite the withholding of wages and the lash. And they would desert the mines in great numbers over the coming several years. No doubt Chinese labor enabled the industry to reach prewar levels of output by 1905 and to expand production to new deep mines. Output increased and profits rose. But these achievements were costly in other, perhaps more significant ways. The Chinese labor program generated an ongoing crisis of social control on the mines and a political crisis in both South Africa and Great Britain. By 1907 the use of Chinese labor on the Rand became untenable. Recruitment of new workers ceased, and the last contracts were run out, with the last Chinese laborers returning home in 1910. The end of the program ensured the triumph of Asiatic exclusion in South Africa.[7]

WITHIN SIX MONTHS of the first shipment of workers on the *Tweeddale,* the Chamber of Mines Labor Importation Agency received 15,199 laborers and distributed them to ten mines; by the end of the first year, there were approximately 28,000 Chinese at twenty-seven mines. The population of Chinese miners on the Rand peaked at 53,838 in 1907. In all, nearly 63,000 Chinese men worked in the South African gold mines under the labor importation program.[8]

Milner had emphasized that Chinese labor would enable a "definite policy of progression." He believed the Chinese presence signaled certainty in the labor supply, without which capital "will never be forthcoming" to develop the mines. Lord Selborne, who took over from Milner as governor of the Transvaal and high commissioner of southern Africa in May 1905, similarly regarded Chinese labor as necessary both for the industry's recovery and for its rapid development and expansion. The CMLIA initially made requests to recruiters in China for 100,000 workers a year for three years. Although officials publicly described the Chinese labor importation program as a short-term and experimental project, they privately discussed the possibility that Chinese labor would become a permanent feature of the industry. Chinese labor served the immediate problem of labor shortage but also held the promise, more long term, of checking both native and white wage rates.[9]

Only three mines used Chinese labor exclusively, notably the huge enterprise Simmer and Jack, part of Cecil Rhodes's Consolidated group. The Chinese workforce there, 4,200 at its peak, was the largest on the Rand. Most of the mining companies used Chinese laborers to supplement their African workforce. The general pattern was to assign Chinese underground, where they drilled, shoveled, and carted rock; and Africans to surface work, where they transported rock to the mills for crushing and worked as "helpers" to skilled white workers in the stamp batteries and in other operations. The workforce was not formally segregated by race, and both groups worked below and aboveground, but many more Chinese worked underground than above (Figures 21 and 22).[10]

The *Illustrated Guide to Chinese Labor in South African Gold Mines,* published in Tianjin for use by recruiters, described jobs in the underground tunnels and in the various departments aboveground—the stamping mill, boiler house, metallurgical processing plant, and storage tower—and claimed that Chinese working at skilled jobs aboveground commanded high wages, as much as fifty yuan per month (100 shillings), double the rate for unskilled labor. The pamphlet was misleading: The law prohibited Chinese from working in skilled jobs; those listed in the pamphlet as "machinist" or "blacksmith" were actually helpers ("boys") to skilled white workers. Moreover, perhaps fewer than 20 percent worked aboveground.[11]

Under the contract, the starting minimum wage was one shilling for a ten-hour day, payable monthly. This was less than half of the daily native wage rate for underground work and one-tenth the wage for unskilled white labor. Ordinance no. 17 stipulated that after six months of work, Chinese wages would rise to the average native wage, fifty shillings per month. Still, the starting daily wage on the Rand, one shilling, was at least twice what laborers earned in China. However, consumer prices in South Africa were also significantly higher than in China. Moreover, some mine companies paid Chinese in scrip (iron tokens) that could be used only at stores on the mine compounds, where goods were shoddy and overpriced, and could be exchanged for sterling only at the end of the contract. The Chinese complained that "after buying milk, sugar, tobacco, and other things which they required there was little or nothing left to send to their families in China."[12]

THE RAND MINES WERE notoriously dangerous and unhealthy, especially as mine managers pushed workers relentlessly to maximize output. The Anglo-Chinese labor convention, the Transvaal Ordinance no. 17, and the terms of each laborer's contract included provisions to protect Chinese workers from abuse. But who would ensure these protections? Xie Zixiu learned quickly that being an "adviser" meant little.

The Foreign Labor Department was officially responsible for monitoring conditions on the mines. Its inspectors were supposed to visit each mine at least once a month and examine the compound (rooms, latrines, kitchens) and the records in the time office, converse with laborers "if possible," and receive money from them to remit to China. But in 1905, one year after the program had started, the department had only two inspectors on staff. By February 1906 the FLD head office in Johannesburg had seven inspectors, still an insufficient force.[13]

On the Chinese side, the Qing consul Liu Yulin arrived in Johannesburg in May 1905, nearly a year after Chinese laborers began going to South Africa. Liu was a cosmopolitan who was educated in China and the United States and had served as a consular official in the United States, Europe, and Southeast Asia. Liu held ongoing meetings with local Chinese merchants, who had long clamored for a consul. He visited the gold mines and investigated complaints from Chinese laborers, though he had no powers of enforcement. The Qing ambassador in London, Zhang Deyi, having lost the battle to ban corporal punishment, continued to press for more support for the Chinese mine laborers. Alarmed at the numbers of Chinese workers who fell sick or died while working on the Rand, he lobbied to get the mine companies to pay a death benefit to the workers' families, but to no avail.[14]

The Chinese merchants of Johannesburg also tried to advocate for the mine laborers. The Cantonese Club continued to send letters to the press in China with exposés of mine conditions. Xie Zixiu, who was originally from Australia, was likely author of a letter sent Melbourne's Chinese-language newspaper, *Aiguo bao* (Chinese Times), which described the mine compounds as prisons. A local laundryman named Ah Bu was arrested at the New Comet Mine after he conferred with the laborers. He was charged with holding an unauthorized meeting with the laborers, inciting them to not work, and trespassing after he refused to leave. He was convicted and sentenced to six weeks in jail.[15]

Isolated on the mining compounds and with little contact with Consul Liu or local merchants and with the FLD woefully understaffed, the Chinese mine laborers were pretty much on their own.

ON A TYPICAL WORKDAY, laborers on the day shift arose before sunrise and took their morning meal in the large dining hall in preparation for the ten-hour workday, which began at five a.m. The same meal was served to workers coming off the night shift, who had gone to work at five p.m. the evening before. A second meal served both shifts in the afternoon. The daily ration, split between these two meals, comprised 1.5 pounds of rice; a half-pound of dried or fresh fish or meat; a quarter-pound of vegetables; a half-ounce of tea, a half-ounce of nut oil, and salt. There was no "lunch" per se; the workers received a can of tea and a loaf of bread to eat while belowground, but reportedly they often used the tea to moisten the hole they were drilling and threw away the bread, which many considered inedible, and instead brought their own food that they purchased with their own money from stores on the mines.[16]

Mine labor was hard labor, physically arduous and dangerous. The Chinese worked at depths of one thousand to two thousand feet, where they attacked the rock face with a chisel and a hand drill to break up the rock. Because the reef dipped at an average of thirty degrees, drillers usually worked on an incline; moreover, the surface was often slippery, which made conditions difficult for drillers and trammers alike. There was water "that pours down on our heads drenching us and giving us cold." Drillers frequently worked in claustrophobic conditions on narrow stopes, which could not accommodate machine drills and where native African workers simply refused to work. Chinese labor thus enabled mine owners to exploit new areas of the reef deep underground, upon which the mining companies had staked their future but that were otherwise difficult to reach.[17]

The performance of the work was measured in inches. At the end of each shift, the white gang supervisor issued each laborer a work ticket that was the evidence of the work he had carried out and the basis for his being paid. As noted, upon arriving at the mines, Chinese drilled on average fifteen inches a day, but they improved quickly. Mines that adopted piecework rates for drillers established a minimum requirement of twenty-four to thirty-six inches for a driller to receive any payment at all. Drilling more than thirty-six inches entitled him to a bonus.[18]

The living quarters, or compounds, mostly were newly built for the program and therefore were of better quality than the older native compounds. Brick or concrete bunkhouses contained large rooms housing up to forty workers; bedding ranged from low cots separated by curtains to tiered bunks made of wire mesh or concrete. The latrines used pails, and bathing houses ran hot and cold water; there were also changing sheds with showers near the mineshaft entrance. The kitchen and a large dining hall stood in the central courtyard. A Chinese staff prepared meals, the head cook recruited specifically for the job in China and assistants drawn from the general ranks. For each table of ten, one man fetched large vessels of rice and "stew" for the table, which method shortened queues and conformed to family-style eating. European observers praised the food as adequate and healthy, although both quantity and quality apparently quickly deteriorated as mine managers skimped on their food budgets. The meat ration at some mines was short by nearly half. By 1905 workers were refusing to eat tasteless meat and rotten vegetables. They may have consumed the rice and supplemented it with food bought at nearby stores, such as jerky and boiled calves' feet, which purchases would have taxed their earnings.[19]

The men did what they could to enliven their surroundings, sometimes growing small flower gardens with plants that they dug up on the veld; a number of men kept birds. The FLD took pains to praise the compounds for being "light and airy," sanitary, and most important, "open" during daylight hours. When not working, the FLD boasted, a laborer was "free to walk in and out [of the compound] just as he pleases" and to roam the "mine premises, which in some cases extends to miles," obscuring the lack of freedom to leave the mine premises to go to town, say, or roam the veld. European observers generally described compound conditions as decent, even "luxurious" and "palatial," in comparison to tin mining camps in the Straits Settlements or to conditions in China itself. The Chinese workers in South Africa seem to have found their living quarters tolerable; they rioted over various issues, but compound conditions was not one of them.[20]

Chinese workers lived separately from both whites and Africans. Skilled white workers lived in boardinghouses in towns near the mines or in separate dormitories on mine properties. African workers lived in separate compounds. Chinese and African workers do not seem to have socialized much with each other during their off hours, but there was some contact. Lionel Phillips, director of Eckstein and Company, wrote that Africans initiated the Chinese to the conventions of gold mining labor, and "each acquire[d] in an incredibly short space of time sufficient of the other's tongue to exchange ideas." The records do not show evidence of friendships across the color line, but critics sometimes blamed Chinese for exercising bad influence over African workers, which suggests a level of engagement between the two groups that was not trivial, even if whites described it in racial stereotypes of depraved Chinese introducing vice to childlike Africans. There are a few reports of Chinese having romantic or sexual affairs with African women in Johannesburg or in native neighborhoods near the mines. These affairs were also a source of conflict among Chinese and African men. Ethnic conflict in the compounds was not uncommon, not only between Chinese and Africans but among Africans and among Chinese, based on regional or clan differences.[21]

There was little recreational activity on the mines. At five or six compounds, laborers formed theater groups that performed Chinese operas on wooden stages erected in the compound courtyards. Elaborate productions took place on holidays. In January 1906 the workers on several mines contributed to a fund that procured from China lavish costumes, umbrellas and banners, paper dragons, fireworks, and special foods. At Glen Deep, where two thousand Chinese worked, the celebration committee raised £250, a considerable sum. Banners and lanterns decorated the bunkhouses and compound. Chinese opera ran for the entire three days alongside games and contests, like tug-of-war, races, pole climbing, and rock drilling (Figure 23).[22]

These festivities came but once or twice a year. The common daily source of entertainment was gambling, the prime activity of male work camps, where boredom and cash reigned. Gambling rackets, which plied the men during the long sea voyage from China, continued to work the compounds, often holding games on payday. Professional gamblers targeted younger and less experienced workers and placed many in their debt. It was said that the professionals often did not even work but paid others to do it for them or exacted labor as payment for debt. The relentless pursuit of debt repayment drove many workers to despair. Cui Guyan, a miner at Simmer and Jack, appealed to the superintendent of the FLD, confessing that, owing to his "foolish disposition," he had incurred debts to sixteen people amounting to "several tens of pounds sterling." His creditors dunned him daily, and one of them took away his work ticket. He wished not to commit suicide, he said, because he had a wife and widowed mother at home, and he begged to be transferred to another worksite.[23]

Everyone looked forward to Sunday, the day of rest. Representatives from several churches visited the mine premises to worship with the small number of Roman Catholics and Protestants, reflecting the late nineteenth-century missionary presence in North China. A few even received baptism in a shallow dam on the Rand. But for most workers, Sunday was the day to go off the mines. Starting at noon, they went out with passes in hand, dressed smartly in outfits brought from China or in Western-style suits purchased locally. They took strolls through the woods, organized picnics on the veld, or visited friends and relatives at other compounds. Some went into town, especially Ferreirastown, the location of Johannesburg's small Chinese quarter. Observers described Chinese from the mines engaged in window shopping, eating at Cantonese restaurants, and riding bicycles through the streets, their queues streaming in the wind. Indian hawkers did a "roaring trade" in fruit and flavored mineral waters. The Chinese freely spent their earnings on cigarettes, foodstuffs, cooking equipment, bicycles, watches, and apparel, their consumption habits indexing their engagement with the modern world. Indeed, storekeepers noted that they were quite knowledgeable about the quality of merchandise and "do not buy rubbish." Most likely the big spenders comprised Chinese in the privileged jobs—policemen, headmen, kitchen workers—who earned higher wages and, importantly, were paid in sterling rather than in scrip. These workers amounted to 10 to 20 percent of the Chinese population on the mines, perhaps five thousand at peak employment, so their conspicuous presence in town would have obscured the fact that ordinary mine laborers lacked the means to enjoy the same pleasures. The consumer habits of the Chinese elicited both praise and disapproval from white South Africans. Some welcomed the boon to the economy; the Chinese at the Witwatersrand Deep Mine alone reportedly spent eight hundred pounds a month at local businesses. Others criticized the Chinese for lacking moral qualities of thrift.[24]

Buying sex was also a Sunday activity. At least two brothels in Ferreirastown catered to Chinese, one run by Cantonese merchants, which employed two "Dutch girls," and another by two European men with two women, one white and one "colored" (mixed race). The latter was site of a sensational police raid in 1907. Chinese solicitation of white women was a violation of the Immorality Ordinance, being considered both a sexual and racial transgression. Police arrested two Chinese men found in the rooms; the court convicted and sentenced one man to twelve months' imprisonment with hard labor and a whipping of ten strokes, but it acquitted the other because he was fully dressed at the time of arrest. It also convicted the two prostitutes and the two white men who managed the brothel. But the authorities decided they could do nothing about the two hundred men who were waiting their turns in the backyard of the house.[25]

If the incident suggested a sex market in which demand far exceeded supply, and if the brothel has always been a staple fixture on the frontier and wherever else all-male work camps are established, we should not assume that it was the only source of sex for Chinese on the Rand. As noted, at least a few Chinese men formed relationships with local African women. Colonial authorities also reported same-sex relationships among Chinese mine laborers, and they criticized the theater groups as meeting grounds for "catamites" and other "bad characters." The British considered same-sex relations to be an "unnatural vice" that was "addictive" and further blamed the Chinese for introducing it to African workers. In fact, male "marriages" in the African compounds predated the arrival of the Chinese. Same-sex practices may have been situational, but they were also not necessarily considered "unnatural" or something shameful that had to be hidden. Although different in their particulars, neither Chinese nor African cultures stigmatized the practice in the extreme manner of Victorian morality.[26]

Among the Chinese mine laborers there were brothers, cousins, and hometown acquaintances, so workers were not altogether without kin or friends while on the Rand. A few Chinese laborers brought wives and children with them to the Transvaal, under a provision of Ordinance no. 17. But Chinese labor emigrants rarely brought wives with them abroad; a central tenet of the Confucian social order was for the wife to live with her husband in the home of his parents. With the rise of mass labor emigration in the nineteenth century, the custom served to keep the sojourner tethered to the home village and the patrilineal family. During the first two years of the program, there were only four women and twenty-six children on the mines. They were likely the families of Chinese headmen or policemen, who had separate rooms. The large number of children relative to women suggests that there were only a few nuclear families. Laborers may have brought children, likely boys old enough to fend for themselves without supervision while their fathers worked, as a way to ease financial pressure on the family household at home.[27]

But most Chinese laborers on the Rand left parents, wives, and children in China. As in other cases of male sojourning abroad, they sent remittances and letters home. But while there were established routes for sending money and mail between northern China and Manchuria, and between southern China and Southeast Asia, Australia and North America, South Africa posed new challenges of distance and organization. Frustrations, worry, and confusion over questions of address, postage, and the like plagued the delivery of mail in both directions. Workers complained they had no word from relatives for months and did not know if their letters or money had arrived; FLD clerks spent considerable energies tracking down laborers whose families had sent mail addressed, simply, to them in "English South Africa." Workers from Tianjin sent letters to parents and wives in care of shops where their loved ones would be known (a tofu shop, a vegetable market, a barbershop); others provided delivery instructions such as "Send the enclosed by way of Hong Kong Post to Guangxi province, to the main road by the northern gate, and give to Wu Shi, from Hu Yulin in the English South African Gold Mine, Letter from afar, please do not lose!"[28]

A system of surveillance and control organized the compounds. European "controllers" seem to have ranged from the dedicated to the cruel. Eugenio Bianchini, the controller at the Witwatersrand Gold Mining Company, had experience in North China as a labor recruiter for the Russian railroads in Manchuria. Although he regarded Chinese paternalistically, he tirelessly represented the workers' complaints (mostly wage disputes) to the mine manager, although usually to no avail. Bianchini eventually quit in protest over treatment of the Chinese. At the other end of the spectrum, H. J. Pless, an American also with experience in China who was the controller at the Nourse Deep Mine, routinely ordered workers who did not drill the requisite number of inches to be whipped. Pless also personally tortured and sexually abused Chinese workers. In one instance he took photographs of his torture victim and bragged that he was going to publish a book called "Slave Driving on the Rand." He returned to China before he could be arrested. Most Chinese controllers likely fell between these two poles. In general, the controllers were not known for their competence, let alone their humanity. Many were hired simply because they had some knowledge of Chinese, even if they lacked managerial skills.[29]

The job of the Chinese policemen was to ensure adherence to sanitary and other regulations on the compounds, to get shifts out to work, and to guard the gates. They were not actually police officers but mine employees and held no legal authority. With one policeman for every fifty to one hundred workers, the Chinese police constituted a sizable stratum of privilege and power. Some had had experience in China working with the British army at Weihaiwei and spoke some English, or at least pidgin. They wore the Weihaiwei regimental uniform in the Transvaal, a variation of the uniforms worn by Sikhs in the imperial army. Selborne considered the police not "oppressive" and only occasionally abusive, but other officials believed they were not only abusive but also unreliable, corrupt, and lacking in authority because they were recruited from same social class as the mass of laborers. The workers resented them, while the mine managers mistrusted them, believing that they were the source of much social instability and discord in the compounds.[30]

Chinese indentured workers held various other nonmining jobs, despite legal prohibitions against their performing anything other than unskilled mining labor. Chinese performed cooking and kitchen work, domestic service for Chinese controllers, and menial work in compound infirmaries. At a number of mines, workers recovering from illnesses or accidents who were not yet able to go back underground were given "light duty" working for white mine employees, including domestic chores, gardening, and the like. The attorney general did not condone the use of generalized "coolie labor" but did not press the point after J. W. Jamieson told him it would be impossible to prosecute. Similar to the Chinese policemen, Chinese working in the kitchens and in other irregular jobs comprised an informal stratum of privileged workers. Their access to contraband goods enabled them to enhance their own situations either through direct consumption or by selling to others.[31]

This sketch of daily life on the mines suggests a routine of arduous labor and confinement, broken only by one afternoon of rest a week. The laborers were bound to the mining company to which they were assigned; they spent ten hours a day engaged in hard and dangerous physical labor underground; and they were subject to control by white controllers and Chinese policemen, who were often abusive. Many undoubtedly suffered from loneliness and depression. Xie Zixiu, who sometimes visited the mines at night, wrote that he heard workers sighing and crying in the dormitories. Very little survives of the workers' correspondence, but one can discern a certain plaintiveness in queries made to the wife: "Why do you not answer my letters?" Depression becomes more visible to us in cases of suicide, which was often induced by opium poisoning. The FLD recorded nineteen deaths by suicide in 1904–5 and forty-nine in 1905–6.[32]

Chen Ziqing wrote a poem before he took his own life on December 20, 1904. A middle-aged and educated man from Tangshan, Guangdong, Chen held a minor rank in the Qing system of honorary military titles. The poem was published and circulated widely in China as evidence of the suffering of Chinese gold mining laborers in South Africa. It was also said that Chen had been kidnapped by recruiters and sold into indenture on the Rand.

> *I lived in China my forty-three years,*
> *By misfortune I came to this foreign land.*
> *Here, not even a hero finds a way.*
> *I can no longer endure.*
> *I say goodbye to this world.*
> *Leaving my countrymen, who continue to suffer in anguish.*
> *Brothers, when your three years are finished, please, then,*
> *Bring my soul back to Tangshan.*[33]

Death on the Rand, whether by suicide, mine accident, or hanging for crimes they may or may not have committed, signaled to contemporaries in China that the Transvaal was a place of cruelty and injustice. But if suicide was an act of refusal, most Chinese laborers resisted their conditions in favor of more positive outcomes. They created spaces of personal and communal autonomy, albeit tenuous, that were beyond the reach of mine managers and the state. Living in bunkhouses and dining communally generated sociability, solidarity, and even intimacy as well as conflict. And the workers formed *yi hui* (righteous societies), similar to the brotherhoods that overseas Chinese formed the world over. The *yi hui* typically signed up members at dues of three pence a week, which enabled the groups to contribute two to three pounds to a deceased member's family. FLD officials linked "undesirables" to "Ko Lo Hut" or "Kuo Lu Whei," likely the Gelaohui (Elder Brothers Society), a secret brotherhood originating in Fujian province. Beyond their basic function as mutual aid organizations, the societies' bonds of solidarity supported a range of collective endeavors, including compound protests and work actions. Brotherhoods formed on nearly all the mines, but they were barely visible to Europeans, who mainly saw them as gangs behind opium trading and gambling rackets and did not understand their complex social character.[34]

✛

THERE WERE TWO MAJOR SOURCES of conflict between the Chinese laborers and the mine companies. The system of calculating wages was complex and perhaps deliberately designed to disadvantage the workers; indeed, laborers often felt cheated of their due. Not paying anything for drilling fewer than twenty-four inches seemed patently unfair. The monthly pay was based on thirty working days, not calendar days, an even greater disappointment to Chinese workers who reckoned a month by the twenty-eight-day lunar calendar. When calculating contracted increases, mine owners used not the individual's but an "average daily wage," a concept that was difficult to parse. Workers who volunteered to work overtime often did not get tickets for the extra work. When wages were scheduled to rise after six months, many companies dragged their feet and delayed giving raises for months.[35]

Second, mine managers and supervisors constantly pressured Chinese to drill more. Chinese reached a daily average of forty inches by 1905, more than the average of thirty-six inches for Mozambique workers and thirty-two for Transvaal Africans. The Chinese achieved greater productivity because they became more skilled with time, but they were also relentlessly pushed, perhaps more than African workers, who could be pushed only so far because they easily deserted the mines. Pressure to drill more was applied, first, by the gang supervisor's exhortations, sometimes combined with a stick or leather prod. The second source of pressure was punishment for failure to drill the daily requisite number of inches, with flogging or the withholding of food or both. It is impossible to know the extent of these practices, but they were neither rare nor exceptional.

Chinese workers hated the whites working in the mines, both the underground bosses and the skilled miners aboveground who worked over nonwhite "helpers." Bianchini believed that as a general rule, white miners treated the Chinese harshly, directing them with contempt and foul language. It was natural, he said, that the Chinese would curse back at them, which resulted in a dynamic of mutual antagonism. Chinese often refused to work with a boss who was known to be of "unenviable character and bad temper," apparently preferring to accept punishment rather than be subjected to ill treatment. Bianchini despaired that unless white miners accepted responsibility for teaching and leading the Chinese, rather than ordering and cursing them, "raw coolies" would never be transformed into "suitable workers." Lionel Phillips, director of Eckstein and Company, observed that Chinese workers recognized their lead supervisor (whom they called "number one") but showed no deference to other whites.[36]

These refusals show that Chinese workers lacked socialization to the South African racial hierarchy, in which whites expected nonwhites to treat them as "masters." Phillips intimated as much when he compared Chinese defiance to the seeming compliance of Africans. Another observer stated flatly, "The Chinese, who call us foreign devils, have more contempt for the white man than the black man has." (Most Europeans did not understand that Africans performed compliance while masking their true thoughts and feelings.)[37]

The Chinese attitude of open contempt for white miners especially angered the latter. At the New Croecus Mine, for example, antagonism between whites and Chinese ran deep. They cursed each other all the time, not only underground but also on the mine premises after work hours. Chinese passing by the whites' living quarters, which were a few hundred yards from the Chinese compound gate, routinely exchanged insults and threats with whites. Chinese workers often lodged complaints about ill treatment by white bosses to the Chinese controller, Charles Duncan Stewart. White miners detested Stewart, believing that "on every available occasion he sides with the Coolies against us." These tensions boiled over on the night of June 7, 1905, when several hundred Chinese laborers attacked the white single men's dormitory, breaking windows with rocks and destroying furniture with pick handles. Richard Bradley, a thirty-two-year-old white miner, died in the fracas, his head bashed by a heavy rock. White mine guards on horses firing shots chased the Chinese back to the compound. It was all over in fifteen minutes, but one man was dead and the dormitory was destroyed.

In fact, the trouble originated in the Chinese laborers' anger that they had not received their wages for the previous month. Late payment was apparently not uncommon, but in this instance the workers had expected their pay in time to celebrate the Dragon Boat Festival, one of the few holidays of the year that they had off. The attack was planned and executed with the aid of Chinese policemen, who unlocked the compound gate, and was possibly abetted by Stewart, who had recently been fired because of his problematic relations with white miners. Stewart was charged with inciting to riot (allegedly calling to the Chinese to come out); he and two Chinese workers, Han Yusun (Han Yu Sen) and Wang Qingsan (Wang Ching San), were also charged with the murder of Bradley. All charges were eventually dropped for lack of evidence.[38]

Stewart denied that he favored the Chinese over whites. He testified that, "I always fairly decided the cases brought before me. . . . When I found the coolies were in the wrong I flogged them." What is of interest here is Stewart's reference to flogging as a routine form of discipline, considered neither cruel nor unusual. Most commonly workers received floggings for refusing to work, for deserting the mines, and for failing to drill the daily requisite number of inches. A controller might administer a flogging with a bamboo cane, a short leather whip, or a *sjambok*, a heavy whip. Many mine managers believed that inflicting corporal punishment was more efficient than bringing formal charges against a worker in the magistrate's court, which process meant hours or days of lost work time. They further reasoned that whereas Chinese understood the meaning of a flogging, they were "confused" by the procedures of Roman-Dutch law. In this way the British classified the Chinese as they did Africans, as uncivilized people who understood only the law of the whip. Although Ordinance no. 17 stated that only a magistrate judge could order flogging as punishment after a court conviction, Superintendent Evans approved the use of "slight corporal punishment . . . of such a nature as permitted in schools in England." J. W. Jamieson, Evans's successor as superintendent, understood that Milner had consented to it, but neither Evans nor Milner committed anything to writing.[39]

Some controllers, like H. J. Pless at Nourse Deep, gained sadistic pleasure from flogging Chinese workers; but in most cases Chinese policemen meted out corporal punishment. This practice kept the Europeans' hands cleaner and gave them a measure of plausible deniability in the event that police used excessive force. Detention was another form of punishment. The clinic doctor at an East Rand Proprietary Mine locked as many as thirty workers he accused of feigning illness into a small room and deprived them of food. After Xie Zixiu protested, FLD officials banned the use of hospital prisons. Some compound managers and other officials also lodged complaints about abuse. In June 1905 Lt. Governor Lawley issued a prohibition against all corporal punishment.[40]

The practice continued, however, and became a public scandal in September 1905, when Frank Boland published in the British *Morning Leader* a sensational exposé of "horrible cruelties" and "barbarities" on the gold mines. Boland's charges made flogging the principal exhibit of the metropolitan campaign against "Chinese slavery" on the Rand. According to the *Leader*, the average number of daily floggings at a single mine, the Witwatersrand Mine, was forty-two. At Witwatersrand Deep, police administered a short bamboo rod against a worker, who was stripped to the waist and knelt with his head to the floor. Chinese policemen at Nourse Deep (working under the supervision of the cruel compound manager Pless) reportedly flogged workers who failed to drill thirty-six inches a day, beating them on the back of the thighs with the heavy *sjambok* or with strips of rubber, which left no marks. Boland also reported forms of "far eastern torture," like tying men by their queues to a stake for several hours. Xie Zixiu witnessed similar punishments at EPRM mines, including chaining workers' feet, confinement in dark spaces, and the withholding of food. Mine managers strenuously denied Boland's charges of torture. Tellingly, they did not deny the floggings but claimed that Boland had exaggerated the numbers, and they placed the blame for extreme cases on Chinese policemen. Boland's article was widely cited throughout Great Britain.[41]

Chapter 10

The Price of Gold

T he use of corporal punishment showed not only the attitude of mine managers; it also indicated the workers' resistance to the conditions of their labor. One could say that the social crisis on the mines resulted from a spiraling dynamic of resistance begetting punishment, punishment begetting more resistance begetting yet harsher punishments, and so forth. Contrary to all expectation of stereotype, the Chinese laborers were not docile. They refused to work with mean bosses and took breaks by deserting for a day or two. At one mine, workers cut down by three inches the measuring rod used to gauge the day's work. Chinese also did not, in general, work overtime, despite management exhortations and financial inducements.[1]

Most broadly, the Chinese resisted by simply not drilling as many inches as their bosses demanded of them. The engineering consultant William Honnold complained that Chinese labor "efficiency is distinctly disappointing. It has so far been impossible to get them beyond a certain point." In the parlance of industrial management the world over, Chinese workers were guilty of "loafing." In one blatant example, a laborer on the night shift at the Nourse Deep Mine "would drill only 24 inches to insure receiving pay and then would go away from his working place to sleep." An observer remarked that Chinese trammers and shovelers

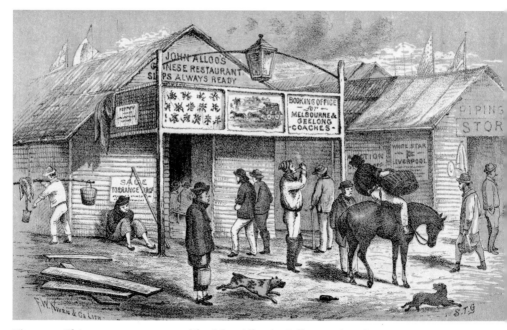

Figure 13. Chinese entrepreneurs, like John Alloo in Ballarat, Victoria, ran restaurants that served both Chinese and European miners.

Figure 14. Chinese communities contributed to building infrastructure in goldfield towns, including hospitals and asylums, and proudly marched in fundraising parades. Ballarat asylum fete, 1875.

Figure 15. Political cartoonist Thomas Nast associated anti-Chinese racism in California in the 1870s with New York City's Irish draft riots of the Civil War. "Columbia—'Hands off, Gentlemen! Americans means Fair Play for All Men.'" *Harper's Weekly,* February 18, 1871.

Figure 16. A race riot in Rock Springs, Wyoming, in 1885, rampaged through the mines and burned the town's Chinese dwellings, leaving twenty-eight Chinese dead and four hundred homeless. Illustration by Thure de Thulstrup for *Harper's Weekly,* September 26, 1885.

Figure 17. Nativists in Australia imagined themselves as a small outpost of the British Empire in Asia, threatened to be overrun by the Chinese Empire's "yellow trash." *Bulletin,* 1895.

Figure 18. Australian nativists also projected images of Chinese in monstrous racial stereotypes. "The Mongolian Octopus—His Grip on Australia," *Bulletin,* 1886.

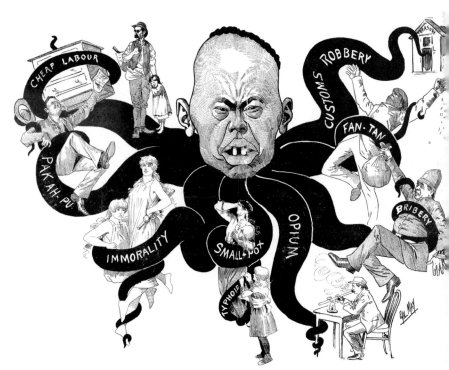

Figure 19. Huang Zunxian (1848–1905) was a scholar, poet, and diplomat who served as Qing consul in San Francisco, Singapore, and Japan. Huang is at center, with Japanese friends, undated photograph.

Figure 20. Zhang Deyi (1847–1918), served in the Qing foreign service for forty years. He began as a student-translator, as shown here in 1866, then traveled to the United States and Europe with the Burlingame mission in 1868. He capped his career as ambassador to Great Britain in 1902. He negotiated the treaty that governed the Chinese labor program in South Africa.

Figure 21. On the Witwatersrand, Transvaal, indentured Chinese worked in deep underground mines, using hand drills to cut into the rockface. They were required to drill at least thirty-six inches a day, c. 1905.

Figure 22. The Simmer and Jack company contracted 4,200 Chinese to work in its mines on the Rand. Roll call, c. 1905.

Figure 23. Chinese laborers on the Rand organized festivals for Chinese holidays, including theatrical and musical performances. Postcard, c. 1905.

Figure 24. In the general elections of 1906, the British Liberal Party and its Labour allies used the Chinese Question as a major campaign issue.

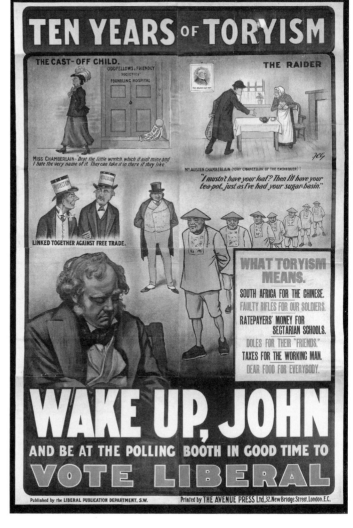

Figure 25. Contrary to stereotypes of docile and powerless coolies, Chinese in Anglo-American societies were real people who worked hard, adapted, and persisted. Muddy Creek, Waikaia, New Zealand, c. 1900.

worked at a much slower pace than their native counterparts, or simply sat down when the supervisor wasn't watching. They "wandered off on loafing expeditions" between breakfast and reporting to work.[2]

"Loafing" was pervasive, as indexed by managers' constant complaints and use of punishments meted out for failure to drill more than the minimum. In 1907 workers at a West Rand mine petitioned the Chinese government to protest punishments for loafing, which included the lash and the withholding of food. The biggest insult, they averred, was that the mine companies treated them not as human beings but as beasts of burden. They added, "Those who drill 3 feet, those who drill one or two feet, are considered loafers. . . . Even of those who could drill 8 or 9 feet, who would be willing to put in the extra effort?"[3]

Chinese mine laborers also resisted collectively. They resorted to riot in the compounds, mostly over wages and work conditions. In the first six months of the program, FLD superintendent Evans reported fourteen disturbances at eight mines. (It will be recalled that there were only ten mines using Chinese labor at the time.) Workers at several mines rioted when they received their first month's wages, which were shockingly low because the companies deducted for the advances the miners had received before embarkation and for the remittances they had signed up for. At Geduld Mine in October 1904, thirty-one workers refused to work with white miners who had "bullied and ill-treated" them and attacked a white supervisor. When police arrived to arrest them, workers turned out en masse to fight the police. After a mine explosion killed two workers on July 22, 1904, at one of the East Rand Proprietary Mines, the night shift refused to turn out and threw stones at mine officials. Other disturbances erupted against Chinese policemen, when meals were not served, and when pay did not arrive in time for holidays. Many incidents involved thousands of workers who fought compound guards and mounted police with stones, bricks, and jumpers (iron rods used to start a drill hole). Workers at Geldenhuis Deep rioted when the mine manager demanded they report for work at midnight on Sunday, their day of rest. The whole compound went into an "uproar"; the workers attacked the Chinese controller and a "furious mob" of 1,400 to 1,600 workers repelled nine European mounted police with jumpers and a "fusillade of stones." Only a second assault by the police, which charged the crowd while firing shots, pushed the workers back into the compound; one worker was killed and several wounded. There were fewer mass disturbances as the program went forward, which may be explained by the increase in individual forms of protest—filing complaints, deserting, loafing—that indicated the workers' adjustment to the reality of the three-year contract. Still, mass protests and rioting continued to take place, if less often, usually in situations where workers wanted immediate redress for a collective complaint.[4]

STRIKES WERE EXPRESSLY PROHIBITED under the terms of Ordinance no. 17, but they did occur. In October 1905 the entire Chinese workforce of three thousand at Witwatersrand Mine refused to work after workers failed to receive a promised wage increase. According to the *Rand Daily Mail*, there was "no trouble"; both shifts remained "quietly in their compound—on strike." Germiston police arrested 47 "ringleaders," charging them with refusal to work.[5]

The most sustained collective work action occurred at the North Randfontein Mine in April 1905. There were 1,965 Chinese workers at the mine and fifty or sixty headmen; more than thirteen hundred worked underground. The mine had a history of labor unrest. In August 1904, shortly after workers arrived on the mine, they had rioted over deductions taken from their wages, for which twenty headmen were prosecuted. By January 1905 desertions were so frequent that the FLD restricted workers to the property of North Randfontein and not the larger premises of Randfontein Estate's mines.[6]

The work action in April 1905 concerned wages. According to the contract, wages were supposed to rise by 50 percent after six months, to fifty shillings a month (or 1s. 6d. per day), but in March, seven months after the Chinese started working at North Randfontein, the average daily wage was still well below 1s. 6d. The company tried to argue over the meaning of the contract, but Lt. Governor Lawley admitted that the section on wages was "clearly understood by every Chinaman and . . . is a very powerful weapon in their hands."[7]

On March 29 the entire night shift drilled exactly twelve inches per man. Lawley called it a "strike," but more properly speaking, it was a "work to rule" action. For refusing to work or for striking, workers risked punishment; by working to rule, they used the letter of the law to diminish production. They reportedly beat into compliance their co-workers who drilled more than twelve inches. The action continued for two more days and nights. When on April 1 the company brought in police to make arrests, the workers set upon them with sticks, rocks, drills, and bottles. A local police officer commented on the tactical prowess of the Chinese: "Each time we charged them they waited for us and threw their missiles when we were almost on to them. All the horses and men were hit several times." The "general riot" lasted an entire day and included a group of several hundred workers who marched off the premises to recruit workers from two neighboring mines. The European police required reinforcements from three towns before they were able to quell the disturbance, drive the workers back to the compound, disarm them, and apprehend fifty-nine "ringleaders."[8]

The ringleaders were the headmen, who led the work gangs. When mine management finally conceded the wage increase, it attempted to wrest from the workers a higher level of output by offering the headmen bonuses for additional inches drilled by their gangs. The headmen refused the incentive to drive their men harder without remunerating the men themselves. When told they could not refuse, they all quit their positions and asked to be reverted to drillers. When the mine manager refused to accept their resignations, the headmen and workers took their action.[9]

The solidarity between the headmen and drillers and the effectiveness of the work action led management to offer a different wage structure. A new offer switched from the day rate to a piece rate system. Terms were finalized on April 14, at a half pence per inch up to thirty-six inches, with bonuses for more than thirty-six inches. As noted above, the daily average for Chinese on the Rand was upward of forty inches. The settlement appeared more generous and fair than all of management's previous offers. Selborne believed it improved the position of Chinese workers and recommended the piecework system for all the mines for work in situations where piecework was applicable.[10]

In fact, piecework removed wages from the supervision of the FLD, as the contract stipulated that piece rates were to be determined by "mutual agreement" between the mining companies and the Chinese laborers. In the coming months, mine managers stepped up their campaign against "loafing" by raising the daily minimum from twenty-four to thirty-six inches. This progression, known by piece rate workers everywhere as a speed-up, suggests that a significant number of workers did not care to drill more than the minimum required of them. The Chinese were not motivated to exhaust themselves simply for more cash. They might work harder when they needed more money, say, for new boots (which wore out after a few months and were expensive), but they seem to have moderated their efforts in light of the long term of the contract. Those with gambling debts knew their earnings would simply be taken by their creditors. In a way, they were similar to African workers, who also could not be motivated simply with higher wages because they were part-time subsistence farmers.[11]

The North Randfontein work action revealed several important qualities of the Chinese laborers: they were well informed as to their contractual rights and resisted being cheated; they were highly organized and capable of near-total solidarity; and they had a sophisticated grasp of tactics both in negotiations and in combat. Their solidarity was characteristic of those bred by lines of kinship, whether close relations or extended families and clan lineages, or the fictive kinship of secret brotherhood societies. In North China, the latter may have included association with the Boxer Rebellion.[12]

BETWEEN JULY 1905 AND JUNE 1906, the Foreign Labor Department reported 7,089 convictions of laborers for desertion from the mines, a rate greater than 10 percent. Desertions were highest in the summer months of January and February, when nearly eight hundred walked off the mines each month, although even during the cold months on the high veld more than two hundred men a month deserted. Regardless of the weather, it was difficult to survive for long on the outside because there was no alternate employment. Unlike the African mine deserter, who found another job or returned to his farm, the Chinese deserter eventually either returned on his own or was apprehended. But some managed to live off the mines for days and even weeks at a time, hiding in mines or outbuildings. A large group of forty to fifty deserters hid in a disused mine shaft on the Princess Mine in the West Rand for months before they were apprehended.[13]

Chinese who had secret relationships with African women might stay with them for extended periods. Rumors held that Cantonese merchants in Johannesburg provided "refuge and employment" to deserters. One worker (recorded only as "Coolie no. 38,695") held the record for desertions: he deserted six times between June 1905 and May 1906, including sojourns of twenty, thirty, and fifty-five days. For his transgressions, he spent a total of twenty-two weeks in jail. Mine managers reported with incredulity that No. 38,695 had been on the Rand for over a year but had logged only forty or fifty work shifts.[14]

While on the outside, deserters sometimes committed crimes against property and persons in order to acquire cash or goods. Some deserters resorted to thievery for personal survival; for others, theft was the object of their leaving the mines. For the same nine-month period, the FLD reported 136 cases of "outrages" against white persons, including house-breaking, theft, damage to property, assault, and murder; and twenty outrages against Africans, either in their own homes or while working in the homes of whites. Chinese also committed crimes against other Chinese as well as Indians and Jews.[15]

Chinese who committed crimes against shopkeepers, householders, and farmers acted in small groups and occasionally in large groups of fifteen or more. They were often armed with knives, sometimes with guns. They almost always acted at night, breaking into shops and homes by smashing windows with stones, bricks, or jumpers; at one store in Boksburg, they used dynamite, destroying the stone veranda. They took cash, from one to ten pounds, and goods that could be consumed or sold—sugar, clothing, watches; in one case, fifty pairs of trousers valued at twenty-five pounds. They slaughtered a sheep at one farm and stole from another "a calf and some mealies" (corn). They sometimes stabbed or beat storekeepers and householders who resisted them, inflicting serious harm on some, even death.[16]

Those apprehended by police were taken to jail and tried before the local magistrate's court. The Witwatersrand high court reviewed all convictions for serious offenses and issued sentences. Those convicted of murder were sentenced to death by hanging; in a few cases, the term was reduced to life in prison. The standard sentencing for theft was three to nine months' imprisonment, usually with hard labor. Conviction for assault carried additional time and sometimes a lashing if the crime was particularly nasty or perpetrated against a white woman.[17]

The number of Chinese who committed crimes against residents of the Rand was actually small—perhaps 1 percent of the total number of Chinese mine laborers. Viewed another way, however, there were on average nearly a dozen incidents a month, or three a week, involving housebreaking, assault, and theft. These incidents received sensational coverage in the local press and fueled the circulation of rumors in the countryside, inciting rural white Afrikaners to hysteria over armed coolies roaming the Rand. Louis Botha led a delegation of twenty Afrikaner leaders from the rural districts to meet with Lt. Governor Lawley in September 1905. They recounted numerous incidents with dramatic details; for example, thirty-two Chinese appeared on a farm at Sterkfontein, near Krugersdorp. The men were away; the women gave them all they asked for, and they took more and slaughtered a calf. Then the Chinese went to Hekport, where they met people with wagons, from whom they "took everything . . . and destroyed everything." There was "great unrest" among the farmers, who said they could not protect their property and families from large gangs. They demanded the immediate repatriation of all Chinese workers on the Rand, projecting the issue of Chinese labor back into the center of the colony's politics.[18]

THROUGHOUT 1905 the mining companies and industry observers lauded the introduction of Chinese labor on the Rand. The recruitment of cheap, unskilled Chinese labor had solved the problem of labor shortage, restored profits to prewar levels, and enabled the expansion of deep-level mining operations. By the spring of 1905, the *Engineering and Mining Journal* reported that working costs on the Rand had dropped two to three shillings per ton from prewar levels and that the "margin of profit is such and the scale of working is so great that [the deep-level] mines on the Rand are today paying out in dividends fully 30% of their total output."[19]

These achievements came at the price of a worsening crisis of labor discipline and social control. A number of factors made containment difficult: relentless pressure to maximize production; ineffective Chinese policemen; and political sensitivity to charges of "slavery." Mine managers and colonial authorities in South Africa grappled with the exigencies posed by the first two factors, whereas the colonial secretary in London considered the latter problem paramount. The differences in priority created rifts between London and Johannesburg that reflected growing tensions within the empire between imperial interests and those of the white settler colonies, tensions that had already led to the Australian colonies to seek autonomy as a federated dominion.

Lord Elgin, a Liberal who succeeded Lyttelton as colonial secretary in 1905, was especially defensive about the outcries in Great Britain about "Chinese slavery" in South Africa. He refused proposals from Johannesburg that seemed to violate the individual rights of laborers, at least the most blatant ones. He also made some proposals of his own, aimed at quashing charges of slavery, in particular that Chinese laborers were detained in South Africa against their will. The press reported that Chinese labor recruits included artisans who were unaccustomed to manual labor and were unaware of the work that lay in store for them in the mines. Although the Ordinance of 1904 allowed for voluntary repatriation at the worker's own expense (£17 6s., a considerable sum), it was said that many who wished to return home did not have the funds to do so. Elgin proposed that the government subsidize repatriation for any laborer lacking the funds to do so on his own. He believed such a provision would eliminate, "in one stroke," all accusations that the British were keeping Chinese on the Rand against their will.[20]

Mine managers reacted with alarm, predicting a mass exodus from the mines and collapse of the industry. Taking a different tack, Jamieson said that the laborers would interpret the proposal as a trick to undermine their contracts and send them home against their will. He believed it was impossible to convey the sincerity of Elgin's motives to the "suspicious Oriental mind." All those actually desiring repatriation, he added, would claim they had no funds. Finally, Elgin and Selborne agreed to a policy that gave the appearance that no one would be kept against his will, while shifting the question of assistance to a case basis. In early 1906 notices were posted in the compounds, informing the laborers that those wishing repatriation but lacking sufficient funds should submit a personal petition, which the superintendent would review and decide whether the government would grant the "gracious favour" of a subsidy. Jamieson added, "This is a matter of exceptional kindness, for which, of course, you ought to be duly grateful."[21]

Meanwhile mine owners and colonial authorities struggled constantly to combat the workers' resistance. At the mundane level, for example, Superintendent Evans considered breaking the large dining halls into smaller messes in order to limit workers' opportunities to conspire. To eliminate cheating, mine managers eliminated the stick method used to measure inches drilled and equipped supervisors with tape measures.[22]

More broadly they sought a major amendment to Ordinance no. 17 in order to more efficiently exercise discipline on the mines. Ordinance no. 27 of September 1905 authorized the FLD superintendent and inspectors to try certain cases on mine company premises rather than in the courts of resident magistrates. These included violations of Ordinance no. 17 (refusal to work, leaving mine premises without a permit, etc.) as well as criminal offenses "ordinarily summarily triable" by the magistrate court. FLD inspectors trying cases also imposed sentences on those they convicted. Ordinance no. 27 further required mine owners to establish lockups for holding laborers before trial. The ordinance did more than shift judicial authority to the mines; it revealed a system of penal sanction for labor discipline. By June 1906, FLD proceedings had tried and convicted some twelve thousand cases involving desertion, traveling without a permit, fraud (faking leave permits or altering work tickets), insulting a superior, and other infractions of the labor ordinance.[23]

The new law also sought to break the solidarity of Chinese workers, first, by requiring headmen to report to management all infractions of labor discipline committed by their workers, on pain of conviction and a fine of five pounds; and second, by authorizing the imposition of a collective fine against the entire gang or section for the conviction of one worker (a provision that Elgin thought legally dubious). In cases where a fine was imposed, the mine company was required to withhold wages and to pay the fine directly to the FLD. This provision eliminated the laborer's option to choose jail time over paying a fine. Many workers preferred jail—when sentences were for a week or two, they were a break from work, which resulted in overcrowded local prisons and lost work time. The ordinance added to the list of punishable violations the use of fraud or deception (forging passes, cutting the measuring stick). The amendments of 1905 also stiffened the rules against opium possession, and a follow-up law, Ordinance no. 12 of 1906, proscribed gambling. Gambling had not been originally prohibited, owing to advice that "all Chinese gamble" and that it was a normative feature of Chinese work camps and compounds. But authorities came to believe it had spiraled out of control.[24]

Finally, Ordinance no. 27 empowered the FLD to cancel the contract and repatriate any laborer believed to be a "danger to the exercise of the proper control of labourers on any mine." Under the original terms of the labor program, repatriations resulted from cases of illness or criminal conviction. The new ordinance gave the FLD unilateral power to repatriate anyone it considered a "bad element" without due process or even the employer's consent. Under these powers, the FLD aggressively removed all those considered undesirable, repatriating several thousand Chinese accused of being gambling racketeers, corrupt policemen, suspected homosexuals, and other "scoundrels," as well as those guilty of more ordinary infractions, including desertion and refusal to work.[25]

DESPITE VIGOROUS EFFORTS to repatriate bad elements, the Foreign Labor Department was unable to quash the growing sense of social crisis on the mines. Two moral panics erupted in 1906, one concerning alleged homosexuality among the Chinese and the other in response to assaults on Afrikaner farmers by Chinese deserters. The panics, especially the latter, proved crucial in unleashing public opposition to the Chinese labor program.

In July 1906 a white Transvaal resident, Leopold Luyt, while visiting London made statements to a member of Parliament and to the Colonial Office about "immoral" and "unnatural vice" practiced by Chinese laborers on the Rand. Luyt claimed that Chinese were frequent customers of European brothels in Johannesburg (the principal violation here being not the purchase of sex but purchasing it from a European). More alarming were Luyt's allegations that same-sex practices among Chinese laborers were widespread on the mines, conducted openly in the bunkhouses and in plain sight on the veld. The prospects of negative publicity and a fresh moral panic prompted the governor to appoint J. A. B. Bucknill, a minor Transvaal official, to conduct a formal inquiry.

Bucknill reported that Chinese solicitation of European women occurred but on rare occasion; and that homosexuality among Chinese mine laborers existed but was neither extensive nor practiced openly. With the flair of an anthropologist, he acknowledged that same-sex practices existed the world over, from England and Europe to China, and noted that "amongst some Oriental peoples this vice is not regarded with the same abhorrence as is evidenced toward it by Western nations." Mine managers and controllers claimed to have no direct knowledge of same-sex practices on the compounds, although some reported hearsay that it took place secretly in places like deserted mine shafts. There was also hearsay that on every large compound, as many as a half-dozen men worked as prostitutes (charging two shillings); these men were thought to come from the "lowest classes," that is, "actors and barbers." Mine doctors reported that although syphilis was widespread among the Chinese laborers, the disease rarely resulted from same-sex relations. Bucknill concluded that Luyt's allegations had been wildly exaggerated and while that same-sex practices existed among the Chinese, they were not "prevalent in any abnormal or grave degree." Moreover, he believed that they were conducted in "so private and unnoticeable a way" that their detection and eradication would be "extremely difficult."[26]

Lord Selborne's office also made inquiries among local mayors, clergy, and other officials. Their replies generally corroborated Bucknill's findings. The results of the inquiry put Selborne and Elgin in a bit of a quandary. They considered releasing Bucknill's report to preempt a public scandal but decided against it because the report affirmed that same-sex relations did exist, even if they were not widespread. At Elgin's request, Selborne wrote a strongly worded letter affirming the Transvaal government's commitment to "stamp out this execrable crime" and to repatriate all "moral undesirables," which entered the record as political cover for the Colonial Office. Meanwhile the FLD closed a half-dozen theaters on the compounds, believing them to harbor "catamites," and rounded up 166 suspected homosexuals for repatriation. The ordinance of September 1905 relieved the FLD of proving charges before a magistrate's court. The FLD simply asked mine managers to report all those they deemed to be of questionable sexual morality and put them on the next outbound ship.[27]

If Selborne and Elgin dodged a major scandal over "unnatural vice," they continued to contend with the ongoing moral panic on the Rand over Chinese "outrages" in the outside districts. To address the problem, the colonial government increased police presence on the Rand and directly enlisted white residents in a war against deserters. The South African Constabulary added 175 policemen around the Rand, bringing the force to four hundred. It operated in a "cordon system," patrolling constantly between posts and "inside the circle." In one week in August 1905, the police apprehended 243 Chinese who were off the mines without passes. The government armed the local Afrikaner population, which was, notably, the first time since disarming them after the South African War; spending nearly £5,300 for fifteen hundred rifles and shotguns to do so.[28]

Furthermore, Ordinance no. 27 authorized "any private white person" to arrest without warrant any laborer outside the Witwatersrand district and to deliver him to the nearest police station. By arming and deputizing the farmers, the government aimed not only to mobilize assistance for the task but also to quell the gathering storm of opposition among rural Afrikaners, who since the end of the war had nursed bitter resentment toward the British. Milner's reconstruction policies had delivered to them neither economic recovery nor a sense of racial security over the African majority. Historian John Higginson argued that these two dimensions of insecurity made poor rural Afrikaners particularly prone to mass hysteria and collective violence.[29]

The various measures taken under the amended ordinance represented an escalation of coercion but did not entirely establish control over
the situation. There were more desertions and outrages in the summer
months (December 1905 through February 1906), and a political crisis
loomed, with more Afrikaner deputations to the government, more mass
meetings in the towns, and a direct appeal by Louis Botha to Lord Elgin.
Hundreds of armed farmers joined the patrols of the South African Constabulary to search the hills for deserters.[30]

In March 1906 colonial officials consulted with mine owners about
the need to better guard their premises. The mine owners were feeling
defensive from public criticism over the seeming ease with which Chinese laborers deserted the mines; they in turn blamed the FLD and the
Colonial Office for insisting that the laborers "enjoy unrestricted and
absolute liberty of movement" on the mines during the daytime in order
to avoid the appearance of slavery. Lord Selborne convened a special committee to address the problem of desertions and outrages. It comprised
local magistrates, police officers, representatives of the FLD and Chamber of Mines, and the Chinese consul, in a rare instance of inclusion. The
committee assumed a moderate tone. It was careful to generally praise
the Chinese for cultivating a higher standard of living and comfort than
the natives and blamed the troubles on gambling and the prevalence of a
"low class" of men in the early stages of recruitment, including many of
the Chinese police. Its recommendations for better control included hiring more European compound police, better patrolling mine properties,
and repatriating "known bad characters."[31]

A committee of mine managers was more blunt. Its foremost recom-
mendation was to erect fences around the mine properties. It also urged
abolishing Chinese theaters in the compounds; cracking down on opium
and gambling; searching workers leaving their shifts for stolen dynamite, pickaxes, and the like; reducing interference of FLD inspectors in
mine management of workforce; imposing harsher penalties for deserters; paying closer attention to attendance, work tickets and leave permits;
making daily instead of weekly roll calls; and hiring white police to aug-
ment mine control.[32]

In May, Selborne urgently requested approval from the Colonial Office to erect fences on the Rand, emphasizing that deserters were not "unhappy workers" but "indebted gamblers." He argued, "The present difficulty arises not from any restrictions on the movements of the coolies, but from the almost total absence of such restrictions." But Elgin— ever sensitive to the charge of slavery—vetoed the idea.[33]

Jamieson despaired that control over the Chinese workforce could ever be established. He wrote wearily to Sir Solomon, the attorney general, "With the exception of Lord Selborne and yourself, no one in the Transvaal realizes how hopeless are the endeavors to lay hands on efficient human machinery for looking after the Chinese." Jamieson resorted to efforts to strike fear into the hearts of the Chinese. He wrote and posted a message in all the compounds, warning the Chinese of the consequences of bad behavior. He listed the names of fifteen Chinese workers who had been sentenced to prison for ten years or more; fourteen "scoundrels" hanged for conviction of murder; and sixteen others who had been shot dead in the course of disturbances or during the commission of a crime. "When your contracts have expired," he intoned in language he thought appealed to Chinese, "you can all joyfully return home, whereas they will have to languish for life or tens of years in an alien gaol, separated by thousands of miles of sea and many intervening mountains from parents and children, whom they will possibly never see more again. . . . Take warning by the fate of these men, and . . . remember that this is a country of law and order, and that all offenders will be most rigorously punished."[34]

In a similar vein, Jamieson wanted to bring Chinese witnesses to the execution of four laborers, who had been convicted and sentenced to death for the murder of Piet Joubert, an Afrikaner farmer at Moabsvelden in August 1905. When the hangings were scheduled in October, Jamieson believed that the mere announcement of the executions would not be believed, "whereas ocular demonstration and the subsequent spreading of the news . . . would have a most beneficial effect." Solomon balked at the idea of compelling anyone to witness an execution, but he authorized "two or three friends of the unfortunate men" to be present if they so desired. The condemned men submitted the names of eight friends, who were brought to Pretoria for a last visit. The government's act of "grace," inspired by a "spirit of compassion," backfired, however, when the visitors returned to the compounds and told their fellow workers that the men had been "innocently condemned." Jamieson issued a "notice forbidding the spreading of rumours," to which he appended the last depositions made by the men as evidence that they had acknowledged their guilt. In fact, only two, Qin Xiangsheng and Liu Huari, had confessed to the crime. The other two, Wang Zhongmin and Xu Houlong, had deposed, simply, "All is finished; All is finished; Fate has ruled it to be thus." Jamieson did not disclose what, if anything, the men said when led to the scaffold. They may well have uttered the phrase that was heard from "almost every condemned man" who was hanged on the Rand: *qu liao*—"I have been wronged."[35]

Chapter 11

The Asiatic Danger in the Colonies

Superintendent Jamieson was right when he declared that supervising Chinese mine laborers was a hopeless endeavor, at least insofar as such supervision had to satisfy both mine production goals and local demands for public safety while, at the same time, not looking like slavery. By 1906 the pace of local and metropolitan politics was fast outstripping the efforts of Jamieson, Solomon, and Selborne to bring order to the Rand. The Chinese labor problem became something quite larger than the specific demands of the mining labor program. It assumed the incendiary symbolic force of the "Chinese Question," building on a half-century of European experience with Chinese emigration to New World settlements while also imbuing it with new features and, in the process, perfecting a global anti-Chinese ideology.

In 1906 and 1907 the Chinese Question on the Rand emerged as a key issue in two major political elections: the general election in Britain and the election for responsible government, or home rule, in the Transvaal. Both elections brought new parties into power that spelled the speedy demise of the Chinese labor program and, moreover, influenced broader political trajectories. In Britain, the Chinese Question helped the Liberal Party overturn more than twenty years of nearly unbroken Conservative rule and galvanized the trade unions to form the Labour Party, which would by the time of the Great War eclipse its Liberal ally as the main opposition to the Tories. The emergence of Labour as an independent political force was inextricably linked to a self-conscious identity that placed it at the center of an imperial white working class. Labour not only acted in solidarity with British workers in the settler colonies, it also expressed a self-interested vision of the colonies as destinations for working-class emigration as a hedge against domestic economic uncertainty. The trade union movement put its own stamp on social imperialism, claiming it from Milner and Chamberlain in a more class-based, yet eminently racialized, politics.[1]

In the Transvaal, the Chinese Question emerged as a common complaint among diverse interests, which hurt the political fortunes of the establishment Progressive Party, dominated by the mining interest. It proved a sensational issue that helped stir Afrikaans-speaking voters to the new Het Volk party organized by the former Boer commandos Jan Smuts and Louis Botha. Het Volk won the election; a few years later, in 1910, Botha would be premier of the newly federated Union of South Africa, with Smuts in his cabinet. Their ascent signaled the electoral strength of Afrikaners in South Africa, even as Afrikaner politics would remain diverse across the subcontinent, from racial hard-liners in the Orange River Colony to moderates in the Cape Colony. Notably, Botha, and especially Smuts, while advocating for white supremacy and racial segregation, committed themselves to the mining interest and more broadly to British imperialism.

South Africa was the most bluntly racist of the British settler colonies. But it was of a piece with Canada, Australia, and New Zealand, all established as dominions of the British Empire, the concept of "dominion" signaling not a colony but a polity akin to a country, and one that indeed signaled its own dominion over native peoples. Dominions possessed maximum autonomy within the British Empire, which protected the rule of local white settlers while conveniently distancing the metropole from the openly racist modus operandi of native removal, racial segregation, and Asiatic exclusion—tenets of white settlerism that had, in fact, been forged in the United States.

⚜

IN THE TRANSVAAL, the Chinese Question brought to the fore basic questions concerning what kind of society white South Africans thought they ought to be building: what should be the route to prosperity and the substantive benefits of white supremacy; the structure of race relations, both between the English- and Dutch-descended populations and between whites and native Africans; and South Africa's relationship to the British Empire. These questions had remained unresolved after the war; the Chinese Question brought simmering tensions to the fore.

Milner's postwar reconstruction policies emphasized industrial development (especially mining), large-scale agriculture, British immigration, and governmental reform. He advocated a native race policy that was "color blind" with regard to the franchise, as practiced in the Cape Colony (where property qualifications in effect excluded nearly all native and colored men from the polity), but was also based on state mobilization and discipline of labor. In the Transvaal, however, the native franchise was effectively foreclosed by the Treaty of Vereeniging, which had settled the South African War. A provision of the treaty delayed the matter until the election of responsible government, that is, a government elected by whites. The British also disarmed natives (who had fought on the side of the British during the war) and removed them from land they had expropriated from the Boers during the war.

Although these measures signaled British intention to reconcile with the defeated Afrikaners, Milner's reconstruction policy did little to improve their economic situation, especially among poor Afrikaners. The quickening of capitalist agriculture had dispossessed many tenants and pushed increasing numbers of them into the towns. Few Afrikaners possessed the skills of the English-speaking miners, whether from Cornwall or New South Wales, who dominated the ranks of white workers on the mines— but neither could unskilled whites compete with Africans in unskilled mining jobs, domestic service, and other menial jobs in the towns, whose wages were typically three or four times less than those paid to unskilled whites. After the war, the urban poor relied on government-subsidized employment on public works for subsistence, but this was not a long-term solution.[2]

Jan Smuts told Selborne that with the Transvaal in a "wretched state," the mines ought to "strengthen the position of the white population in the country. . . . If yellow labour were abolished plenty of whites would be found willing to work in the mines, and the mines as well as the white population would prosper." But the Randlords persisted in their belief that using white labor in unskilled jobs would simply be too costly to be profitable, especially in low-grade gold mining, for which the labor cost per ton was highest. Many Afrikaners believed that the government's show of favoritism to the mining interest had brought the Chinese to South Africa and worsened the problem of white unemployment and poverty—not to mention exposing farmers to "outrages" committed by Chinese who deserted the mines.[3]

The trade unions also opposed Chinese labor. Despite skilled British miners' privilege on the mines and in local society, they bore many grievances: seasonal unemployment, a high cost of living, and miner's phthisis (silicosis), the "white death," which became common with the introduction of underground machine drilling in the 1890s. Skilled workers also resented efforts by the mining companies, led by their engineers, to wrest from them control over production and to increase productivity. Rather than enjoying unalloyed prosperity and privilege, these workers viewed their situation as precarious.[4]

While the unions feared that Chinese would creep into skilled positions and depress the wages of whites, their larger worry was that such a trend would lead to native Africans working in semiskilled and skilled jobs. In fact, at some mines Africans did work in semiskilled jobs, and mine owners might well replace much of the white workforce with far cheaper black labor. Since the 1890s, the unions had tried to codify an occupational color bar, but they were as yet unsuccessful. The Chinese labor program's explicit exclusion of Chinese from all but unskilled mining labor was the first of its kind.[5]

The trade unions' view was shared by British elites, who believed the future prosperity of the white population in South Africa lay in the continued immigration of skilled British workers, not in the employment of poor whites in unskilled jobs, which they imagined to be the province of Africans. They believed that only a strict racial division would preserve whites' high status—as Milner had famously said, "We do not want a white proletariat in this country." The American mining engineer Ross E. Browne, who consulted for the Corner House on the Rand in 1905, recognized the importance of racial segregation on the mines. Browne's father was J. Ross Browne, who surveyed western mines for the U.S. government and served as American envoy in China. Neither father nor son had a history of racial animus toward Chinese. But in South Africa, the younger Browne wrote, "A distinct line of separation in the duties of skilled white and unskilled coloured labour is of paramount importance.... Only in this way that a high average wage of skilled labour can be maintained, and a desirable status for the white man can be upheld." The other side of this calculus was that employing Africans in unskilled work kept overall labor costs low.[6]

By advocating for the employment of unskilled whites on the mines, Afrikaners did not mean that they were willing to work side by side with Africans in the mines, doing the same work. The Afrikaners would have sent Africans back to the farms to work under white control. The agricultural sector, both Afrikaner family farms and large-scale British-owned farms, competed fiercely for African labor as sharecroppers and wage workers, respectively. As the Transvaal became increasingly industrialized and urbanized, whites' demands for African labor grew.[7]

THE MOST VOCAL CHAMPION of employing unskilled whites in the mines was Frederic H. P. Creswell, a mining engineer and former manager of the Village Main Reef mining company. Creswell, born in Gibraltar to a British official and trained at the Royal School of Mines, worked in Venezuela, Asia Minor, and Rhodesia before settling on the Rand. He was an ardent and persistent critic of the mining industry's use of Chinese labor. Like the unions, he aimed his fire at the big groups that dominated the Chamber of Mines and their backers in colonial government. Because he was both an insider and an outsider to the industry, the Randlords spent considerable energy trying to discredit his claim that he had profitably employed unskilled whites at Village Main. Some critics charged that he had falsified or distorted his data. Creswell in turn accused the Chamber of Mines of inflating the number of workers needed on the mines, and hence the cost of labor. He argued that mining could be profitable with a different calculus that involved fewer men working more efficiently and with greater use of machinery. Creswell understood the general tendency that capitalists with access to cheap labor that was plentiful and controllable (enslaved, indentured, undocumented) had little incentive to mechanize.[8]

Creswell's larger point was that the big mining groups and their overseas financial investors based the industry on the indenture of very cheap, colored labor in order to make the greatest profits and to return the greatest dividends in the short term. The same interest drove "speculative and share-market" practices by absentee financial corporations, such as holding undeveloped mining lands in order to drive up property values rather than develop them into producing mines, which required investments of capital and time. Pecuniary interests of the financial sector now held the "very real power, over the destinies of the Colony," interests that could not be expected to have "any genuine sympathy with the real political feelings and aspirations of the people for the Colony." Creswell advocated for a colony "in which white men of every class are welcomed" and not just a small class of wealthy whites who controlled both politics and the economy.[9]

The white labor position had a democratic sheen insofar as it criticized the mining magnates for practices of monopoly and indenture. But its vision of democracy was for whites only, shaped by the idea that was central to South African politics, that South Africa was a "white man's country" or, more precisely, a country ruled entirely by whites. This view was held across the white political spectrum, from liberal paternalism in the Cape Colony to racial hard-liners in the former Boer republics. The requirements of sustaining white minority rule, however, especially with increased industrialization, steadily pushed politics to the right. A South African writer, I. Dobbie, wrote, "The theories of the Social Democrats cannot be put into practice in a case like this without the disappearance of the highest in the lower. So long as the black preponderates and is at a lower level of mental culture, so long must South Africa be an oligarchy and not a democracy. . . . For the white man to descend to the level of the Kaffir and to share his avocations would be suicidal from a racial point of view."[10]

There was, in fact, a history of unskilled whites working in the mines, both before and after the South African War, and not just at Village Main Reef. In the early 1890s, John X. Merriman experimented with unskilled white labor on the Langlaate Estate. He hired "first-class" Cornish men on contract for drilling and shoveling, but after a month they had not earned enough to subsist. For many mine managers, the problem was not just cost but their opinion that unskilled whites were an inferior class of workers, unreliable and "extremely incompetent." In fact, some 2,300 unskilled whites were working on the mines when the Chinese labor program began. But the government mining engineer acknowledged that with Chinese labor, mine managers no longer felt any compulsion to hire whites in unskilled jobs.[11]

THE ARGUMENT AGAINST Chinese labor was not just that it cost whites jobs. Critics believed that an additional, if not greater, danger lay in the prospect that indentured Asian labor would lead to a settled Asian population of merchants and traders. The use of indentured Indians on the Natal sugar plantations was an object lesson in the consequences of importing indentured colored labor. Indian indenture had led inexorably to a free, settled population, including merchants and traders who undersold white businesses. By 1905 there were more Indians than whites in Natal, and they were migrating to the Transvaal. Whites worried that the small population of Chinese merchants in Johannesburg would likewise grow, especially with an indentured labor force potentially offering an ethnic market. They warned that the "imported Asiatic gains a grip on a country with wonderful rapidity." Although Natal passed laws to restrict immigration of Asiatics, the colony was "a back door wide open" because indentured Indian laborers were not required to repatriate at term: "the indentured coolie of to-day is the free man of tomorrow, and the free man becomes the trader."[12]

In a sense, South Africa presented the same geographical problem as Australia, where plantations were not on isolated tropical islands but in provinces that were contiguous to more temperate areas. Dobbie articulated the common racialist argument about the Indian and Chinese that complemented the theory of "cheap Asiatic labor" with a theory of the "underselling Asiatic trader." The Indian, he said, "industrious, thrift, with no wants, with the acute, over-trained brain of centuries and the commercial immorality from the same cause . . . have overmatched the

Kaffir at every turn and undersold the European." They held the retail trade in fruits and vegetables and were "formidable competitors" with small English traders. Dobbie considered the Chinese an even greater threat: the "hardest-headed businessmen in the world, older by several centuries than the Indians; their industry is proverbial, their plodding patience with small profits inimitable—all very good qualities in themselves but dangerous to introduce into a land occupied already by two different races, of which one is too uncivilized, and the other too impatient, to exercise them." Dobbie's reasoning reflected the crisis in contemporary Social Darwinism, which had, by the late nineteenth century, begun to worry that the white race might have become overly civilized and hence gone soft. He warned that Chinese would oust Africans from lowly employment and poorer Europeans from all the petty trades. Some went farther, predicting that the Chinese could intrude "even into the ranks of the greater merchants," as they had in Hong Kong and Singapore.[13]

Agitation against Chinese and Indian traders in the Transvaal predated the labor importation program. Alleged competition rationalized additional head taxes and restrictions that had been imposed by the ZAR Volkstaad. In 1902 white storekeepers on the Rand formed the White League with the chief concern "to prevent any coloured Oriental from setting up a rival store and underselling them." The White League succeeded in driving Indian traders out of many towns along the reef. When Chinese labor was proposed in 1903, the league joined the fray, making the link between Chinese traders and labor. "It was absurd," railed E. O. Hutchinson of the league, to say that Chinese would be employed only in unskilled labor. Once imported, they would become "proficient" and then would take over all the skilled jobs from the whites, and the Chinese compounds on the mines would become "fetid" Chinatowns filled with the fumes of crude opium.[14]

Opposition to Chinese labor fed nationalist politics and opposition to South Africa's ties to the British Empire. The South African Party (formerly the Afrikaner Bond), a politically moderate group, gathered in Cape Town in January 1906 to protest accusations made in the British press that Afrikaners were disloyal to Britain. In fact, they plainly advocated cutting ties to the empire on grounds of British interference in Transvaal affairs. The meeting welcomed an address by John X. Merriman, who had long opposed importing Chinese labor. Most tellingly, Merriman predicted that, "Sooner or later, English opinion would insist on the removal of the restrictions on the coolies, then good-bye to the chances of the white man." In fact, English opinion against indentured Chinese labor was already mobilizing.[15]

✻

THE BRITISH GENERAL ELECTIONS of 1906 brought the Liberal Party and its Labour allies to power, ending twenty years of nearly unbroken Conservative rule. The watershed election has received considerable attention from historians of British politics, but there has been scant analysis of the role that the Chinese Question played in the Liberal-Labour victory. Traditional accounts, when they consider it at all, describe it as "emotive if somewhat ephemeral," that is, as uncharacteristic of British temperament and anomalous to the key, substantive Liberal issues of free trade and education policy. To be sure, controversy over Chinese labor in South Africa shot into British politics with seeming suddenness and alacrity in 1904, only to seemingly disappear from prominence after the elections. Yet perhaps more than any other election issue, the Chinese Question galvanized support for Labour candidates, who took seats in traditionally Conservative districts where workers had historically voted Tory. These victories were critical to the Liberal-Labour landside and were all the more important because they reflected the late nineteenth-century expansion of the franchise and the unionization of unskilled workers. While both parties courted working-class voters, in 1906 Labour announced its arrival as an independent political force and hastened the official formation of its own political party. If the Chinese Question was the powerful symbol that motored this achievement, the question remains, why was it so potent? If the Chinese Question performed some kind of ideological work for British labor, we ought to ask, in service to what ends?[16]

The core of Liberal opposition to Chinese labor in South Africa was the view that Chinese labor had been brought to South Africa under conditions "akin to slavery." In this view, it represented a stain on the honorable tradition of British abolitionism, a tradition held dearly by both

radicals and religious nonconformists in the Liberal Party. The "slavery" trope pervaded debate as early as 1904, when plans for the Chinese
labor importation ordinance were drawn, and continued through 1905–
6, during the run-up to the general elections. The opposition found it
a blunt instrument to attack the Conservative-Unionist government by
linking the moral tradition of abolitionism to the recent sacrifices made
by British soldiers (50,000 casualties) and taxpayers (£250 million spent)
in the recent war against the tyrannical Boer republics—waving the
bloody shirt, as it were. The trade unions adopted the antislavery refrain.
In March 1904 a mass demonstration of the British Trade Union Congress gathered eighty thousand people in London's Hyde Park to oppose
the passage of the Chinese labor importation ordinance. The congress
declared its "emphatic protest against the importation of forced, fettered,
and cheap labour into South Africa, such importation being a violation
of the principles of Trade Unionism," and it appealed to the "previous
splendid record of our race" in "freeing the civilized world from slavery."[17]

Criticism of the program reached a crescendo of outrage in late 1905 and
early 1906 after the metropolitan press revealed the flogging of Chinese
laborers on the one hand, and Chinese desertions and crimes committed
against white farmers, on the other. The Liberal Party connected the two
developments in a single indictment of a disastrous policy: "We brought the
Chinamen into the mines and we cannot prevent them from being at once
the victims and authors of lawlessness." A furious debate ensued in the press
and on the floor of Parliament over the alleged abuses of Chinese mine laborers. Lyttelton, the colonial secretary, claimed the charges were either lies or
exaggerations—citing assurances from mine managers—but soon there
were too many reports and corroborations for the government to dismiss.[18]

Frederick Mackarness, an Englishman living in South Africa, wrote to
the *Westminster Gazette* (a Liberal publication) that he supported the use
of Chinese mine labor but not flogging and tying laborers up, practices
that he said were "not rare or secret, but open, if not general," adding that
he had seen photographs of coolies tied up. "If the casual visitor can see
these things, why cannot a government inspector?" he asked. "If not slavery, what is it?" By early 1906 the Chinese Question elicited more excite-

ment than any other issue at Liberal campaign rallies; the Sunday *Sun* commented that "no subject attracts more interest at public meetings" (Figure 24).[19]

Notwithstanding the embarrassment, Conservatives attacked the Liberals for hypocrisy and for using the Chinese Question for partisan purposes. They fought back with a deluge of newspaper reports and pamphlets of their own, with photographs of clean quarters in the compounds and the like, while also invoking the protections of the contract. They warned that the withdrawal of Chinese labor would ruin the colony's future prosperity. A typical Conservative leaflet succinctly iterated the reasons to support the government's policy: "to assure the solvency of the youngest British Colony, . . . [to] refuse to consent to the degradation of British workmen by making them work side by side with Kaffirs in the mines, . . . [and] because there will be 150 more places open to British skilled labourers for every 1,000 Chinamen who go to the Transvaal."[20]

But the charges of Liberal hypocrisy and partisan opportunism were not far off the mark. Skeptics of the Liberals' "vapourings" pointed out that indenture had long been a feature of imperial policy; indeed, Liberals had authored the legislation governing indentured labor in British Guiana. The Liberals countered that Chinese indentured labor on the Rand bore no resemblance to indentured labor in the plantation colonies. They argued that the latter had, over the course of the nineteenth century, been reformed by extensive state regulation; moreover, the government, not private interests, administered the Guiana contracts. (This is not to say that Indian indentured labor rights in British Guiana, the West Indies, and Mauritius were honored other than in the breach; but the appeal to legalism and contract, long obsessions of English political culture, had satisfied public opinion.) By contrast, the Radicals averred, the Chinese Labor Ordinance contained few explicit labor protections, excluded Chinese laborers from all other employments, and required repatriation at term.[21] The Radical Liberal MP John Burns explained further,

It is no excuse to say that indentured labor has been sanctioned before. Where it has been, the labour performed has been agricultural or pastoral, and not accompanied by the loathsome compound system, with its physical restriction and its moral degradation. This differentiates all other indentured labour from what is now being imposed upon Africa, and makes that the industrial slavery it is.[22]

The Chinese ordinance's "general tenour," Burns continued, "is based on force, compulsion, penalties, restrictions. Confinement is, in a word, the negation of personal freedom and industrial liberty, and is for the benefit of one side only—the mine magnates."[23]

The Liberal opposition to "slavery" was also hypocritical insofar as it did not support free labor, free immigration, or equal rights for Asians in the settler colonies as alternatives to indenture. Its proposed solution was exclusion. If Indian coolies settled in the Caribbean colonies after their contracts expired, they were exercising their rights as imperial subjects. More important, they posed no competition for British workers or shopkeepers, who did not emigrate to the tropics. But the presence of Asiatics in the settler colonies was another matter. Liberals' moral opposition to "Chinese slavery" in the Transvaal conceded to, while also giving cover to, the belief that British working men were, by their own rights of empire and race, entitled to populate, work, and prosper in the settler colonies of Canada, Australia, New Zealand, and South Africa. It was an article of faith that they could not exercise their rights if they had to compete with Asiatics.[24]

English emigration to the colonies was not new, of course, as it dated to the first colonizations in the New World in the seventeenth century and then, after the American revolution and the Napoleonic wars in the early nineteenth century, the more systematic development of Canada and Australasia. Assisted emigration to the Australian colonies in the 1830s and '40s to increase the laboring population and to address the sex imbalance created by convict transportation is well known. John Stuart Mill famously supported emigration and colonization for the "future and permanent interests of civilization" as well as providing a practical solution to domestic overpopulation. From the 1860s, British trade unions and elite reformers (especially neo-Malthusians) explicitly advocated for emigration as a strategy to raise domestic wages and to combat the danger of socialism. Emigrants did not really need official prodding or assistance; in the 1870s and '80s as many as 250,000 people a year were leaving the British Isles. Notably, however, more than half of British emigrants were going to the United States and not to the empire's so-called settlement colonies. By the 1890s emigration had slowed considerably, down to as little as ten thousand a year to Canada.[25]

Although Charles Dilke celebrated the Anglo-Saxon affinities of the United States and Britain in his triumphalist book *Greater Britain* (1869), proponents of a Greater Britain in the 1880s and '90s were interested in strengthening the ties between Britain and its settler colonies, not the United States. The issue gained increasing importance in British politics, owing to twin concerns that responsible government (self-rule) was leading the colonies to drift away and that the United States and Germany were emerging as formidable economic competitors. Some advocated a formal imperial federation, others an "alliance of independent states." Regardless of specific proposals, there was broad consensus that emigration and trade with the settler colonies were vital for strengthening both empire and the self-governing colonies.[26]

By the turn of the century a new vision of imperialism emerged, with Colonial Secretary Joseph Chamberlain staking the empire's future not on its traditional jewel, India (which through the nineteenth century had carried the burden of Britain's balance of trade), but on the settler colonies. Richard Jebb hailed the shift as "marking a fresh epoch" in imperialist thinking. Jebb focused on the synergies of nationalism and imperial patriotism that defined colonial identity, but the more hardheaded iteration envisioned population and economic growth in Canada, Australasia, and South Africa based on emigration and tariff reform to protect British and dominion products. These policies, together with the City of London's leading role in global finance and credit (based not least on gold), were seen as the keys to British competition against rising American and German industrial might.[27]

None of the parties during the 1906 election campaign promoted emigration. As a strategy for combatting domestic poverty, it was eclipsed by the belief that the time for domestic social reform was nigh (especially old-age pensions), although social insurance was decidedly a nonissue

during the elections. But emigration as a working-class prerogative arguably lurked behind the trade unions' emotive embrace of the Chinese
Question. The question of colored labor in the colonies had not been an
issue in domestic labor politics in the past, but by the turn of the twentieth century the British working class was more closely linked to emigration circuits in the empire. British labor in the colonies was not an
abstraction. There was enough historical and contemporary connection
to emigration, especially in certain industrial regions, that even those
who did not intend to go abroad likely had relatives or otherwise knew
people who had emigrated or contemplated emigrating. These long-
standing circuits of migration laid the basis for what sociologist Jonathan
Hyslop has dubbed the "imperial working class." Far from being ephemeral or merely symbolic of Conservative-Unionist rule, Asiatic exclusion
in the colonies spoke directly to the perceived material interests of British
workers—wages, job competition, and standard of living.[28]

Britons did not usually speak explicitly of, or dwell on, the racial character of the settler colonies. Viewing the colonies as direct offspring of
the mother country, they simply assumed them to be inhabited by whites
or, rather, by those of the "British race," a special branch of European
civilization. Contemporaries called them "settlement colonies" to distinguish them from India and the plantation colonies. They considered
them to be colonizations based on transplantation (natural and benign),
not colonialisms based on conquest (problematic but bringing a duty to
uplift). Seeley had emphasized that colonization spread British civilization, whereas colonialism involved incommensurable difference, and
hence conflict, between British and "natives."[29]

British emigration throughout the empire carried ideas about race and
civilization generated not only from the metropole but from settler experiences as well. The Transvaal attracted British settlers from across the
empire, and those with experience with "coloured labor" in other locations
were quick to claim authority on the Chinese Question when it emerged on
the Rand. The Australian case wielded particular influence on white South
Africans' thinking about the Chinese Question. If anything, the "White
Australia" policy seemed to make even more sense in the South African con-

text. The Australian and New Zealand parliaments took the unusual steps of commenting on the affairs of another colony in 1903, when they passed resolutions opposing the importation of Chinese labor to South Africa, and prime ministers Deakin and Seddon sent a joint telegram to London expressing their concern. By 1905 an English writer predicted, "Apprehension of such consequences [Chinese competition in labor and commerce] has evidently been by far the most potent cause for the exclusion of this race from Australia, and a similar fear will almost certainly unite the white people of South Africa in precluding coolies from permanent settlement."[30]

More directly, recent Australian emigrants to the Transvaal personally carried racial politics with them from the antipodes to the Rand. Australians were visible in the ranks of skilled labor in the Transvaal and in the leadership of the unions; the most prominent, Peter Whiteside, head of the Witwatersrand Trades Council, was born in Ballarat. Whiteside co-authored the minority report of the Transvaal Labour Commission in 1903, disagreeing with the majority's endorsement of Chinese labor. For white South African labor, Australia offered the model of a "militantly egalitarian polity, backed by an interventionist state."[31]

But if the Australian case inspired Transvaal trade unionists, it was a negative exemplar for elites. Percy Tarbut, a director of Consolidated Goldfields, conceded to Creswell that among the mining magnates, "the feeling seems to be one of fear that, having a large number of white men employed on the Rand in the position of labourers, the same troubles will arise that are prevalent in the Australian colonies, viz., that the combination of the labourers will become so strong as to be able to more or less dictate not only on the question for wages, but also on political questions by the power of their votes when a representative government is established."[32]

White laborism also operated through the Cornish diaspora. In 1905 there were seven thousand Cornish miners on the Rand, nearly 45 percent of all skilled mining labor. Many Cornish miners in South Africa had previously worked in Australia or the United States, like Tom Matthews, the leader of the Transvaal Miners' Association. Matthews had worked in the United States and was a socialist member of the Montana legislature. Adding to these loops, white South Africans also traveled around the settler colonies and back to the metropole. Creswell's writings were known in Australia, and he personally stumped in England during the election season, speaking at trade union rallies and receiving wide coverage in the press. The secretary of the White League, one MacDonald, made a grand "anti-Chinese crusade" to Australia, New Zealand, and Britain in 1906, the latter specifically to help the Liberal Party during the elections.[33]

The conflict between white labor and capital was, at one level, over the distribution of resources and power within the context of the white settler state. Milner had once pointed out the obvious fact that a "white man's country" as a "practical statement was practically useless" in South Africa, where Africans outnumbered whites five to one. What it really meant, he explained, was that "the white man must rule." The white labor constituency promoted a vision of "white rule" that was democratic and not, as in Milner's vision, dominated by the mining interest. At another level, racial nationalism expressed the view that racial entitlement unified national identity and purpose across class lines. Charles Pearson had sounded this theme with the 1893 publication of *National Life and Character*. Pearson warned that the "temperate zones" were the last and only hope for the white race under global population pressure from Africans and Asians. If not excluded by force of law, the argument went, Asiatics would inundate and overwhelm the white settler colonies with cheap labor and commerce. In the global context, Australia was the central battleground between two races, the European and Chinese, for domination. Pearson's analysis was rehearsed *tout court* in Britain during the election season. For example, M. A. Stobart wrote that what was at stake in South Africa was the "existence of the country as a Colony of Great Britain or as a dumping ground for Asia." The Transvaal, with its temperate climate and riches, must be preserved as a "nursery for the highest form of civilizing influence the world can boast."[34]

If the Liberal Party made easy use of the Chinese Question during the election campaign by invoking the moral authority of abolitionism, its embrace by British labor may be explained perhaps less by the symbolic politics of antislavery than by the emergence and circulation of an imperial working-class interest that was defined in no small part by Asiatic exclusion. British workingmen may have thought it extreme that Chinese coolies would be imported to the Welsh mines, as David Lloyd George predicted, but they were alarmed by stories of British emigrants living in abject poverty on the streets of Johannesburg, their unemployment supposedly the result of Chinese labor. They were their kith and kin, figuratively and literally. When the Liberal candidate Thomas Horridge campaigned in Manchester, audience members shouted out, "I had two relatives in South Africa supplanted by Chinese" and "I have a son in South Africa engaged in hunting Chinese [deserters]." (Horridge spectacularly defeated Prime Minister Arthur Balfour in his home district.) If the trade unions' primary election program was for domestic social reform (old age pensions, unemployment insurance, etc.), racial protectionism in the colonies could be seen as another kind of statist reform, a government guarantee that the peripheries of the empire would be reserved for British settlement. In fact, emigration between 1903 and 1913 rose to unprecedented levels, with over 3 million people leaving England for the colonies, half of them bound for Canada, the closest of the dominions.[35]

It may credit the Liberals with too much political savvy to suggest that they drummed up the Chinese Question in order to motivate working-class voters, that they understood that labor's material interest in the colonies would be just as salient, if not more than, the moral appeal of antislavery. The Chinese Question did conveniently obscure the fact that the "Liberal programme offered virtually nothing to the working-class electorate" in terms of social reform. In the event, the Chinese Question consolidated working-class interest in preserving the settler colonies as white. Moreover, by constructing a unified racial interest among British workers across the empire, the Chinese Question provided a source of domestic support for the racial logics that underlay settler-colonial home rule, federation, and dominion, processes that were already in motion but not yet fully settled.[36]

THE CHINESE QUESTION was a prominent feature in discussions over the bringing of responsible government (self-rule) in the Transvaal. Metropolitans and white South Africans alike agreed that self-government was the goal for the South African colonies, but the timing of elections depended on many things, including the state of Anglo-Boer relations and the progress of reconstruction. Self-government was also a step toward the larger goal of South African federation. Local British and Afrikaner political figures (if not their popular constituencies) both supported reconciliation and union, but the terms of sharing power would have to be negotiated.[37]

The controversy over Chinese labor during the general elections in Britain provoked protest among whites in the Transvaal that London was violating the principle of colonial autonomy by interfering in local affairs. These protests continued after the Liberals took office, especially after the colonial secretary, Lord Elgin, issued policies to freeze licenses for importing Chinese, which stopped all new recruitment, and to subsidize repatriation of any Chinese laborer who wished to return home. Elgin was trying to walk a narrow path between satisfying domestic demand to immediately end Chinese "slavery" and Transvaal insistence on noninterference. In fact, Elgin was not eager to abruptly terminate the program, mindful of the mining companies' warnings that the industry would suffer. More broadly, deferring the decision to an elected responsible government was befitting to a strategy not just of noninterference but of distancing London from the racial policies of the colonies.[38]

Between 1905 and 1907, four main parties competed in the Transvaal in the runup to the elections for responsible government. Three of them—the Nationalists, with roots in the Rand Pioneers, an old *uitlander* white supremacist group; the Labour Party, headed by Creswell; and Het Volk (The People), led by Botha and Smuts—represented diverse interests, but they agreed on the Chinese Question, which crystallized opposition against the mining industry's power over Transvaal affairs. It was especially potent for Het Volk, which had formed in 1905 and was striving to revive Afrikaner politics around self-government, language rights, and the "poor white" problem. The fourth party, the Progressives, was the British establishment party representing the mining interest, led by two of the biggest magnates, George Farrar and Percy Fitzpatrick. They alone supported the use of Chinese labor, as well as a more limited form of self-government in order to prevent a possible Afrikaner electoral majority.[39]

During the election campaign, the Chinese Question provided a key motive for cooperation between the Nationalists, Het Volk, and Labour against the Progressives. They agreed to not oppose each other in districts where their candidates overlapped, and in some cases, they campaigned together. These alignments show the evolution of South African politics, in which British and Afrikaner ethnic distinctions were becoming secondary to a white "national" interest. As much was noticed by the conservative-leaning British *Saturday Review,* which criticized the Liberal government for having "deliberately armed those [Afrikaners] whom we conquered, not with Mauser rifles, but with the more deadly weapons of constitutional power. . . . [They] will gradually push the British out of all posts of emolument and power."[40]

The elections for responsible government held in February 1907 resulted in Het Volk winning a majority of seats. The Progressives won one-third, the Nationalists won 10 percent, and Labour, less than 5 percent. Creswell was defeated, but he would win in 1910 and remain the leader of the Labour Party into the 1930s. Louis Botha became prime minister, and Jan Smuts the colonial secretary. In one of its first acts, the new government terminated the Chinese labor program save for existing contracts, which it allowed to run out by 1910.[41]

THE SMUTS-BOTHA GOVERNMENT enacted legislation restricting new Asiatic immigration as well as the rights of Indians and Chinese already residing in the colony. The Transvaal Immigration Act of 1907, modeled on Natal's, required prospective immigrants to pass a literacy test in a European language. A second law required fingerprinting and registration of all Asiatics. The Chinese Association, led by Johannesburg Cantonese merchants, and the British Indian Association, led by M. K. Gandhi, both hotly opposed the requirements, but they perceived their interests differently. The Chinese claimed the law violated their rights under Anglo-Chinese treaties; China's formal position as a diplomatic equal to Britain gave the Chinese a sense of racial superiority to Africans and "colored" people. The Indians believed their status as British subjects set them apart from others.

Previously, each group had protested anti-Asiatic measures separately.

But in 1907 they came together in what Gandhi called an alliance of "strange bedfellows." In April Chinese leaders met with Gandhi in his office, where they discussed Gandhi's proposed *satyagraha* campaign of passive resistance. The following month Gandhi spoke to a large meeting at the Cantonese Club in Johannesburg. The Chinese agreed to the principles of peaceful disobedience, including their willingness to submit to "extreme penalty of the law, namely liability to imprisonment and also to boycott the permit [registration] office." Nine hundred Chinese signed a document committing themselves to the resistance; the Chinese consul-general Liu also wrote to Gandhi expressing his support. Gandhi acknowledged the unity and resolve of the Chinese in his newspaper, *Indian Opinion*. In fact, Chinese were well versed in the boycott tactic. They had deployed it in the 1850s against discriminatory taxes in Victoria, Australia, and more recently in Shanghai and other Chinese cities, to protest the exclusion laws in the United States.

In the Transvaal, the two groups picketed registration offices and spoke at each other's meetings, while also organizing their own communities. By the time of the November deadline for registration, only 8 percent of the Asian population in the Transvaal had complied. Over the course of the next few months, the government arrested and convicted over two thousand Chinese and Indians for not having registration permits, including Gandhi and Leung Quinn, head of the Chinese Association, who were both imprisoned. Jan Smuts agreed to a compromise agreement in February 1908, providing for voluntary registration and no fingerprinting, but he then reneged on his promise to repeal the registration act. The Chinese, who had voluntarily registered, publicly burned their papers. Leung Quinn was arrested and jailed several times over the next two years and was deported in 1910.[42]

The matter was not resolved until after the federation of the four colonies as the Union of South Africa in 1910. As was the case with federation in Australia, South Africa moved with due haste to impose restrictions on Asiatics. The Indian Question was of paramount importance, owing to the large population in Natal and, increasingly, in the Transvaal. The Chinese Question had diminished in importance after the repatriation of virtually all Chinese gold mining laborers by 1910 and previous exclusion laws that limited Chinese immigration across the colonies.

Jan Smuts, now a key figure in the Union cabinet, consulted with Gandhi and others and made a few concessions. He released from prison Indians and Chinese who had been convicted of noncompliance with registration. In 1911 the registration requirement was modified to exempt educated persons and to accept a signature in lieu of a fingerprint. The Immigration Act of 1913 was based on the literacy test pioneered by Natal and adopted by the Transvaal. It gave immigration inspectors discretion in applying the test: in some cases a simple signature sufficed to admit a European, while a dictation of fifty words in a European language might be used to exclude an unwanted Asian. For good measure, South Africa ended indentured labor importation in order to stanch Indian population growth and recognized only Christian marriages, to prevent Indians from immigrating their wives. The law also included provisions that allowed for immigration checkpoints between the provinces. That was intended to keep Indians out of the Cape and the Orange River Colony, but its greater application would be to control the internal mobility of native Africans.[43]

IN GENERAL, Botha and especially Smuts committed to the British Empire and to the mining interest. With the notable exception of a limited native franchise, many of Milner's reconstruction policies were realized under Afrikaner-majority rule. The resolution of the Chinese Question cleared the way for white South Africans to tackle the underlying problems of mine labor—the recruitment and retention of African labor and the employment of unskilled whites in mining—while ensuring that South Africa would be built as a "white man's country." The ruling party of Botha and Smuts, now named the South African Party, implemented a social order based on systematic racial segregation, the term copied from the American South but with distinctive South African features. Most important, the Native Land Act of 1913 outlawed native land ownership and tenancy on all but 7 percent of the land, which was designated as "reserves." Never large enough for Africans to be agriculturally self-sufficient, they were envisioned as "sovereign" entities under the rule of tribal chiefs. Calling them sovereign "homelands" was but a thin veil over a massive dispossession intended to finally sever Africans from the land and turn them into a migratory proletariat for mining and urban employment. Residential and occupational segregation and the notorious pass laws sustained the system. The repeal of the colored franchise in the Cape Colony foreclosed the possibility that Africans would be members of the polity.[44]

The mines continued to import African workers, principally from Mozambique. In 1910 the number of African mining workers on the Rand was already over 143,000, more than twice the number in 1904, and it would reach a peak of 200,000 in 1928. The number of Afrikaans-speaking workers on the mines also increased. They were not employed in unskilled jobs, for which there were now adequate supplies of African labor, but in skilled positions, in part to replace the British immigrant workforce decimated by silicosis. (Because it takes time for the dust particles to accumulate in the lungs, the deadly disease did not become apparent among Afrikaners until the 1920s.) In time Afrikaner workers constituted 50 to 75 percent of the white mining workforce; they became assimilated into the white industrial working class and brought their own traditions of militancy to the trade union movement. But the "poor white" problem persisted—white unemployment in Johannesburg remained at 25 percent throughout the 1920s.[45]

Both processes of native dispossession and working-class formation were marked by ongoing labor strife and rural unrest through the Great War and into the 1920s. The mining industry's continued efforts to reduce the cost of white labor through wage cuts, layoffs, and the introduction of native Africans into semiskilled positions provoked militant strikes in 1913 and 1914 and a general strike and armed revolt in 1922. On more than one occasion Smuts called out the army to put down striking workers. African workers, although legally forbidden to join trade unions, nonetheless organized their own unions; in 1920, seventy thousand struck for nearly two weeks for better wages. They, too, were brutally suppressed.[46]

⊕

THE CONSOLIDATION OF Asiatic exclusion in the United States and in the British settler colonies perfected an ideology that cast all Chinese as a "coolie race" and as "slaves" regardless of status or condition. To be sure, a precise definition of slavery eluded the 1906 British election campaign; vague phrases like "general tenour," "feeling of slavery," "conditions akin to slavery," "partaking of slavery," and the like studded the writings and speeches of critics. When asked to define "slavery," John Burns resorted to citing the American experience. Burns quoted the California state constitution, that "'Asiatic Coolieism is a form of human slavery, and is forever prohibited in this state, and all contracts for Coolie labor shall be void'." Even as individual contracts were voided, Burns continued, Chinese were free to live and work where they liked. But they had become a "moral menace and industrial evil" such that their importation, whether free or under contract, had to be prohibited altogether.[47]

In this way the Chinese Question circumnavigated the Anglo-American world, justifying immigration exclusion with a theory that defined "slavery" not as a mode of property and exploitation but as a racial condition. "Slavery" remained the central organizing concept of a global discourse against Chinese immigration. Americans and British alike opposed the "slavery" of the Chinese—but did not support their freedom.

PART IV

THE CHINESE DIASPORA
IN THE WEST

The myriad nations all trade with each other;

So how can the Chinese be refused?

—HUANG ZUNXIAN,
"EXPULSION OF THE IMMIGRANTS"

Chapter 12

✳

Exclusion and the Open Door

I n July 1900 the Chinese minister to the United States, Wu Ting-fang, published an article in the *North American Review* arguing that immigration and trade were matters of "mutual helpfulness" between China and the United States. Wu listed the major American imports to China in the late nineteenth century: cotton goods, kerosene oil, and other consumer goods, and more recently, iron and steel products, especially train locomotives. Appealing to American business interests, he observed that there were enormous opportunities for further American trade and investment in China, from manufactured goods to railroads, mines, harbor improvements, street lighting, and other infra-structural works, now that China was "fast . . . getting into the swing of the world's forward movement."[1]

Every nation conducted its foreign trade on the basis of self-interest; yet, Wu pointed out, "transactions cannot be one-sided affairs, for the simple reason that it takes two to make a bargain." Confucius had deemed "reciprocity" the guiding principle of life, what Americans would agree was the "golden rule." But "true reciprocity demands the 'open door,'" wrote Wu. Yet China "is singled out [by the United States] for discrimination and made the subject of hostile legislation. [China's] door is wide open to the people of the United States, but their door is slammed in the face of her people."[2]

Wu was not the first to argue against exclusion from the standpoint of commerce and reciprocity. Since the mid-nineteenth century, opponents of exclusion, both Euro-American and Chinese, had argued that migration and trade went hand in hand. Cut off the former, they warned, and the latter would suffer. But if the notion that exclusion would harm trade was a fixture in the debates over the Chinese Question, there has been little examination of the actual effects of exclusion on commerce and trade. Answering this question requires a consideration of its various dimensions. Exclusion had both direct and indirect effects on global trade and commercial relations, in different realms of economic activity, and at different scales. One aspect concerns the effects of exclusion on Chinese merchant trade and capital investment in the United States and the British settler colonies. Another lies in the consequences of exclusion for China's foreign trade. A further question lies in the consequences that the adoption of gold as the international monetary standard had for China, which remained on the silver standard, for its balance of trade and its general position in the global economy.

MOST DIRECTLY, exclusion meant fewer outlets for Chinese merchants and investors abroad. Chinese merchants operating between China (and Hong Kong) and Australia and the United States settled into ethnic markets, which were not inconsiderable but remained outside the commercial mainstream. During the 1850s, Chinese merchants and shipping entrepreneurs in both San Francisco and Hong Kong had enjoyed a lucrative business in the export of all manner of goods from China to California— not just the proverbial teas and silks but also granite, lumber, flour, cotton goods, and other consumer items for the general population. Chinese also profited from shipping; a few purchased their own vessels and others consigned ships from Americans. Through the 1870s, Chinese merchants and shippers carried passengers (in both directions); imported rice (a $1 million-a-year business), tea, and opium; and exported wheat, flour, ginseng, mercury, and "treasure," including Chinese miners' gold dust and bullion sent by European and American banks.[3]

China remained one of San Francisco's three largest trading partners until at least 1880. By that time there were twenty-five Chinese-owned import-export firms in San Francisco doing business with Hong Kong. Each of the most prosperous was worth a half-million dollars, and many had seats on the city's Merchants Exchange, including seven who were stockholders. Some successful Chinese miners and merchants invested in mining operations through the 1870s, but they never had access to large-scale capital projects. Their roles in agriculture and urban manufacturing were limited to tenancy and subcontracting, respectively.[4]

Anti-Chinese animus and the exclusion laws adversely affected Chinese immigrant merchants and small capitalists in myriad ways. The shrinking Chinese population meant a shrinking market. There were discriminations. San Francisco's fire insurance companies began canceling their policies with Chinese business owners in the 1870s. The city passed numerous laws to harass Chinese businesses, such as the ban against walking on a sidewalk with a pole on one's shoulder and the notorious laundry ordinance, which discriminated against Chinese-owned washhouses built from wood.[5]

During the late 1880s and '90s, the Bureau of Immigration changed its interpretation of the exclusion laws, expanding the definition of *laborer* and narrowing the definition of *merchant*. In the early 1900s, it treated arriving merchants with newfound hostility, detaining them, interrogating them, and in many cases denying them entry. Wu Panzhao (Ng Poon Chew), editor of San Francisco's *Zhongxi ribao* (Chung Sai Yat Bo) claimed that the "ill treatment" of the merchant class produced "irritation and unfriendly feeling" that was "disastrous also to commercial interests. Because of the injustice all the great Chinese merchants, who formerly paid one-third of the customs duties at the port of San Francisco, have gone back to China or do business in other countries." In the early twentieth century, there were just a handful of successful Chinese capitalist enterprises in the United States—a few large-scale commercial farmers and cannery owners, one bank (Canton Bank, established in 1906 in San Francisco), and one steamship company (the China Mail, established in 1915 in San Francisco).[6]

In Australia, Chinese capitalists in the 1870s invested at a larger scale in mining and plantation agriculture in the far north, but by the turn of the century these opportunities narrowed as immigration restrictions constrained the availability of Chinese labor, upon which they depended.

The Australian historian Paul Griffith argues that elite Anglo-Australian interests chose to destroy the economy of the Northern Territory rather than let Chinese develop it. After federation, Queensland, with substantial capital already invested in agricultural development, replaced Chinese and Pacific Islander workers with white workers at higher wages supported by government subsidies. Public health officials introduced new theories that countered older ones about white racial degeneration in the tropics, theories that had long served as an alibi for using colored labor. Raphael Cilento, head of the Australian Institute for Tropical Medicine, boasted in 1925 that white men thrived in the tropics with hard work, cleanliness, and "purity of race." In this view, nonwhites, formerly deemed biologically able to endure the tropics, were now considered too dirty and germ-ridden to benefit from medical progress in the prevention and treatment of tropical disease. In Melbourne and other southern cities, Chinese remained confined to the ethnic market, with just a few niches that served non-Chinese consumers: garden farming and furniture making. Cooktown, which had thrived as a port connecting northern Queensland to Singapore and Hong Kong, declined after 1890.[7]

But Chinese storeowners persisted in Australia. Many were able to obtain exemption certificates in order to immigrate partners and family members, which sustained and even grew their business. Taam Sze Pui's eponymous store in Innisfail, See Poy, was the largest department store in northern Queensland. He was also was a successful banana and sugar planter in Fiji and the New Hebrides. Taam thus had a hand in two exceptional areas where Chinese Australian capital found success—department stores and the banana trade. Another successful retailer, Hong Yuen, ran a successful dry goods store in the small town of Inverell, in northern New South Wales. From there he established a chain of "cash and carry" stores throughout the NSW-Queensland border region, which his family operated at least until the 1930s.[8]

But other Chinese retailers left Australia for better investment opportunities in Hong Kong and China. Ma Ying Piu (Ma Yingbiao) left Sydney in 1900 to found Sincere, the first department store in Hong Kong. The brothers James and Philip Kwok (Guo Le and Guo Quan), who owned a fruit and nuts store in Sydney, left Australia and established the Wing On department store in Hong Kong in 1907. Both Sincere and Wing On would soon expand to Shanghai's fanciest shopping district, Nanjing East Road, and establish veritable retail empires with branches from Jakarta to Macao to Singapore.⁹

Chinese Australians' success with department stores in Hong Kong and Southeast Asia was part of a larger trend that redirected the energies of Chinese emigrant labor and capital. Notably, migration from southern China to Southeast Asia dramatically increased after 1870 and reached a peak around the turn of the century. Southeast Asia had a long history of Chinese trade and settlement dating to the seventeenth century, with Chinese economic partnerships based on kinship or fictive kin relations establishing in trade, mining, and farming. In the early nineteenth century, Europeans adapted to these structures, as the Chinese adapted to new demands and opportunities with the spread of sugar, tea, and coffee plantations.¹⁰

The late nineteenth- and early twentieth-century booms in tin mining and rubber production for European industrial markets required ever larger numbers of workers. The tin mining industry in Malaya and in parts of the East Indies relied not only on Chinese labor but also on ethnic Chinese capitalists known as *toujia* (towkay), who financed labor recruitment and small Chinese mining companies that were the mainstay of tin mining. Both Chinese and Indian migration networks played a vital role in the development of an interdependent Southeast Asian economy involving Burma, the Straits Settlements, Malaya, Siam, French Indochina, Dutch East Indies, and the Philippines. Migration to Southeast Asia from India was comparable to that from China, about 14 million between the 1890s and 1938.¹¹

At comparable scale, migration from northern China to Manchuria numbered some 25 million between the 1890s and World War II, in response to Russian and Japanese industrial and mining development in the region. Chinese migration to Manchuria comprised both permanent settlement and seasonal labor. As we have seen, the recruitment of northern Chinese for the Transvaal mining program resulted from the disruption of the seasonal labor market in Manchuria during the Russo-Japanese War. Some Chinese who were excluded from the United States

and Canada diverted to Mexico and Latin America; however, restriction-
ist sentiment followed them, so those communities remained small.[12]

Exclusion thus resulted, first, in greatly diminished economic opportunities for Chinese merchants and capitalists in the West; and second,
in the concentration of Chinese labor and mercantile emigration to
Southeast and North Asia. The first did not directly cause the second,
but neither are the two trends merely coincidental. Both were integral to
a broad reorganization of global migration in the early twentieth century:
British settler emigration to the white dominions; eastern and southern European emigration to the industrializing centers of the West; and
Asian migration to the colonial economies of Southeast and North Asia.
The new ethno-racial patterns of migration were not simply spontaneous
responses to labor and capital market demands. Rather, they resulted
from a confluence of political and economic measures that directed labor
and commercial energies in certain directions and not others.

These actions included negative policies, such as Chinese exclusion, as
well as positive ones, such as deliberate efforts to divert British emigration
from the United States to Canada and the tireless work of industrialists, agriculturalists, labor agents, and shipping companies to recruit labor for states
and employers. In some cases, they built on older migrations but at a far
greater scale (British emigration to Canada, Chinese to Southeast Asia); in
other cases, new migration streams developed (Italians to the United States
and Argentina). Once these patterns were established, they reproduced
through ongoing demand and chain migration. A global redivision of labor
resulted from the exigencies of Euro-American capital, nations, and empire.

Global migration in the early twentieth century is also notable for the
decline in the use of Asian indentured labor. The use of Chinese and Indian
coolies, established in the 1830s in the wake of slave emancipation in the
European plantation colonies, waned in the late nineteenth century and was
practically eliminated by World War I. The Qing ended Chinese indenture
to Peru and Cuba in the 1870s after its investigations into the condition of
Chinese labor. The Transvaal gold mining project of 1904–10 was one of
the last contract labor programs sanctioned by the Chinese government,
although subterfuge and corruption underwrote a sporadic practice in other

African colonies as late as the 1920s. Indian indentured migration to the Caribbean declined in the late nineteenth century but actually increased between 1890 and 1910 as the British mobilized Indians for work in new colonial plantations areas (sugar in Natal and Fiji, rubber in Malaya).[13]

Notwithstanding, around the turn of the century indentured Asian labor became increasingly untenable, politically and economically. Indians and Chinese workers protested their conditions, sometimes with strikes, as did metropolitan and colonial reformers, most famously Gandhi in Natal. In Malaya, European capital took direct control over the tin industry with larger holdings, mechanization, shorter contracts, and voluntary labor edging out the towkay; emigration of Chinese on three-year labor contracts destined for Singapore and Penang began to decline after 1890.[14]

In general, indentured labor became harder to sustain when workers had other options. Indians and Chinese from Guyana to Natal to Malaya established themselves after their contracts expired as free persons, working for wages or starting small farms and businesses. Rubber producers in British Malaya and French Indochina, finding indentured labor insufficient, switched to free wage labor by 1910. This is not to say that harsh labor conditions or social discriminations ceased to exist. The rubber and tin mining camps in Malaya, for example, were notorious for mean conditions.[15]

A similar observation can be made about the eastern and southern European laborers who provided the brawn for the industrialization and urbanization of the United States in the late nineteenth and early twentieth centuries. Although the Foran Act of 1885 outlawed foreign contract labor, new European immigrants still toiled as unskilled and low-wage labor in a segmented labor market, lived in ethnic enclaves, and suffered myriad discriminations. Like their counterparts in Southeast Asia, many (upward of 50 percent) were seasonal or temporary migrants, who worked abroad to earn remittances. Although Asian labor migrants were presumed to be indentured coolies and Europeans were presumed to be voluntary immigrants and wage workers, they bore many basic commonalities in the early twentieth century.[16]

⁜

THE IMPACT OF the exclusion laws on China's trade with the Anglo-American world varied. The differences can be seen in the case of tea, long China's number-one export item. The primacy of the tea trade dated to the early eighteenth century, when the British needed a Chinese product to purchase in exchange for silver. By the late nineteenth century, tea was still China's largest export; in 1874 it accounted for 55 percent of total exports. Silk was second, at 15 percent. The preponderance of these items signaled China's lack of interest in or necessity for a diverse export-oriented economy. Yet as China imported more foreign products (opium accounted for over 40 percent of all imports in 1867), tea and silk exports were important to its balance of trade.[17]

Between 1886 and 1905, the volume of China's annual tea exports fell by more than half, from 246 million pounds to 112 million pounds. China's export of tea to Great Britain, Australia, and the United States declined dramatically, though for different reasons. The British began cultivating tea in India (Assam) around 1840 as a replacement for Chinese tea in order to improve its balance of trade position with China—part of the same strategy that drove the opium trade. It took some time to establish Indian tea, but by 1857 India was exporting one million pounds of tea; with increasing production in Assam and the introduction of Ceylon tea in the 1880s, tea from the subcontinent steadily took over the British home market. By 1905 China supplied just one-fortieth of the tea consumed by Great Britain. Hosea Morse of the Chinese Maritime Customs lamented that India tea—plantation grown, industrially processed, and capable of two "equally robust" infusions—had rendered English taste "so perverted and insensible of the delicacy and cleanness of flavor characteristic of the Chinese tea that the market can never be recovered, even at reduced price."[18]

Australians, who were said to drink more tea per capita than any other country in the world, including England, continued to buy tea from China until the late 1880s, despite British efforts to advertise Indian tea as the "patriotic" beverage in the antipodes. Chinese tea was cheaper and considered to be of superior quality to India tea. Australians did not follow British practices in lockstep. It was after the Afghan affair of 1886 that Australians switched their tea allegiance. In New South Wales, Chinese tea consumption dropped by nearly 60 percent between 1888 and 1897, part of a general decline in Chinese exports to Australia. A contemporary analyst noted that hostility toward China "outweigh[ed] . . . all other considerations, including those of a commercial nature."[19]

During the same period when Chinese tea exports to Britain declined, British imports into China more than doubled, in part a result of the opening of more ports to foreign trade. By 1903 Britain had established a trade surplus of 35.5 million taels (£5.3 million) with China. In keeping with general trends, British economic activity in China and Hong Kong increasingly concentrated on service industries, especially finance. British banks in Shanghai and Hong Kong absorbed Chinese capital and invested it in Southeast Asia and elsewhere.[20]

Americans drank far less tea per capita than their British counterparts, but tea was also the single largest import from China to the United States. As a share of total tea imports to the United States, China's share fell from 65 percent in 1867 to 23 percent in 1905. The shift went not to India but to Japan, especially after the U.S.-Japan Treaty of Commerce and Navigation of 1894 and was likely not a direct consequence of anti-Chinese animus as in the Australian case.[21]

In contrast to Great Britain, the United States continued to run a trade deficit with China at the turn of the century. However, the volume of the U.S.-China trade was small, as was overall American foreign trade in the late nineteenth century. Yet, American elites, worried about overproduction and the closing of the frontier, looked to the Pacific for new markets, especially China. Hence American strategists advocated for building naval power, the colonization of the Philippines, and an open door policy in China, all of which aimed to achieve a better competitive position vis-à-vis European and Japanese interests in the Asia-Pacific.[22]

The value of American exports to China grew from $3.6 million in 1895 to $53.6 million in 1905. Cotton cloth was the most important (accounting for 57 percent of the total in 1900), followed by kerosene, wheat flour, and tobacco. Around the turn of the century, the United States began to export to China iron and steel products, especially train locomotives and machinery, and after 1913 the U.S.-China trade rapidly expanded again, with more diverse American producer and consumer goods, including paper, cars and train carriages, electrical machinery, chemicals, drugs, and rubber manufactures.[23]

＊

THE DECLINE IN SILVER PRICES relative to the price of gold in the late nineteenth century had a direct impact on China, whose monetary system continued to be based on silver when the gold standard came to dominate international trade. The declining gold-price of silver meant that China's imports were costlier. This was a vast change in China's position from the late sixteenth to the late eighteenth centuries, when it was not only the largest economy in the world but also dictated the terms of trade in the emerging global economy. Silver from the world's two major producing regions in the late sixteenth and seventeenth centuries, Japan and Spanish America, poured into China, drawn by the latter's need for silver for fiscal and commercial purposes. Andre Gunder Frank estimates sixty thousand tons of silver went to China between 1545 and 1800, about half the world's production for the period. The drive for silver arbitrage underwrote the early modern silver trade from Japan and the Americas and the East India Company's brutal colonization of India and the draining of its silver in the eighteenth century.[24]

These were difficult levers for the British to maintain, especially as the silver arbitrage advantage slowed by the late eighteenth century. Britain (now hooked on tea) faced a balance of payments deficit—hence its decisions to grow opium in India for sale in China, to use gunboats to open Chinese ports to foreign trade, and to produce tea in India. Britain rewrote the rules of the game by reversing the flow of silver and by establishing sterling (that is, gold) as the medium of international trade. This was, above all, a feat of empire, which involved subordinating its various colonies' trade and monetary interests to those of the metropole. Most notably, Britain manipulated India's currency and trade (net deficit to Britain, net surplus to the world) and used the colonies as export markets for British goods and capital investment.[25]

The City of London—the Bank of England as well as numerous private banking houses like Barings and Rothschilds—was the center of the international financial transactions that fueled the expansion of the global trade and investment. It was also the world's largest gold market. Beginning in the 1870s, because of Britain's preeminence in international finance and the high transaction costs of trade for nongold countries, the European powers and the United States switched from silver or bimetallism to the gold standard. That movement was a response to Britain's command of global finance and trade, but it was made possible by the increase in the world's supply of gold. Thus the British imperial standard became the international gold standard.[26]

Classical economists lauded the gold standard for its anti-inflationary character, which promoted price stability and international trade cooperation. But the theory masked the historical and political relations that powered the viability of the gold standard. Moreover, the gold standard does not advantage every sector; because gold is relatively scarce, it favors creditors over debtors. The international gold standard accelerated European investment in their colonies and enabled them to exploit the flexible monetary arrangements of nongold countries, especially as the gold-price of silver declined in the late nineteenth century, China being but one case in point. Domestically in the gold countries there were also losers, especially farmers, who depended on credit. In the United States that problem fueled the great political controversies over greenbacks (fiat money), gold, and silver during the late nineteenth century. Britain's aging domestic industrial plant suffered from want of updating because capital fetched far higher returns on investment abroad, although the British mitigated the problem by exporting wares at artificially high prices to its colonies, at least until World War I.[27]

The movement of the advanced capitalist countries of the West to the gold standard in the 1870s involved their demonetization of silver and, as a consequence, a glut of silver on the world market at falling prices relative to gold. Britain addressed this problem in part by its control over India, which it kept on silver: while depreciating silver currency favored exporters and Britain's balance of international accounts, India was still required to pay its annual "home charges" to London in gold. The United States, one of the largest silver producers in the world in the late nineteenth century, exported silver to China and also continued to its long practice of trading Mexican silver dollars there. These silver exports helped the United States' balance of trade and also augmented China's money supply.[28]

⚜

THE INTERNATIONAL GOLD STANDARD also influenced the second major round of war indemnities imposed upon China around the turn of the century. The Opium War indemnities of £7.5 million were reckoned in silver dollars and taels. After the first Sino-Japanese war (1896), Japan demanded a £50 million indemnity, an enormous increase, and furthermore demanded that it be paid in gold. That required China to borrow on the international market at a time when the price of silver relative to gold was declining. The indemnity enabled Japan not only to pay for its cost of the war and but also to establish sufficient reserves to adopt gold as its monetary standard. Its deposits in London established credit for construction of its first steel mill.[29]

The Boxer Protocol of 1901 was even more punishing. The eight powers (Europe, the United States, and Japan) demanded an indemnity of 450 million taels, negotiated at £67.5 million in gold over thirty-nine years at 4 percent annual interest. China's obligation to the powers from 1895 through 1918 was £28 million a year (42 million to 45 million taels depending on the exchange rate). Even with the cancelation of the German and Russian debts in the 1920s, China paid out 652 million taels (£91 million) by 1938. The famous remissions later negotiated with the powers, such as the American Boxer scholarships, did not cancel debt. China still had to pay, but the funds were directed to education, railroad construction, and other projects of "mutual benefit." In other words, China underwrote direct foreign investment.[30]

Although the fluctuating gold-price of silver disadvantaged China in its payment of the Boxer indemnities, there were also disadvantages to the West, which desired price stability in order to promote investment. It thus became a matter of mutual interest to establish a stable exchange rate. In 1903 China and Mexico (which shared a long history of exchange, in which China was an open market for the Mexican silver dollar) concurrently asked the United States to lead an effort to bring about a fixed standard of silver to gold. The U.S. Congress formed the Commission on International Exchange to address the issue, headed by Hugh C. Hanna, Charles Conant, and Jeremiah Jenks. The commission recommended that China be placed on a gold-exchange standard.[31]

Under a gold-exchange standard, a nation fixes its local currency (coin, paper) to gold but does not circulate gold domestically; maintains a gold reserve for foreign payments (which reserve is typically held in a London or New York bank); and submits its monetary affairs to foreign supervision. The United States had recently placed the Philippines on the gold-exchange standard; it was already in use in the Dutch East Indies and British India. Under pressure from foreign bankers and investors, Mexico accepted the gold-exchange standard in 1905. Putting China on a gold-exchange standard would have supported the open door policy and, more broadly, contributed to the creation of the gold-dollar bloc based in New York that could compete with sterling.[32]

The colonial nature of the gold-exchange model was not lost on China. Viceroy Zhang Zhidong of Hubei province advised the Qing court that China should remain on a silver standard. China had insufficient gold resources, he stated, and although declining silver prices relative to gold hurt China in reparations, foreign debts, and imports, it favored its exports. Zhang argued that remaining on silver would encourage China to boycott foreign products and develop its domestic industries. Imperial proclamations in 1905 and 1907 expressed China's need for a uniform value for copper and silver currencies, not a gold or gold-exchange standard. Thus China asserted its sovereignty, even under the crumbling Qing regime. China remained on silver during the Republican era until it switched to a gold-exchange standard in 1935, when the Great Depression rippled from the West across the world. By this time, it should be noted, the international gold standard was in irreversible decline, the result not just of the depression but of the general demise of Great Britain as world hegemon.[33]

⊹

WRITING ABOUT CHINA's foreign trade, Hosea Morse tallied China's liabilities and assets for the year 1903. For China's liabilities, he counted merchandise, bullion, and coin imported; foreign debt payment (44 million
taels that year); and invisible liabilities such as the net profits of foreign
merchants and foreign shipping and insurance companies, for an estimated total of 424 million taels (£63.6 million).[34]

Morse counted as assets merchandise, bullion, and coin exported;
overland trade to Russia (a net surplus); and Western investments in
China in railroads and mines that he considered a future liability. He
then considered "China's most important invisible asset, her export of
brawn and brains in the emigration of a portion of her redundant population," whether as traders or as laborers. He quoted Fujian customs
commissioners who called attention to "cash assets" derived from remittances, including those "made by the 2,500,000 Amoy men who are
earning money in Manila, Java, and the Straits," amounting to over 10
million dollars [yuan] a year (13.8 million taels). Morse estimated that
Chinese overseas were "remitting to their homes the fruit of their labor
in an annual sum, which on the lowest possible estimate, is 73 million
taels" (about £11 million). He calculated China's total assets for 1903
at 440 million taels, which figure exceeded its liabilities. According to
Morse, China actually carried a modest net surplus in its balance of 16
million taels (£2.3 million).[35]

Morse's analysis was flawed in some respects; most important, he did
not account for transshipments through Hong Kong and Singapore or
for the coastal Chinese junk (sailing) trade. Morse was aware of the omis-
sions, which were unavoidable because these data were not collected.
But both were considerable elements of the Southeast Asian economy,
in which China had long been the central node of a dense network that
spanned the region. Hong Kong and Singapore also connected China to
India, Europe, Great Britain, and Australia. Nonetheless Morse's inclusion of remittances as part of China's assets was an important recognition of Chinese emigrants' ties and contributions to China. It certainly

amounted to a significant infusion of household income and capital, especially in Guangdong and Fujian provinces.[36]

Morse was not the only analyst to credit overseas Chinese remittances for balancing China's trade accounts. The economist C. F. Remer of the University of Michigan, writing in 1933, believed that some 4 to 5 million overseas Chinese (perhaps 60 percent of the total emigrant population) regularly sent remittances home to China. Remer revised Morse's figures upward, based on his own investigation, to an estimated average annual remittances of 100 million taels ($50 million) per year for the period 1902–13. In the late 1920s, remittances neared 200 million taels a year. Remer acknowledged that the small remittances of individual laborers, from laundry workers in America to rubber plantation workers in Malaya, constituted a considerable amount in the aggregate. But the "great sums," he posited, "are remittances of business profits and of income from property holdings," especially in Southeast Asia. Chinese comprised the "wealthiest group" in the British Straits Settlements and were the "great middlemen" of foreign trade across Southeast Asia. The prosperity of emigrant-sending regions in Guangdong and Fujian provinces testified to the power of overseas remittances. Remer noted, "The Chinese have built up business investments abroad with practically no out-payments from China. These investments bring into China payments from outside which are of the greatest importance in her balance of payments."[37]

Remittances from the United States were not as great as those from Southeast Asia, but they were still considerable. Huang Zunxian estimated that during the 1880s California's Chinese sent $1.2 million a year in remittances to Guangzhou. Anticipating the conclusions of Morse and Remer, Huang too figured that total yearly remittances from overseas Chinese equaled the amount of silver that left China every year.[38]

Morse, Remer, and Huang's claims that credited remittances (and by extension, the Chinese overseas who sent money home) for China's balance of payments was more a political statement than an economic certainty, for no single source is decisive, unless it is something huge, like silver, opium, or tea. Nevertheless, even as exclusion policies shut

Chinese out of the social and economic mainstream in the West, the emigrants carried gold dust home in the linings of their jackets and sent foreign exchange through "silver letters." The fluctuating rates of exchange between gold and silver were not just matters for accountants and financiers. Chinese emigrants followed them as well; they always knew how remittances sent in foreign exchange would translate into local currency. One of the greatest ironies of the Chinese Question is that overseas Chinese in the United States, Australia, and Southeast Asia held on to their savings and remitted large amounts to China when the price of silver dropped.[39]

Chapter 13

Becoming Chinese, Becoming China

Remittance was but one of the threads that bound Chinese abroad to their homeland. Politics was another, and politics also was not without an economic dimension. At the turn of the twentieth century, the question of the treatment of overseas Chinese emerged as a prominent theme in China's political discourse. Reformers associated the oppression of overseas Chinese to the weakness of the Qing, viewing Chinese exclusion in the West as one of the many humiliations imposed on China by the Western powers since the Opium Wars. A flurry of agitation in China against the Chinese exclusion laws in the United States led to a boycott of American-made goods in China in 1905–6. The boycott was, in effect, a protest against the United States' one-way open door policy. The action expressed an emergent nationalist politics in China and throughout the diaspora.[1]

The link between the Chinese Question abroad and homeland politics was created through overlapping networks of native-place associations (*huiguan*), secret societies, merchant guilds, and political parties. Two of the most prominent political leaders of the anti-Qing movement were active abroad. Kang Youwei, one of the most brilliant philosophers of nineteenth-century China, reinterpreted Confucius to promote progress and reform and developed a global utopianism based on the Confucian ideal of *datong*, "great unity." A proponent of a constitutional monarchy and capitalist development, Kang had advised—some say, authored—Emperor Guangxu's famous "one hundred days of reform" before the Dowager Empress Cixi ousted him in 1898. As part of the coup, Cixi executed six associates of Kang Youwei, but Kang and his disciple Liang Qichao managed to escape to Japan. The other prominent figure of the era was the young Cantonese doctor Sun Yatsen, who also operated from exile abroad in Hawaii and North America. Sun, a revolutionary, advocated the overthrow of the Qing and the establishment of a constitutional democracy. He would famously succeed in those aims in the 1911 Republican revolution, but in the early 1900s Kang Youwei's reform party was more influential. According to some accounts, Kang "orchestrated" the boycott movement from abroad, where he was exiled—at the time, on a private island off the coast of Sweden.[2]

Kang Youwei and Liang Qichao remained in exile for some fifteen years. Liang made Japan his base, while Kang went to Canada, where he founded the reform party, the Baohuanghui (Protect the Emperor Society) in 1899. Both men traveled extensively throughout the Chinese diaspora, setting up party chapters (over 175 around the world) and establishing newspapers, schools, and businesses. Its Commercial Corporation's investment and business activities included real estate, restaurants, banks, and railway and mining ventures in the United States, Canada, Mexico, and Southeast Asia. The corporation's mobilization of capital from across the Chinese diaspora not only raised money for the party but also provided new outlets for overseas Chinese wealth. Kang Youwei envisioned the diaspora as integral to China's modernization. An article written in 1902, "The Grand Trend of World Economic Competition," also expressed that view, considering emigration a kind of economic expansion, based on the remittances of working people and not on colonialism. The exclusionary policies of the United States and other Western countries, however, threatened China's survival and expansion.[3]

From Japan, Liang Qichao edited *Xinmin congbao* (New Citizen), a radical periodical that was part of an energetic urban print culture in China. A proliferation of newspapers and magazines ran the gamut from moderate to radical and from intellectual to popular; they took up issues from foreign relations to the examination system and foot binding. Most writers thought about China's position in the world in a framework of emerging nationalism and Social Darwinism. *Waijiao bao* (Diplomatic Review) published the texts of treaties and foreign laws and translated articles from *The Times* of London and the *North American Review.* Liang Qichao's *Xinmin congbao* was enormously influential, known for clear analysis, direct advocacy, and strong writing about China's position in the world. Huang Zunxian praised Liang's writings for their power to "move hearts and shock minds.... Everybody feels what he has to say. Even a man of iron and stone is moved."[4]

Liang Qichao made extended tours of both Australia and the United States. He spent six months in Australia in 1900–1, visiting the major cities as well as Bendigo and Ballarat in Victoria's gold country. His trip coincided with the inauguration of Australian Federation. It may seem odd that Australian leaders, with their commitment to Chinese exclusion, would invite Liang to sit at the formal federation dinner at Sydney town hall, presided over by the new prime minister. Or perhaps even more odd that Liang found much to praise in Australia—its enfranchisement of women, its labor protections, and its influential workers movement. Historian John Fitzgerald views Liang's perspective as that of a metropolitan elite, versed in the classical imperative of moral improvement, who was relating "universal concerns to the new and unfamiliar world of nationalism and nationstates." Liang cherished equality, and Australia had embraced equality in greater measure than many other nations, but he recognized that racial discrimination showed that it had not yet embraced the ethic of equality of all humankind. Liang operated very much from a moral high ground.[5]

In 1903 Liang toured twenty-two U.S. and Canadian cities. His "Travelogue of the New Continent," published serially by *Xinmin congbao* in 1904, offered a comprehensive description and analysis of Chinese communities in North America and a thorough critique of exclusion policies. Again, Liang focused on the question of equality: he did not oppose on principle the United States' right to restrict immigration, but he criticized its discriminatory nature, singling out Chinese for exclusion by denying Chinese laborers and merchants access to jobs and business opportunities outside the confines of the ethnic market.[6]

The importance of the activities abroad of Kang Youwei and Liang Qichao, as well as those of the revolutionary Sun Yatsen, was not lost on the Qing government. By driving them into exile, Cixi had unwittingly sped the growth of anti-Qing nationalist politics among Chinese emigrants. In 1902 the Qing ambassador to Great Britain, Luo Fenglu, warned the Foreign Ministry, "There are more and more overseas Chinese. We need to prevent them from following Kang-Liang and Sun." He proposed that the Qing send officers to Singapore, Penang, Australia, and Canada. The ambassador suggested that one way to counter the influence of anti-Qing activists would be to support Chinese living abroad, especially in Australia and Canada, where they suffered from discrimination and mistreatment but had no consular representation.[7]

THE BAOHUANGHUI AND *Xinmin congbao* were not the only voices that brought the plight of overseas Chinese to the attention of China's urban intellectuals, professionals, and reformers and connected it to China's weakness. The antislavery novel *Uncle Tom's Cabin* was published in Chinese translation in 1901, under the title "A Black Slave's Cry to Heaven." The translator, Lin Shu, wrote in the preface that he hoped Chinese readers would read it as a mirror to reflect on their own situation. "Recently," he wrote, "the treatment of blacks in America has been carried over to yellow people. When a cobra is unable to release its poison fully it vents its anger by biting wood and grass. Afterward no one who touches the poisoned dead branches will escape death. We the yellow people, have we touched its dead branches?"

Lin observed, "Of the Americans, the more calculating ones are alarmed at the draining of their silver and so treat Chinese workers cruelly so as to stop them from coming." Although the "prospect of enslavement is threatening our race," he argued, the Qing did nothing. "Do not our Chinese officials realize that their own nationals, though guiltless, are ignominiously being put into prison and wasting to death there? . . . Our national prestige has been wounded; what more be said?" A review of the book in a Shanghai newspaper sounded the same theme: "The book is not really about the sufferings of the black race as it is about all races under the whites. The novel is a wake-up bell to rouse us from a deep dream. . . . White men talk about civilization while doing barbaric things."[8]

Zou Rong, a young Sichuanese who had recently returned from studying in Japan, published a pamphlet titled "Revolutionary Army" in 1904. Zong wrote passionately about the coolies sent to Cuba and other Chinese workers who were ill-treated abroad. Chinese were "banned from America, then from Honolulu and Melbourne, living in abject poverty, dying without land for a grave." He criticized China's lack of democracy and its supine posture when abused by the West. "Do we not see that when a missionary is killed, land is ceded and an indemnity is paid. Or when a foreigner is insulted, trouble is taken to issue a decree instituting inquiries. But our fellow countrymen settled abroad are humiliated by foreigners in ways we would not tolerate toward bird or beast. Yet the Manchu government remains practically blind and deaf to this. . . . I dare say: Our ill-treatment is at the hands of the Manchus." Although banned by the Qing government, Zuo's pamphlet reportedly sold a million copies in China and abroad. Wu Panzhao, editor of San Francisco's *Zhongxi ribao,* printed and distributed eleven thousand copies. The pro-republican newspaper *Aiguo bao* (Chinese Times) of Melbourne serialized it.[9]

An escalation in American hostility toward Chinese immigration fueled outcry in China over the exclusion laws. In 1900 the Qing government tried but was unable to prevent the extension of the Chinese exclusion laws to the Philippines and Hawaii, both recently acquired American territories. The treatment of Chinese arriving in San Francisco worsened after 1897, when Terence Powderly, former head of the Knights of Labor and an avowed Chinese exclusionist, became commissioner of immigration. Powderly embarked on a determined campaign to tighten the noose around merchant and student arrivals. Detention in the notorious wooden sheds at the San Francisco docks; the use of Bertillon measurements, a prison procedure; and harassment of merchants and students (both exempt classes), including the humiliation of high-class merchants and officials who arrived to prepare China's exhibition at the St. Louis world's fair and the refusal to land four siblings from a wealthy Shanghai family and educated in London—all these were detailed for Chinese readers.[10]

It was in this political climate that the idea for a boycott of American goods in China emerged as a weapon to push the United States to amend its exclusion policy. As early as 1900, Chinese in America, including newspaper editor Wu Panzhao, the Six Companies, and Chinese Christians, as well as China's representative to the United States, Wu Tingfang, pressed for a renegotiation of the Gresham-Yang Treaty, which authorized exclusion legislation and was scheduled to expire in 1904.[11]

The idea of a boycott of American goods as a pressure tactic was floated on a few occasions in overseas Chinese newspapers in Honolulu and San Francisco, but activity focused mainly on gathering signatures for a mass petition, which Chinese in America presented to the Qing government in 1903. Wu Tingfang's successor in the United States, Liang Cheng, drafted a new treaty and presented it to Secretary of State John Hay in 1904. Liang Cheng's treaty would have allowed for the exclusion of laborers, but it added protections both for resident laborers and for nonlaborers, including legal rights to counsel, bail, and appeal. From China's perspective, it was eminently reasonable, acknowledging the United States' right to regulate immigration but opposing mistreatment and discrimination, much like the proposals put forth by Liang Qichao in his "Travelogue of the New Continent." But Liang Cheng's proposed treaty and other appeals made by the Qing to American representatives in China fell on deaf ears. Congress let the Gresham-Yang Treaty expire and tacked Chinese exclusion onto an appropriations bill in 1904, making it permanent and permanently mooting any input from China via a treaty process.[12]

While Chinese in America despaired, the course of events galvanized reformers and merchants in Shanghai. Support for a boycott of American goods grew, prompted by nationalist sentiment as well as support from some Qing officials and native capitalists, such as a nascent flour milling industry, which aimed to promote domestic products to compete with imports. In May 1905 merchant leaders in Shanghai called for a boycott to commence in July if the United States did not agree by then to change the exclusion policy. President Theodore Roosevelt—under pressure from American business interests in China—prodded the State Department and the Bureau of Immigration to treat arriving merchants and students with the "fullest courtesy and consideration" in June. But it was not enough to stop the momentum of the boycott.[13]

The boycott's leadership came from the older, established native-place *huiguan* in Shanghai, many of which were represented on the city's fledgling chamber of commerce. The movement quickly galvanized a broad swath of urban society, including students, professionals, women's organizations, literary societies, and Christian groups—groups long familiar with Western consumer goods and styles. The boycott crystallized the idea that foreign goods symbolized foreign imperialism. It spread to at least ten cities in China and was strongest in Shanghai, Guangzhou, and Xiamen. Shanghai was China's most cosmopolitan city and the port through which most American products entered the country. Guangdong and Fujian, of course, were the home provinces of most Chinese in North America, Southeast Asia, and Australia.[14]

American products—cotton cloth, cigarettes, flour, and kerosene—were highly visible consumer items in Chinese cities. American cotton constituted 90 percent of all coarse cotton imports in China, selling under at least eleven brands, in addition to thirty-one brands of cotton sheeting, four of fine cotton cloth, and ten of twill. Shanghai businessmen who worked with U.S. companies not only sold American goods in Shanghai but also distributed them to retailers in other cities. The Shanghai Chamber of Commerce chose one of its members, the prominent Fujianese businessman Zeng Shaoqing, to head the boycott committee. Zeng was a good choice because he had no conflict of interest; his own business dealings were in Southeast Asia, not in the American trade.[15]

Thousands of people attended mass meetings and pledged to boycott American-made goods. Returned emigrant merchants spoke at public meetings in Guangzhou. Eight hundred student and merchant representatives met in Tianjin to organize boycott activities. The nationalistic newspaper *Anhui suhua bao* published a twenty-four-page article, with historical background on the oppression of Chinese in the United States and nine pages of the American brand names to be boycotted. The press reported on meetings, speeches, and resolutions, while a fresh round of pamphlets and short novels kept the reading public engaged with the plight of Chinese in

America. Even the "old monks" at a mountaintop monastery in Guangdong wanted to talk with visitors about the exclusion treaty.[16]

Handbills urging support were mass-distributed in the cities. Shops
and homes in Guangzhou displayed placards: "This shop/home does
not sell/use American goods. . . . Anyone who trades in American goods
is without shame." A Suzhou cigarette merchant announced he would
burn his stock of American cigarettes in public. In Jiaxing, Zhejiang,
every store displayed boycott posters; the press reported there were "no
traces of American goods in the city anymore." As far away as the Man-
churian port city of Yingko, local compradors and dockworkers refused
to unload a ship bearing eighty thousand cans of Standard Oil kerosene.[17]

Chinese in the United States rallied to the cause, which was, after all, their
own, now enveloped in a rising tide of nationalist politics in China. In California, the Six Companies, Zhigongdang, Baohuanghui, and several newspapers came together to form a boycott-support group and raised at least
$15,000. Support rallied across the diaspora as well. Kang Youwei wrote an
open letter to Chinese abroad, expressing humiliation and anger over the
U.S. exclusion laws. If Chinese exclusion continued, he wrote, China would
lose some $80 million to $90 million a year in the remittances now flowing through Hong Kong, funds badly needed for China's development—for
conducting business, opening schools, building a navy. Chinese exclusion
was intolerable, he continued, especially as Japanese, Indians, and Koreans
could all travel to the United States, even with their dogs.[18]

Chinese merchants in Thailand refused shiploads of American flour
and cigarettes; Chinese in Kobe, Japan, refused to handle American goods
and in Yokohama boycotted American banks and insurance companies. In
Australia, the Chinese-language press avidly followed the progress of the
boycott. Chinese Australians, who had welcomed Liang Qichao to their
communities in 1900–1, were no strangers to Chinese nationalist politics. They were alert both to the boycott against the American exclusion
act and to the travails of the Chinese mine laborers in South Africa, both
generating attention in 1904 and 1905. They understood that they were all
connected: "If exclusion continues [in the United States] there will be no
hope for Australia. . . . The Qing government may not be able to help us

since they are busy flattering the Westerners. Therefore, we should rely on ourselves and unite as a community," wrote a Chinese Australian.[19]

The boycott movement began to falter in the fall of 1905, although it persisted in Guangdong through early 1906. The merchant-gentry elite that had initiated it began to waver in their commitment, especially those who stood to lose from the stagnation in business. While popular support continued, internal divisions also weakened the movement. The Qing government, under pressure from the United States, officially opposed the boycott but took few steps to suppress it until late 1905.[20]

Was the boycott effective? In terms of its explicit aims, the U.S. Bureau of Immigration made a few procedural changes that were face-saving for Chinese elites but not substantive. President Roosevelt continued to call for fairness and courtesy in the treatment of merchants and students, but hardliners controlled the bureau and Congress as well. Although students would begin coming to the United States in 1909 to study under scholarships provided by the Boxer indemnity, merchants continued to fare poorly. Wu Panzhao wrote in 1908 that the "great" Chinese merchants had all left the United States to do business elsewhere.[21]

The political results went beyond the boycott's immediate aim, however. The boycott heralded the birth of modern Chinese urban politics and protest, with its vibrant print culture and diverse social composition, ranging from reform-minded merchants and literati to the middle classes, including women's associations, students, and intellectuals. Its bywords, *gongli* (public interest) and *gongyi* (public good), captured the spirit of emergent Chinese nationalism. The popular aspirations for national sovereignty that were unleashed against the United States' exclusion laws and American-made products were easily rechanneled against the Qing, leading to its revolutionary overthrow in 1911.[22]

Economically, the boycott had a definite short-term impact on American businesses. Overall, the value of American imports fell from 77 million taels in 1905 to 44.4 million in 1906, a decline of 35.2 million ($44 million). In his study of the boycott, the American economist C. F. Remer did not consider the decline to be entirely attributable to the boycott, but he concluded that there was definite effect against certain products in

Shanghai, Guangzhou, and a few other cities. U.S. consular officials noted in 1905 that the boycott had seriously disrupted trade in Shanghai, describing "heavy loss" and "complete stagnation of business" in cotton piece goods. Unsold stocks of kerosene accumulated in Shanghai, Guangzhou, and Xiamen; twenty thousand sacks of wheat flour piled up in Hong Kong warehouses for want of a market. In Hong Kong, the U.S. consul reported, American goods were purchased solely by the foreign population or transshipped to French Indochina. In hindsight we can see that these effects were specific and temporary; the volume and value of the U.S.-China trade continued to grow, especially after 1913. But American exporters and diplomats worried a great deal at the time about the potential for long-term damage to U.S. trade interests.[23]

The anti-American boycott heralded a "national products movement" that called for the domestic manufacture and consumption of products as anti-imperialist and patriotic acts for the nation. Chinese boycotts against Japan in 1908, 1915, and 1919 over insults and losses of territory exacted a toll such that Japan told the Lytton Commission of the League of Nations that continued boycotting would "make the economic activities of all foreign nations in China very difficult, if not impossible to carry on." Indeed, Chinese boycotts of Japanese goods and commercial relations continued during the 1920s, culminating in the great boycott of 1931–32 in response to Japan's invasion of Manchuria. That was the most successful of the Chinese economic boycotts against a foreign power, but the distinction pales in light of the war that followed.[24]

THE SECOND SINO-JAPANESE WAR, followed by civil war between Chinese Nationalists and Communists and culminating in the Chinese Communist Revolution of 1949, ended China's century of humiliation that had begun with the first Opium War. During that century, China had experienced one of world history's greatest reversals in geopolitical and economic fortune.

After the Opium Wars, the Qing had struggled to figure out how to relate to the West, how to develop domestic industry, how to enact administrative reforms. But even as foreign businesses and culture were implanted in

China, especially in the treaty ports and in industrializing areas, modernizing efforts were slowed by internal divisions within the Qing and by the weight of vested bureaucratic interests, not to mention the inertia of China's long dynastic tradition. By the late nineteenth century, the Qing teetered on the brink of fiscal insolvency, the result of the high cost of the military suppression of the Taiping and other domestic rebellions, which had ravaged southern and central China (1850–64), and of its foreign indemnities.

Chinese emigrants living abroad in the Anglo-American world were not marginal actors in the history of the late Qing. Those who went to the gold rushes were among the first Chinese to experience the West first hand. Their participation in the gold rushes in North America and Australasia in the late nineteenth century and in the revival of the gold industry in South Africa in the early twentieth were integral to a new era of long-distance migrations and global trade that transformed international finance and political relations. Chinese gold miners contributed to the global financial hegemony of Great Britain, and then the United States, based on the power of the gold. Their contribution was doubly ironic. At one level, the gold rushes both materially and symbolically consolidated the shift to gold-based trade and investment in the global economy, which disadvantaged China. At another level, the presence of Chinese on the goldfields and in other industries gave rise to racial conflict and discrimination, violence, and finally, legal policies of exclusion from immigration and citizenship, which policies also disadvantaged China. Chinese exclusion did not directly cause either the West's rise or China's decline. But it was part of a constellation of policies that privileged Anglo-American settler nationalism, and that contributed to China's oppression in myriad ways. The exclusion laws, moreover, loom large in nineteenth-century Chinese history because they were, along with the unequal treaties, the most potent symbols of China's humiliation on the global stage.

But if Chinese emigrants were despised and marginalized by Euro-American societies, they were also conduits of knowledge and resources to their hometowns and regions. They built dense networks—migration, commercial, and political networks—across the Pacific that contributed to an emergent Chinese nationalism at the turn of the twentieth century. The

anti-American boycott exemplified this national consciousness, which connected diasporic communities with the urban middle classes in China and
linked the injustice of the exclusion laws to China's weakness as a nation.

The Qing, while fiscally enfeebled and burdened by a sclerotic bureaucracy, did try to assert its independence in the face of foreign encroachment
and aggression. China refused to adopt the gold-exchange standard; it mat-
tered that China was not a colony, like India or the Philippines, where imperialism arbitrarily imposed monetary policies that inscribed dependency.
Qing diplomats intervened to protect Chinese merchants and laborers living
and working abroad from discrimination and abuse, although not always
successfully. European and American encroachments were bad enough;
the Japanese were, in turn, arguably even more rapacious, seizing Taiwan,
going to war to take Korea, long a Chinese tributary state, and building up
its forces in Manchuria. The stakes became even greater with the Boxer
Rebellion of 1900–1, a peasant uprising in North China against foreign
missionaries that split the Qing court, led the Western powers and Japan to
send troops into Beijing, and resulted in another raft of indemnities.

In 1905 the Empress Dowager Cixi initiated a series of reforms, including abolishing the examination system, building up the military, and
streamlining the bureaucracy. But they were slow to be implemented (in
part because the Qing could not pay for them), and popular opposition
to the Qing only grew. By decade's end, the idea of reforming the monarchy had given way to popular demands to overthrow it. Armed uprisings
throughout China in the summer and fall of 1911, many associated with
Sun Yatsen's revolutionary party, finally toppled the Qing and with it,
four thousand years of dynastic rule. The new Republic of China faced
myriad challenges, from how to form a modern government on the ash
heap of the Qing to how to end fighting among warlords and corruption
at high levels. The Republican era saw the establishment of a constitution, a modern university system, investments in domestic industry, the
end of foot binding, and a cultural renaissance. But the needs of the peasantry, the vast majority of the population, remained largely unaddressed.
Instability, both political and economic, was endemic, especially with the
burden of foreign indemnity payments continuing well into the 1920s.

Just as the Qing had run out of time, so did the republic, when Japan seized Manchuria in 1931 and then invaded China proper in 1937.

During the ensuing Sino-Japanese War and World War II, Chinese living abroad rallied to support the homeland. During the civil war that followed and the Chinese Communist revolution of 1949, their loyalties were divided. During the Cold War, Chinese living in the anglophone world, regardless of their political inclinations, were largely cut off from their families in mainland China, and China removed itself from the global capitalist economy. Not until after the Cultural Revolution (1966–76) did China again "open" to the West. After a long hiatus, Chinese living in the West began to visit their families and hometowns and to send remittances and investments. Restrictions on emigration from the People's Republic of China relaxed beginning in the 1980s. Chinese living abroad, both old and new emigrants, sending remittances and participating in cultural and intellectual exchanges, would again contribute to China's development and standing in the world.

RECENT CHINESE EMIGRANTS know little, if anything, about their predecessors, who were the first to venture to the West and whose experiences influenced the course of late nineteenth-century global politics. Chinese emigrants working for gold on the bars of the Yuba River in California; in the gullies of Castlemaine, Victoria; and in the depths of the Simmer and Jack Mine on the Witwatersrand all knew they were part of a big international event, a happening, a movement, even as their immediate interests were personal. As American forty-niners would say, they came to make their "pile." And like all gold seekers, their success depended on both hard work and good luck. And like everyone else, they confronted gold seekers from other nations.

But Chinese gold miners also learned quickly that the rules of engagement on the goldfields were often unjust. Who could belong, who was worthy of rights, who could be a citizen? When whites argued that Chinese did not belong to the new communities and nations that gold was making on the Anglo-American frontiers, they offered reasons to explain why, whether an incompatibility between "heathenism" and "Christian values" or between "coolieism" and "free labor." These ideas embodied the Chinese Question—as it arose in different local contexts over the course of the late nineteenth century—and gave rise to a global race theory. Chinese abroad had but few Euro-American allies: missionaries; at times, business interests; and a few liberal advocates. The Chinese Question was fueled by popular racism, theorized by elite thinkers, and weaponized by politicians. In the United States and the British settler colonies, the Chinese Question pushed against established principles of equality to marginalize China within the family of nations and to cast Chinese people as racial inferiors within the family of humankind. Exclusion was a necessary feature of the West's containment of China.

Chinese everywhere resisted racism and exclusion—with petitions, memorials, and lawsuits; with acts of solidarity and self-defense; and with appeals to Western publics and the Chinese government. Not least, they persisted. Chinese living abroad created ethnic communities and adapted traditional organizations, like native-place associations and secret brotherhood societies, to attend to their needs. Chinese merchants, low in the traditional Confucian social order, exercised new-found power as mining investors, community leaders, and culture brokers. San Francisco's Yuan Sheng, Melbourne's Lowe Kong Meng, and Johannesburg's Xie Zixiu advocated for the recognition and interests of Chinese emigrants as part of their host countries and as part of China. These laborers and merchants forged the modern Chinese diaspora amid the global contours drawn by race and money.

Epilogue

⁜

The Specter of the Yellow Peril, Redux

I n May 2013 President John Dramani Mahama of Ghana formed a military task force to crack down on illegal small-scale gold mining throughout the country. The task force took down several hundred illegal mining sites, seized cash and destroyed equipment, and evicted and arrested thousands of miners, local Ghanaian and Chinese. Ghana deported over 4,500 Chinese in the scandal, which raised alarms about Chinese predation, exploitation, and even colonialism, in Africa. The arrests and deportations dampened but did not eliminate illegal Chinese mining, however, as prospectors moved to remote areas, where they received protection from local chiefs. Another raid in the Ashanti region in 2018 snared a thousand illegal miners.[1]

Between the mid-1990s and 2013, fifty thousand Chinese went to Ghana to work in small-scale gold mining. The vast majority of participants in Ghana's Chinese gold rush hail from Shanglin county, Guangxi province in southern China, where alluvial gold mining has a long history but was recently curtailed by the government in response to environmental damage. Although in Ghana only Ghanaian citizens may legally practice small-scale or artisanal mining, many Ghanaians form illicit partnerships with Chinese companies, in which Ghanaians hold the legal permits while Chinese provide capital, equipment, and technical expertise. They operate in a legal gray zone, where Ghanaian citizens own land but the state owns minerals below the ground.[2]

The Chinese companies have eight to ten partners, who contribute family savings and borrowed money to capitalize their enterprises. They bring in their wake a chain migration of workers, who are connected by kinship networks and aided by brokers, who arrange for tourist visas. A Chinese company typically works an alluvial operation on twenty-five acres with ten to fifteen Ghanaian and Chinese workers. The company may have an initial capital expenditure of $500,000, mostly for equipment (excavators, generators, sand pumps, pickup trucks). Ongoing expenses include profit sharing with the Ghanaian license holder (typically 10 percent), labor costs, and fees and bribes to various local officials.[3]

The modest scale of these enterprises contrasts with industrial gold mining by multinational corporations, which are responsible for over 70 percent of Ghana's gold production. For example, AngloGold Ashanti, a publicly traded company on the NYSE, is capitalized at over $700 million, operates on over 28,000 acres, utilizes sophisticated deep-mining technologies, and employs nearly 7,000 people in Ghana. Still, Chinese technical skills and capital enabled a significant increase in output from alluvial mining, which created wealth for both Chinese and locals but also resulted in complaints about environmental degradation and labor abuses.[4]

The contours of Chinese small-scale gold mining in twenty-first-century Ghana and other gold-rich areas of West and Central Africa bear some uncanny resemblances to Chinese gold-mining and migration practices in the mid-nineteenth century: small companies with partners pooling resources; network-based migrations and brokers that pave the journey from home to foreign goldfields; and uneasy relations with citizens and governments in destination countries. These economic and cultural patterns are remarkable for their persistence and adaptability.

But the Chinese gold rush to Ghana is quite different from the gold rushes of the nineteenth century. Gold is no longer the money-commodity and hence does not generate the same kind of global fever that it did in the past. Nevertheless, gold remains a premier store of value and is highly sought during economic recessions. Thus, Chinese mining entrepreneurs rushed to Ghana between 2008 and 2013 because the world price of gold hit historic highs after the 2008 financial crisis. Gold remains valuable, furthermore, for use in some industrial applications and especially for ornament. China and India are the two largest consumers of gold in the world, nearly all of it for jewelry. China is actually the world's largest producer of gold (400 tons in 2018), but its declining reserves cannot keep up with domestic demand.[5]

Chinese participation in small-scale gold mining, while not insignificant, is just one aspect of China's mining interest in Africa. China also engages in industrial gold mining, with investments in South African mines, which are still producing after 150 years on the Witwatersrand but now at nearly two miles below the surface. In addition, copper, cobalt, manganese, bauxite, coltan (used in electronics and mobile phones), and dozens of other minerals and metals are critical elements in Chinese manufacturing, especially in top sectors like electronics, vehicles, and steel production. Africa's rich mineral reserves and China's voracious industrial appetite have made China the largest importer of minerals from sub-Saharan Africa.[6]

Still, mining ranks but third in China's African interests, after infrastructure (roads, railroads, ports) and energy (oil and gas). China's annual foreign direct investment in Africa is enormous, growing from $75 million in 2003 to $5.4 billion in 2018. Approximately one-half of the capital comes from the central government's state-owned enterprises and banks. Other Chinese investors and contractors include provincial-level state-owned enterprises and private companies and, at the bottom of the hierarchy, small entrepreneurial ventures like those in artisanal mining.[7]

These projects in Africa form part of China's global economic strategy called the Belt and Road Initiative, announced by President Xi Jinping in 2013. Originally envisioned as a "new silk road" to Central Asia and a "new maritime silk road" through Southeast Asia, it recalls the ancient trade routes that connected China to other parts of the world. The Belt and Road Initiative comprises infrastructural projects from Tajikistan to Istanbul and from Jakarta to Djibouti—high-speed railways, highways, ports, pipelines, power stations, and airports—a strategy that promotes economic development in tertiary regions and provides an outlet for China's surplus currency reserves and excess industrial capacity. China also plans to develop "corridors" off the main belt through Pakistan, Bangladesh, and Mongolia; terminal points in Moscow, Rotterdam, and Venice; and fifty special economic zones for factory production. As of 2019, China had spent $30 billion, mostly low-interest governmental loans in exchange for long-term leases and rights. It intends to invest upward of $1 trillion by 2027, although projects and loans slowed in 2020 in response to the coronavirus pandemic. China also started the Asian Infrastructure Investment Bank in 2015, pledging to seed it with 1 trillion yuan ($160 billion), which it claims will complement, rather than subvert, the World Bank.[8]

PRESIDENT XI JINPING'S EVOCATION of the old overland and maritime silk roads is a central trope in China's recent nationalistic rhetoric and agenda. All nationalisms rely on grand historical narratives to anchor the nation's special nature, imagined as a through-line from time immemorial to the present and onward into the future. Xi Jinping also emphasizes China's century of humiliation under Western imperialism in order to situate China's new global role as a repair of deep historical injustice. In Xi's words, "rejuvenation" of China's "greatness" is the "Chinese dream."

One need not subscribe to the nationalism of present ambitions to recognize how it resonates with the outlines of China's history. Between 1550 and 1750, China was the single largest domestic economy in the world and the center of early modern global trade. This book has focused on the greater portion of China's century of humiliation, from the Opium Wars to the fall of the Qing, a period also bookended by the discovery of gold in California and the end of the Chinese labor project in South Africa. These proximate events shaped China and Chinese people's entry into the world's family of nations, which was dominated by Anglo-American power, power that was at once extractive, commercial, and financial. China's position in the global economy during the nineteenth and early twentieth centuries was essentially a colonial one, characterized by intrusion and plunder by the West and Japan. The new Republic of China, founded in 1911, struggled to end China's two biggest international humiliations—the unequal treaties and the exclusion laws—but with scant success. The unequal treaties were not abrogated until World War II. The exclusion laws were slower to fall: the United States repealed its exclusion law in 1943, but Australia and South Africa did not end their Chinese exclusions until the 1970s. The Republic of China made reforms, notably in law and education, and promoted industrialization, but it was also plagued by political factionalism, armed conflict and corruption. The ongoing conflict between Nationalist Party (Guomindang) and Communists that had brewed since the 1920s erupted into civil war at the end of World War II, leading to the Communists' victory in 1949.[9]

When the Chinese Communist Party took power, Mao Zedong famously declared that "the Chinese people, comprising one quarter of humanity, have now stood up. Ours will no longer be a nation subject to insult and humiliation. We have stood up." By linking China's impoverishment to its abject position in the world, Mao recalled sentiments expressed by reformers and revolutionaries since the late nineteenth century. But whereas late Qing and Republican nationalists sought to modernize China in the image of the West and Japan, the Chinese Communist Party rejected capitalism and imperialism. It pursued instead a socialist model based on the mobilization of peasants and workers, agrarian land reform, and a self-sufficient path of economic development. During the Mao era (1949–76), China made notable achievements, including land reform and a more egalitarian distribution and increased production of food; improvements in the standard of living, education, healthcare, and life expectancy; and in the status of women. China also provided inspiration and material support for anti-imperialist movements around the world.[10]

But progress was hampered by the limitations of Soviet-style central planning, the use of agricultural surplus to underwrite industrialization, and relative international isolation by the West and Japan during the Cold War. Just as important were ideological excesses that emphasized human will (that is, revolutionary commitment and iron discipline) as the key to realizing socialist prosperity and equality. The Great Leap Forward of the late 1950s caused agricultural production to plummet and led to catastrophic famine (1959–61), which claimed at least 15 million and possibly

over 40 million lives. During the Cultural Revolution (1966–76), the punishment of intellectuals and other "capitalist roaders" resulted in upward
of 2 million deaths and a lost generation of educated people, necessary
for any kind of social progress. By the 1970s, agricultural production had
not kept up with population growth; food consumption per capita in 1979
was no better than in 1955. China was still a very poor, agrarian country.[11]

After Mao Zedong died in 1976 Deng Xiaoping, a veteran of the revolution, seized leadership of the party. He threw out the Marxist-Leninist
orthodoxy, as well as the Maoist emphasis on political mobilization, and
began a pragmatic program of economic reform. Under what was called
"socialism with Chinese characteristics," China shifted from a command
economy to a market-driven one. The state devolved greater economic
authority to provincial and local levels, encouraged private companies
and cooperatives, and energized rural economies. It promoted massive
infrastructural and urban construction, with local governments buying land from small farmers and using it as collateral for loans from
the China Development Bank. It invited foreign capital and global trade;
Apple and Walmart are just the best-known foreign companies in China
that produce both for the Chinese consumer market and for global
export. "Opening up" also included greater artistic freedoms, international travel and intellectual exchange, and an immense expansion of
civic discourse, much of it through online social media in the 2000s.
China lifted some 600 million people out of poverty and created a new
middle class as well as millionaires and billionaires. The reform strategy produced annual double-digit growth for more than two decades. By
2010 China overtook Japan to become the second-largest economy in the
world, after the United States.[12]

But phenomenal economic growth also created new problems and tensions in Chinese society: increased economic inequality, the dismantling
of the social welfare net, horrible pollution, rampant corruption, and with
them, a buildup of popular grievance. While many Western observers
believed China's economic reforms would lead to political reforms, China's leadership has not allowed that path to be pursued. Its brutal suppression of popular protesters at Tiananmen in Beijing (and elsewhere in

the country) in June 1989 foreclosed the possibility of democratic political engagement. Since the 1990s, politics became increasingly marginalized, the result of both state repression and a culture emphasizing getting rich and getting rich quick.[13]

Mao had defined China's role in the world as an alternative to capitalism and imperialism; in contrast, China's leaders from Deng Xiaoping to Xi Jinping redefined "greatness" on the capitalist West's terms. The current strategy emphasizes productivity, profit, and accumulation; extraction of raw materials in the developing world; and investment in foreign debt. China's aggressive development agenda is potentially fractious both domestically and abroad; hence, under Xi Jinping's presidency (2012–present), censorship and arrest of dissidents have increased. Beijing authorities have pursued a shocking oppression of Uighur Muslim people in Xinjiang province in northwestern China, including a massive inmigration of ethnic Han people to deracinate the local population, high-tech surveillance, and the detention of more than 2 million Uighurs in "re-education" centers. It bears noting that the main artery of the inland Belt and Road initiative goes straight through Xinjiang.

CHINA'S ECONOMIC POWER results from unleashing the labor power and creative energies of its huge population and strategic decisions to engage with, indeed to dominate, the supply chains of the contemporary global economy. Economic historians are now thinking about recent successes in China (and other East Asian economies since the late twentieth century) as echoes of early modern East Asian practices of "industriousness" and "industrious revolutions." In this view, labor-intensive agriculture and domestic craft and textile production, supported by vibrant local and regional commercial markets and credit networks, represented an alternative to the capital-intensive European path to industrialization. Each path derived from contingent factors—relative availability of land and energy resources, exigencies of war—and not from any inherent superiority or inferiority of Western versus Asian civilizations or from any normative development of capitalism. Critical political economic histories emphasize that European empires used various strategies of race and money for capital accumulation—African slavery, silver and gold, opium and gunboats—which were central in the creation of divergence within the emerging global economy. This book has tried to illuminate how the politics of the Chinese Question was part of the "great divergence" between the West and China in the nineteenth century.[14]

A long view of the political economies of race and money also invites us to think about global economic change broadly, in world-historical terms. Empires rise and fall, and one global hegemon becomes eclipsed by another, seldom peaceably. These processes overlap, and the rise of a new center of power is not preordained but contingent on many factors.

But the sun did set on the British Empire, and the American Century did not last one hundred years. China's strategy is to build an Asian center of the global economy and to move outward from there, but whether China will become in the twenty-first century the new global hegemon remains to be seen. It is perhaps more likely that no single country will dominate and that the global economy will continue to be characterized by a multipolar distribution of power (United States, Europe, and East Asia).[15]

With the rising prominence of the European Union and East Asia in global trade since the 1990s, the U.S. share of world gross domestic product declined—from 35 percent in 1985 to 24 percent in 2018. Nevertheless, the U.S. GDP remains by far the largest in the world. Just as important, it still dominates the high end of the value chain (science and technology) in the global division of labor. In large measure, China's growth resulted from its manufacturing for consumption in the West, the traditional position for colonies and developing countries. As the economist Isabella Weber points out, the back of every iPhone states, "Designed in California, Assembled in China." Thus, China's efforts to move up the value chain are hot spots in U.S.-China economic competition, as evidenced in controversies over Huawei and 5G technology, artificial intelligence, and research collaborations between Chinese and American scientists.[16]

China's ambitions face other tensions. As Chinese workers in export manufacturing have demanded higher wages, multinational corporations have moved production to areas with cheaper labor, such as Cambodia and Bangladesh. The Belt and Road Initiative faces criticisms of unfair competition, rent seeking, and unsustainable debt borne by host countries. In 2020 some partners—Egypt, Bangladesh, Tanzania, Nigeria—asked to renegotiate or forgive sovereign debts and have postponed and even canceled projects. China points out that its loans carry lower interest rates than the World Bank and that it pays attention to creating jobs and wealth in developing nations. Still, there is something rather different in tone and substance between China's extractive role in Africa today and its previous projects in Africa, such as the construction of the Tanzania-Zambia Railway during the Mao era (1968–76). The railroad involved a massive interest-free loan, the deployment of fifty thousand Chinese technicians and workers, and complete transfer of ownership to the African nations.[17]

THE ECONOMIC RELATIONSHIP between the United States and China in the twenty-first century is both interdependent and competitive. It is especially interdependent with regard to consumer goods and machinery, such as electronics, clothing, plastics, and medical equipment. Products are manufactured in China (often for U.S. multinationals, using East Asian subcontractors or joint ventures with Chinese companies) and consumed in the United States and other countries of the global North. China has benefited from this relationship by providing employment for its massive population and raising the standard of living. But rising wages and educational attainment push China toward higher-value sectors (human services, knowledge production), which employ relatively fewer people and face opposition from the advanced industrial countries. Consumers in the West benefit from low-cost products, especially as China has kept the value of its currency (renminbi) low relative to the dollar. But that also makes U.S. exports to China relatively more expensive, which affects industries like agriculture, whose exports (soybeans, sorghum, poultry, wheat) compete with other countries for market share in China.[18]

Another major area of interdependence is debt financing. The federal debt of the United States was $23 trillion at the end of 2019. Because domestic resources are insufficient to finance its deficit, the United States has depended on foreign countries to buy its bonds, especially since the turn of the twenty-first century. In 2019 foreign countries held 28 percent of U.S. public debt ($6.8 trillion), with China being the second largest, after Japan. China, whose exports generate a surplus of foreign exchange reserves, holds about one-third of its foreign reserves in U.S. Treasury securities.[19]

At the same time, China competes with the United States (and other countries) in a global scramble for raw materials and energy resources in the developing world (especially oil and gas), for global investment opportunities, and for control over scientific and technical knowledge. China's relationship with the United States is fraught with tension, stemming from instability in the balance of their interdependencies as well as from direct competition. The leadership of China and the United States both engage in heavy nationalist rhetoric: each blames the other for unfair competition and invokes their respective nation's "greatness" in the world, whether as something to protect or to rejuvenate. Upon taking office in 2017, U.S. president Donald Trump instigated a trade war with China, although the constraints of interdependence limited how far he could go with protectionist tariffs. But U.S.-China trade relations are not the concern solely of the Republican Party. The Democratic Party, which is also invested in protecting the United States's status as global economic hegemon, is no stranger to China-bashing.

Thus the Chinese Question has been revived and repurposed in the twenty-first century. The specter of a new yellow peril infuses contemporary depictions of China and its alleged threat to American (and world) security. Chinese ownership of American debt is exaggerated—China's share is about 4.5 percent of the total U.S. public debt. Japan is the largest foreign holder of American debt; the U.K., Switzerland, and Brazil are also major holders. But none of these holdings are considered threats to U.S. national security.[20]

The figure of the coolie has returned as the embodiment of unfair competition. Today's "coolies" are workers in China's manufacturing export zones and Chinese and Chinese American students at American universities. Both are imagined as automatons who endure arduous labor without complaint, assembling semiconductor boards or studying for exams, eighty hours or more a week.

Chinese Americans are again feared as disloyal and are alleged to be spies, from scientists like the Taiwanese American Wen-ho Lee at Los Alamos to Chinese American donors to the Democratic Party during Bill Clinton's presidential election campaign. In 2019 the Trump administration asked American universities to surveil Chinese American scholars, especially those in STEM fields, and blocked visas for visiting scholars from China.[21]

During the coronavirus pandemic, President Trump repeatedly called the coronavirus the "Chinese virus," "Wuhan virus," and "Kung-flu virus," in order to deflect attention from his mismanagement of the crisis. He invoked a long racist association of Chinese with disease, resulting in a spate of verbal and physical assault against Chinese and other Asian Americans across the country. During the pandemic, anti-Chinese and anti-Asian racism also erupted in Australia, Britain, and continental Europe.

⚓

GEOPOLITICS HAS ALWAYS FRAMED the Chinese Question, including its trade and immigration dimensions. The United States repealed its Chinese exclusion law during World War II, when China was a war ally. After the Chinese Revolution, American geopolitics required subtler distinctions between "good" Chinese (the Nationalists or Guomindang on Taiwan) and "bad" Chinese (mainland Communists), and immigration restrictions gradually eased. After the United Nations recognized the People's Republic of China in 1971 and booted the Guomindang government from the organization, the Taiwan regime had few friends in the world; one of them was apartheid South Africa, which courted Taiwan capital and immigrants. In the post-apartheid era, South Africa–China trade relations steadily grew after South Africa established formal relations with the People's Republic in 1998. By 2002 China was South Africa's top trading partner; the value of bilateral trade in 2017 was $39 billion.[22]

Since the 1970s, Australia has strived to refashion itself with a Pacific-world identity; it repealed its White Australia immigration policies in the 1973 and began to reckon with China as a trading partner. By 2007 China had become Australia's largest trading partner and in 2009 became Australia's largest export market, led by iron, coal, natural gas, barley, and beef. In 2015 Australia joined China's regional banking initiative, the Asian Infrastructure and Investment Bank, and leased the port of Darwin to a Chinese company for ninety-nine years.[23]

The West's attitudes toward China became less overtly racial in the middle decades of the twentieth century, turning more on ideological distinctions during the Cold War than on simplistic racial stereotypes, and as China's trade with the United States and other countries grew in the early twenty-first century. But the Chinese Question never really went away. The idea that China poses a threat to Euro-American civilizations remained just beneath the surface. In the 1980s, Americans called upon it to service protectionism against Japanese electronics and automotive imports. But whereas Sony and Toyota were easily recognizable as foreign imports, Chinese-made products arrived in America with American labels—Nike, Apple, Levi's, Walmart—their origin undetected (or ignored) until Americans seemed to wake up one day in the early twenty-first century to realize that "everything" sold in the United States was made in China. That's not true, of course: Chinese products accounted for 21 percent of all U.S. imports in 2018.[24]

But in the United States and throughout the West, the specter of a China as a new "yellow peril" grew in the 2010s, especially in the wake of the 2008 financial crisis and recession, which China weathered far better than the United States and Europe. Anxiety over China's rise as a global economic power rests in large part on China's size—the enormous scale of its domestic economy, the global reach of its supply chains and investments, the spectacular double-digit rates of its growth, and the new wave of emigration of both professionals and lower-skilled workers to the United States, Australia, Canada, and Europe. Anti-China discourse is laced with the notion that China's rise in global power is somehow unfair because the Communist government manipulates China's large population, updating nineteenth-century stereotypes of despotic bosses controlling servile coolies and fears of the "sleeping giant" awakened. The Chinese Question, originating in late nineteenth-century politics of racism, colonialism, and capitalism, informs nationalist competition between China and the West in our own time.

Acknowledgments

This book would not have been possible without the financial and intellectual support from a great many institutions and individuals. I thank Columbia University for its generous support, which enabled me to take time from teaching in order to conduct research and to write. Research funds also paid for traveling to distant archives and for hiring research assistants. These resources are often unavailable to scholars at nonelite institutions or in developing countries, and I am grateful to have had these privileges.

For fellowship awards, I thank the John Simon Guggenheim Memorial Foundation (2009); the Institute for Advanced Study (2009); the Dorothy and Lewis B. Cullman Center at the New York Public Library (2012); the Chiang Ching Kuo Foundation (2012); the Woodrow Wilson Center for International Scholars (2013); the Huntington Library and Cheng Family Foundation (2017); and the Shelby Collum Davis Center at Princeton University (2018). I was honored to serve as Kluge Chair at the Library of Congress (2017) and as Wayne Morse Chair at the University of Oregon (2019).

I am grateful to the archivists and librarians who helped me navigate records in their collections. I owe special thanks to Peter Blodgett and Li Wei Yang at the Huntington Library; Michele Matthews at the Bendigo

Regional Archive Centre; and Leigh McKinnon at the Golden Dragon museum in Bendigo.

I benefited enormously from critical readings of draft chapters by Sven Beckert, Sue Fawn Chung, Andrew Edwards, Madeline Hsu, Rebecca Karl, Benjamin Mountford, and Marcia Wright. For research tips, rich conversation, and learned advice, I thank Timothy Alborn, Warwick Anderson, David Atkinson, Gordon Bakken, Manuel Bautista Gonzalez, Katie Benton-Cohen, Elizabeth Blackmar, Angela Creager, Saul Dubow, Alec Dubro, John Fitzgerald, Natalie Fong, Hongdeng Gao, Gary Gerstle, Bryna Goodman, John Higginson, Marilyn Lake, Sophie Loy-Wilson, Valerie Lovejoy, Julia Martínez, Susan Pederson, Jean Pfaelzer, Keir Reeves, Dan Rodgers, Elizabeth Sinn, David Torres-Rouff, Teemu Ruskola, Michele Shover, and Carl Wennerlind. Patrick Wolfe welcomed me to his home in Wurundjeri country in Victoria in 2013. I am sorry he did not live to see his imprint on my thinking.

I thank the following for research assistance: Zabeth Botha, Rebecca Bonner, Miesha Brooks, Catherine Choi, Cailin Hong, Maria John, Nick Juravich, Jennifer Keltz, Rob Konkel, Gina Lam, Brenna McKallick, Dan Miller, Nancy Ng Tam, Yuki Oda, Alexandra Smith, Jiaxian Jessie Wang, and Atlas Tian Xu.

For assistance with research and translation of Chinese-language sources, many thanks to Jack Neubauer (*Xinmin congbao*, Zhang Deyi's writings, remittance letters), Jo Hsuan Wang (Qing Foreign Ministry records), Siwei Wang (Chinese-language newspapers in China and Australia), and Chengji Sally Xing (documentary history collections on modern Chinese history, Chinese language newspapers, Xie Zixiu's South Africa account).

I had the good fortune and opportunity to present my research findings to diverse audiences as this book was in progress. I thank sponsors and participants at the University of Oxford conference on global gold rushes (2008); the University Lecture at Columbia University (2015); the University of Cambridge U.S.—Global History seminar (2017); the Queen Mary University symposium on U.S. history (2017); the Cheng Lecture at the Huntington Library (2017); the Society for Historians of

American Foreign Relations (2017); the Harvard world history workshop (2018); New York University's nineteenth-century history seminar (2019); and the Lowell Humanities Lecture at Boston College (2020).

I thank my readers and interlocutors for their wise advice. All errors remaining are mine.

My deepest gratitude goes to my agent, Sandy Dijkstra, for always cheering me on, and to the team at W. W. Norton, especially my editor, Tom Mayer, who understood from the beginning what I was trying to say and helped me say it.

Glossary of Chinese Proper Names

Aiguo bao 爱国报

Anhui suhua bao 安徽俗话报

Baohuanghui 保皇会

Beiguo chunqiu 北国春秋

Beiximiao (Bok Kai Mui) 北溪庙

Cen Chunxuan 岑春煊

Chen Le (Chan Lok) 陈乐

Chen Ziqing 陈子卿

Dabu (Dai Fow) 大埠

Dongfang zazhi 东方杂志

Donghuabao 东华报

Erbu (Yi Fow) 二埠

Gelaohui 哥老会

Guanghetang (Kwong Hok Tong) 光和堂

Guo Le (Kwok Lok) 郭乐

Guo Quan (Kwok Chuen) 郭泉

Hangzhou baihuabao 杭州白话报

Hehe Huiguan (Hop Wo) 合和会馆

He Yale (Ho A Low) 何亚乐

He Yamei (Ho A Mei) 何亚美

Hongmen (Hungmen) 洪门

Huang Zunxian 黄遵宪

Ji Long (Chy Lung) 济隆

Jiaohui xinbao 教会新报

Jiujinshan 旧金山

Kaiping 开平

Kang Youwei 康有为

Lei Yamei (Louis Ah Mouy) 雷亚枚

Li Gen (Lee Kan) 李根

Liang Cheng 梁诚

Liang Qichao 梁启超

Lin Shu 林纾

Lin Zexu 林则徐

Liu Guangming (Lowe Kong Meng) 刘光明

Liu Yulin (Lew Yuk Lin) 刘玉麟

Luo Fenglu 罗丰禄

Ma Yiingbiao (Ma Ying Piu)
　马应彪

Mei Zhen (Ping Que) 美珍

Renjinglu shicao jianzhu
　人境庐诗草笺注

Rong Hong (Yung Wing) 荣闳

Sanbu (Sam Fow) 三埠

Sanyi (Sam Yup) 三邑

Shanghai Xinbao 上海新报

Shantou (Swatow) 汕头

Shi Jiriu 施吉瑞

Siyi (Sze Yup) 四邑

Taishan (Toishan) 台山

Tang Tinggui (Tong K. Achick)
　唐廷桂

Tiandihui 天地会

Waijiao bao 外交报

Waiwubu 外务部

Wanguo gongbao 万国公报

Wenxiang 文祥

Wu Panzhao (Ng Poon Chew)
　伍盘照

Wu Tingfang 伍廷芳

Wuyi 五邑

Xiamen (Amoy) 厦门

Xiang Sheng Hang (Tseang Sing
　Hong) 祥胜行

Xie Zixiu 谢子修

Xingzhonghui 兴中会

Xinjinshan 新金山

Xinmin congbao 新民丛报

Xinning (Sunning) 新宁

Xue Fucheng 薛福成

Yang Feihong (Yeung Ku-Wan)
　杨飞鸿

Yanghe Huiguan (Yeong Wo)
　洋河会馆

Yantai (Chefoo) 烟台

Yixing (Yee Hing) 义兴

Yuan Sheng 袁生

Zeng Jize (Tseng Chi-tse) 曾纪泽

Zhang Deyi 张德彝

Zhang Zhuoxiong (Cheok Hong
　Cheong) 张桌雄

Zhang Zhidong 张之洞

Zheng Yuxuan 郑玉轩

Zhigongdang (Chee Kung Tong)
　致公党

Zhonghua Huiguan 中华会馆

Zhongshan 中山

Zhongwai xinwen qiri bao
　中外新闻七日报

Zhongxi ribao (*Chung Sai Yat Bo*)
　中西日报

Zongli Yamen 总理衙门

Zou Rong 邹容

Notes

ABBREVIATIONS

Alta	*Daily Alta California*
AS	Academia Sinica
BANC	Bancroft Library
BL	Bodleian Library
BRAC	Bendigo Regional Archives Centre
CAB	Cabinet Office Files, UK
CAJ	California Legislative Journals
CCO	Conservative Central Office, UK
CDB	China Development Bank
CHS	California Historical Society
CMC	Chinese Maritime Customs
CO	Colonial Office, UK
CRL	Center for Research Libraries
CSA	California State Archives
CSL	California State Library
EMJ	*Engineering and Mining Journal*
FLD	Foreign Labour Department, Transvaal
FO	Foreign Office, UK
FRUS	*Foreign Relations of the United States*
GOV	Governor's Office, Transvaal
HL	Huntington Library
KAB	Western Cape Archives, Cape Town
LD	Law Department, Transvaal

NA	National Archives, UK
NASA	National Archives of South Africa
NLA	National Library of Australia
NSW	State Library of New South Wales
PP	*Parliamentary Papers*, UK
PROV	Public Record Office Victoria, North Melbourne
PROV-B	Public Record Office of Victoria, Ballarat
SMH	*Sydney Morning Herald*
TAB	Public Records of Transvaal Province
TCM	Transvaal Chamber of Mines
Union	*Sacramento Daily Union*
VIC	State Library of Victoria
Vic-PP	Victoria Parliamentary Papers
WH	William Honnold Papers

NOTE ON ROMANIZATION AND CURRENCIES

1. Historical Chinese currency: "Tael," *Wikipedia*, https://en.wikipedia.org/wiki/Tael. On gold prices: Lawrence Officer, "What Was the Price of Gold Then? A Data Study," https://www.measuringworth.com/docs/GoldBackground.pdf; "Historical Gold Prices 1833–Present," http://piketty.pse.ens.fr/files/capital21c/xls/RawDataFiles/GoldPrices17922012.pdf. On the gold-price of silver: Hsiao, *China's Foreign Trade Statistics*, table 9a.

INTRODUCTION: YELLOW AND GOLD

1. Schmidt, *In the Human Realm*, 27–29; Huang, "Expulsion of the Immigrants."
2. Lockard, "Chinese Migration and Settlement in SE Asia," 765–781. Chinese in Southeast Asia have long been described as the oldest Chinese diaspora; sociologist Robin Cohen calls it the prototypical "trading" diaspora. Both Republican and Communist Chinese governments use the term *huaqiao* (Chinese overseas), which claims an ongoing national affiliation and identity. Some scholars eschew *diaspora* as a general concept referring to all ethnic Chinese communities abroad, recognizing historical, linguistic, and political differences among them. This book uses *diaspora* specifically to reference Chinese communities in the Anglo-American West, whose historical experience and identities were not only strikingly similar but also coincided with, and were constituting of, late Qing and Republican Chinese nationalism. Cohen, *Global Diasporas*; Shih et al., eds., *Sinophone Studies*; Hsu, "Decoupling Peripheries from the Center"; Kuhn, *Chinese Among Others*; Wang, *Don't Leave Home*, chap. 7.
3. Igler, *Great Ocean*, 17–22.
4. Notable works include Thomas Carlyle, *Occasional Discourse on the Negro Question* (1849); Karl Marx, *On the Jewish Question* (Zur Judenfrage, 1844). Debates over the Woman Question (Querelle des femmes) in Europe date to the seventeenth century,

and in nineteenth-century Britain and United States they were associated with woman suffrage.

5. Classic works on mining include Shinn, *Mining Camps;* Paul, *California Gold;* and Serle, *Golden Age.* More recent works on the California and Australian gold rushes take a more critical approach to nationalist historiography: Rohrbough, *Days of Gold;* and Goodman, *Gold Seeking.* Johnson, *Roaring Camp,* is an exceptional work that gives due attention to Chinese gold seekers in context of a broader history of the California gold rush. For economic histories, see Eichengreen and Flandreau, *Gold Standard in Theory and History;* Flandreau, *Glitter of Gold;* Desan, *Making Money;* Dodd, *Social Life of Money;* Frank, *ReOrient;* Flynn and Giráldez, "Cycles of Silver"; Flynn and Giráldez, "Born with a Silver Spoon"; Schell, "Silver Symbiosis." Alborn, *All That Glittered,* is a rare book that combines cultural and economic history.

6. Lynch, *Mining in World History,* chap. 1; Frank, *ReOrient,* chap. 3; Tutino, *Mexican Heartland,* 39–48.

7. On the Brazilian gold rush: Alborn, *All That Glittered,* 16–17.

8. Total world production of gold from 2000 BCE (in Egypt) through the mid-nineteenth century has been estimated at 10,000 metric tons. Of that amount, about 850 metric tons came from the eighteenth-century Brazilian gold rush. Gold production from the 1848 rush in California through the opening of the goldfields in Yukon Territory in 1891 totaled 13,540 metric tons (435.32 million ounces). See "Gold Production Through History," GoldFeverProspecting.com, http://www.goldfeverprospecting.com/goprthhi.html; David Zurbuchen, "The World's Cumulative Gold and Silver Production," January 14, 2006, Gold-Eagle.com, http://www.gold-eagle.com/editorials_05/zurbuchen011506.html.

9. Newmarch and Tooke are quoted in Daunton, "Britain and Globalization," 15–18; Van Helten, "Empire and High Finance," 533.

10. Curle, *Gold Mines of World,* 2, 16.

11. Mitchell, "Gold Standard in Nineteenth Century," 369–76; Carruthers and Babb, "Color of Money"; O'Malley, "Specie and Species," 369–95.

12. Flynn and Giráldez, "Cycles of Silver"; Flynn and Giráldez, "Born with a Silver Spoon"; Frank, *ReOrient,* chap. 2; Tutino, *Mexican Heartland,* chap. 1.

13. Morse, *Chronicles of East India Company,* 1:26, 45. Morse stated that gold "was cheap in China circa 1700, being only two-thirds of the European mint price," another way of stating silver's arbitrage advantage. Ibid., 1:69. "Multiple arbitrage": Flynn and Giràldez, "Cycles of Silver," 402.

14. Liu, *Tea War,* chap. 1. See also Yong, "Dutch East India Company's Tea." On sugar and food drugs: Mintz, *Sweetness and Power,* 108–9. On tea as a mass consumer good and import to American colonies: Merritt, *Trouble with Tea,* chaps. 1–2; Bello, *Opium and Limits of Empire,* 22–24.

15. Ghosh, *Sea of Poppies,* 85–91.

16. Bello, *Opium and Limits of Empire,* 1–2, 14. Production of opium in Sichuan, Yunnan, and Guizhou would surpass the total of foreign import by 1879. Import data: "Opium Trade," https://www.britannica.com/topic/opium-trade. A chest comprised about 140 pounds of opium.

17. "coveting profit": Translations of Lin Zexu's letter to Queen Victoria (1839) vary. This quote is from S. Teng and J. Fairbank, *China's Response to the West* (1954), published by DigitalChina/Harvard, https://cyber.harvard.edu/ChinaDragon/lin_xexu.html.

18. Hamashita, "Intra-Regional System," 127–28.

19. *Zongli Yamen* was shorthand for *Zongli geguo shiwu yamen*, or "Office in charge of affairs of all nations." On the institutional history of the Zongli Yamen: Rudolph, *Negotiated Power*.

20. Huang, "Writing My Anger" (one poem of five), c. 1890s, in Schmidt, *In the Human Realm*, 295.

21. "What is real": Huangfu, "Internalizing the West," 11. Western inventions: Xue Fucheng, *European Diary*, tenth day of the fourth month, sixteenth year of the Guangxu Emperor (1890). "Chinese learning": Zhang Zhidong, *Exhortation to Study* (1898). On the relative conservativism of Zhang's position: Zarrow, *After Empire*, chap. 4. On the evolution of Huang's views: Huangfu, "Internalizing the West," 5; Schmidt, *In the Human Realm*, 36–40.

22. Average yield was nine dollars per ton. See Penrose, "Witwatersrand Gold Region," 745.

23. Eichengreen and Temin, "Gold Standard and Great Depression," 183–207; see also Eichengreen and Flandreau, *Gold Standard in Theory and History*.

24. Keynes, *General Theory of Employment*, 129–30.

25. Ibid., 130; Simmel, *Philosophy of Money*, 176; Desan, *Making Money*; Skidelsky, *Money and Government*, 23–32; Dodd, *Social Life of Money*; Ingham, "Money Is a Social Relation," 507–29.

CHAPTER 1: TWO GOLD MOUNTAINS

1. Spoehr, "Hawai'i and Gold Rush," 123–32. Allan cited $16/ounce although the price of gold throughout the nineteenth and early twentieth century remained constant at $20.67/ounce. At that rate, 420 ounces equaled 2.6 cups in volume. http://onlygold.com/Info/Historical-Gold-Prices.asp; https://www.aqua-calc.com/calculate/weight-to-volume. Allan's letter, dated October 7, 1848, accompanied the payment to Hudson's Bay, Honolulu, on the schooner *Julia*, the next outbound ship to the islands, which left San Francisco October 23 and arrived at Honolulu on November 12, 1848. Departure and arrival are reported respectively in "Marine Intelligence," *Californian*, November 4, 1848, 3, and "Commercial Statistics," *Polynesian*, January 20, 1849. The next outbound ship from Honolulu to Hong Kong was the *Amelia*, which departed November 20, 1848. "Commercial Statistics," *Polynesian*, January 20, 1849. I calculated *Amelia*'s arrival in Hong Kong based on sailing time from Honolulu to Hong Kong of thirty to thirty-six days, from two contemporary sailings: the *Thomas W. Sears*, Honolulu to Hong Kong, October 1 to November 6, 1850 (thirty-six days), and the *Ocean Pearl*, Honolulu to Hong Kong, April 28 to May 29, 1855 (thirty days). Edward Horatio Faucon, Log of *T. W. Sears*, in Logbooks 1850–1863, Ms. N-1216, Massachusetts Historical Society, http://www.cap.amdigital.co.uk/Documents/

Details/MHS_EdwardSFaucon_Logs_1850; Alfred Tufts, *"Ocean Pearl* Logbook," Tufts Family Papers, Massachusetts Historical Society, http://www.cap.amdigital.co .uk/Documents/Details/MHS_TuftsFamily_OceanPearl_Alfred.

2. "California," *Friend of China,* January 6, 1849, 6; "Gold and Silver," *Polynesian,* November 11, 1848; "California" and "Gold Hunting," *Polynesian,* November 18, 1849; Sinn, *Pacific Crossing,* 44. Arrival at San Francisco of *Richard and William*: "Marine Journal," *Alta,* March 22, 1849, p. 2.

3. On the *Swallow*: Sinn, *Pacific Crossing,* 55; "Marine Journal," *Alta,* July 19, 1849, 2. On Yuan Sheng: Lai, "Potato King."

4. In some accounts, "Asing."

5. Seven arrivals: Bancroft, *History of California,* 7:336. The *Alta* reported that there were fifty-five Chinese in California as of February 1, 1849. "The Chinese Emigration," *Alta* second supplement, May 15, 1852, p. 7. Weekly shipping reports account for forty passengers arriving from Hong Kong and China between January and August, although the names and nationalities of the passengers are not listed. "Marine Journal," *Alta,* July 2, 1849, p. 2, and August 2, 1849, p. 3. Polyglot scenes: Borthwick, *Three Years in California,* 30, 51–56.

6. "Agreement between the English Merchant and Chinamen," 29th year of Taou Kwang [1849], Wells Fargo corporate archives.

7. The company was probably among the 101 passengers on the English ship *Amazon,* which arrived from China on October 15. "Merchant Ships in Port, 1849," *Maritime Heritage Project,* http://www.maritimeheritage.org/inport/1849.html. The name of the ship in the agreement was transliterated as "Ah-mah-san." Five hundred Chinese: Chiu, *Chinese Labor in California,* 3, 11–12; Barron, "Celestial Empire." Jinshan among Chinese Americans is mostly known in Siyi dialect as Gum Saam.

8. On Sutter: Spoehr, "Hawaii and Gold Rush," 124–27; Dillion, "Fool's Gold, the Decline and Fall of Captain John Sutter of California," https://en.wikipedia.org/ wiki/John_Sutter#Beginnings_of_Sutter.27s_Fort. On Marshall's discovery: Marshall to Hutchings, January 24, 1848, in Egenhoff, *Elephant as They Saw It,* 27–29. Indian Jim: Rawls, "Gold Diggers," 30.

9. Scholars estimate that the precontact indigenous population of California was about 300,000 and that by 1846 it was reduced to half that number as the result of disease, violence, and maltreatment by Spanish and Mexican missions. Madley, *American Genocide,* introduction; Chan, "People of Exceptional Character," 50; Rohrbough, *Days of Gold,* 7–16.

10. Chan, "People of Exceptional Character," 50–52; Rawls, "Gold Diggers," 30–32.

11. Rohrbough, *Days of Gold,* 24–25; Chan, "People of Exceptional Character," 57; "Travel Routes," Gold Rush of California, http://goldrushofcalifornia.weebly.com/ travel-routes.html; Barbara Maranzani, "8 Things You May Not Know About the California Gold Rush." History.com, January 24, 2013, https://www.history.com/ news/8-things-you-may-not-know-about-the-california-gold-rush.

12. On LeMott: Rohrbough, *Days of Gold,* 167. On Hawaii, Chile, and Australia imports: Chan, "People of Exceptional Character," 51–54. On Hong Kong: Sinn, *Pacific Crossing,* 141–47. On flour: Meissner, "Bridging the Pacific," 82–93.

13. "Mexican Prizes," *California Star,* January 1, 1848, p. 2; Spoehr, "Hawaii and Gold Rush," 126–27; Greer, "California Gold," 157–73.

14. *Californian,* October 7, 1848, p. 2.

15. Sinn, *Pacific Crossing,* 35–47, 143–45.

16. Ibid., 309–11; Bibb, "China Houses"; Augustin Hale diary, entry for August 9, 1850, Box 6, Augustin Hale Papers, HL.

17. Sinn, *Pacific Crossing,* 309–11, 147–48.

18. Peter McAllister, "Sydney Ducks." *Monthly,* February 2015, https://www.themonthly .com.au/issue/2015/february/1422709200/peter-mcallister/sydney-ducks; Ricards and Blackburn, "The Sydney Ducks: A Demographic Analysis," 12–31; Monaghan, *Australians and Gold Rush.*

19. Mitchell, "Hargraves, Edward Hammond."

20. Serle, *Golden Age,* 10–12; "Rumours of Gold," in *Eureka!*

21. Mitchell, "Hargraves, Edward Hammond"; Hargraves to William Northwood, "Rumours of Gold," in *Eureka!* Hargraves also received an annual pension of £250 to begin in 1877 and was appointed colonial commissioner of the goldfields. His three assistants, John Lister and the brothers James and Henry Tom, bitter and resentful at their exclusion from acknowledgment and reward, petitioned the government and, after a lengthy investigation, received a thousand pounds each in 1853 and, in 1890, official recognition as the first to have discovered gold.

22. Serle, *Golden Age,* 10–11; Fahey, "Peopling Victorian Goldfields," 148–61.

23. Serle, *Golden Age,* 67–71, 95.

24. Mountford, *Britain, China, and Colonial Australia,* 17, 25, 48–49, 68–70; Broadbent et al., *India, China, Australia,* 22, 42; Serle, *Golden Age,* 42, 121. Import statistics from Macgregor, "Lowe and Chinese Engagement." The Navigation Acts, which required all trade to the British colonies to be routed through England, were repealed in 1850.

25. Serle, *Golden Age,* 2–3; Wolfe, "Settler Colonialism"; Hunter, "Aboriginal Legacy."

26. On Djadjawurrung and Wathawrrung: Cahir, *Black Gold,* 23. Milne quoted in Goodman, "Making an Edgier History," 32–33.

27. Estimates by Evans and Ørsted-Jensen, "'I Cannot Say the Numbers That Were Killed,'" 4–5. "Multiply and replenish": Henry Mort to his mother and sister, January 28, 1844, quoted in Reynolds, *Dispossession,* 4. On Aboriginal resistance to white settlers, white reprisals and punitive expeditions, and the use of spears and rifles: *Dispossession,* 31–49. On forced occupation: *Queensland Guardian,* May 4, 1861, quoted ibid., 12.

28. Rawls, "Gold Diggers," 4; Augustin Hale Diary, entries for February 22, August 8, 10, 30, 1850, box 6, Hale Papers, HL.

29. Madley, *American Genocide,* chap. 4; Peter Burnett, State of the State Address, January 6, 1851, https://governors.library.ca.gov/addresses/s_01-Burnett2.html.

30. Serle, *Golden Age,* 321; Cronin, *Colonial Casualties,* 19.

31. Johnson, *Roaring Camp,* 193–95; Rohrbough, *Days of Gold,* 125; Rawls, "Gold Diggers," 31; Sisson, "Bound for California," 259–305; Pitt, *Decline of Californios;* Gonzalez, "'My Brother's Keeper,'" 118–41; Standart, "Sonoran Migration to Cal-

ifornia," 333–57; Pérez Rosales, "Diary of Journey to California," 3–100; Navarro, *Gold Rush Diary.*

32. Fifteen coolies: Lucett, *Rovings in the Pacific,* 2:363; Navarro, *Gold Rush Diary,* 6–8. Chinese *huiguan* leaders stated as early as 1852 that contracting workers "was done to some extent at one time, yet it was not found to be as profitable as was anticipated and is now abandoned." California Committee on Mines and Mining Interests, *Report* (1853).

33. "Prospects of California," *California Star,* March 25, 1848, p. 4; Borthwick, *Three Years in California,* 66; Navarro, *Gold Rush Diary,* 10. Port Phillip Bay: Mountford, *Britain, China, and Colonial Australia,* 49. Ship captains: Serle, *Golden Age,* 66.

34. Siyi (Sze Yup in Cantonese). Xinning (Sunning) was later renamed Taishan (Toishan). Mei, "Socioeconomic Origins," 463–99; Hsu, *Dreaming of Gold,* 16–27.

35. Wang, *Chinese Overseas,* chap. 1; Mei, "Socioeconomic Origins." On Taiping Rebellion: Spence, *God's Chinese Son.*

36. Look Lai, *Indentured Labor;* Meagher, *Coolie Trade;* Hu DeHart, "From Slavery to Freedom," 31–51; Yun, *Coolie Speaks;* McKeown, "Global Migration."

37. Morse, *International Relations of Chinese Empire,* 2:166.

38. Ibid., 165. Lowe Kong Meng estimated that two-thirds of the Chinese emigrants in Victoria were from farming background and one-third were traders. *Report of the Select Committee of the Legislative Council on the Subject of Chinese Immigration 1857,* p. 10, Vic-PP. On women: Johnson, *Roaring Camp,* 169–76; Rohrbough, *Days of Gold,* 95–99; Serle, *Golden Age,* 320–21; McKeown, "Transnational Chinese Families," 73–110.

39. Lee Chew, "The Biography of a Chinaman," *Independent* 15 (February 19, 1903): 417–23.

40. Loan for steamship ticket, 1856: Wuyi Overseas Chinese Museum. Huang contract: Chang and Fishkin, *Chinese and the Iron Road,* 60–61. See also Zo Kil Young, *Chinese Emigration,* 93–96. On late Qing contracts and loans: Zelin, "Structures of the Chinese Economy," 31–67.

41. "Upwards of 800 Chinese": White, December 26, 1853, quoted in Morse, *International Relations of Chinese Empire,* 2:166. On *Xia'er guanzhen*: Sinn, "Beyond 'Tianxia,'" 94.

42. Customs data cited in Chiu, *Chinese Labor,* 13; Chan, "People of Exceptional Character," 73. On Australia: Serle cites government reports of 42,000 Chinese in 1859, roughly 20 percent of total, in *Golden Age,* 330. Walker estimates 50,000 Chinese in 1859, or 25 percent, in *Anxious Nation,* 36; Mountford and Tuffnell, *Global History of Gold Rushes,* 11; Reeves, "Sojourners or a New Diaspora?," 181; Fahey, "Peopling Victorian Goldfields," 149.

CHAPTER 2: ON THE DIGGINGS

1. Nicolini et al., "Chinese Camp," 47–67; "Charlie" to "My dear sister" (1856), in Sheafer, *Chinese and Gold Rush,* 53; Barron, "Celestial Empire"; Hoover et al., *Historic Spots in California,* 574–75; Speer, *Humble Plea,* 26–28.

2. Occupations and description of town: U.S. Census of 1860, Tuolumne County, Township 5 (Chinese Camp); "Chinese Camp," *Sonora Herald*, March 31, 1866; Nicolini, "When East Met West." Plantings: Bloomfield, *History of Chinese Camp*, 45, 58–61.

3. U.S. Population Census of 1870, Tuolumne County, Township 3 (Chinese Camp), p. 35, shows the family of Ah Son, a miner, and Chun Kee, with two children, age 4 and 10; and Sing Tong, a miner, and Sa Soo, with three children, age 6, 10 and 12. Duck Mary and China Lena: Nicolini et al., "Chinese Camp," 57. Ah Sam and Yo Sup Marriage Certificate, MS 23, CHS, http://www.oac.cdlib.org/ark:/13030/hb6d5nb1g0/?brand=oac4. U.S. Population Census, 1860, Tuolumne County; men named Ah Sam are listed in Townships 2, 3, 5 and 6; Ah Yow in Township 5 (Chinese Camp), p. 38.

4. Tom and Tom, *Marysville's Chinatown*, 17–34; "Sacramento News," *Alta*, May 13, 1852, p. 2; California state census of 1852, Yuba County.

5. *U.S. Population Census, 1860*, Butte County, Oroville.

6. Borthwick, *Three Years in California*, 143, 319; *Register of Mining Claims, Calaveras County*, 1854, Rare Books, CSL; *U.S. Population Census, 1860*, Calaveras County, California, Township 5.

7. Williams, "Chinese in California Mines," 39–40. Chinese quarters may also be found in contemporary Sanborn fire insurance maps and census records, including Weaverville, Sonora, Goodyears Bar, San Andreas, Angels Camp, Mokelumne Hill, Shasta, and other towns. On Angels Camp and other Calaveras County towns, Costello, "Calaveras Chinese." Daniel Latimer, originally from Michigan, is listed as a merchant in the 1852 California census, Calaveras County, 1. The Lower Log Cabin district convened meetings at his store and kept its mining ledger there. On Petersburg: "Terrible Affray with Chinese," *Union*, May 14, 1861, 4; Costello, "Calaveras Chinese"; "Greasertown, California," https://en.wikipedia.org/wiki/Greasertown,_California. The town no longer exists after it was flooded for the creation of the Hogan Dam on the Calaveras River, 1924–30.

8. Sidney Hardy and his brothers put up a tent and called it an "inn" on the road to Wood's Creek in Tuolumne County. Hardy journal, 1849–50, mssHM 62959, HL. On folk houses: Bloomfield, *History of Chinese Camp*, 67–68. On Sun Sun Wo (*xinxinhe*): "Mariposa County Points of Interest: Sun Sun Wo Co.," NoeHill Travels in California, http://noehill.com/mariposa/poi_sun_sun_wo_company.asp; "The Sun Sun Wo Store," Coulterville, http://malakoff.com/goldcountry/mccvssws.htm.

9. Ledger from Bidwell's Bar, 1860–62, HM79058, HL; Andrew Brown, Account Books for the Chinamen, 1873–77 and 1886–88 (Whisky Flat), MssBrown Papers, HL; account ledgers of Sun Sun Wo Co, 1876, 1889, 1901, Mariposa Museum and History Center. I thank David Torres-Rouff for sharing this source. The butcher ("S____") is quoted in Speer, *Humble Plea*, 24. See also Chung, *In Pursuit of Gold*, 14–18.

10. Rohrbough, *Days of Gold*, 124. *Xie jin*: "Jinshan kaikuang de ju jin" (Big gold found in gold mountain mining), *Jiaohui xinbao*, no. 112 (1870), 11.

11. Rohe, "After the Gold Rush," 7.

12. "Mining Technology: Overview," *Encyclopedia of Gold in Australia*, http://www
.egold.net.au/biogs/EG00009b.htm.

13. Limbaugh, "Making Old Tools Work Better," 24–51; Chung, *In Pursuit of Gold*,
10–11. Borthwick, *Three Years in Cali*fornia, 265, 261–62. "Watch the miners":
Bloomfield, *History of Chinese Camp*, 56. The *Bendigo Advertiser* is cited by Lovejoy,
"Fortune Seekers," 157–58. On water technologies in Australia: McGowan, "Economics and Organisation," 119–38.

14. McGowan, "Economics and Organisation," 121; Rohrbough, *Days of Gold*, 125;
Rasmussen, "Chinese in Nation and Community," 80; Serle, *Golden Age*, 73; Limbaugh, "Making Old Tools Work Better," 24–51. For an example of American partnerships: Diary of John Eagle, mssEGL 1–49, HL.

15. On kinship: Chung, *In Pursuit of Gold*, 13–14, 20. Lovejoy, "Things that Unite,"
showed only 7 of 97 cases in inquest hearings where miners had no relatives or
mates. Calaveras claims, Mining Records of Calaveras County, 1854–1857, Rare
Books, CSL. The Tuolumne County manufacturing schedule in the 1860 census
lists only one Chinese miner, W. Chang, with an "employee" (who was more likely
a partner). *U.S. Census, 1860*, Schedule of Industry, California, Tuolumne County,
Township 2 and Township 3.

16. Claim no. 1786, Ah Ping and Low Ying, 1868, *Mining Registrar's Register of Claims*,
Sandhurst, VPRS6946, P0001/2, PROV. See also Sluicing claim no. 1693, Ah Hee,
March 21, 1865, 600 x 120 feet (1/10 acre), Sailor's Creek, *Court of Mines Register of
Mining Claims*, Daylesford, VPRS3719, P0000/1, PROV-B. On Chinese and European miners working in close proximity: Lovejoy, "Fortune Seekers," 154; "Plan
of Golden Point Section of Forest Creek," 1859, Department of Economic Development, Jobs, Transport, and Resources, Victoria, http://earthresources.vic.gov.au/
earth-resources/geology-of-victoria/exhibitions-and-Imagery/beneath-our-feet/the
-early-years.

17. Chinese claims along the Klamath River in Siskiyou County: California Bureau of
Mines, *Eighth Annual Report of State Mineralogist* (1888). Approximately one thousand Chinese mined in Siskiyou County, with an aggregate annual income of at
least $365,000. Chiu, *Chinese Labor*, 24, 30–31; Chung, *In Pursuit of Gold*, 17–18.

18. Description of cooperatives in river placers: U.S. Census Bureau, *Report on Mineral
Industries in the United States: Gold and Silver* (1890), 109. See also claims registers
for Lower Log Cabin District, *Mining Records of Calaveras County*, Rare Books, CSL.
At Smith's Flat, Chinese recorded cooperative claims and claims by preemption,
El Dorado County, Mining Claims Register (1864–68), *El Dorado County Records*,
vol. 165, HL. Mining cooperative members in Sacramento County in 1860 earned
shares of approximately $40 to $50 per month. U.S. Census Bureau, *Schedule of
Industry, California, Sacramento County, Cosumnes Township*, 1860. Yuba county
preemption claims: Chan, "Chinese Livelihood in Rural California," 57–82.

19. Ah Fock, testimony, December 12, 1887, *People v. Ah Jake*, trial transcript, 106–7,
file F3659-13, Executive Pardons, CSA. Forty-pound nugget: Chung, *In Pursuit of
Gold*, 12.

20. Young, *Report on Conditions of Chinese Population*, 40, 42–43. Heads of Chinese

mining companies in southern New South Wales took a 20 to 25 percent share and charged miners for weekly board. Small companies also worked on shares instead of paying wages. McGowan, "Economics and Organisation," 121, 123. On puddling and tailing: Serle, *Golden Age,* 321. Serle's use of the term *cooperatively* would have applied to egalitarian cooperatives and proportional share companies, as distinguished from employees earning a wage.

21. Ah Ling's claim, August 25, 1865, *Register of Mining Claims,* Daylesford, 3719/P0000/1, PROV-B. One-quarter shares registered by Let Chook, Kin Lin, Fong Ming, and Ah King, for puddling claim #2125, January 29, 1866, Blind Creek, *Mining Registrar's Register of Claims,* Daylesford Mining Division, VPRS3719, P0000/1 (January 1865–October 1868), PROV-B. The Portuguese Flat cooperative is described in testimonies of Ah Su and Ah Ter, "Inquest Held upon the Body of Ah Yung at Creswick," February 2, 1863, Inquest Deposition Files, VPRS24 P0000/24, PROV. Thirty shillings per week was the average earning for a Chinese miner through the 1860s and '70s. Lovejoy, "Fortune Seekers," 159.

22. Qing-era mining merchant-investors allotted as much as 40 percent of the profits to their workers. Sun, "Mining Labor in Ch'ing Period"; Valentine, "Chinese Placer Mining," 37–53; Bowen, "Merchants," 25–44. On share division in China: Gardella, "Contracting Business Partnerships," 329.

23. Heidhues, *Golddiggers, Farmers, and Traders;* Heidhues, "Chinese Organizations"; Jackson, *Chinese in West Borneo Goldfields.* Kongsi were also prevalent in the tin-mining industry on the Malaysian peninsula. Reid, "Chinese on Mining Frontier," 29.

24. Southern China economy: Mei, "Socioeconomic Origins," 481; Wong, *China Transformed,* 19–20. By the mid-eighteenth century, most hired farmhands were legally considered free persons. Wu, "On Embryonic Capitalism," in Xu and Wu, *Chinese Capitalism,* 11–12; California's southern mines: Chiu, *Chinese Labor,* 34–37; Raymond, *Statistics of Mines and Mining* (1870), 4.

25. Isenberg, *Mining California,* 23–35; Rohe, "Chinese and Hydraulic Mining," 73–91; Chiu, *Chinese Labor,* 36–38. Generally, whites worked as skilled labor and Chinese as semiskilled and unskilled labor; standard wage rates in the 1860s and '70s were $3.00 to $3.50 per day for whites and $1.50 per day for Chinese, with mill hands earning $2 and $1 per day, respectively. Chinese were commonly hired through a headman, but some companies hired and paid Chinese individually. There are no extant payroll records for North Bloomfield Mining and Gravel, but records from other companies illustrate general hiring, work, and pay patterns: for example, Alturus Mining Company workman's time book, Charles William Hendel Collection, 10/675, CSL; Little York Gold-Washing and Water Company payroll ledger, 1873–75, vol. 4, William Maguire Mining Records, banc mss 90/163c, BANC; Chinese time book, 1875, El Dorado Water and Deep Gravel Company, El Dorado County, vol. 156, HL.

26. *Woodruff v. North Bloomfield Mining and Gravel Company,* 18 F. 753 (C.C.D. Cal. 1884); Isenberg, *Mining California,* 39–51; Rohe, "Chinese and Hydraulic Mining," 88–89; *Mining and Scientific Press,* January 28, 1882.

27. H. L. Hurlbut to wife, February 10, 1853, CHS MS 32, letter 12, Hurlbut Family Correspondence, CHS. The letter does not specify how many Chinese they hired. The average daily pay was $2.50. The going rate for Chinese was $1 to $1.25 a day. It is hard to imagine they would have had employed than two or three Chinese, but even four Chinese would have earned more than $12 each for three weeks work. H. B. Lansing, Diary, 1853, HM 70409, HL.

28. Young, *Report on Conditions of Chinese Population*, 40, 42–43, 33–43. Chinese labored underground for Chinese-owned quartz companies and for European companies such as the Reform Mining Company, near Ballarat. Lovejoy, "Fortune Seekers," 160. On tailings work: Application of Ah Wah, Nov. 7, 1871, Applications to Mine 26 and 27a, VPRS16936/P0001, BRAC; Rasmussen, "Chinese in Nation and Community," 84–87.

29. Miles, *Capitalism and Unfree Labour*; Brass and van der Linden, *Free and Unfree Labor*, 11; Stanley, *From Bondage to Contract*; Jung, *Coolies and Cane*; Follett et al., *Slavery's Ghost*. On Chinese native place associations: Lai, *Becoming Chinese American*, 41; Chung, *In Pursuit of Gold*, 19; Kian, "Chinese Economic Dominance," 8.

30. Chung, *In Pursuit of Gold*, 16–17. On Wong Kee: Valentine, "Historical and Archeological Excavations," 33–34, 40–41.

31. Sinn, *Pacific Crossing*, 55; Lai, "Potato King," Achick and Hab Wa to Governor Bigler (1852), in *Analysis of Chinese Question*, 7.

32. "Meeting of the Chinese Residents of San Francisco," *Alta*, December 10, 1849, p. 1.

33. Woodworth: "Selim E. Woodworth," *Wikipedia*, https://en.wikipedia.org/wiki/Selim_E._Woodworth.

34. "Meeting of the Chinese Residents of San Francisco," *Alta*, December 10, 1849, p. 1; "The Celebration," *Alta*, October 31, 1850.

35. Lai, "Potato King."

36. Goodman, *Native Place, City, and Nation*.

37. Lai, *Becoming Chinese American*, chap. 3. The Siyi Huiguan was formed in 1851 but split into as many as ten groups, then was finally organized in the early twentieth century as the Ning Yung, Hop Wo (Hehe), Kong Chow, and Sue Hing associations. The Sanyi Huiguan included people from Nanhai, Panyu, and Shunde counties. In San Francisco the CCBA continued to be called the Six Companies regardless of the number of *huiguan*. On Victoria *huiguan*: Young, *Report on Conditions of Chinese Population*, 40.

38. "Jinshan huaren zi song laorun ku min huiguo" (San Francisco Chinese support elders and miserable to return home), *Jiaohui xinbao*, no. 299 (1874), 13–14; Loomis, "Six Chinese Companies," 221–27; Speer, *Humble Plea*, 6.

39. California Committee on Mines and Mining Interests, *Report* (1853); Young, *Report on Conditions of Chinese Population*; Fitzgerald, *Big White Lie*, 66. On paying off credit-ticket in a year: Cronin, *Colonial Casualties*, 19–20.

40. Lai, *Becoming Chinese American*, 46–47.

41. Ownby, *Brotherhoods and Secret Societies*; Murray, *Origins of Tiandihui*; Ownby and Heidhues, *"Secret Societies" Reconsidered*. On the Zhigongdang: Chung, "Between Two Worlds"; McKeown, *Chinese Migrant Networks*; Jin, *Hung Men Handbook*.

42. "Notice to every villager" (Charlie Fun Chung note), signed by Zhong Jinrui (n.d.), Golden Dragon Museum; Telegram to a Chinese in Sierra City, October 7, 1874, MSS C-Y 209, BANC. For various cases over payment and rent disputes, see Los Angeles Area Court Cases, HL.

43. Cai, "From Mutual Aid to Public Interest," 133–52; Fitzgerald, *Big White Lie*, 69–76, 93–94; Crawford, *Notes by Mr. Crawford.*

44. Cai, "From Mutual Aid to Public Interest," 139; Fitzgerald, *Big White Lie*, 60.

45. Benton and Liu, *Dear China*, chap. 2; Guoth and Macgregor, "Getting Chinese Gold," 129–50; Young, *Report on Conditions of Chinese Population*, 50.

46. Loy-Wilson, "Coolie Alibis," 28–45. Unfortunately for these men, customs officials seized their gold because they allegedly had not paid a newly established gold export fee but kept it even after the men agreed to pay the duty. The Chinese finally prevailed after a lengthy court battle but were returned only a third of their gold, as the rest had been divided among corrupt officers and deemed impossible to recover.

47. Gold shipped from Melbourne to Hong Kong, July 1857 through December 1859, 215,989 ounces, most of which was shipped as "crude gold," not coin. "Chinese Passengers and Gold Shipped by the Chinese," 1859/A1, Vic-PP. Lowe Kong Meng, testimony, *Report of the Select Committee of the Legislative Council on the Subject of Chinese Immigration*, p. 10, 1856-57/D19, Vic-PP. On gold shipped in late 1870s: Crawford, *Notes by Mr. Crawford*, 18. On California remittances: Mei, "Socioeconomic Origins," 489.

48. Kaiping, *Kaiping yinxin*, chap. 3; Li, *Shijie jiyi yichan.* For a social history of a remittance society of Taishan county and its ties to California in the late nineteenth and early twentieth centuries, see Hsu, *Dreaming of Gold.* The Kaiping watchtowers are now a UNESCO world heritage site.

49. In Wuyi (five counties including Taishan and Kaiping), the first couriers were called water guests and horses patrolling the city. Kaiping, *Kaiping yinxin*, chap. 2; Liu, *Taishan lishi wenhua ji.* Teochew couriers in Fujian were called "water carriers" and "feet." Qiaopi agencies working for Teochow emigrants lasted until 1979, when banks took over the entire process. *Teochew Letters*, http://www.teochewletters.org/.

50. Macgregor, "Lowe Kong Meng."

51. *Argus* (1863) quoted ibid. Lowe Kong Meng, testimony, *Report of the Select Committee of Legislative Council on the Subject of Chinese Immigration*, p. 12, 1856-57/17, Vic-PP; Fitzgerald, *Big White Lie*, 64–66.

52. Fitzgerald, *Big White Lie*, 66–69; Macgregor, "Lowe Kong Meng"; Gouth and Macgregor, "Getting Chinese Gold"; Bowen, "Merchants," 40.

53. Bowen, "Merchants," 39–40; Macgregor, "Chinese Political Values," 62. Louis and Mary had two children, but she died early, at the age of twenty-three. Louis later married a Chinese woman, with whom he had eleven children.

54. Robert Bowie testimony, *Report of the Select Committee of the Legislative Council on the Subject of Chinese Immigration*, pp. 7–8, 1856-57/19, Vic-PP; "Population of the Goldfields," table V, Victoria Census of 1857. The goldfield districts were formal administrative units under the charge of colonial goldfield commissioners and magistrates.

55. Young, *Report on Conditions of Chinese Population;* Young, "Tabular Statement of Chinese Population, and Particulars of their Employments, as furnished by the Chinese Interpreters on the different Goldfields, for 1866 and 1867," 1868/56, Vic-PP.

56. *Precis of Reports of Chinese Protectors with Respect to Diversity of Chinese Dialects* (1857), VSRP1189/P0000/502/57–94, PROV; Cronin, *Colonial Casualties,* 25–26; Serle, *Golden Age,* 332.

57. Young, *Report on Conditions of Chinese Population.* Ironbark Village: Lovejoy, "Fortune Seekers," chap. 8; Yixing hall: Crawford, *Notes by Mr. Crawford,* 10. The original Chinese on the scrolls is unknown. There are no obvious correspondences in the Hung Men Handbook translated by Jin.

58. Denny, "Mud, Sludge and Town Water"; "Population of the Goldfields," table V, Victoria Census of 1857.

59. Jones, "Ping Que: Mining Magnate." Ping Que's Chinese name is somewhat elusive. "Pin Qui—Mei Zhen" signed a petition at Creswick in 1867. "Humble Petition of Storekeepers and Rate-payers on Black Lead 30 April 1869," VPRS5921/P0000/2, PROV.

60. Lovejoy, "Fortune Seekers," chap. 4.

61. On James Ni Gan: Lovejoy, "Fortune Seekers," chap. 7; Rasmussen, "Rise of Labor"; James Ni Gan, Claims no. 39398–403 (amalgamated sluicing claim) showing partners John Saville, Hen Loy, Ah Choon, Patrick Mooney, Ni Gook, James Ni Gan, Fourth White Hill, *Sandhurst Mining Registrar's Register of Claims,* VPRS 6946/7, PROV; Jones, "Ping Que: Mining Magnate."

62. Rescued prostitutes: Pascoe, *Relations of Rescue.* Merchants' wives: Yung, *Unbound Feet.* Working wives: Nicolini, "When East Met West."

63. On masculinity: Johnson, *Roaring Camp,* 121–39; Bryson to Stoddard, December 3, 1851, HM 16387, HL. Third sex: Lee, *Orientals,* 88–89; Shah, *Contagious Divides,* chap. 3.

64. Ko, *Teachers of Inner Chambers;* Ransmeier, "Body-Price," 209–26.

65. Sommer, *Sex, Law, and Society,* 30–31, 154–56. On corporate form of the family: Ruskola, *Legal Orientalism,* chap. 3; Bernhardt, *Women and Property in China, 960–1949.* On sex and same-sex relations in China before the twentieth century: Chou, *Tongzhi,* 1–55.

66. *People v. Ah Jake,* examination transcript, in Dressler, *California Chinese Chatter,* 51–52; *People v. Ah Jake,* transcript of testimony, December 12, 1887, pp. 50–57, 61, 100, file F3659-13, Executive Pardons, CSA.

CHAPTER 3: TALKING TO WHITE PEOPLE

1. *People v. Ah Jake,* examination transcript upon a charge of murder, in Dressler, *California Chinese Chatter,* 51–52.

2. Ibid., 45.

3. Instruction to ignore defendant: ibid., 44. "You want to ask him": ibid., 47.

4. Ibid., 50–51, 54–55.

5. Hunter, *"Fan Kwae" at Canton*, 60–62; Spence, *God's Chinese Son*, 7–8; Ghosh, *Sea of Poppies*, 490. Spence writes that, when a comprador informs an American trader that a visiting official is expecting a large bribe, "'Mant-a-le [mandarin] sendee one piece chop. He come tomollo, wantee two-lac dollar,' everyone knows what he means." Pidgin is a simplified contact language and not a creole, a mature language that is the primary language of a group, such as Gullah spoken in the Georgia Sea Islands, Jamaican *patwah* (patois), or Hawaiian *pidgin*. According to linguists, for a language to be a true pidgin, "two conditions must be met: its grammatical structure and vocabulary must be sharply reduced . . . and also the resultant language must be native to none of those who use it." Hall, *Pidgin and Creole Languages*, vii.

6. I thank Teemu Ruskola for information on translators in nineteenth-century Chinese courts. On treaty writing: Liu, *Clash of Empires*, 112. The treaty also notoriously banned use in any Chinese official documents of the Chinese word *yi*, meaning generally "foreigner" but translated by the British to mean "barbarian," to refer to the British government or persons. Ibid., 31–69.

7. The *OED* defines the verb *to savvy* as "slang, trans., To know; to understand, comprehend. Freq. used in the interrogative (= 'do you understand?') following an explanation to a foreigner or to one considered slow-witted.)" "Few necessary words": William Speer, "Claims of the Chinese on Our Common Schools," San Francisco *Evening Bulletin*, January 20, 1857. See also Rusling, *Across America*, 303.

8. Thomason and Kaufman, *Language Contact*, 167–88.

9. Not until 1978 did the United States require federal courts to provide interpreters for defendants and witnesses whose primary language was not English (Court Interpreters Act of 1978, 28 USCS § 1827). However, electronic sound recording of interpretation is not mandatory but at the court's discretion. Sec (d)(2). Lack of translation and mistranslation are grounds for appeal, but higher courts seldom find that translation errors reach the threshold for what they consider constitutionally an unfair trial.

10. *People v. Ah Jake*, trial transcript, December 12, 1887, p. 3, file F3659-13, Executive Pardons, CSA (hereafter cited as Ah Jake pardon file); Hall and Millard, "History of California Pioneer"; quotes from Millard letter, August 17, 1881. On Millard's work for Charles Crocker, see also Alisa Judd, "CPRR Ah Henge & J. Millard" (blogpost), Central Pacific Railroad Photographic History Museum, CPRR Discussion Group, March 28, 2005, http://cprr.org/CPRR_Discussion_Group/2005/03/cprr-ah-henge -jmillard.html. I thank Alisa Judd for sharing photographs and information about her great-grandfather Jerome Millard.

11. *People v. Ah Jake*, trial transcript, 49–52, Ah Jake pardon file.

12. Ibid., 78–80, 109–14.

13. Ibid., 120. I thank Gordon Bakken for clarifying that these strange instructions do conform to the California criminal code. In a fight situation, a person may be deemed to have acted in self-defense if he/she killed the initiator of the fight in the course of combat. However, if the initiator has been incapacitated by a blow or a fall and the other person takes advantage of the situation to then kill him/her, the state of mind is considered to have changed from self-defense to premeditation.

The judge did not make these distinctions clear to the jury. *People v. Ah Jake*, death warrant, December 23, 1887, Ah Jake pardon file. Motion for new trial denied: *People v. Ah Jake*, afternoon session, December 22, 1887, Ah Jake prison file, Folsom commitment papers, CSA; *Mountain Messenger*, December 24, 1887, p. 2.

14. The first Protestant missionaries in California, Revs. Wiliam Speer, A. W. Loomis, and Ira Condit (Presbyterian) and Otis Gibson (Methodist) all served in China. Woo, "Presbyterian Mission." On Gibson: Thomson, *Our Oriental Missions*, 235–36. In Victoria, Rev. William Young joined the London Missionary Society in Batavia; Rev. A. A. Herbert had worked in Shanghai. "Christian Missions to the Chinese in Australia and New Zealand, 1855–c. 1900," Chinese Australia, Asian Studies Program, LaTrobe University, https://arrow.latrobe.edu.au/store/3/4/5/1/public/welch/missionaries.htm.

15. Fitzgerald, *Big White Lie*, 69; Timothy Coffin Osborn, Journal, entry for December 26, 1850, MSS C-F 81, BANC; Hall and Millard, "History of California Pioneer."

16. *Diary of Jong Ah Sing* (1866), p. 16, VIC. Translation by the author.

17. "Claims of Chinese on Our Common Schools," *San Francisco Evening Bulletin*, June 20, 1857.

18. Ngai, *Lucky Ones*, 119–21.

19. "The Children of the Sun," *Sacramento Transcript*, January 1, 1851, p. 2; "Chinese Case," *Alta*, May 24, 1851, p. 2; "Law Courts," *Alta*, October 9, 1851, p. 2.

20. Resident Warden Beechworth to chief secretary, April 22, 1857, doc. 57-115, VPRS1189/P0000/482, PROV; Rule, "Transformative Effect." Young is quoted in Cronin, *Colonial Casualties*, 86.

21. Cronin, *Colonial Casualties*, 85–88.

22. Wong, *English-Chinese Phrase Book*.

23. Zhu, *Guangzhao yingyu*.

CHAPTER 4: BIGLER'S GAMBIT

1. "John Bigler," Governors' Gallery, CSL, http://governors.library.ca.gov/03-bigler.html.

2. Memorial to the U.S. Congress from the People of California, *CAJ*, 3rd sess. (1852), appendix, 585.

3. On agricultural potential: Special Message from the Governor, January 30, 1852, *CAJ*, 3rd sess. (1852), 78. "Vast, safe and beautiful": "Prospects of California," *California Star*, March 25, 1848, p. 4. "Alaska to Chili": Speer, *Humble Plea*, 10.

4. Quinn, *Rivals*; Ellison, *Self-Governing Dominion*, 309–14; McArthur, *Enemy Never Came*, 17; St. John, "Unpredictable America," 56–84.

5. Speer, *Oldest and Newest Empire*, 483–528, quote at 527.

6. Jung, *Coolies and Cane*, chap. 3.

7. "Commerce and Coolies at the Sandwich Islands," *Alta*, February 24, 1852, p. 2; "The Labor Contract Law," *Alta*, March 21, 1852, p. 2. On Tingley: Shuck, *History of Bench and Bar*, 590; Smith, *Freedom's Frontier*, 99–100.

8. Bryson to Stoddard, December 3, 1851, California File, box 17, HL.

9. "Legislative Intelligence," *Alta*, April 24, 1852, p. 2. On senate opposition: "Minority Report of the Select Committee on Senate Bill no. 63," March 20, 1852, *CAJ*, 3rd sess. (1852), 669.

10. "The Robert Browne Story," Takao Club, http://www.takaoclub.com/bowne/index .htm. On mutinies: Meagher, *Coolie Trade*, 100, 145.

11. "The China Boys," *Alta*, May 12, 1851, p. 2.

12. "The Chinese Immigration," *Alta*, April 26, 1852, p. 2; "The Cooley Trade," *Alta*, May 4, 1852, p. 2.

13. "Legislative Intelligence," *Alta*, April 24, 1852; "Governor's Special Message," April 23, 1852, *CAJ*, 3rd sess. (1852), 376.

14. "The Chinese Emigration," *Alta* second supplement, May 15, 1852, p. 7. Statistics of arrivals and departures were prepared by S. E. Woodworth, who was "agent and consul" for Chinese in California.

15. Bancroft, *History of California*, 6:679.

16. Smith, *Freedom's Frontier*, 71–79.

17. Chun Aching and Tong Achick to Governor Bigler, May 16, 1852, in *Analysis of the Chinese Question;* "Governor's Special Message," *Alta*, April 25, 1852, p. 2; "Meeting at Columbia," *Alta*, May 15, 1852, p. 2. "Vamose the ranche": "Anti-Chinese Meeting at Foster's Bar," *Union*, May 3, 1852, p. 3. On miners meeting in Centreville, El Dorado: "Sacramento News," *Alta*, May 15, 1852, p. 2. See also Chiu, *Chinese Labor*, 13, 15; Paul, "Origin of Chinese Issue," 190.

18. Counties that went solidly for Bigler: Tuolumne (53.9 percent), Calaveras (53.5 percent), Sierra (55.7 percent), and Mariposa, Nevada, El Dorado, and Yuba (51 percent or more each). Bigler even won San Francisco, a Whig stronghold, by five votes. "Election Returns," *Alta*, September 12 and October 1, 1853. On corruption: Caxton, Letter to Bigler, *Alta*, July 2, 1853, p. 2; Editorial, "Gov. Bigler and the Extension Scheme," *Union*, August 24, 1853, p. 2. On Tammany Hall tactics: Editorial, *Alta*, September 15, 1853, p. 2; "Biglerism," *Alta*, May–September 1853, *passim.*

19. Henry George, speech delivered at Metropolitan Hall in San Francisco, February 4, 1890, in George, *Life of Henry George*, 80.

20. Lai, "Potato King"; Yin, *Chinese American Literature*, 18–20.

21. Hab Wa and Tong K. Achick to Governor Bigler, April 29, 1852, in *Analysis of the Chinese Question.*

22. "Memorial to the Legislature on the Chinese Question," in *Analysis of the Chinese Question*, 9.

23. "China-men in America," *New York Times*, June 9, 1852.

24. Norman Asing (*sic*), "To His Excellency Gov. Bigler," *Alta*, May 5, 1852, p. 2.

25. Ibid., emphasis in original.

26. *Analysis of the Chinese Question*, 10.

27. Chun Aching and Tong K. Achick to Govenor Bigler, May 16, 1852, in *Analysis of the Chinese Question*, 11.

28. Ibid.; "Off for the Mines," *Alta*, May 3, 1852, p. 2. Drop in population from 25,000 to 21,000: California Committee on Mines and Mining Interests, *Report* (1853).

29. Foreign Miners License Tax Act, 1852 Ca. Stat. 84; Chun and Tong to Bigler, May 16, 1852, *Analysis of the Chinese Question,* 12.

30. Foreign Miners License Tax Act, 1850 Ca. Stat. 221; Smith, *Freedom's Frontier,* 93–94; "Importation of Coolies" (letter to the editor), *Alta,* April 27, 1852, p. 2.

31. Foreign Miners License Tax Act, 1852 Ca. Stat. 84; "Passage of the School and Foreign Miners' Tax Bill," *Alta* supplement, May 1, 1852, p. 7; "The Tax on Foreign Miners and the Policy of Expulsion," *Alta* supplement, May 15, 1852, p. 4; Smith, *Freedom's Frontier,* 106–7; Chiu, *Chinese Labor,* 13.

32. Chiu, *Chinese Labor,* 15; California Committee on Mines and Mining Interests, *Report* (1853), appendix.

33. California Committee on Mines and Mining Interests, *Report* (1853), pp. 9–10. The Chinese attending the meeting were: Gee Atai and Lee Chuen of the Siyi Huiguan; Tong K. Achick and Lum Tween-Kwei of the Yanghe Huiguan; Tam San and Chun Aching of the Sanyi Huiguan; and Wong Sing and Lee Yuk of the Xin'an Huiguan (Sun On), the four existing *huiguan* representing the major dialect groups and regions of Guangdong present in California in 1852. Lai, *Becoming Chinese American,* 40–41.

34. California Committee on Mines and Mining Interests, *Report* (1853), p. 10.

35. Ibid., 9–10.

36. Ibid., 10–12.

37. Ibid., 10.

38. An Act to Provide for the Protection of Foreigners, and to Define their Liabilities and Privileges, 1853 Ca. Stat. 44. On revenues, see Chiu, *Chinese Labor,* 23. Tax receipts were highest in Calaveras, El Dorado, Placer, Tuolumne, and Yuba counties.

39. "An Extensive Swindle," *Alta,* November 19, 1855; *Report of Joint Select Committee Relative to the Population of Chinese of the State of California,* March 11, 1862, p. 7.

40. *U.S. Census of Population, 1860,* California, Yuba County, Foster's Bar, 6–7, 10–11, 14, 16, 2–23. On preemption: Chan, "Chinese Livelihood in Rural California," 57–83. On urban goods and services: U.S. Census of Population, 1860, California, Yuba County, Marysville, showed four washerwomen (p. 4) and washmen (p. 16) in ward 3; eighteen gardeners and one peddler in ward 4 (p. 10).

41. *Miners and Businessman's Directory,* Tuolumne County, 1856, HL. On Woods Creek: "San Joaquin News," *Alta* supplement, May 1, 1852, p. 1. For "lightly once over": Paden, *Big Oak Flat Road,* 67–70.

42. H. B. Lansing, Diary, entries for January 12 and 18, 1855, HM 70410, HL; Valentine, "Historical and Archaeological Investigations," 156–57; *Report of Joint Select Committee Relative to the Population of Chinese of the State of California,* March 11, 1862.

43. Raymond, *Statistics of Mines and Mining* (1870), 2–6.

44. Chiu, *Chinese Labor,* 3; Chan, *This Bittersweet Soil;* Chan, "Early Chinese in Oroville"; Chang, *Ghosts of Gold Mountain;* Chen, *Chinese San Francisco.*

45. California Joint Select Committee, *Report Relative to the Chinese Population,* 3; Rohe, "Chinese and Hydraulic Mining," 83–85; *Scientific and Mining Press,* January 28, 1882.

46. Rohe, "Chinese Mining and Settlement at Lava Beds," 52.

47. Ibid., 53–55.

48. Ibid, 56–59.

49. California Joint Select Committee, *Report Relative to the Chinese Population,* 4.

50. Figures reported in *"Jinshan yikou jin yi zong dan"* (Total Gold and Silver Inventory from San Francisco Port), *Wanguo gongbao,* no. 314 (1874), 19.

51. "Is it Practicable?" *Union,* April 8, 1882, p. 4.

52. J. A. Vaughn to M. D. Baruck, August 15, 1888; Rev. C. H. Kirkbride to Governor Waterman, August 8, 1888; N. B. Fish, foreman, Robert Forbes, Samuel Tym, William Perryman, Edward Perryman, William Box, petition to R. M. Waterman (1888); William P. McCarty, petition to Governor Waterman, October 12, 1888; L. Barnett, petition to Governor Waterman (n.d.); petitions from 1888 and 1889, all in file F3659-13, Executive Pardons, CSA (hereafter cited as Ah Jake pardon file).

53. *People v. Ah Jake,* death warrant, December 23, 1887, Ah Jake pardon file; "Historic Sierra County Gallows," http://www.sierracounty.ws/index .php?module=pagemaster&PAGE_user_op=view_page&PAGE_id=28&MMN_ position=44:37; Soward to Waterman, August 18, 1888, Ah Jake pardon file. On Downieville gallows: "Sierra County History," Sierra County Gold, http://www .sierracountygold.com/History/index.html.

54. Samuel C. Stewart, affidavit, August 7, 1888; F. D. Soward, petition to Governor Waterman, August 18, 1888, Ah Jake pardon file.

55. Vaughn, however, told the governor that he did not know Ah Jake, either to make his appeal appear unbiased or because he worried about retribution from local anti-Chinese elements, who campaigned against the employment of Chinese in the county. Ah Jake to Waterman, November 27, 1890; Vaughn to Baruck, August 15, 1888; Bouther testimony, *People v. Ah Jake,* trial transcript, 99–100, all in Ah Jake pardon file. On Wah Chuck: *People v. Ah Jake,* trial transcript, 52, 104–109, Ah Jake pardon file; "A Curious Pardon," *Mountain Messenger,* December 1, 1888, p. 2.

56. *Mountain Messenger* reported that Lo Kay paid out $100 in reward to Henry Hartling, who arrested Ah Jake. October 29, 1887, p. 3; *People v. Ah Jake,* trial transcript, 42, 98, Ah Jake pardon file; F. D. Soward to Governor Waterman, September 1, 1889, ibid. On shared Hop Wo membership: *People v. Ah Jake,* examination transcript, in Dressler, *California Chinese Chatter,* 55. The Sanborn Fire Insurance Company map for Downieville, California, 1902, shows a Chinese quarter, at the end of Main Street, with four structures, the largest of which, a two-story building labeled "joss house," likely belonged to the Zhigongdang. Beyond are a few additional dwellings, including one marked "fem. bldg" (i.e., brothel) and "old and dil[api-date]'d." On Zhigongdang, see Chapter 2.

57. Waterman, order of commutation of Ah Jake, November 14, 1888, Ah Jake pardon file; *Folsom Prison Register 1882–97,* MF 1:9 (12), CSA. On March 1, 1890, for reasons unknown, he was transferred to San Quentin. San Quentin prison register 1880–96, MF 1:9 (1), CSA.

58. Soward to Waterman, September 1, 1889, Ah Jake pardon file; "Ah Jake's Case," *Mountain Messenger,* December 1, 1888, p. 2.

59. Ah Jake to Waterman, September 14 and November 27, 1890; McComb to Waterman, December 1, 1890, all in Ah Jake pardon file. Spaulding, a grocer in Downie-

ville, had signed petitions on Ah Jake's behalf. The warden reported that Ah Jake's conduct "while in prison has been good, never having been reported for punishment for violation of prison rules and has discharged his duties faithfully." Ah Jake also worked in the prison jute mill. Doughtery to McComb, December 1, 1890, Ah Jake pardon file.

60. Executive pardon, December 30, 1890, Ah Jake pardon file; San Quentin prison register 1880–96, MF 1:9 (1), CSA; Lavezzola to Dressler, May 4, 1927, in Dressler, *California Chinese Chatter*, 60–61; Mason to Dressler, April 29, 1927, CSL.

61. *CAJ*, 1853–85. Aggregate pardon data are included in the state prison director's reports, published in *CAJ* appendices; names of prisoners pardoned appear in *CAJ* as part of the governor's annual reports to the legislature. In 1860 Song Ah Pong, who served four years of a ten-year sentence for murder in the second degree, was pardoned for good behavior and the governor's belief that the time served was adequate. *California Senate Journal*, 12th sess. (1861), 51. Many whites received pardons for good behavior. The practice, which addressed both overcrowding in the state prison and the belief that the possibility of pardon promoted prison discipline, was similar to what we now know as parole. It was codified in 1864 with a law that granted a credit of five days for each month of "fruitful labor and good behavior," enabling an accelerated expiration of the prisoner's sentence. Act to confer Further Powers upon the Governor of this State in Relation to the Pardon of Criminals, April 4, 1864. Ah Fong, serving a twelve-year sentence for murder in second degree, suffering from consumption, and close to death, was pardoned in 1868. *California Journal of the Assembly*, 18th sess. (1869–70), 66. Ah Lin, convicted of robbery, dying of heart disease, was pardoned in 1870, *California Senate Journal*, 19th sess. (1871–72), 59. Yung Toy, sentenced to seven years for robbery, *California Senate Journal*, 20th sess. (1873–74), 104. Legal historian Clare McKanna's study of homicide cases in seven California counties during the late nineteenth century revealed that pardons and convictions vacated by appeals courts in Chinese cases often resulted from revelations that Chinese witnesses, usually members of rival clans or brotherhoods, had perjured their testimony. McKanna, *Race and Homicide*, 32–51.

62. Doubt as to guilt was most commonly cited. "Doubt": pardon of Ah Yik, *California Senate Journal*, 19th sess. (1871–72), 66; "conspiracy," pardon of Ah Chee, *California Senate Journal*, 21st sess. (1875–76), appendix, 4:37. "Circumstances have come to light": pardon of Ah Wong, *California Senate Journal*, 19th sess. (1871–72), 79.

63. *People v. Hall*, 4 Cal. 339 (1854).

64. Pun Chi, "Remonstrance to Congress," c. 1860, quoted in Speer, *Oldest and Newest Empires*, 591–603.

65. Wunder, "Chinese in Trouble," 25–41.

CHAPTER 5: THE LIMITS OF PROTECTION

1. "A Chinese Demonstration," *Empire*, August 13, 1857, p. 5; Kyi, "'Most Determined, Sustained.'" The newspaper reported 1,200 to 1,300 Chinese at the meeting, but

the petition bore 2,873 signatures. The population of Castlemaine was about 1,500 according to Rev. William Young's census, *Report on Conditions of Chinese Population,* 38–39.

2. Loy-Wilson, "Coolie Alibis," 30–31; Cronin, *Colonial Casualties,* 9–12.

3. "Grave injustice": quoted in Cronin, *Colonial Casualties,* 7. "Convicts and Chinese," *Empire,* November 24, 1851. "Trampled into beggary": quoted in Ohlsson, "Origins of White Australia," 203–19. See also "Sworn to No Master, of No Sect Am I," *SMH,* October 3, 1848; "Chinese Immigration," *Empire,* November 20, 1851; "Convicts and Chinese," ibid., November 24, 1851. Antitransportation: Cronin, *Colonial Casualties,* 7. "Supply of really eligible": Earl Grey to Sir Charles Fitz Roy, December 18, 1847, *Historical Records of Australia,* series 1, vol. 26, 104–8.

4. Cronin, *Colonial Casualties,* 6. In fact, Nicholson was being disingenuous: free labor was expensive, convict labor had run out, and former convicts were considered too rowdy and disobedient to be reliable workers.

5. "Morbid craving": quoted in Loy-Wilson, "Coolie Alibis," 32. See also "Chinese Immigration," *SMH,* February 28, 1852, p. 2; "Chinese Slavery," *SMH,* January 18, 1853, p. 2; "The Chinese—The Yellow Slave," *Empire,* June 18, 1853, p. 4.

6. Serle, *Golden Age,* 44–54, 75–76.

7. Ibid., 323; Curthoys, "'Men of All Nations"; Markus, *Fear and Hatred.*

8. Henry Melville, testimony to the Commission on Conditions of Goldfields of Victoria, p. 9, 1855/1, Vic-PP. William Hopkins, testimony, ibid., 10. The "water holes" were built by Europeans to hold fresh water for drinking. Serle, *Golden Age,* 323. The Chinese, who came from rice-growing southern China and brought agricultural irrigation techniques with them to the goldfields, probably did not consider water a scarce resource.

9. Quoted in Serle, *Golden Age,* 327.

10. "Plan of Golden Point Section of Forest Creek," 1859, Department of Economic Development, Jobs, Transport, and Resources, Victoria http://earthresources.vic .gov.au/earth-resources/geology-of-victoria/exhibitions-and-Imagery/beneath-our -feet/the-early-years; Goodman, *Gold Seeking,* 65–88, 189–202. "Quiet, inoffensive": George Henry Gibson, testimony to Goldfield Commission, p. 7, 1855/1, Vic-PP. "Not insolent": "Chinese in Victoria," *Bendigo Advertiser* supplement, August 23, 1856, 1. "Thieves and gamblers": Charles James Kenworthy, testimony to Goldfield Commission, p. 8, 1855/1, Vic-PP.

11. Reports of Chinese population figures vary in the historical record. Gillies, Memorandum for the Governor, April 11, 1888, *Correspondence relating to Chinese Immigration into the Australasian Colonies,* 1888 C. 5448, p. 25, *PP.* See also table of census figures in Cronin, *Colonial Casualties,* appendix 2. Monster meeting: Serle, *Golden Age,* 322–23.

12. "Australia and the Chinese," *Empire,* July 28, 1857, p. 6; "Convicts and Chinese," *Empire,* November 24, 1851; "The Chinese in Victoria," *SMH,* May 7, 1855, p. 8. "Absurd to suppose": "Chinese in Victoria," *SMH,* May 7, 1855, 8; Home-Stayer, "The Chinese," *Empire,* July 13, 1858, p. 5.

13. Hopkins testimony to Goldfield Commission, p. 10, 1855/1, Vic-PP. On religious

difference: "Chinese Emigration," *Goulburn Herald and Argyle Advertiser*, March 6, 1852, p. 4. Doubting conversion: "Interior, Chinese Labour—Public Meeting," *Empire*, April 2, 1852.

14. Christian morals: Goodman, *Gold Seeking*, 149–78; Johnson, *Roaring Camp*, chap. 2. "Piebald": "Chinese Emigration," *Goulburn Herald and Argyle Advertiser*, March 6, 1852, p. 4.

15. On slavery: "Convicts and Chinese," *Empire*, November 24, 1851, p. 2. Others hesitated and asked for clarification as to whether Chinese were slaves. "Chinese Immigration," *SMH*, February 28, 1852, p. 2. Hotham is quoted in Serle, *Golden Age*, 320. Serle considered Hotham's claim an exaggeration. On general use of credit in immigration: Taylor, *Distant Magnet*, 97–102; Kobrin, "A Credit to Their Nation," 69–90; Kobrin, "Currents and Currency," 87–104. "Sulky": Loy-Wilson, "Coolie Alibis," 38–40. Public outcry and petitioning by the Chinese forced an official investigation, which ruled in favor of the Chinese and ordered that £3,160 of the gold be restored to the Chinese, the rest having been distributed among the takers and impossible to trace.

16. Editorial, *Argus*, January 6, 1879, p. 4.

17. "Great number . . . countless throng": *Goldfield Commission Report*, par. 161–64, 1855/1, Vic-PP. "Swarmed": Westgarth, quoted in Serle, *Golden Age*, 327. Ten to one: "Chinese Immigration into Victoria," *SMH*, April 21, 1855. *"One or two millions"*: Henry Melville, testimony to Goldfield Commission, 1855/1, Vic-PP. "Mass of foreign": "Convicts and Chinese," *Empire*, November 24, 1851, p. 2. "Vast influx . . . inexhaustible": "Chinese in Victoria," *SMH*, May 7, 1855, p. 8. All emphases are added.

18. "Chinese Disturbances in Singapore," *Argus*, April 8, 1857, p. 5; "Treatment of Chinese," *Mount Alexander Mail*, July 24, 1857; Serle, *Golden Age*, 325. On crisis of confidence: Mountford, *Britain, China and Colonial Australia*, 61.

19. Serle, *Golden Age*, chaps. 5–6; Proceedings and reports compiled in Anderson, *Eureka*.

20. *Report of Goldfield Commission*, par. 166, 1855/1, Vic-PP; An Act to Make Provision for Certain Immigrants, 18 Vic. 39 (June 12, 1855), secs. 3 and 4. The act defined *immigrant* as "any male adult native of China or its dependencies or of any islands in the Chinese seas or any person born of Chinese parents." An Act to Regulate the Residence of the Chinese Population in Victoria, 21 Vic. 41 (November 24, 1857), sec. 3.

21. Humble Petition, Chinese Storekeepers, November 26, 1856, 1856/4, Vic-PP. The number of signatures represents about a third of the Bendigo population, which had increased dramatically from 1854 (3,000) to 1855 (17,000). Serle, *Golden Age*, 323; Kyi, "Most Determined."

22. Webster to chief secretary, September 6, 1856, VPRS1189/P0000 W56/7831, PROV; Nicholson to chief commissioner of police (Melbourne), July 23, 1856, VPRS1189/P0000, X56/6748, PROV; Serle, *Golden Age*, 325; "The Walk from Robe," *GOLD!, Victorian Cultural Collaboration*, https://www.sbs.com.au/gold/story.php?storyid=57.

23. 'Statement of the number of Chinese reported to have arrived in this Colony overland to avoid the payment of the capitation tax authorized to be levied under the Act 18 Victoria no. 39, August 21, 1856," VPRS1189/P0000/467 K56/7026, PROV; "The Walk from Robe."

24. Serle, *Golden Age*, 325–30.

25. In addition to the Bendigo, Ballarat, and Castlemaine petitions mentioned above, petitions came from Fryer's Creek, Campbell's Creek, Forest Creek, Jim Crow goldfields, Geelong, and Sandy Creek. Kyi, "Most Determined," n27. On arguments and justifications: Ibid.; On language of rights: *Argus*, May 13, 1859, quoted in Messner, "Popular Constitutionalism," 63. Petition of [Bendigo] Chinese Storekeepers (November 26, 1856).

26. Pon Sa, "A Chinese Demonstration," *Empire*, August 13, 1857, p. 5; Lowe Kong Meng, testimony before Select Committee on Subject of Chinese Immigration, pp. 10–12, 1857/6, Vic-PP.

27. An Act to Regulate the Residence of Chinese in Victoria, 21 Vic. 41, December 24, 1857. New petition: Kyi, "Most Determined"; Chamber of Commerce, cited in Mountford, *Britain, China, and Colonial Australia*, 60.

28. An Act to Consolidate and Amend the Laws Affecting the Chinese Emigrating to or Resident in Victoria, 22 Vic. 80, February 24, 1859; Cronin, *Colonial Casualties*, 98. Penal sanctions: John O'Shanassy, "Regulations for the Guidance of Chinese Protectors," February 28, 1859 (Min 59.27), VPRS1189/P0000/522 J56/1988, PROV.

29. Quoted in Kyi, "Most Determined."

30. Messner, "Popular Constitutionalism," 75; United Confederacy: Serle, *Golden Age*, 330–31.

31. Serle, *Golden Age*, 331; Macgregor, "Lowe Kong Meng."

32. Serle, *Golden Age*, 331.

33. Messner, "Popular Constitutionalism"; Serle, *Golden Age*, 330.

34. Cronin, *Colonial Casualties*, 80–81.

35. McCulloch, "Sir George Gipps"; Earl Grey to Charles Fitz Roy, February 11, 1848, noting "regret . . . that but little progress appears to have been made towards any effectual improvement in the condition of the natives in your Colony." Earl Grey also reiterated that leases granted for purposes of pasturing cattle or agriculture did not give grantees "exclusive rights" and that such leases were not meant to "deprive the natives of their former right to hunt over these Districts, or to wander over them in search of subsistence . . . except over land actually cultivated or fenced in for that purpose." *Historical Records of Australia*, series 1, vol. 26, at 223, 225. This might have seemed reasonable in London, but settler colonials believed control over land and territory was a zero-sum proposition. On theories of extinction, see Wolfe, "Settler Colonialism"; Markus, *Fear and Hatred*.

36. Memorandum of conversation (colonial governor) with [Melbourne] Chamber of Commerce on the Chinese Question, May 8, 1855, VPRS1095/P0000/3, PROV.

37. Rede to Kaye, September 24, 1854, file "petitions of Amoy etc.," VPRS1095/P000/3, PROV; Matson, "Common Law Abroad"; Buxbaum, *Family Law and Customary Law*; Collyer, "Straits Settlements," 82–84. It should be noted that the promulgation of

dual governance necessitated the British production and codification of racialized knowledges about "tribes," "ethnicities," and "custom." See also Kuhn, *Chinese Among Others,* chap. 2; Carstens, "Chinese Culture and Polity." Cronin also cites as antecedents both the Port Phillip Aboriginal Protectorate and practices in Southeast Asia, but in positing Chinese "compounds" in Asia (which were uncommon) suggests a closer similarity to the Australian protectorates than actually existed. *Colonial Casualties,* 82.

38. Rede to Kaye, September 24, 1854, file "petitions of Amoy etc.," VPRS1095/P000/3, PROV.

39. "Chinese Demonstration," *Empire,* June 13, 1857, p. 5; Serle, *Golden Age,* 326. "Leading men": quoted in Cronin, *Colonial Casualties,* 83.

40. O Cheong, letter to private secretary [Kay] to the Lieutenant Governor [Hotham], December 23, 1854, VPRS1095/P0000/3 "Petitions of Amoy etc.," PROV. The placement of Cheong's letter in this file suggests that he was not from the Siyi of Guangdong but from the neighboring province of Fujian, the location of Xiamen, its treaty port.

41. Hotham acted under authority of the Act to Make Provision for Certain Immigrants, 18 Vic. 39 (June 22, 1855), secs. 6–8. The protectorate system was codified in "Regulations for the Chinese on the Gold Fields," December 2, 1856, A.13/1856–57, Vic-PP. See also "Regulations for the Chinese on the Victoria Gold Fields," *SMH,* April 4, 1856, 3.

42. Military background: Cronin, *Colonial Casualties,* 84; William Foster, Diary for the Fortnight Ending Saturday, March 1, 1856, VPRS1189/P0000/467 J56/1791, PROV.

43. Each branch budgeted for the European protector's salary at £750 a year; that of a European clerk at £500; an interpreter, at £500 for Europeans, £350 for Chinese; a Chinese scribe at £60; numerous headmen at £120 each; and two police constables at 10s. 6d. per diem each. Frederick Standish, "Estimated Expenditures for the Protection of the Chinese for 1856" [1855], VPRS1189/P0000/467 R55/14,639, PROV; Standish to chief secretary, October 22, 1855, VPRS1189/P0000 R55/13,887, PROV; "Precis of Recommendations of Chinese Protectors Regarding Payment of Chinese Headmen of Villages" (December 31, 1855), VPRS1189/P0000/467 Y562028, PROV; *Fortnightly Report of the Resident Warden, Ballarat,* Period Ending March 1, 1856, VPRS1189/P0000/467 J56/1791, PROV.

44. Chinese protector to Resident Warden, Castlemaine, October 22, 1855, VPRS1189/P0000/R13, 871, PROV. Standish is quoted in Cronin, *Colonial Casualties,* 87.

45. Standish to colonial secretary, July 9, 1855, VPRS1189/P0000/467 P55/8757, PROV. Standish conceded that imposing a fee to bring a complaint was unjust, especially since "in the great majority of cases the Chinese complainants are in the right." Standish, September 5, 1855, VPRS1189/P0000/467, T56/243, PROV. According to Cronin, the government's Chinese funds recorded a surplus every year save for one. *Colonial Casualties,* 93.

46. Drummond, "Regulations for Keeping the Camp Clean," September 2, 1858, VPRS1189/P0000/522 A58/266, PROV; see also Cronin, *Colonial Casualties,* 90–91.

47. Standish to colonial secretary, November 30, 1855, VPRS1189/P0000/467 R55/15,543, PROV; Webster to resident warden (Avoca), July 28, 1856, VPRS1189/P0000/W6629, PROV.

48. Smith to resident warden, October 22, 1855, VPRS1189/P0000 R13/871, PROV; Smith to resident warden, July 21, 1856, VPRS1189/P0000 X6233, PROV.

49. Resident warden to chief secretary, October 7, 1858, VPRS1189/P0000/522 G8441, PROV.

50. Acts Consolidating and Amending the Laws Affecting the Chinese Emigrating to and Resident in Victoria, 25 Vic 132, 1862, and 27 Vic. 170, 1863.

51. Young, *Report on Conditions of Chinese Population,* 31–58; Fitzgerald, *Big White Lie;* Rasmussen, "Chinese in Nation and Community"; Cai, "From Mutual Aid to Public Interest."

52. Goodman, *Gold Seeking,* 25; Messner, "Popular Constitutionalism." Similarly, Fitzgerald has argued that Chinese Australians in the late nineteenth century were modernizing subjects, their associations and fraternities "as egalitarian and democratic as their counterparts in the white labor movement, in Irish-Catholic sodalities and in local lodges of colonial and federation Freemasonry." *Big White Lie,* 28–29.

53. DianaTalbot, "Trouble in the Buckland," http://www.dianntalbotauthor.com/buckland-riots/.

54. Taylor to chief secretary, *Report of the Board Appointed to Inquire into Losses Sustained by Chinese at Ararat,* December 7, 1857, VPRS1189/P0000/502, PROV.

55. Serle, *Golden Age,* 325–26; Taylor to chief secretary, December 7, 1858; *Argus* quoted in Talbot, "Trouble in Buckland."

56. Serle, *Golden Age,* 326.

57. "Anti-Chinese Riots and Rorts," Gold!, https://www.sbs.com.au/gold/story.php?storyid=56; Taylor to Chief Secretary Melbourne, December 7, 1858; "List of Property Stated to Have Been Destroyed Belonging to Chinese Storekeepers at the Buckland on 4th July 1857" (n.d.), VPRS1189/P0000/502, PROV.

CHAPTER 6: THE ROAR OF THE SANDLOT

1. "John Bigler," *Wikipedia,* https://en.wikipedia.org/wiki/John_Bigler. Chinese work on the transcontinental railroad: Chang, *Ghosts of Gold Mountain.*

2. Editorial, "The Elections," *Alta,* September 5, 1861, p. 1. On California politics in the era of the Civil War and Reconstruction: Saxton, *Indispensable Enemy;* Smith, *Freedom's Frontier.*

3. California Joint Select Committee, *Report Relative to the Chinese Population.* The committee was co-chaired by two Republicans and consisted entirely of Republicans and Union Democrats.

4. Chiu, *Chinese Labor,* 23–29.

5. Saxton, *Indispensable Enemy,* 68–71; Chiu, *Chinese Labor,* 54–55.

6. "Disgraceful Riot in San Francisco," *Union,* February 14, 1867, p. 3; "Trial of the Rioters," *Alta,* February 24, 1867, p. 1; Saxton, *Indispensable Enemy,* 72.

7. "Memorial and Joint Resolution in Relation to Chinese Immigration to the State of California," *CAJ*, 17th sess. (1867–68), appendix, 2:4; "Anti-Coolie Memorial," March 12, 1868, in ibid.

8. Henry George, "The Chinese in California," *New York Tribune*, May 1, 1869, pp. 1–2.

9. Mill to George, October 23, 1869, in George, *Complete Works*, 10:198–200.

10. *Oakland Daily Transcript*, November 20–21, 1869, quoted in George, *Complete Works*, 10:200–1. See also Shelton, *Squatter's Republic*, 86–87.

11. "Crude," in George, *Complete Works*, 10:195. On Chinese demands for higher wages: Raymond, *Statistics of Mines and Mining* (1870), chap. 1; George Robert, testimony, "Memorial of the Six Chinese Companies," 17–18. Later writing on Chinese by George: *Complete Works*, 9:202–3. See also Beck, "Henry George and Immigration."

12. Saxton, *Indispensable Enemy*, 106; Deverell, *Railroad Crossing*, 34–36.

13. Saxton, *Indispensable Enemy*, 74–76.

14. "Anti-Chinese Song," *Marin County Journal*, May 25, 1876.

15. Brooks, "Chinese Labor Problem," 407–19; Condit, *Chinaman as We See Him*, 83.

16. Kurashige, *Two Faces of Exclusion*, while recognizing discrete interests, calls them "egalitarians"; "Memorial of the Six Chinese Companies," 22–24.

17. "Memorial of the Six Chinese Companies," 18; Rusling, *Across America*, 317–18.

18. Speer, *Humble Plea*; Condit, *Chinaman as We See Him*; Gibson, *"Chinaman or White Man, Which?,"* 28.

19. Gibson, *Chinese in America*, 76–77.

20. Williams, *Our Relations with Chinese Empire*, 14.

21. Daniel Cleveland, "Chinese in California" (1868), HM72176, HL; Clyde, "China Policy of Browne."

22. Wong Ar Chong to Garrison, February 28, 1879, at "Rediscovered: An Eloquent Voice against Chinese Exclusion," Smithsonian Asian Pacific American Center, http://smithsonianapa.org/now/wong-ar-chong.

23. Burlingame to Williams, quoted in Xu, *Chinese and Americans*, 72–73; Wenxiang quoted in Haddad, *America's First Adventure*, 221.

24. Haddad, *America's First Adventure*, 221–26.

25. Saxton, *Indispensable Enemy*, 104–5. Kurashige discusses the turn to national exclusion legislation as a "perfect storm" of events, *Two Faces of Exclusion*, 8–9.

26. California State Senate, *Chinese Immigration: Its Social, Moral, and Political Effect* (1876); U.S. Senate, *Report of the Joint Special Committee to Investigate Chinese Immigration* (1877).

27. Amendment to strike ban on naturalization defeated, April 28, 13 *Cong. Rec.* (March–April 1882), p. 3411; final bill House/Senate, April 29, p. 3440.

28. Ibid., pp. 2027, 2028; veto (April 4, 1882), p. 2551.

29. "Chinese Consul-General," *Union*, March 27, 1882; Shi, "Jinshan sannian ku"; "Senators Investigating Chinese Labor Conditions," *Wanguo gongbao*, no. 437–40 (1877).

30. "On Protecting the People" (Baomin shuo), *Zhongwai xinwen qiri bao*, June 3, 1871, p. 8.

31. "Anti-Chinese Riot at Martinez," *Weekly Butte Record*, May 6, 1882, p. 1; "The Irrepressible Conflict," *Los Angeles Herald*, April 28, 1882, p. 1.

32. "The Trouble at Martinez," *Union*, April 28, 188, p. 2; *Sonoma Democrat*, April 29, 1882, p. 2; "Distinction without a Difference," *Los Angeles Herald*, May 3, 1882, p. 2.

33. "Complaint of the Chinese Minister," *Los Angeles Herald*, July 2, 1882, p. 1; "Martinez Riot," *Union*, May 9, 1882, p. 2; "Pacific Coast Items," *San Jose Herald*, December 7, 1882, p. 3; *Daily Morning Times* (San Jose), December 8, 1882, p. 2.

34. An Act to Execute Certain Treaty Stipulations Relating to Chinese, May 6, 1882. Just a few months later, President Arthur signed into law the Immigration Act of 1882, the nation's first general immigration law, which imposed a "head tax" on each new arrival and excluded from entry paupers, convicts, lunatics, and persons likely to become a public charge, and required them to be returned to their place of origin by the steamship company that brought them. That law built on decades of head taxes and exclusion and removal policies of various states, especially indigent Irish from Massachusetts and New York. On the related influences of anti-Chinese and anti-Irish nativisms and exclusions: Hirota, *Expelling the Poor.*

35. On exclusion of Chinese regardless of country of origin: *In re Ah Lung* 18 F. 28 (1883); "Chinese from Hong Kong," *Alta*, June 1, 1884, p. 2. On conflicts over enforcement: Salyer, *Laws Harsh as Tigers*, chap. 4; McKeown, *Melancholy Order*, chap. 5; Ngai, *Impossible Subjects*, chap. 6. The Supreme Court ruling in *U.S. v. Ju Toy* (1906) gave broad discretion to immigration officials and limited immigrants' rights to court review; *U.S. v. Wong Kim Ark* (1898) upheld birthright citizenship of Chinese born in the United States.

36. "Victory at Last!," *Alta*, March 24, 1882, p. 1.

37. Huang, *Renjinglu shicao jianzhu*. Selection trans. by John Guo in Frederick Bee History Project, http://frederickbee.com/huangpoem.html.

38. Section 6 of the Exclusion Act specified the exempt classes and the requirement for a certificate for entry.

39. *Case of the Chinese Cabin Waiter, In re Ah Sing*, 13 F.286 (1882); *Case of the Chinese Laborers on Shipboard, In re Ah Tie and others*, 13 F.291 (1882); *Case of the Chinese Merchant, In re Low Yam Chow*, 13 F.605 (1882).

40. Huang to Zheng, report no. 19, August 3, 1882, in *Jindaishi ziliao*, vol. 55. Translation by Jack Neubauer. 13 F.286, 289 (1882).

41. 13 F.605, 608, 611 (1882).

42. Huang to Zheng, reports no. 22, 23, 24, 26 (September to November 1882), *Jindaishi ziliao*, vol. 55.

43. Huang to Zheng, reports no. 34, 35 (January 1886), ibid.; *Yick Wo v. Hopkins*, 18 U.S. 356 (1886).

44. Shi, "Jinshan sannian ku." On formation of the Chinese Consolidated Benevolent Association: Lai, *Becoming Chinese American*, 47–48. On school exclusion: *Tape v. Hurley* 66 Cal. 473 (1885); Ngai, *Lucky Ones*, chap. 4.

45. Lew-Williams, *Chinese Must Go*, appendix A, showing 439 cases and 84 murders in California, Idaho, Montana, Nevada, New Mexico, Oregon, Washington, and Wyoming in 1885–87.

46. Ibid., 120–25.

47. Snake River: Pfaelzer, *Driven Out*, 287; Rock Springs, ibid., 209–11.

48. "Memorial of Chinese Laborers, Resident at Rock Springs."
49. Ibid.
50. Frederick Bee, Report and accompanying documents, September 30, 1885, Cheng to Bayard, November 30, 1885, doc. 64 encl., Chinese Legation correspondence, *FRUS*.
51. Cheng to Bayard, November 30, 1885, ibid.
52. Bayard to Cheng Tsao Ju, February 18, 1886, doc. 67, Chinese Legation, *FRUS*; Denby to Bayard, March 10, 1886, doc. 50, China, *FRUS*; Denby to Bayard, March 29, 1886, doc. 52, China, *FRUS*.
53. Pfaelzer, *Driven Out*, 214–15.
54. George to Garrison, November 30, 1893, in George, *Complete Works*, 9:202–3.
55. The arguments varied. Some justified Chinese exclusion as an "antislavery" measure, continuous with abolitionism. Others, especially after the demise of Reconstruction, opposed granting the franchise to both. Justice Harlan's famous dissent in *Plessy v. Ferguson* (1896) praised African Americans' citizenship as a reward for their military service in the Civil War but argued that Chinese were an undeserving race. Smith, *Freedom's Frontier*; Aarim-Heriot, *Chinese Immigrants*; Wong, *Racial Reconstruction*.
56. *Chae Chan Ping v. U.S.* (1889), 130 U.S. 581; *Fong Yue Ting v. U.S.* (1893), 149 U.S. 698.

CHAPTER 7: THE YELLOW AGONY

1. Australian newspapers from the 1850s to the '70s occasionally covered the Chinese in California, but beginning in the late 1870s, there was a significant uptick in the number of articles. Using the keywords *Chinese* and *California*, a search of Australia's national newspaper database Trove yielded 2,378 hits for the thirteen years between 1857 and 1870 and 2,436 for the four years between 1878 and 1882. For example, "The Labor Movement in California," *Argus*, February 5, 1878, p. 7; "The Chinese in California," *Queenslander*, December 14, 1878, p. 23. See also Markus, *Fear and Hatred*, 80–83, 124–25; Lake and Reynolds, *Drawing the Global Colour Line*, chap. 6. "The Chinese in Australia: Their Vices and Victims," *Bulletin*, August 21, 1886, p. 4, 11–14; Editorial, "The Chinese Must Go," ibid., p. 2.
2. Convention of Peking between Great Britain and China (October 24, 1860), Article 5: "Chinese choosing to take service in the British colonies, or other parts beyond sea, are at perfect liberty to enter into engagements with British subjects for that purpose, and to ship themselves and their families on board any British vessel at any port of the open ports of China; also, that the high authorities aforesaid shall, in concert with Her Britannic Majesty's representative in China, frame such regulations for the protection of Chinese emigrating, as above, as the circumstances of the different open ports may demand."
3. Lowe et al., *Chinese Question in Australia*, 26–28.
4. Decline in gold mining: Battellino, "Mining Booms," 63. The Chinese population declined during the 1860s, from 24,700 to 17,800 in Victoria and from 13,000 to

7,200 in New South Wales. Repeals of restrictions in 1863 in Victoria and 1867 in New South Wales: Mountford, *Britain, China, and Colonial Australia,* 64.

5. *Times* (London), November 18, 1857, p. 8, cited Mountford, *Britain, China, and Colonial Australia,* 62.

6. The so-called Wallace Line that marks the division between "Indonesian" and "Australian" ecologies in fact joins eastern Indonesia and New Guinea to Australia. Martínez and Vickers, *Pearl Frontier,* 24–25. On Marege: Ganter, *Mixed Relations,* chaps. 1–2. Macassan (Makassan) is the collective name of a multiethnic trading culture from Sulawesi, including peoples from the Gowa and Bone Kingdoms and adjacent islands. The following discussion of the Top End draws from Ganter, chaps. 2–4, and Martínez and Vickers, chap. 2.

7. Jones, *Chinese in Northern Territory,* 5–13; Jones, "Ping Que: Mining Magnate." The government paid a £14/7s per head to labor contractors in Singapore , covering commissions, passage, and medical fees. The workers were paid three pounds a month, including food and medical care, and headmen five pounds per month, on two-year contracts, with a five-pound bonus or return passage at term. The government committed to engage those not hired by companies on public works and to shelter them in tents.

8. Jones, "Ping Que"; Jones, *Chinese in Northern Territory,* 37.

9. Jones, "Ping Que."

10. Ganter, *Mixed Relations,* 69; "Chung Wah Society, Darwin, Northern Territory," Chung Wah Society, http://www.chungwahnt.asn.au/index.php?page=short-history.

11. Jones, *Chinese in Northern Territory,* 31, 53–54; Ganter, *Mixed Relations,* 70, 118.

12. Number of Aboriginal peoples killed: Evans and Ørsted-Jensen, " 'I Cannot Say the Numbers.' " On violence on the Queensland frontier: Henry Reynolds, "Other Side of the Frontier" and Reynolds, "Unrecorded Battlefields of Queensland," in Reynolds, *Race Relations in North Queensland.*

13. Kong Shing Yung, "A Chinese Letter Home," *Rockhampton Bulletin and Central Queensland Advertiser,* September 26, 1865, pp. 2–3. The letter was translated into English by a local Christian missionary.

14. "The Palmer River Goldfield: North Queensland Outback" (n.d.), Tropical Tableland Netguide, http://www.athertontablelandnetguide.com/outback/gold/palmer-river-gold.htm; William Hill, "The Palmer Goldfield: Early Day Experiences" (n.d.), http://www.chapelhill.homeip.net/FamilyHistory/Other/QueenslandHistory/ThePalmerRiverGoldfieldEarlyDayExperiences.htm. On Chinese entering Queensland from the Northern Territory: Jones, *Chinese in Northern Territory,* 53–55; Crawford, *Notes by Mr. Crawford.* On racial myths about Pacific Islanders: Banivanua-Mar, *Violence and Colonial Dialogue.*

15. Crawford, *Notes by Mr. Crawford,* 4, 18–20.

16. Kirkman, "Chinese Miners on Palmer," 49–62.

17. Loy-Wilson, "Rural Geographies," 414; Comber, "Chinese Sites on Palmer," 207, 209.

18. Kirkman, "Chinese Miners on Palmer," 49; Hill, "Palmer Goldfield." On violence:

Noreen Kirkman, "From Minority to Majority," in Reynolds, *Race Relations in North Queensland*, 238–39, 243. Mining wardens: Comber, "Chinese Sites on Palmer," 205.

19. Cathie May, "Chinese in the Cairns District," in Reynolds, *Race Relations in North Queensland*. On Cooktown: Crawford, *Notes by Mr. Crawford*, 27. On market gardens and shops: Loy-Wilson, "Rural Geographies," 415. On banana trade: Fitzgerald, *Big White Lie*, 155–56. On racial theory of climate: Anderson, "Coolie Therapeutics."

20. Huttenback, *Racism and Empire*, 241–50; An Act to Amend the Goldfields Amendment Act of 1874 (1876); Queensland Act 2 of 1878. The inclusion of Africans in the bill was a prophylactic against all nonwhite immigrants, existing and potential. There were no Africans in Queensland goldfields at the time. See also Griffiths, "Strategic Fears of Ruling Class."

21. "The Kanaka Question at Mackay," *Week*, December 8, 1877, pp. 21–22; Huttenback, *Racism and Empire*, 42–49. Queensland Acts 47 of 1868 and 17 of 1880. On conditions on plantations as late as 1901: "The Kanaka Problem," *North Queensland Register*, June 24, 1901, p. 39.

22. "In Townsville," *Worker*, December 17, 1892, 3; "The Kanaka Question," *Telegraph*, January 29, 1876, p. 6. See also Huttenback, *Racism and Empire*, 246–47. "Black and yellow agony": "Black Labour and the Farmers," *Worker*, May 28, 1892, p. 2.

23. Markus, "Divided We Fall," 1–10.

24. Curthoys, "Conflict and Consensus."

25. Ibid.

26. Cameron, member of the NSW legislative assembly, quoted ibid., 56.

27. Anderson, "Coolie Therapeutics"; Editorial, *Brisbane Courier*, August 18, 1877, 4. On anti-Chinese racism as constitutive of nationalism: Auerbach, *Race, Law, and "Chinese Puzzle,"* 16–27.

28. *South Australian Register*, February 20, 1888, cited in Mountford, *Britain, China, and Colonial Australia*, 100.

29. Non-European population in 1891: Queensland, 5.05 percent; Western Australia, 4.65 percent; New South Wales, 1.29 percent; Victoria, 0.86 percent. Markus, *Fear and Hatred*, 160.

30. Lowe et al., *Chinese Question in Australia*, 20–21.

31. Ibid.

32. Kong Shing Yung, "A Chinese Letter Home," *Rockhampton Bulletin and Central Queensland Advertiser*, September 26, 1865, pp. 2–3. Battery hands: Jones, *Chinese in Northern Territory*, 70. An *SMH* survey found that among cabinetmakers, European wages averaged £2 10s. and Chinese about £2 with food and lodging provided by the employer. Markus, "Divided We Fall," 7.

33. On San Francisco and Rock Springs, see the discussion in Chapter 6; Zhang, *Gaoben hang hai shu*, entry for the twenty-second day, sixth month [1878], 553.

34. Cuba Commission, *Report of the Commission*; Yun, *Coolie Speaks*. On the Burlingame Treaty, see Chapter 6.

35. Mountford, *Britain, China, and Colonial Australia*, 96–99, 102; Tseng, "China— Sleep and Awakening."

36. Lowe Keng Meng et al., "Petition to their Excellencies General Wong Yung Ho and U Tsing," cited in Lake, "Chinese Empire Encounters British Empire," , "Chinese Empire Encounters British Empire," 107. See also Fitzgerald, "Advance Australia Fairly," 66–67, 104.

37. *Argus*, May 27, 1887, cited in Lake, "Chinese Empire Encounters Brtish Empire," 105.

38. Ibid., 104.

39. Toasts: *Argus*, May 28, 1887, cited ibid., 104–5.

40. Ibid., 107–8; Fitzgerald, "Advance Australia Fairly," 69.

41. Mountford, *Britain, China, and Colonial Australia*, chap. 4; Cheong, *Chinese Remonstrance*, 8–14.

42. Cheong, *Chinese Remonstrance*, 5–7.

43. Cheong, "Address to Australasian Conference," in ibid., 15.

44. Mountford, *Britain, China, and Colonial Australia*, 130–31.

45. Ibid., 136–42; Finnane, "'Habeas Corpus Mongols.'"

46. Mountford, *Britain, China, and Colonial Australia*, chap. 5.

47. Ibid., 153.

48. Griffiths, "Making of White Australia," 516–31. Griffiths argues that elite Anglo-Australian interests chose to destroy the economy of the Northern Territory rather than let Chinese people develop it (535). Markus, *Australian Race Relations*, 74; Markus, *Fear and Hatred*, 195; Lake and Reynolds, *Drawing Global Colour Line*, chap. 6. By the turn of the century, the Queensland sugar industry's investment in capital-intensive technology allowed it to eliminate Pacific Islander field labor. Denoon and Wyndham, "Australia and Western Pacific," 550. On Tasmania: Irving, *Constitute a Nation*, 102.

49. Mountford, *Britain, China, and Colonial Australia*, 183.

50. Markus, "Divided We Fall," 10; "Coloured Alien Curse," *Worker*, July 29, 1899, p. 2; "Sticking to the Chinese! The Capitalists' Conference Decides to Put White Labour Down—If Possible," *Worker*, March 21, 1891, p. 4. On minimum wage: Lake, "Challenging 'Slave-Driving.'" Australia continues to have one of the highest minimum wages in the world (US$12.14), surpassed only by Luxembourg (US$13.78) in 2020. "Minimum Wage by Country 2020," *World Population Review*, https://worldpopulationreview.com/country-rankings/minimum-wage-by-country. On white labor protectionism: Hyslop, "Imperial Working Class."

51. Fitzgerald, "Advance Australia Fairly," 59–74.

52. "Huagong Nanzuo" (letter), *Hangzhou baihuabao*, no. 8, August 1, 1901, p. 1.

53. Luo Zhongyao, *Report*, in Luo Fenglu to Foreign Ministry, July 29, 1902, File 3, no. 02-13-008-01-061, Qing Foreign Ministry Records, AS.

54. Lake and Reynolds, *Drawing Global Color Line*, chap. 6.

55. "The Slippery Chinese," *Western Mail*, February 20, 1904, p. 13; "Prohibited Immigrants: Eleven Chinese Deported," *West Australian*, September 16, 1904, p. 2; "Chinese Stowaways," *Northern Territory Times and Gazette*, January 29, 1904, p. 3. On pearling industry: Tang Entong to Foreign Ministry, April 15, 1911, File no. 02-12-015-01-015, Qing Foreign Ministry Records, AS. See also Martínez, "End of Indenture?" The pearling industry won exemption from the immigration restriction law

of 1901 and continued to recruit indentured Asian workers until the 1970s. On other demands: "Chinese Competition," *Albany Advertiser* (WA), April 2, 1904, p. 3; "Sunday Labour by Chinese," *Goulburn Evening Penny Post* (NSW), November 5, 1904, p. 2; "Future Trouble of Overseas Chinese," *Aiguo bao*, September 21, 1904, p. 2; Letters to Editor, *Aiguo bao*, November 23, 1904, p. 2; *Aiguo bao*, December 7, 1904, p. 2.

56. "Public Morals," *SMH*, November 1, 1904, p. 3; "Early Morning Raid. Chinese Gamblers Secured," *Evening News* (Sydney), November 26, 1904, p. 4; "Future Trouble of Overseas Chinese," *Aiguo bao*, September 21, 1904, p. 2; "Resistance Against Cruel Laws," *Aiguo bao*, November 23, 1904, p. 2. Zhong letter, *Aiguo bao*, December 7, 1904, p. 2.

57. On consuls: Liang Lanxun to Foreign Ministry, May 18, 1909, File no. 02-12-014-02-018; Li Jingfang to Foreign Ministry, June 3, 1910, File no. 02-12-014-03-009; Huang Rongliang to Foreign Ministry, July 5, 1911, File no. 02-12-015-01-023; all in Qing Foreign Ministry Records, AS. Act of 1905: Lake and Reynolds, *Drawing Global Colour Line*, 162.

58. Dilke, *Greater Britain;* Belich, *Replenishing the Earth*, 320–21.

CHAPTER 8: THE RICHEST SPOT ON EARTH

1. Evans, *Report*, June 27, 1904, Cd. 2183/doc. 13, *PP* 1905; Richardson, "Recruiting Chinese Indentured Labour," 94.

2. Evans, June 27, 1904, Cd. 2183/13, *PP* 1904; Evans, November 1904, Cd. 2401/22, *PP* 1905; Evans, *General Report*, February 13, 1905, Cd. 2401/49, *PP* 1905.

3. Evans, *General Report*, February 13, 1905, Cd. 2401/49, *PP* 1905.

4. Marks and Trapido, "Milner and South African State," 58. Farrar was knighted for his service in the South African War and was created a baronet in 1911. Farrar papers, BL.

5. Higginson, "Privileging the Machines," 12–16; Hamill, *Strange Career of Hoover*, 162; Peng, "Qingdai yingguo wei nanfei."

6. Xie, *Youli nanfeizhou ji*, 278–89. For background on the Xie family, I thank Chengji Xing.

7. Evans, June 27, 1904, Cd. 2183/13, *PP* 1904.

8. On fatalities: Yap and Man, *Colour*, 117; Richardson, *Chinese Mine Labour*, 256n5. Convictions for desertion, refusing to work, absent without permit, failure to show permit, and rioting, for the period June 22, 1904 to January 31, 1907, Cd. 2786 /28, *PP* 1905; Cd. 3338, appendix 2, *PP* 1907; Cd. 3528/6, 12, 17, 25, 38, *PP* 1907. As of June 1906, fifteen were sentenced to ten years to life; fourteen were executed for murder; sixteen were shot dead during riots. "Notice Addressed to Chinese Indentured Laborers from Foreign Labor Department Superintendent Jamieson," appended lists, TAB/GOV 990 PS 37-17-06 Part I, NASA.

9. Saunders and Smith, "Southern Africa," 597–623. The British annexed the Transvaal in 1877 and held it briefly until it conceded it back to the Afrikaners after the first Anglo-Boer War in 1881.

10. Erthington et al., "From Colonial Hegemonies to Imperial Conquest," 319–91; Dubow, "South Africa and South Africans."

11. Stephens, *Fueling the Empire*, 92–94.

12. Saunders and Smith, "Southern Africa," 609. "Hell room": Stephens, *Fueling the Empire*, 165. Chinese denied mining licenses: Yap and Man, *Colour*, 73–75. Refusal of gold licenses was informal until 1898, when Gold Law no. 15 expressly prevented any colored person from obtaining a license to dig for precious metals.

13. S. Herbert Frankel, "Fifty Years on the Rand." *Economist*, September 19, 1936, p. 523; "The Transvaal Gold Mines—XV: The Rand East of Boksburg," *Economist*, Feb. 11, 1905, p. 218. Industrial needs: Marks and Trapido, "Milner and South African State," 60–61; Richardson and Van Helton, "Development of South African Gold-Mining," 319–40. Reaching the reef: Stephens, *Fueling the Empire*, 166.

14. Stephens, *Fueling the Empire*, 165–67; Delius, "Migrant Labor and Pedi," 295–303; Higginson, "Privileging the Machine," 16–22. "Scientific industry": Burt, *Visit to Transvaal*, 27.

15. "Statement Showing Increase in the Number of Whites, Coloured, and Chinese Employed by all the Gold Mines on the Witwatersrand," Cd. 2401/47, *PP* 1905. On output: Yap and Man, *Colour*, 134; TCM, *15th Annual Report for the Year 1904*, xxxix, Richardson, "Recruiting of Chinese Indentured Labour," 87. By 1914 the Rand would account for 40 percent of the world's gold output. Saunders and Smith, "Southern Africa," 609.

16. Van-Helten, "Empire and High Finance," 533.

17. The classic work in this regard is J. A. Hobson's *Imperialism: A Study* (London, 1890); see also Ally, *Gold and Empire*. On the British strategy to forsake modernizing its domestic industry in favor of relying on its "growing power as the hub of international lending, trade and settlements": Hobsbawm, *Industry and Empire*, 169.

18. De Cecco, *International Gold Standard*, 30–38.

19. Erthington et al., "Colonial Hegemonies to Imperial Conquest," 372.

20. Selborne quoted in Meredith, *Diamonds, Gold, and War*, 366.

21. The high cost of living also resulted in high wages for whites on the mines. Although whites were a minority of the workforce, white wages comprised a far greater expense than native wages. ZAR Witwatersrand Chamber of Mines, *Report of Industrial Commission*, 447–48, 452–55. On mining capitalism and the ZAR state: Denoon, "Capital and Capitalists," 111–32. Kruger outburst at 1899 Bloemfontein conference: Marks and Trapido, "Milner and South African State," 61.

22. Trapido, "Imperialism, Settler Identities," 66–101; Marks and Trapido, "Milner and South African State," 55–57. On the debate among historians over the role of gold in the South African War: Marks and Trapido, "Milner and South African State Reconsidered," 80–94.

23. Saunders and Smith, "Southern Africa," 610–15; Trapido, "Imperialism, Settler Identities," 90–97. Scholars of British and South African history have argued over the origins of the South African war for decades, in particular over whether it was driven primarily by political (imperial) or economic (gold mining) interests. The

debate has largely failed to understand that economic interests are constitutive of imperial power. Robinson and Gallagher, *Africa and Victorians;* Marks and Trapido, *Politics of Race;* Porter, *"Cultural Imperialism";* Smith, *Origins of South African War.*

24. Milner quoted in Marks and Trapido, "Milner and South African State," 52. See also Dubow, "Colonial Nationalism"; Bright, *Chinese Labour,* 38–47.

25. Lawley to Milner, May 14, 1904, Cd. 2104/11, *PP* 1904; *Reports of Transvaal Labour Commission,* Cd. 1894, p. 33, *PP* 1904; Higginson, *Collective Violence,* 69–71, 87–88.

26. *Reports of Transvaal Labour Commission,* Cd. 1894, pp. 33, 39, *PP* 1904. "Fraught with danger": "Worker," letter to Johannesburg *Star:* "The only thing that will 'drive' the Kaffirs to the mines is economic pressure. In other words, we must be prepared to increase the hut tax, and to face the consequence of such a step, if we must have Kaffir labour to work the mines. I venture to say that such a solution of the labour problem is fraught with more danger to the white population of South Africa than the importation of a hundred thousand Chinese." "Chinese Labour," *Star,* March 3, 1906, in "History of Chinese Labour, January to November 12, 1906," clipping album, Farrar papers, BL. The process of dispossession was long and uneven, and native-peasant farming and share-tenancy persisted in rural Transvaal. The Native Land Act of 1913 aimed to achieve land dispossession by limiting African ownership to 13 percent of land in the country. The mines also lengthened the minimum term of contract to seven months in 1919 and to nine months in 1924. Martin Legassick and Francine de Clercq, "Capitalism and Migrant Labour in Southern Africa: The Origins and Nature of the System," in Marks and Richardson, *International Labour Migration,* 148–49; Higginson, *Collective Violence.*

27. On wages: Marks, "War and Union," 169. On prods and whips: *Report of Native Deputation Inspection from Cape Colony to Transvaal,* October 15, 1903, Milner to Lyttelton, January 24, 1904, Cd. 2788/3 encl., *PP* 1906. On drills: Marks and Trapido, "Milner and South African State," 65. On Native Passes: Transvaal Proc. no. 37, 1901. On Liquor Law Amendment: Transvaal Proc. no. 36, 1901. On mortality rates: Lyttelton to Milner, February 22, 1904, Cd. 2025/4, *PP* 1904; Milner to Lyttelton, February 27, 1904, Cd. 2025/5, *PP* 1904. On investors: Richardson, *Chinese Mine Labour,* 15–21.

28. Transvaal Labor Commission, 9; Honnold to Rickard, June 30, 1903, letterbook A, box 77, H.Mss.03381, WM, Claremont Colleges Library. On India: Bright, *Chinese Labour,* 33.

29. TCM, *Report for 1900–1,* xxxviii–xxxix; Richardson, "Recruiting Chinese Indentured Labour," 89.

30. H. Ross Skinner, *Report Furnished to the Witwatersrand Native Labour Association,* September 22, 1903, in TCM, *Report for 1903,* 155–69. On brokering arrangements: Richardson, *Chinese Mine Labour,* chap. 3. On draft legislation: Ibid., 29. Skinner would go on to be Transvaal director of munitions during World War I, a service for which he would be knighted in 1917.

31. Skinner, *Report,* 161, 166–67.

32. Ibid, 163.

33. Li, *History of Overseas Chinese,* 92; Yap and Man, *Colour,* 14–24. Occupations: Harris, "History of Chinese," 218.

34. Yap and Man, *Colour*, 71–80.

35. Ibid., 79.

36. Ibid., 89–93. Yeung directed Sun Yatsen's failed 1895 uprising in Guangzhou, after which the British banished him and Sun from Hong Kong for five years. Yeung went to South Africa and returned to Hong Kong in 1899. In 1900 he started another uprising in Guangdong. In 1901 he was assassinated by a Qing agent.

37. Harris, "History of Chinese," 220–32; resolutions from Dordrecht, Wodehouse, Hanover, and George, December 1903 to February 1904, KAB GH 1/358/16, NASA. The 1904 law remained on the Cape Colony's books for two decades after the Chinese mine program ended, effectively ending Chinese immigration to the Cape and stunting community growth in the Cape and beyond.

38. Farrar quoted in *Rand Daily Mail*, April 1, 1903, Milner to Chamberlain, April 25, 1903, Cd. 1895/8, encl. 1, *PP* 1904.

39. "Flood us" and "neutrality": Milner to Chamberlain, April 6, 1903. Mining engineers: Milner to Chamberlain, December 20, 1902, both in MSS Milner dep. 171, BL. "Leave nothing": Milner to Gell, December 13, 1903, in Milner, *Papers*, 2:481. Lobbying CO: Phillips to Reyersbach, November 13, 1903, in Phillips, *All that Glittered*, 121; Bloemfontein resolution, *Report of Executive Committee*, in TCM, *Annual Report for 1903*, xxxi.

40. Minority report, *Statement of the Chamber Presented to the Transvaal Labor Commission*, in appendix, TCM, *Annual Report for 1903*, 49–57. On Whiteside: Bright, *Chinese Labour*, 34–35; Majority report, Cd. 1896, p. 40, *PP* 1904; *Report of the Executive Committee*, TCM, *Annual Report for 1903*, xxx–xxxi.

41. Trade unions: Bright, *Chinese Labour*, 44–46. Banners: Yap and Man, *Colour*, 107. White League: *Transvaal Leader*, April 2, 1903, Milner to Chamberlain, April 6, 1903, MSS Milner dep. 171, BL.

42. Resolution cited in Bright, *Chinese Labour*, 56; Smuts to Hobhouse, February 21, 1904, cited ibid., 58.

43. Ibid., 42.

44. Phillips, *Transvaal Problems*, 49; Bright, *Chinese Labour*, 42–44.

45. Bright, *Chinese Labour*, 35–37. Richardson, *Chinese Mine Labour*, 28–29, quoting Farrar at 28.

46. Ordinance no. 17 of 1904, Transvaal, *Handbook of Ordinances*.

47. Regulations issued under Section 29 of Ordinance no. 17 of 1904; Government Notice 777, June 10, 1904, all ibid.

48. Hyde Park: Yap and Man, *Colour*, 107; Richardson, "Recruiting Chinese Indentured Labour," 93–97. Yantai recruitment: Zhang to Waiwubu, January 8, 1904, in Chen, *Huagong chuguo shiliao huibian*, 1:1653.

49. Zhang to Waiwubu, February 18, 1904, ibid., 1:1656–57. The Convention of Peking of 1860 recognized that Chinese were at "perfect liberty" to enter into service in "British colonies or other parts beyond the sea," under regulations framed by Chinese and British officials for the "protection of Chinese emigrating as above" (Article 5). "Unexpected": *Report of the Executive Committee*, TCM, *Annual Report for 1904*, xxvii.

50. Zhang, *Gaoben hang hai shu qi huibian*. On Zhang's early training and career, see also Zhang, *Diary of Chinese Diplomat*.

51. Zhang to Waiwubu, February 6, May 1, August 26, September 4, October 16, and December 4, 1903; January 8 and 22, 1904, all in Chen, *Huagong chuguo shiliao huibian*, 1:1643–55.

52. Emigration Convention of Great Britain and China of 1904, in Transvaal, *Handbook of Ordinances*, 31–37.

53. Zhang to Waiwubu, March 18, 1904, in Chen, *Huagong chuguo shiliao huibian*, 1:1661; Villiers, Sixth meeting of [negotiating] committee, April 8, 1904, Cd. 1945, *PP* 1904.

54. Richardson, *Chinese Mine Labour*, 51–72; *General Report on Chinese Labour*, March 13, 1905, Cd. 2401/49, *PP* 1905. In the port city of Yantai in Shandong, the CMLIA engaged Cornabe Eckford and Co. and Silas-Schwabe and Co. and in Tianjin, the Chinese Engineering and Mining Company. Richardson, *Chinese Mine Labour*, 114–15. The latter was a British firm that had subsumed the Kaiping Mining Company, established in 1877 as one of China's first modern industrial firms, after a hostile takeover from Kaiping's Chinese shareholders in 1901. Hoover, chief engineer for Kaiping, had played a central role in the takeover. He had connections to British mining and financial interests—with Moreing and Werner Beit in London, and Walter Nathan, recently of South Africa and the new director of Kaiping Mining, and brother of Sir Matthew Nathan, governor of Hong Kong—that greased his recruitment contract for the Transvaal gold mines. Carlson, *Kaiping Mines*, 57–83; *Times* (London), March 2, 1905, p. 9; Peng, "Qingdai yingguo wei nanfei." In the first year of recruitment, Chinese Mining and Engineering made a net profit of 72,071 yuan and in the following year 22,000 yuan. Walter Nathan, *Chinese Mining and Engineering Company Annual Report 1904–1905*, and 1905–6 annual report, reprinted in Zhonggong Kailuan meikuang weiyuanhui kuangshi bianweihui (History Editorial Board of CCP Kailuan Mining Committee), "Qian kai luan meikuang ying, bi diguo zhuyi fenzi fanmai huagong de yixie ziliao" (Selected documents on labor trafficking by British and Belgian imperialists from the former Kailuan coal mine), *Beiguo chunqiu*, no. 2 (1960), pp. 76–94.

55. Xie, *Youli nanfeizhou ji*, 278–81. "Tyrannical": *Chung Kwok Po*, May 29, 1903, and "living hell," in *Swatow* (Shantou) *Daily News*, May 20, 1903, quoted in Yap and Man, *Colour*, 100.

56. *Waijiao bao* printed translations of British news articles and the text of Ordinance no. 17 and would continue to publish subsequent ordinances issued in relation to the Chinese labor program in Transvaal. Translation of Ordinance no. 17, *Waijiao bao*, June 8, 1904. *Dongfang zazhi* was directly critical, writing about the Chinese laborers' suffering, their exploitation as beasts of burden, and China's humiliation. For example, "Shu nanfei yingshu jinzhi huagong rujing xinli hou" (New Regulations Forbidding Chinese Labor from South Africa), *Dongfang zazhi* 1, no. 10 (October 25, 1904): 161–64; "You wuding zhaomu huagong zhiyue" (Chinese Labor Contract Signed Wrongly Again), *Dongfang zazhi* 1, no. 5 (July 8, 1904): 19. "Nan feizhou hua qiao can zhuang ji" (A Record of the Miserable Condition of the Over-

seas Chinese in South Africa), *Xinmin congbao* 3, no. 1–2 (June–July 1904), trans. Jack Neubauer. This letter, and a second letter published in October, were signed by Chinese Association of South Africa and were likely written by Xie Zixiu. On Social Darwinism and Chinese nationalism: Duara, *Rescuing History*, chap. 4; Karl, *Staging the World*, chap. 7.

57. Richardson, *Chinese Mine Labour*, 85–88; "Nanfeizhou di er tongxin" (A Second Letter from South Africa), *Xinmin congbao* 3, no. 6 (1904).

58. Under-Secretary of State, Foreign Office, to Under Secretary of State, Colonial Office, June 22, 1905, *Intelligence Report for March Quarter*, TAB/FLD 19 AG11/05, NASA. Between 1847 and 1874, 125,000 indentured Chinese shipped to Cuba and 95,000 went to Peru. The Qing abolished labor contracts to Cuba and Peru in 1874 after a delegation visited the Cuban site and found widespread abuse. Hu DeHart, "Chinese Coolie Labor in Cuba"; Martínez, "'Unwanted Scraps.'"

59. Richardson, *Chinese Mine Labour*, 93–97; CMLIA cited in Yap and Man, *Colour*, 105.

60. On provincial officials: Johnson to Commissioner no. 260, re Chinese emigration to Transvaal, Weihaiwei area port of embarkation, August 29 and September 1, 5, 12, and 13, 1904, CO 873/136, NA; *Nanfeizhou jinkuang huagong xintu*. Rosters are reprinted in Li, *Fei zhou huaqiao huaren*, 60–63, 65–67, 70–75.

61. Richardson, *Chinese Mine Labour*, 125–26, FLD and Skinner quoted at 126.

62. Xie, *Youli nanfeizhou ji*, 279; Burt, *Visit to Transvaal*, 61; Richardson, *Chinese Mine Labour*, 145.

63. Richardson, *Chinese Mine Labour*, 141–43; *Shandong ribao*, translation in FO 2/971, p. 194, NA.

64. Richardson, *Chinese Mine Labour*, 148.

65. Ibid., 156–57.

66. Ship surgeon's journal quoted in ibid., 158–59.

67. Ibid., 161–62.

68. Evans, *Report*, June 27, 1904, Cd. 2183/13, *PP* 1904; Milner to Lyttelton, July 29, 1904, Cd. 2401/6, *PP* 1905.

CHAPTER 9: COOLIES ON THE RAND

1. Xie, *Youli nanfeizhou ji*, 284.

2. Thomas Ah Sze to Higgins, April 3, 1905, FO 2/971, p. 250, NA.

3. Higgins to Bagot, April 5, 1905; Bagot to Perry, April 6, 1905; interview at Farrar Brothers Offices (Johannesburg), March 29, 1905; Thomas Ah Sze to W. G. Higgins, April 3, 1905; McCartney to Perry, May 26, 1905; all FO 2/971, pp. 242–58, NA.

4. Thomas Ah Sze to Higgins, April 3, 1905.

5. Xie, *Youli nanfeizhou ji*, 278–89; Chen, *Huagong chuguo shiliao huibian*, 1:1757.

6. Milner to Lyttelton, July 29, 1904, Cd. 2401/6, *PP* 1905.

7. List of beriberi patients sent back from Durban per SS *Ikbal* (November 18, 1904), TAB/FLD 41, 5/54, NASA. Output and profits: Richardson, *Chinese Mine Labour*, 202, table A.12.

8. Evans, *General Report,* February 13, 1905, Cd. 2401/49, *PP* 1905. Richardson, *Chinese Mine Labour,* 167–68. Data on workers imported: Bright, *Chinese Labour,* 91.

9. "Definite policy": Milner to Lyttelton, January 30, 1905, Cd. 2401/41, *PP* 1905. CMLIA requests: *Report of Chinese English Mining Co. General Manager W. Nathan,* May 25, 1905, in "Qian Kailuan meikuang Ying/Bi diguozhuyi fenzi fanmai huagong de yixie ziliao" (Selected Documents from the Former Kailuan Coal Mine on Foreign Labor Recruitment), *Beiguo chunqiu* no. 2 (1905), 76–94. Permanent feature: Elgin to Selborne, January 5, 1906, Cd. 2788/15, *PP* 1906; Selborne to Elgin, January 20, 1906, Cd. 2819/39, *PP* 1906; Davenport, *Digging Deep,* 294.

10. Richardson, *Chinese Mine Labour,* 169–72.

11. *Extracts from Report of the Government Mining Engineer for Year Ending 30 June 1905,* Cd. 2819/71, *PP* 1906, showed 79.18 percent of Chinese working underground, 20.82 percent aboveground; 67.18 of native workers underground, 32.82 percent aboveground; 42.15 percent of white workers underground (mostly as foremen of Chinese and native labor), 57.85 percent aboveground. *Nanfeizhou jinkuang huagong xintu*'s samples of workers at various mines bear out these data: 80 Chinese laborers at the Angelo mine of East Rand Proprietary comprising 49 rock drillers, 14 cart pushers, and 7 rock carriers (underground); and 3 machine assistants and one blacksmith's assistant (aboveground); and 3 foremen and one policeman. The sample of 49 workers at Geldenhuis Deep of Wernher Beit listed 41 drillers, 4 carters, one rock carrier, one blaster, and 3 foremen. *Nanfeizhou jinkuang huagong xintu.*

12. Regulations issued under section 29 of Ordinance no. 17 of 1904, Form no. 1, Contract of Service, par. 4–6; Second Schedule to Contract, Schedule of Native Wages, Transvaal *Handbook of Ordinances.* White miners earned daily wages of 9 to 10 shillings for unskilled work and 17 to 20 shillings or more for skilled labor, Burt, *Visit to Transvaal,* 40. Wages in late Qing China differed by region, and data are inconsistent. The daily wage in Beijing in 1905 was equivalent to 5 grams silver or a half shilling. Allen et al., "Wages, Prices, and Living Standards," fig. 3, p. 20. Lionel Phillips put the daily wage at 2 pence in China and 5 pence (nearly a half shilling) in Korea, but he probably meant Manchuria. Phillips, *Transvaal Problems,* 111. On "buying milk," see Gim Ah Chun, Chinese interpreter at New Comet, in Burt, *Visit to Transvaal,* 61. Xie Zixiu reported that nothing could be had on the Rand for less than 3 pence and that prices for everyday goods at the stores on the mines were ten times higher than in town. Xie, *Youli nanfeizhou ji,* 281; "Nanfeizhou di er tongxin."

13. Evans, *General Report,* February 13, 1905, Cd. 2401/49, *PP* 1905; Selborne to Lyttelton, September 18, 1905, Cd. 2786/25, *PP* 1905; *Annual Report of the FLD, 1905–6,* Cd. 3338, appendix 8, *PP* 1907.

14. Yap and Man, *Colour,* 110; Bright, *Chinese Labour,* 80–82; Zhang to Waiwubu, June 19, 1905, file no. 02-29-003-04-018; Liu Yulin to Waiwubu, April 11, 1906, file no. 02-29-001-08-001, both in Qing Foreign Ministry Records, AS. On Liu's investigations, see enclosures in Zhang to Waiwubu, October 14, 1905, doc. 374, *Qingji huagong chuguo shiliao.* Death benefits: Zhang Deyi to Waiwubu, June 19, 1905, file no. 02-29-003-04-018, Qing Foreign Ministry Records, AS.

15. "Nanfeizhou di er tongxin" (A Second Letter from South Africa), *Xinmin congbao,* 3,

no. 6 (1904); Letter to editor, *Aiguo bao,* September 28, 1904, p. 2. On Ah Bu: Naylor, "Yellow Labour: The Truth about the Chinese in the Transvaal," dd-22487, CRL.

16. Food rations: Regulations issued under section 29 of Ordinance no. 17 of 1904, Form no. 1, par. 7. Lunch: Evans, *Report,* November, 28, 1904, Cd. 2401/22, *PP* 1905; Evans, *General Report,* February 13, 1905, Cd. 2401/49, *PP* 1905. Evans called the bread "first class," but workers complained to Xie Zixiu that it was so coarse, they could not swallow it. Xie, *Youli nanfeizhou ji,* 280.

17. Stopes: Burt, *Visit to Transvaal,* 57–58. Water: "Complaints by Chinese December 7, 1905," quoted in Harris, "History of Chinese," 173. The government mining engineer reported that only fifteen out of seventy-one producing mines on the Rand could productively use machine drills. Milner to Lyttelton, February 13, 1905, Cd. 2401/47, *PP* 1905. By 1905, some twenty-two deep mines, at an average depth of 2,600 feet, were running on a second reef line. Chinese worked on them and also prepared to bring into production mines along a third reef line, at depths of 4,000 to 5,000 feet. Leggett, "South African Methods," *EMJ,* April 20, 1905, pp. 754–56.

18. Eugenio Bianchini, report, October 28, 1905, Cd. 2819/29, *PP* 1906.

19. Compounds: Evans, *Report,* November 28, 1904, Cd. 2401/22, *PP* 1905; Evans, *General Report,* February 13, 1905, Cd. 2401/49, *PP* 1905. Stew: Phillips, *Transvaal Problems,* 110. Meat ration: "Wu gao zhi min" (A People with Nowhere to Turn), *Xinmin congbao* 3, no. 11 (1904). Tasteless meat: Xie, *Youli nanfeizhou ji,* 280. Outside food purchases: Chinese controller, New Heriot to Sir John Walsham Bart, Inspector FLD, April 29, 1909, TAB/FLD 251 83/32, NASA.

20. Flowers and birds: Phillips, *Transvaal Problems,* 104. Light and airy: Evans, *Report,* November 28, 1904, Cd. 2401/22, *PP* 1905; Evans, *General Report,* February 13, 1905, Cd. 2401/49, *PP* 1905. Luxurious and palatial: McCallum to Selborne, January 10, 1906, TAB/FLD 22/115-05, NASA. Lane Carter, manager of the French Rand Company, believed Chinese in South Africa were living "in clover." Phillips, *Transvaal Problems,* 110.

21. On exchange of ideas: Phillips, *Transvaal Problems,* 103, 112. On vice: Malcolm to local mayors, clergy, and Chamber of Mines, August 7, 1906, and response correspondence, TAB/FLD 210/51-51-27, NASA. Most refuted the idea that the Chinese had anything new to teach Africans in the way of vice. On relations with African women: Rose to Malcolm, August 24, 1906, TAB/SNA 248 147–56, NASA; District Controller, Native Affairs to Pass Commissioner (n.d.), TAB/SNA 248 NA 70/105, NASA; Acting Secretary For Native Affairs to Private Secretary of Lieutenant Governor, January 17, 1905, TAB/SNA, 248 NA70/05. NASA. See also Harris, "Private and Confidential," 125–26. Examples of ethnic conflicts include fighting between Chinese and Africans bathing in the dam near the compound, after the latter pulled the Chinese workers' queues; Grant-Smith, "Disturbance at the Van Ryn Gold Mines and Estate Limited, 14th May 1905," TAB/FLD 29, AG 2553-3491/05, NASA. Arrest of seven Chinese workers picnicking on the veld after a group of Africans accused them of theft: "Petition of 7 Witwatersrand Deep Coolies Sentenced at Germiston to 10 Lashes Each and 6 Months," May 28, 1906, TAB/FLD 240/76-76-15, NASA.

22. *Nanfeizhou jinkuang huagong xintu;* Phillips, *Transvaal Problems,* 113; "Is it Slavery?" (1906), Cambridge University Library, CCO; Yap and Man, *Colour,* 122.

23. Professional gamblers: *Report of the Special Committee Appointed to Consider and Report upon the Present Conditions in Regard to the Control of Chinese Indentured Labourers on the Mine Premises of the Witwatersrand Area* (1906), Cd. 3025/101, *PP* 1906; Memorandum, superintendent FLD, January 5, 1906, TAB/FLD 22/115-05, NASA; petition of Ts'ui Ku-yan (translation), July 25, 1906, TAB/FLD 240/76-11, NASA. It is impossible to know whether Cui actually contemplated committing suicide or used the rhetoric of suicide to strengthen his appeal.

24. Baptism: Yap and Man, *Colour,* 123. Going to town: Evans, *General Report,* February 13, 1905, Cd. 2401/49, *PP* 1905; Yap and Man, *Colour,* 120; Phillips, *Transvaal Problems,* 104, 113. Praise and disapproval: McCallum to Selborne, January 10, 1906, TAB/FLD 22/115-05, NASA; Harris, "Private and Confidential," 122–24.

25. Selborne to Elgin, July 2, 1906, TAB/GOV 990 PS 37-17-06 Part 1, NASA; A. G. de Villiers, *Report,* May 4, 1907, TAB/LD AG 1524/07, NASA; Yap and Man, *Colour,* 122. The Immorality Ordinance of 1903 forbade any white woman to have "unlawful carnal connection with any Native" (defined as any "person manifestly belonging to any of the native of Coloured races of Africa, Asia, America, or St. Helena"). See also Harris, "Private and Confidential," 123–26.

26. Epprecht, "'Unnatural Vice'"; Moodie et al., "Migrancy and Male Sexuality"; Harris, "Private and Confidential," 127–31; Chou, *Tongzhi,* 1–55.

27. Records often mention laborers going to visit relatives at other mines on Sundays. Because recruitment was concentrated in certain areas, laborers would have come from the same counties and even the same villages and hence from extended families and clan lineages. On patrilineal customs: McKeown, "Transnational Chinese Families," 73–110. Data on women and children: *Annual Report of the FLD, 1904–5,* Cd. 3025, appendix 4, p. 167, *PP* 1906; *Annual Report of the FLD, 1905–6,* Cd. 3338/32, *PP* 1907. *Nanfeizhou jinkuang huagong xintu* includes depictions of boys, who appear to be twelve or thirteen years of age at Simmer and Jack. It states there is a school for them, but the archives make no mention of any school on the mines.

28. Transmission of letters: TAB/FLD 188–90, NASA. Mail addressed to Tianjin shops: Record of Chinese laborers' correspondence from South Nourse (1904–6), TAB/FLD 189/40/8, NASA; letter of Hu Yulin, in Li, *Fei zhou huaqiao huaren,* 112. Hu Yulin wrote to his wife that he had twice wired money to her in care of the "Xie Family home on the street in front of the courtyard" and asked her, "How is it that my wife did not reply upon receipt of these letters?" Hu may have known how to direct his letter to his wife's home in Guangxi, but he gave her scant information in the way of a return address.

29. Bianchini Report, Cd. 2819/29, *PP* 1906. On Pless: Affidavits of Alexander McCarthy, Chang Chan Yin, Li Yu Cheng, Liu An Pan, and Yao Li Kung (November 1905–February 1906); sundry correspondence between Selborne and Elgin; Law Office and Lieutenant Governor's Office, February 1906, TAB/FLD 22/115-05, NASA. The torture case came to light after McCarthy, a hospital attendant who boarded with Pless, witnessed and reported Pless's torture of Li Yu Cheng. Li had deserted the

mine for two days. Upon his return, Pless took him to his house, where he stripped him and hosed him with cold and then hot water. He then tied him up from a nail on the dining room door for over twelve hours, broken only by a period when he coerced him to his bed. Liu An Pan, Pless's house servant, was sexually abused by Pless. Controllers, *Report on Control of Chinese Labourers*, Cd. 3025/101, *PP* 1906; *Annual Report of the FLD, 1905–6*, Cd. 3338/8, *PP* 1907.

30. Selborne to Elgin, February 17, 1906, Cd. 2819/70, *PP* 1906; Bright, *Chinese Labour*, 102, 147; Milner to Lyttelton, October 22, 1904, Cd. 2401/14, *PP* 1905; *Report on Control of Chinese Laborers*, Cd. 3025/101, *PP* 1906; Selborne to Elgin, February 17, 1906, Cd. 2819/70, *PP* 1906.

31. Solomon put his foot down, however, at a request by a local Christian mission to hire Wang Che from the Lancaster mine as an evangelist; that, he said, would be the "thin end of the wedge" of permanent settlement. Baker to Jamieson (n.d.); secretary FLD to private secretary Solomon, August 3, 1905; secretary Law Department to superintendent FLD (n.d.); all in TAB/FLD 19, AG 20/05, NASA. Kitchen workers: Evans, *Report on Disturbances*, December 1904, Cd. 2401/28, *PP* 1905.

32. Xie, *Youli nanfeizhou ji*, 285; *Annual Report of the FLD, 1904–5*, April 21, 1906, Cd. 3025, appendix IV, *PP* 1906; *Annual Report of the FLD, 1905–6*, Cd. 3338, appendix 6, *PP* 1907.

33. Cheng's poem in Xie, *Youli nanfeizhou ji*, translation by Chengji Xing. See discussion also in Peng, "Qingdai yingguo wei nanfei," 184.

34. On *yi hui*: Joint petition of SP nos. 9027, 9049, 9011, et al., Labourers of the South Nourse Mine to superintendent FLD, April 2, 1906, TAB/FLD 240/76-76/15, NASA; Bright, *Chinese Labour*, 46–147. On *gelaohui*: Hyunh, "We are Not a Docile People," 156. At Simmer and Jack, thirty-two Chinese were arrested for forming a secret society, but the matter was dropped after authorities determined it was unimportant. London's main concern was whether it was "in the nature of a trade union." Governor to secretary of state, March 11, 1905, TAB/FLD 4/147-7-11, NASA. A "triad society" was reportedly responsible for a disturbance at French Rand Gold Mining Company in November 1904. Evans, *Report on Disturbances*, December 1904, Cd. 2401/28, *PP* 1905.

35. Bianchini Report, Cd. 2819/29, *PP* 1906; see also Bright, *Chinese Labour*, 82.

36. Phillips, *Transvaal Problems*, 108–9; Selborne to Lyttelton, September 18, 1905, Cd. 2786/25, *PP* 1905; Bianchini Report, Cd. 2819/29, *PP* 1906.

37. Phillips, *Transvaal Problems*, 109; Browne, *South Africa: Glance*, 190.

38. Affidavits and Preparatory Examination, "Rex v. Charles Duncan Stewart and two Chinese coolies," TAB/GOV 990 PS 37-17-06 Part 1, NASA. A witness, William Taylor, swore out an affidavit that Stewart called out "shangoli" (*shang guolai*, or "come on up"). Taylor also identified Han and Wang but later could not be found to testify against them.

39. Lyttelton to Selborne, October 24, 1905, Cd. 2786/36, *PP* 1905.

40. Charles Stewart, testimony, TAB/GOV 990 PS 37-17-06 Part 1, NASA; Xie, *Youli nanfeizhou ji*, 284; Lyttelton to Selborne, October 24, 1905, Cd. 2786/36, *PP* 1905. On complaints, for example, the director of prisons informed the Law Department

that a Chinese worker, jailed on charges of rioting at Simmer and Jack, arrived at the Germiston prison suffering from effects of a severe beating, which he received from Chinese police after the riot. Prison officials did not want to be blamed for the flogging. Director of prisons to secretary Law Department, February 8, 1905, TBD/LD 1009, NASA. Lawley's order: Lyttelton to Selborne, October 24, 1905, Cd. 2786/36, *PP* 1905.

41. Frank Boland, "The Price of Gold. Flogging of the Rand Yellow Serf. Horrible Cruelties. Babarities Practised in the Mine Compounds. Terror on the Rand. Measures for Preserving Life and Property," *Morning Leader*, September 6, 1905, enclosure in C. H. Norman to Lyttelton, September 6, 1905, Cd. 2819/1, encl., *PP* 1906; Xie, *Youli nanfeizhou ji*, 288; Selborne to Lyttelton, November 20, 1905, Cd. 2819/14, *PP* 1906.

CHAPTER 10: THE PRICE OF GOLD

1. Measuring rod: Phillips to F. Eckstein, March 5, 1905, in Phillips, *All that Glittered*, 131. Overtime: Phillips, *Transvaal Problems*, 104.

2. Honnold to Wetzlar, February 13, 1905, box 4, folder 2, H.Mss.03381, WH, Claremont Colleges Library. On Nourse Deep: Manager, Nourse Deep, to Gibson, re: Coolie no. 30407, April 14, 1906, TAB/FLD 241/76-18, NASA. On working slowly and wandering off: "The Mining Problem. The Handling of Unskilled Labour," by "underground contractor," Johannesburg *Star*, February 8, 1906, clipping album, Farrar papers, BL.

3. "Xilande jin kuang huagong qing yuan shu" (Petition by Chinese miners in West Rand Mines), 1907, in Li, *Fei zhou huaqiao huaren*, 113–114.

4. Disturbances over wages deducted, bullying and ill treatment, explosion, policemen, meals not served: Evans, *Report on Disturbances*, December 1904, 1905 Cd. 2401/28. On Geldenhuis Deep: Lloyd to inspector, September 18, 1905, TAB/FLD 19, AG 10/05, NASA. At Simmer and Jack East in June 1908, workers rioted when mine management ordered men to work on the day of the dragon boat festival, a contracted holiday. Police and troopers put down the disturbance, but the workers succeeded in getting the day off. Yap and Man, *Colour*, 121.

5. "In Minor Key. Wit. Chinese Dissatisfied. Trouble all Over," *Rand Daily Mail*, October 7, 1905.

6. Evans, *Report on Disturbances*, December 1904, Cd. 2401/28, *PP* 1905; Richardson, "Coolies and Randlords," 164, 166.

7. Meaning of contract: Lawley to Lyttelton, April 6, 1905, Cd. 2401/58, *PP* 1905. "Clearly understood": Lawley to Lyttelton, April 18, 1905, cited in Richardson, "Coolies and Randlords," 168.

8. Lawley to Lyttelton, April 6, 1905, Cd. 2401/58, *PP* 1905; Richardson, "Coolies and Randlords," 171; *EMJ*, May 11, 1905, p. 932.

9. Richardson, "Coolies and Randlords," 164–65. The proposal was for a bonus of "one penny for each hole of twenty-four inches or over drilled by any member of their gang, plus a bonus of sixpence per shift if all coolies in their gang drilled thirty-six inches or over."

10. Bonus schedule, threepence (per shift) for 36 to 47 inches; fivepence for 48 inches to 59 inches, and so on up to a ninepence maximum. Richardson, "Coolies and Randlords," 172; Selborne to Lyttelton, July 1905, TAB/FLD 29, AG 2553-3491/05, NASA. See also correspondence between Selborne and Lyttelton, October 25, November 24, and December 5, 1905, Cd. 2819/4/8/12, *PP* 1906.

11. On expense of boots and work clothes, see "Xilande jin kuang Huagong qing yuan shu" (Petition by Chinese Miners in West Rand Mines), 1907, in Li, *Fei zhou huaqiao huaren,* 113–114.

12. Authorities often asserted that bad elements on the Rand were "ex-Boxers," though without evidence. Selborne to Lyttelton, September 18, 1905, Cd. 2786/25, *PP* 1905.

13. Data on desertions are from *Annual Report of the FLD, 1905–6,* Cd. 3338, appendix 2, *PP* 1907. See also "Return of Monthly Convictions of Chinese Labourers for Desertion, 1905," TAB/FLD 25/47-1906, NASA. The monthly average of the number of Chinese workers at Rand mines was 45,730. On return of deserters, see Selborne to Lyttelton, September 18, 1905, Cd. 2786/25, *PP* 1905. On the five deserters hiding in the old mill house of West Rand Mines, see Returns to Work, December 6, 1906, TAB/FLD 120 15/11, NASA. "This coolie had been hiding down this mine" of Aurora West: Returns to Work, December 6, 1905, TAB/FLD 120 15/11, NASA. On deserters convicted and sentenced for one month's desertion, see W. W. R. Jago, secretary of Association of Mine Managers, to Selborne, May 19, 1906, attached Schedule, TAB/GOV 990 PS 37-17-06 Part 1, NASA. On the Princess Mine, see Jamieson to Solomon, February 16, 1906, TAB/FLD 24 AG 27/06, NASA. In another case, six deserters hid in a mine shaft during the day and allegedly robbed farmsteads at night. Inspector to superintendent FLD, September 22, 1906, TAB/FLD 54 6/78, NASA.

14. On relations with African women, see Rose to Malcolm, August 24, 1906, TAB/SNA 248 147–56, NASA. On "refuge and employment": "Chinese on the Rand," *Manchester Guardian,* September 26, 1905. On Coolie no. 38,695: Jago to Selborne, May 19, 1906, TAB/GOV 990 PS 37-17-06 Part 1, NASA.

15. Reports show 107 outrages committed in Transvaal Town Police Area and 29 committed outside the town police area. "Transvaal Town Police Area, Return of Chinese Outrages from June 1, 1905, to February 28, 1906" (hereafter "Return of Chinese Outrages 1905–6"), TAB/FLD 25/47-1906, NASA; "Districts Outside the Transvaal Town Police Area," attachments to Selborne to Elgin, March 26, 1906, TAB/GOV 990/37-17-06 Part 1, NASA. A number of crimes took place on mine premises and hence were not committed by deserters. Some involved breaking into stores that operated on the mines. Attacks on individuals appear to be opportunistic: a "gang of coolies" attacked a white man who was asleep under his wagon at Simmer and Jack and robbed him of five pounds; a Chinese laborer "snatched a sovereign" from a native at the Angelo gold mine. Personal grudges rather than theft may have motivated some cases, as when fifteen Chinese attacked an African at the Witwatersrand Deep, stabbing him with a knife in the left side, forehead, and hand but stealing nothing. "Return of Chinese Outrages 1905–6," case nos. 2, 7, 8, 18, 22, 40.

16. Jamieson reported that it was "an undoubted fact that knives and revolvers are being freely sold to Chinese" by unknown purveyors. Jamieson to Solomon, February 16, 1906, TAB/FLD 24, AG 27/06, NASA. A white farmer wrote that a group of Chinese that attacked the "natives" at his farm were armed with "5 big knives, 1 hammer, a piece of piping, 1 tin dynamite caps, and about 100 dynamite cartridges." Meyer to Botha, May 25, 1906, TAB/GOV 990/37-17-06 Part 1, NASA. Outrages committed: "Return of Chinese Outrages 1905–6," case nos. 22, 31, 44, 45; "Return of Chinese Outrages Committed 1905–6," case no. 1; *Report of Proceedings, Deputation to His Excellency the Lieutenant-Governor on the Question of Desertion of Chinese Labourers from the Mines*, September 6, 1905, Cd. 2786/22, *PP* 1905.

17. "Return of Chinese Outrages 1905–6," case nos. 30, 37, 45.

18. *Annual Report of the FLD, 1905–6*, appendix 2 (listing two homicides and twenty-six murders), Cd. 3338, *PP* 1907; *Report of Proceedings, Deputation to His Excellency the Lieutenant Governor*, September 6, 1905, Cd. 2786/22, *PP* 1905. See also Botha to Elgin, May 16, 1906, TAB/GOV 990/37-17-06 Part 1, NASA.

19. Leggett, "South African Methods," *EMJ*, April 20, 1905, p. 756.

20. Elgin, "Chinese Labour—Proposal for Repatriation," January 1, 1906, CAB 37/82, 1906, no. 2, NA.

21. Selborne to Elgin, March 31, 1905, Cd. 3025/38, *PP* 1906; TCM, *Repatriation Proposals of His Majesty's Government*, Cd. 3025/72, *PP* 1906; Selborne to Elgin, April 28, 1906, Cd. 3025/67, *PP* 1906. Translation of notice published in *Manchester Guardian*, June 15, 1906, reprinted Cd. 3025, appendix I, *PP* 1906. By January 1907, 1,550 Chinese applied for state-assisted repatriation, of whom 766 returned, the balance of petitions rejected or withdrawn. Selborne to Elgin, February 20, 1907, Cd. 3528/31, *PP* 1907.

22. On dining halls: Evans, *General Report*, February 13, 1905, Cd. 2401/49, *PP* 1905. On measuring stick: Phillips to F. Eckstein, March 5, 1905, in Phillips, *All that Glittered*, 131.

23. Violations of ordinances and regulations included leaving premises without a permit; failing to produce a passport or tin ticket; refusal to be repatriated; aiding or abetting someone evading provisions of the ordinance; obstructing an officer from performance of duties; aiding and abetting a laborer to desert; desertion from service; refusal to work when required; unlawful absence from work; performing work other than unskilled work in mines; entering the service of persons other than importer or transferee; engaging in any kind of trade or business; making a frivolous complaint against an employer; failure of the head boy of gang or section to report any offense committed by any laborer of his gang; failure of laborers belonging to a gang or section to report an offense committed by any member to the mine manager; possession of gum opium or extract opium. Crimes "ordinarily summarily triable" by the magistrate court included "ordinary crimes committed on mine premises, excluding cases for which punishment is fine more than 75 pounds or imprisonment of more than six months." Ordinance no. 27 of 1905, Transvaal *Handbook of Ordinances*, 23–28. For lockups, see Ordinance no. 27 of 1905, sec. 1, 5. Data on trials and convictions is from *Annual Report of the FLD, 1905–6*, Cd. 3338, appendix 2, *PP* 1907.

24. Ordinance no. 27 of 1905, sec. 6, 8, 10. On gambling: Ordinance no. 12 of 1906, sec. 1; "Notes on Northern Chinese and Notes on Southern China" (no author), 1904, TAB/FLD 276/356-04, NASA. The report also recommended allowing the use of opium and importing a certain number of prostitutes for the compounds but these were not followed.

25. Ordinance no. 27 of 1905, sec. 7; Selborne to Lyttelton, September 18, 1905, Cd. 2786/25, *PP* 1905; Attorney general's testimony before legislature on proposed amendments to labor importation ordinance, Cd. 2786/46, encl. 2, *PP* 1905. Ordinance no. 17 of 1904, sec. 26, provided for the repatriation for laborers convicted of crimes, those declared to be of "unsound mind," and those "permanently incapacitated for work by physical infirmity or disease." These are borne out in reasons cited in returns, including beriberi, phthisis, amputation of limbs, "mania," "weakness in intellect," and "refusal to work." "Repatriations from Durban of Chinese Labourers Who Have Not Been Despatched to the Rand," sent on *SS Indravelei*, June 29, 1905, TAB/FLD 41/5-51, NASA. With its new powers of repatriation, the FLD did not bother to report cases of same-sex practices to the police, which required some evidence, such as a medical report, but merely asked mine managers for lists of suspected homosexuals and ordered them repatriated. Governor of Transvaal to secretary of state, November 16, 1906, TAB/EC (Executive Council) 101, NASA. In 1907 the FLD reported that it had repatriated to date 131 laborers who were "under suspicion of being addicted to [unnatural] crime" and was holding another eight for removal. Suggested Draft Reply to Telegram from Secretary of State of February 14, 1907 no. 1, TAB/FLD 236/73-73/32, NASA. Ordinary infractions: Selborne to Elgin, January 7, 1907, Cd 3528/19, *PP* 1907.

26. "Strictly Confidential Report of an Enquiry held by Mr. JAS Bucknill into Certain Allegations as to the Prevalence of Unnatural Vice and Other Immorality Amongst the Chinese Indentured Labourers Employed on the Mines of the Witwatersrand" (September 1906), Transvaal 38767, October 1, 1906, CO 537/540, NA. See also Harris, "Private and Confidential"; Chua, "'Open and Public Scandal.'" On prostitution and syphilis, see also Brammer to Malcolm, August 15, 1906, pp. 28–29, CO 537/540, NA.

27. Malcolm to mayors of Johannesburg, Germiston, Boksburg, Roodeport-Maraisburg, Springs, Krugerdorp; Rev. Amos Burnet; Rev. N. Audley Ross; Archdeacon of Johannesburg; president, Chamber of Mines; inspector general, South African Constabulary, August 7, 1906, and responses, CO 537/540, NA. On repatriation of suspected homosexuals: Selborne to Elgin, November 15, 1906, Confidential Telegrams Relating to Affairs in South Africa, 1906, CO 879/106, no. 1025, NA.

28. Selborne to Lyttelton, September 18, 1905, Cd. 2786/16, *PP* 1905; *Report on Control of Chinese Labourers*, Cd. 3025/101, *PP* 1906. The government at first loaned out firearms at no charge but then required a deposit of one hundred pounds because some people were borrowing guns and then reselling them. *Report of Proceedings*, Deputation to His Excellency the Lieutenant Governor, Cd. 2786/22, *PP* 1905. Funds expended last financial year (October to June) in "purchase of arms for issue to farmers and others for protection against Chinese Marauders": total £5,297/9s/5d for 1,250 Martini-Henry rifles; 358 shotguns; 208,000 ball cartridges; 3,630 shot

cartridges, plan to spend another £200 on shotguns. Assistant colonial secretary to private secretary, acting lieutenant general (1906), TAB/FLD 16 147/81/13, NASA.

29. Ordinance no. 27 of 1905, sec. 10; Higginson, *Collective Violence*, 125–29.

30. Copy of Resolution of Public Meeting held on April 12th, 1906, from town meeting of four hundred people, Heidelberg municipality; Resolution Passed at a Meeting Held at Pretoria on Friday, May 4, 1906; Selborne to Elgin, May 7, 1906 (on deputation from Het Volk); Louis Botha to Lord Elgin, May 16, 1906; Curtis to Solomon, April 22, 1906; all in TAB/GOV 990 PS 37-17-06 Part 1, NASA.

31. Solomon to Malcolm, March 15, 1906; Deputation Received (by Solomon) to Discuss Matters Relating to the More Effective Control of Wandering Chinese Coolies and the Prevention of Outrages Committed by Such Coolies (March 1905); Solomon to Selborne, June 1, 1906; all in TAB/GOV 990 PS 37-17-06 Part 1, NASA; *Report on Control of Chinese Labourers*, Cd. 3025/101, *PP* 1906.

32. *Report of Committee of Mine Managers*, May 28, 1906, TAB/GOV 990 PS 37-17-06 Part 1, NASA.

33. Selborne to Elgin, May 12, 1906, Cd. 3025/82, *PP* 1906; Elgin to Selborne, May 16, 1906, Cd. 3025/84, *PP* 1906.

34. "hopeless": Jamieson to Solomon, March 8, 1906, TAB/FLD 24, AG32/06, NASA; Jamieson, "Notification Addressed to All Chinese Indentured Labourers on the Witwatersrand Gold Mines," June 25, 1906, TAB/GOV 990 PS 37-17-06 Part 1, NASA.

35. "ocular": Jamieson to Solomon, October 26, 1905, TAB/FLD 22 AG 3161/05, NASA. "Two or three friends": Solomon to Jamieson, October 27, 1905, ibid. "Notice forbidding spreading of rumours": Jamieson to Chinese employed at Simmer and Jack and New Kleinfontien mines (n.d.), TAB/FLD 22 AG 3161/05, NASA. "Every condemned man," *Annual Report of the FLD*, 1905–6, Cd. 3338/5, *PP* 1907.

CHAPTER 11: THE ASIATIC DANGER IN THE COLONIES

1. Hyslop, "Imperial Working Class"; Semmel, *Imperialism and Social Reform.*

2. Van Onselen, *New Babylon,* 309–26, 366; Katz, "Underground Route," 467.

3. Smuts quoted in Selborne to Elgin, April 18, 1906, Cd. 3025/101 encl. 4, *PP* 1906. The excavation of one ton of rock was required to yield on average nine dollars of gold ore in 1905. Penrose, "Witwatersrand Gold Region," 745.

4. White labor grievances: Marks, "War and Union," 172; Katz, *White Death*; Katz, "Underground Route." White men working underground, whether with machine drills or supervising African hand drillers, typically worked on contract and controlled the pace of work, which engineers considered too slow to meet their aggressive production goals. By switching to hand drilling by Chinese workers and by imposing upon them a thirty-six-inch minimum daily requirement, the mine companies aimed to directly control production. Some white drill men became supervisors of Chinese gangs while others were moved to jobs aboveground, but not a few were laid off, causing alarm and consternation among the unions and other critics. Higginson, "Privileging the Machines"; Marks and Trapido, "Milner and South African State"; Phillips to Eckstein, March 5, 1905, in Phillips, *All That Glittered,* 128.

5. Freund, "South Africa: Union Years," 225.

6. Milner, *Papers*, 2:458–59; Katz, *Trade Union Aristocracy*, 117–18; Browne quoted in Katz, "Underground Route," 479.

7. Evans, *Cultures of Violence*, 93–95. See also Curle, *Gold Mines*, 135–37.

8. Creswell, *Chinese Labour Question from Within*, 24–34, 56–58; "Chinese Labour. Speech by Mr. Creswell [*sic*]. Meeting at Potchefstroom. Repatriation Resolution," *Rand Daily Mail*, October 6, 1905, p. 8. Critics pointed out that Village Main Reef enjoyed wide stopes and high-grade ore, whereas most mines had low-grade ore, which required a large supply of cheap labor to turn a profit, and narrow stopes, which did not allow for machine drills. Charles Sydney Goldmann, "South Africa and Her Labour Problem," *Nineteenth Century and After* 55 (May 1904): 848–62, at 857. See also "Chinese and Whites. Chamber of Mines Memorandum. Creswell Controverted," *Transvaal Leader*, January 5, 1906; "Mr. Creswell's Fallacies Exposed," Johannesburg *Star*, January 5, 1906; "Chinese Labour. Interesting Correspondence" [from Creswell], *Transvaal Leader*, February 17, 1906, all in clipping album, Farrar papers, BL. Not all criticisms defended the mining industry's interest. A letter from "Worker" to the *Star* criticized Creswell's proposals for an "open labor market" as laissez-faire doctrine that had brought impoverishment to the English working class. "Chinese Labour," *Star*, March 3, 1906, ibid. On the politics of "labor shortages" and preference for cheap labor to mechanization: Ngai, *Impossible Subjects*, chap. 4; Hahamovitch, *No Man's Land*, chap. 2.

9. Creswell, *Chinese Labour Question from Within*, 66, 75–76.

10. Dobbie, "Chinese Labour," *Macmillan's*, August 1906, pp. 787–800.

11. "Incompetent": Phillips to Selborne, January 24, 1906, in Phillips, *All that Glittered*. "Unskilled whites working": Richardson, *Chinese Mine Labour*, 177; "GME's Report for Last Administrative Year. Wages and Salaries," *Transvaal Leader*, January 24, 1906, clipping album, Farrar papers, BL. See also Katz, "Underground Route."

12. L.E.N., "About Indentured Labour, the Best System," *Transvaal Leader*, January 17, 1906, clipping album, Farrar papers, BL.

13. Dobbie, "Chinese Labour." "Ranks of greater merchants": Des Voeux, "Chinese Labour in Transvaal," 584. See also Bederman, *Manliness and Civilization*.

14. F. G. Stone, "A White South Africa," *North American Review* (June 1905), 880; Hutchinson quoted in *Transvaal Leader*, April 2, 1903, in Cd. 1895/8 encl. 2, *PP* 1904.

15. "Cutting the Painter. Loyalty and Chinese Labour," *South African News* (Cape Town), January 10, 1906, Cd. 2819/71 encl., *PP* 1905. See also Dubow, "Colonial Nationalism."

16. The formal labor electoral group was the Labour Representation Committee, which negotiated with the Liberal Party over tickets. "Emotive": Pelling and Reid, *Short History of Labour Party*, 12. Tanner, *Political Change and Labour Party*, does not mention the Chinese labor question in South Africa at all. Others historians who portray it as a symbolic appeal to the Labour vote without lasting consequence include Clarke, *Hope and Glory*, 33; Russell, *Liberal Landslide*, 106–13, 196. For recent work with greater analysis of the dynamics of race and empire in the 1906

election, see Grant, *Civilised Savagery*; Auerbach, *Race, Law and "Chinese Puzzle"*; Bright, *Chinese Labour*; Atkinson, *Burden of White Supremacy*. On expanded franchise: Russell, *Liberal Landslide*, 15–21.

17. Central Federation of Trade Unions, "White Labour or Yellow Slaves? Analysis of Division," March 9, 1904, dds-22478, CRL; Yap and Man, *Colour*, 107.

18. The most incendiary was the article by Boland, "The Price of Gold," published in the *Morning Leader*, September 6, 1905. The various "tortures" were again described and illustrated with lurid drawings in "Eyewitness" (probably Boland), *John Chinaman on the Rand*. On the Liberal Party: "The Government and Chinese Labour," *Speaker: Liberal Review* (June 16, 1906), 240. Debate in Parliament: "Mr. Lyttelton and Chinese Labour," *Times* (London), September 27, 1905, p. 6; "Chinese Labour in the Transvaal," *Anti-Slavery Reporter* 25 (August–October 1905): 95–100.

19. "The Undesirable Ordinance," *Westminster Gazette*, September 7, 1905, Cd 2819/3 encl., *PP* 1906; Russell, *Liberal Landslide*, 103, 107–8; *Sun* quoted at 108.

20. "South Africa and Party Politics," *Saturday Review*, February 24, 1906, pp. 224–25; "Chinese Labour. Five Reasons for Supporting the Government on Chinese Labour," Imperial South Africa Association Pamphlets no. 60 (1904), dds-22458, CRL.

21. "Vapourings": Blyth, letter to editor, *Times* (London), October 31, 1905, p. 15; Sidney Buxton, *Chinese Labour. The Transvaal Ordinance Analysed Together with the British Guiana Ordinance* (1904), Cambridge University Library, Liberal Pub. Department.

22. John Burns, "Slavery in South Africa," *Independent Review*, May 1904, pp. 594–611, at 595.

23. Ibid., 602.

24. Only the *Anti-Slavery Reporter* supported free Chinese immigration to the colonies. "Chinese Labour in the Transvaal," *Anti-Slavery Reporter* 25 (August–October 1905): 95–100. On Asiatic competition: Des Voeux, "Chinese Labour in Transvaal," 583–84.

25. Labor emigration was a key component of the so-called Wakefield plan, which considered the supply of labor and the sale of public land key to attracting capital for developing the colonies. Thousands of people from Irish poorhouses and orphanages went to Australia with state assistance, including three thousand young women between 1832 and 1836. Egerton, *Short History of Colonial Policy*, 282–84. Mill, *Principles of Political Economy* (1848), is quoted in Bell, *Idea of Greater Britain*, 50; Erickson, "Encouragement of Emigration"; Malchow, "Trade Unions and Emigration." On emigration trends in 1880s and '90s: Clarke, *Hope and Glory*, 17–18. On the major effects of colonization and emigration in a global history context: Belich, *Replenishing the Earth*.

26. Various luminaries supported imperial federation including J. R. Seeley, J. A. Hobson, James Bryce, Alfred Tennyson, and Cecil Rhodes. Bell, *Idea of Greater Britain*, 12. Others, notably Richard Jebb, advocated for more equal partnerships or associations of independent states. Jebb, *Studies in Colonial Nationalism*. Seeley's *Expansion of England* (1883) was the most popular text expounding this view.

27. Jebb, *Studies in Colonial Nationalism*, viii; Clarke, *Hope and Glory*, 12, 16. On Chamberlain's support for tariff reform: Semmel, *Imperialism and Social Reform*, 245.

28. Tanner, *Political Change,*" 23–30; Hyslop, "Imperial Working Class."

29. Seeley, *Expansion of England,* 10–12. See also Mantena, "Crisis of Liberal Imperialism."

30. Bright, *Chinese Labour,* 59; R. A. Durand, "Indentured Labour Under British Rule," *Monthly Review* 23 (May 1906): 39–46. "Apprehension": Des Voeux, "Chinese Labour in Transvaal," 584; Auerbach, *Race, Law and "Chinese Puzzle,"* 24.

31. Other Australians active in South African unions and labor politics included James Briggs, president of the Pretoria Trades Council; J. Forrester Brown of the mine workers' union; and Robert Burns Waterston, an officer of the South African Labour Party. Hyslop, "Imperial Working Class," 408.

32. Tarbut to Creswell (1903), cited in Central Federation of Trade Unions, "White Labour or Yellow Slaves?" (London, 1904), 5, dds-22478 (emphasis in original), CRL. See also Everard Digby, "The Drift Towards State-Socialism in Australia," *Empire Review* 10 (1905): 38–46.

33. Hyslop speaks of three "vectors" of transempire migrations that circulated white labor politics: Australian trade unionists, Cornish miners, and engineers. Creswell, it will be recalled, was a mining engineer. Gill Burke, "The Cornish Diaspora of the Nineteenth Century," in Marks and Richardson, *International Labour Migration,* 62–65; Nauright, "Cornish Miners in Witwatersrand"; Payton, *Making of Modern Cornwall,* 108–12; Hyslop, "Imperial Working Class," 411–12. On Creswell: "Chinese Labour Question," *West Australian,* June 5, 1905; Russell, *Liberal Landslide,* 108. On Macdonald: "White Leaguers. Meeting at Fordsburg. Anti-Chinese Crusade," *Rand Daily Mail,* September 28, 1906, clipping album, Farrar papers, BL.

34. Milner, address to the Municipal Congress of Johannesburg, May 18, 1903, also known as the Watch Tower Speech, in Milner, *Papers,* 2:465–70. See also Pearson, *National Life and Character;* Neame, *Asiatic Danger;* Lake and Reynolds, *Drawing Global Color Line,* especially chap. 3; Auerbach, *Race, Law and "Chinese Puzzle,"* 20; M. A. Stobart, "The Asiatic Invasion of the Transvaal," *Fortnightly Review,* February 1907, pp. 296–97.

35. Russell, *Liberal Landslide,* 106, 108; Des Voeux, "Chinese Labour in Transvaal," 593. On white unemployment: "Yellow v. White Labour," *Western Daily Press,* January 2, 1906, clipping album, Farrar papers, BL; English Emigration to Canada, http://englishemigrationtocanada.blogspot.com.

36. On the Liberal program: Clarke, *Hope and Glory,* 33

37. Dubow, "Colonial Nationalism."

38. Bright, *Chinese Labour,* 162–63.

39. Ibid, 167–71. The Nationalist Party was initially called the Responsible Party, which Denoon characterized as a collection of "ill-assorted malcontents, united mainly by their opposition to the prevailing alliance of government and Chamber of Mines, and reflecting the interests of dissident economic interest groups, of which the diamond lobby was probably the largest." Denoon, *Grand Illusion,* 222–23. On Het Volk and the revival of Afrikaner politics: Marks, "War and Union," 180–81.

40. "The Transvaal for the Boers," *Saturday Review,* February 9, 1907.

41. Bright, *Chinese Labour,* 174.

42. Selborne to Secretary of State, January 24, 1908, Cd. 3887/64-65, *PP* 1908; Harris, "History of Chinese in South Africa," 315–27.

43. Klotz, *Migration and National Identity*, 59–112.

44. Dubow, "Colonial Nationalism"; Freund, "South Africa: Union Years," 213, 221; Bonner, "South African Society and Culture," 256–59.

45. Davenport, *Digging Deep*, 294; Freund, "South Africa: Union Years," 220, 226–27.

46. Davenport, *Digging Deep*, 304–8; Bonner, "South African Society and Culture," 255.

47. John Burns, "Slavery in South Africa," *Independent Review* 8 (May 1904): 602–3. It should be noted that indenture was rare in California, and so the claim that individual contracts were canceled is misleading.

CHAPTER 12: EXCLUSION AND THE OPEN DOOR

1. Wu, "Mutual Helpfulness," 7.

2. Ibid., 2, 8–9.

3. Sinn, *Pacific Crossing*, chap. 3; Ma, "Big Business," 101–2.

4. Ma, "Big Business," 102. On agriculture: Chan, *Bittersweet Soil*. On manufacturing: Chen, *Chinese San Francisco*.

5. Shrinking market: Ma, "Big Business," 103. The laundry ordinance led to the Supreme Court ruling in *Yick Wo v. Hopkins* (1886), which found the application of the law to be discriminatory and upheld that the Fourteenth Amendment applied to all persons, not just citizens. See the discussion in Chapter 6.

6. On scope of *laborer* and *merchant*: Kramer, "Imperial Openings," 323; Ng, *Treatment of Exempt Classes*, 13. Successful entrepreneurs: Ma, "Big Business," 103–5; Chan, "Chinese American Entrepreneur." These entrepreneurs included Thomas Foon Chew, owner of Bayside Canning, by 1930 the third largest cannery in the United States, with an annual gross income of $3 million; Chin Lung, the "Chinese Potato King," who leased over one thousand acres in San Joaquin County and employed five hundred Chinese farmworkers; Lew Hing, another commercial farmer and owner of Pacific Fruit Cannery, who was president of Canton Bank in 1919 and also an investor in the China Mail; and Look Tin Eli, founder of the China Mail. Both the bank and the shipping line failed in the late 1920s.

7. Griffiths, "Making of White Australia," 535. Queensland banned all new indentures in 1901 and granted subsidies of two pounds a ton for sugar grown exclusively with white labor. Northrop, *Indentured Labor*, 146–47. Cilento is quoted in Anderson, "Coolie Therapeutics," 52–53. On Cooktown: Ormston, "Rise and Fall of a Frontier Mining Town."

8. Loy-Wilson, "Rural Geographies," 417–18. On banana trade: Fitzgerald, *Big White Lie*, 155–56. On Hong Yuen: Wilton, "Chinese Stores in Rural Australia," 98–105.

9. Fitzgerald, *Big White Lie*, 156.

10. Sugihara, "Patterns of Chinese Emigration," 245–46; Trocki, *Opium and Empire*, 30–35.

11. *Towkay* is Hokkien dialect for *toujia*, "boss." Wong Lin Ken describes towkay in Malaya as advancers of emigration credit as well as mineralogists, prospectors,

mining experts, and moneylenders. Wong, *Malayan Tin Industry*, 60, and chap. 2 passim; Loh, *Beyond the Tin Mines*, chap. 1; Heidhues, *Banga Tin and Mentok Pepper*. Between 1891 and 1930, 16 million Chinese and 14 million Indians migrated to Southeast Asia. Sugihara, "Patterns of Chinese Emigration," 245.

12. McKeown, "Global Migration"; Pan, *Encyclopedia of Overseas Chinese*, 248–58; Park, "Chinese Migrants in Latin America." By the late nineteenth century, former indentured Chinese in the Caribbean and Peru were engaged in agriculture and urban trades; Chinese also helped develop the Peruvian Amazon, much as they did the Northern Territory of Australia.

13. Martínez, "'Unwanted Scraps'"; Northrop, *Indentured Labor*, 143 and table A1, 156–58; Tinker, *New System of Slavery*, 315–66; Manhattan, "Plantation Dispossessions."

14. Tinker, *New System of Slavery*, 314–15; Hamashita, "Geopolitics of Hong Kong Economy," table 8, p. 121.

15. Hagan and Wells, "British and Rubber in Malaya," 145. On rubber in Vietnam: Murphy, "White Gold or White Blood?"; Wong, *Malayan Tin Industry*, 76.

16. On the Foran Act: Peck, *Reinventing Free Labor*, 84–90.

17. Values of Chinese exports in 1874: tea, 40 million taels; silk, 25 million taels, other, 8 million taels. Morse, *Trade and Administration*, chart following 271; Merritt, *Trouble with Tea*, 7; Liu, *Tea War*, 32–34.

18. Morse, *Trade and Administration*, 291–93. CMC figures are in piculs: 1.846 million in 1886; 839,000 in 1905. I have used a conversion rate of 1:133 to arrive at figures in pounds.

19. Per capita consumption: Morse, *Trade and Administration*, 293. Decline in tea imports after 1888: Tweedie, *Trading Partners*, 26–27. The value of Chinese exports to Australia fell from 3.14 million taels (£475,000) in 1886 by over one-third the following year and continued to drop, reaching a low of 24,000 taels (£3,600) in 1902, the year after federation. Hsiao, *China's Foreign Trade Statistics*, 138–39. The Chinese ethnic market likely accounted for a large share of ongoing imports. That trade also may have been larger as it included transshipments through Hong Kong and Singapore, not recorded in CMC data. "Outweigh [ed]": Archibald Colquhoun quoted in Mountford, *Britain, China, and Colonial Australia*, 198.

    The Australian colonies similarly refused to participate in the Anglo-Japan treaty of 1896, which would have opened a lucrative Japanese market to Australian wool. Queensland brokered a side agreement that exchanged access to the Japanese market for a freeze in the Japanese population in the colony at three thousand. That is, one Japanese could enter only after one Japanese left. However, the deal became moot in 1901, when Queensland became subordinate to federation policy. "Agreement Between the Japanese and Queensland Governments," January 14, 1902, with appendices; Nelson to chief secretary, May 27, 1896, and June 19, 1896; Satow to Salisbury, "Japan: Treaty Revision, Confidential," October 8, 1896; all in Prime Minister's Department, Pacific Branch, Volume of Papers on External Relations: "External Relations. Volume 2 B-N," 1918; Commonwealth Archives Office: CRS A2219, vol. 2 B-N. I thank David Atkinson for the reference.

20. Morse, *Trade and Administration*, chart following 271. Chinese exports to Britain

declined from 37 million taels in 1874 (£5.5 million) to 10.5 million taels in 1903 (£1.57 million). During the same period the value of British imports into China increased from 22 million taels (£3 million) to 50 million taels (£7.5 million). The change was exacerbated by the declining gold value of silver. CMC data do not include exports from Hong Kong and Singapore and also exclude the coastwise junk (sailing) trade. Remer calculated that Britain commanded 60 percent of foreign and Chinese (coastwise) shipping in 1899. Remer, *Foreign Investment in China*, 355. On financial services: Hamashita, "Geopolitics of Hong Kong Economy," 105.

21. Morse, *Trade and Administration*, 292; Pan, *Trade of United States with China*, 129–30. An accounting correction also shifted tea from Taiwan from China to Japan after the latter colonized it.

22. Between 1865 and 1900, the U.S. share of Chinese imports was only 2.65 percent; its share of Chinese exports was 11.07 percent. Keller et al., "China's Foreign Trade," 864–69; Schran, "Minor Significance." U.S. economic growth after the Civil War derived not from foreign trade but from internal commodity chains and a massive integrated domestic market: Between 1890 and 1914 the value of U.S. exports contributed only 7.3 percent of GNP, and imports equaled only 6.6 percent. Beckert, "American Danger," 1140–41; David and Wright, "Increasing Returns." Classic works on late nineteenth-century American overtures into the Pacific include Williams, *Tragedy of American Diplomacy*; LeFeber, *New Empire*; Hunt, *Making of Special Relationship*.

23. The leading American exports to China in the 1890s and 1900s were cotton cloth, which comprised 40 to 50 percent of all exports, followed by kerosene, which made up a quarter to a third. Still, American goods comprised a small portion of China's imports, about 10 percent. Pan, *Trade of United States with China*, 59–60, 106–7. See also the chapters on cotton cloth, cigarettes, and petroleum trade in May and Fairbank, *America's China Trade in Perspective*.

24. Frank, *ReOrient*, 149; see also Flynn and Giráldez, "Born with Silver Spoon"; Von Glahn, *Fountain of Fortune*, 125–33.

25. Keynes, *Indian Currency and Finance*, chap. 5; Daunton, "Britain and Globalization," 25–30; De Cecco, *International Gold Standard*, chap. 4. Tea production in India, grown on large plantations and factory processed, is an exemplary case of British overseas capital investment.

26. Germany 1872, Netherlands 1875, Belgium and France 1878, the United States 1879, Italy 1884, Japan and Russia 1897. Daunton, "Britain and Globalization," 21–23; Davies, *History of Money*, 356–65; Meissner, "New World Order."

27. British banks and foreign investment: Davies, *History of Money*, 350–64. On money in American politics: Carruthers and Babb, "Color of Money."

28. On India: De Cecco, *International Gold Standard*, chap. 4. On Mexican silver: Schell, "Silver Symbiosis."

29. Metzler, *Lever of Empire*, chap. 1; Bytheway and Metzler, *Central Banks and Gold*, chap. 1.

30. Russia 28.9 percent, Germany 20.02 percent, France 15.75 percent, United Kingdom 11.25 percent, Japan 7.73 percent, United States, 7.32 percent, Italy 7.32 percent,

Belgium 1.89 percent, Austria-Hungary 0.89 percent, Netherlands 0.17 percent, Spain 0.03 percent, Portugal 0.02 percent, Sweden and Norway 0.014 percent. The German and Austria-Hungary indemnities were canceled after World War I; the Soviet Union canceled the Russian debt in 1924. King, "Boxer Indemnities," 668–75; Morse, *Trade and Administration,* 299.

31. On the need for price stability: Anderson, "Chinese Exchange and Foreign Trade"; Jenks, "Suggestions of Plan for China," in Hanna et al., *Gold Standard,* 80-105; Jenks, "Consideration on Monetary System."

32. On India and the gold-exchange standard, see Keynes, *Indian Currency,* chap. 2. On Mexico currency reform: Passananti, "Politics of Silver and Gold"; Lai et al., "Professor Jeremiah Jenks." Jenks's PhD student Edwin Kemmerer would be the most famous of the "money doctors," responsible for engineering the gold-exchange standard for Latin America and elsewhere. Rosenberg, *Financial Missionaries;* Flandreau, *Money Doctors.* On China and Mexico: Schell, "Silver Symbiosis."

33. Lai et al., "Professor Jeremiah Jenks," 41–42. On China adoption of gold standard: Matsuoka, "China's Currency Reform," 77. Financial instability and havoc in China resulted from myriad factors, including the persistence of diverse regional currencies and inefficient revenue collection. Due to resistance to raising taxes and widespread corruption from the sale of gentry titles, only a small percentage of both actually made it into government coffers.

   The international gold standard was suspended during World War I, reinstituted afterward, and suspended again during World War II, but its general demise resulted from a reordering of world economic power: myriad pressures on Great Britain from competing nations, decolonization, and the rise of the United States. The Bretton Woods agreement of 1944 acknowledged the ascent of the United States as the premier capitalist power by establishing an international monetary system based on both gold and the U.S. dollar. In 1971 the United States unilaterally ended convertibility of the dollar to gold, thus establishing the dollar as a fiat currency, backed by nothing but itself and the economic and geopolitical power of its issuer.

34. Morse, *Trade and Administration,* 299–301. These figures reflect an exchange rate of £1 = 7 taels, a depreciation of about 50 percent between 1875 and 1899.

35. Ibid.; "Amoy men," in Hamashita, "Geopolitics of Hong Kong Economy," 113.

36. Hamashita, "Geopolitics of Hong Kong Economy," 107-10.

37. Remer, *Foreign Investment in China,* 180–88; Hsiao, *China's Foreign Trade Statistics,* table 13, "China's International Balance of Payments," showing remittances for 1928 of 167.1 million taels; for 1929, 187.1 million, for 1930, 210.9 million, and for 1931, 232.2 million ($80 to $115 million). Remer (like Morse before him) compiled remittance data from bank reports and interviews. Most monies sent back to China made their way to Hong Kong banks, although in the nineteenth century an unknown amount was hand-carried by returnees or couriers.

38. Huang based his calculation on an investigation of San Francisco banks' remittance practices over a period of four years. Kamachi, "American Influences on Reform Thought," 256.

39. Remer, *Foreign Investment in China*, 185, 188. This was especially the case during the interwar period, when there was unusual prosperity in emigration countries followed by a great decline in the price of silver.

CHAPTER 13: BECOMING CHINESE, BECOMING CHINA

1. During the Late Qing a "self-strengthening" movement had begun efforts to modernize China, but it paid little political attention to emigration, which was still officially illegal. Self-strengthening emphasized modernizing diplomacy, customs and the military, and industrial development. Many of the first Chinese who studied abroad in the late nineteenth century, notably more than one hundred young men who studied at Yale and other New England colleges, returned to China to work as diplomats or for enterprises like the China Steam Navigation Company. After the Empress Dowager Cixi and her conservative backers ousted the Emperor Guangxu in 1898 and ended the latter's ambitious Hundred Days Reform program, the anti-Qing movement grew.

2. Kang's works include *Xinxue weijing kao* (Forged Classics), 1891; *Kongzi gaizhi kao* (Confucius as a Reformer), 1897; and *Datongshu* (The Great Commonwealth), 1900. See also Zarrow, *After Empire*. On Kang's sojourn in Sweden and his role in the boycott movement: Evans Chan, interview by William Cheung, http://www.chinaheritagequarterly.org/articles.php?searchterm=027_datong.inc&issue=027.

3. Kang went first to Japan, then to Canada (1899–1905). He was in Sweden from 1905 to 1908. He did not return to China until 1913, after the Republican revolution. The Baohuanghui established chapters in Canada, the United States, Mexico, Central America, Hawaii, Australia, Southeast Asia, Japan, and South Africa, as well as Hong Kong and Macao, and in China itself. "Mapping the Baohuanghui," *Baohuanghui Blogspot*, https://baohuanghui.blogspot.com/; Ma, *Revolutionaries, Monarchists*, 109–11; Yu Chen Zi, "The Grand Trend of World Economic Competition," *Xinmin congbao* (1902), cited in Wang, *In Search of Justice*, 55. Kang Youwei was influenced by the nineteenth-century German economist Friedrich List, who supported a strong state and protectionism and opposed free trade, which he believed was an alibi for British hegemony. The statist orientation may also account for Kang Youwei's relationship with Mexican president Porfirio Díaz.

4. Influence of Social Darwinism: Wang, *In Search of Justice*, 144; Karl, *Staging the World*, 14, 122. Huang is quoted in Wang, *In Search of Justice*, 55.

5. Fitzgerald, "Advance Australia Fairly," 70. See also Fitzgerald, *Big White Lie*, chap. 5.

6. Liang, *Xin dalu youji*.

7. Luo Fonglu to Foreign Ministry, September 1, 1902, file no. 02-13-008-02-061, Qing Foreign Ministry Records, AS.

8. Lin, *Heinu yu tian lu*. Quotes from translator's preface and afterword: Arkush and Lee, *Land Without Ghosts*, 77–80. Review quoted in Wang, *In Search of Justice*, 60.

9. Zou Rong, *Geming zun* (Revolutionary Army), quoted in Wang, *In Search of Justice*, 59; *Aiguo bao*, January–February 1904.

10. On Hawaii and Philippines: Wu to Waiwubu, June 8, 1900, File no. 01-35-002-03-

006, and Liang Cheng to Waiwubu, February 22, 1905, file no. 02-29-002-01-00, both in Qing Foreign Ministry Records, AS. On harassment of arrivals: Ng, *Treatment of the Exempt Classes*. On merchants going to St. Louis fair: Ngai, *Lucky Ones*, 105–6. See also Wang, *In Search of Justice*, 51–55; Kramer, "Imperial Openings," 332.

11. Gresham-Yang (1894) was the latest iteration of the Sino-American treaties governing immigration, following the Angell Treaty (1880) and the Burlingame Treaty (1868). Although the Supreme Court ruled in *Chae Chan Ping v. United States* (1889) that legislation trumped treaties, the Qing continued to use treaty negotiations to influence each renewal of the exclusion laws.

12. Liang Cheng to Waiwubu, May 24, 1906, File no. 02-29-001-08-019; Liang Cheng to Waiwubu, February 22, 1905, File no. 02-29-002-01-001, both in Qing Foreign Ministry Records, AS. See also McKee, "Chinese Boycott Reconsidered"; Wang, *In Search of Justice*, 124, 131.

13. Qing and native capitalists: Meissner, "1905 Anti-American Boycott," 176–79. On business pressure on Roosevelt: Lorence, "Business and Reform," 425; Roosevelt to Metcalf, June 16, 1905, in Roosevelt, *Letters*, 4:1235–36; Roosevelt to Pierce, June 24, 1905, ibid., 4:1251–52; Liang Cheng to Waiwubu, August 13, 1905, F11: 02-29-003-02-004, Qing Foreign Ministry Records, AS; McKee, "Chinese Boycott Reconsidered," 180–82.

14. Goodman, "Locality as Microcosm," 394; Gerth, *China Made*, 128–29.

15. Wang, *In Search of Justice*, 89–90, 105; Remer, *Chinese Boycotts*, 33.

16. Telegram from Chinese in London, *Donghuabao*, June 24, 1905, p. 3; *Anhui suhua bao*, no. 21–22 (1905): 1–24. The paper's editor, Chen Duxiu, later became dean of humanities at Peking University and a co-founder of the Chinese Communist Party. "Old Monks": Arkush and Lee, *Land Without Ghosts*, 58–59.

17. Arkush and Lee, *Land Without Ghosts*, 59; Wang *In Search of Justice*, 171.

18. "General Society at San Francisco for Opposing the Exclusion Treaty": McKee, "Chinese Boycott Reconsidered," 177–78, 188; Kang Youwei, letter, *Donghuabao*, June 17, 1905, p. 2.

19. Support in Southeast Asia and Japan: Wang, *In Search of Justice*, 171–72. South Africa: "Petition Letter from Chinese Workers in South Africa and Chinese Officials Response," *Donghuabao*, March 11, 1905; "Recent News about Chinese Workers in Africa," *Donghuabao*, November 18, 1905; "The Miserable Situation of Chinese Workers in South Africa," *Donghuabao*, December 2, 1905 (this appears to be taken from *Xinmin congbao*'s critique). Coverage of boycott: "Chinese Americans Petition to Repeal Chinese Exclusion Act," *Donghuabao*, December 14, 1904; "Anti-American Boycott Meeting," and "Workers Refuse to Carry American Products," *Donghuabao*, September 9, 1905; Editorial supporting boycott, *Donghuabao*, October 21, 1905; "Chinese Immigrants Who Participated in the Anti-American Boycott Movement," *Donghuabao*, November 4, 1905; "Strategy of Boycott in China and Overseas," *Donghuabao*, November 11, 1905; Lishanqiaozi, "If Exclusion Continues" (letter), *Donghuabao*, August 5, 1905.

20. Wang, *In Search of Justice*, 178–91; Remer, *Chinese Boycotts*, 33–34.

21. Roosevelt's State of the Union address, December 5, 1905, made brief mention of the

boycott and advocated for "equity" in the treatment of merchants, while emphasizing his commitment to exclude laborers. Changes in policy included: no longer requiring photographs of members of exempt classes in transit, eliminating Bertillon photographs, eliminating rejection on minor technical errors in exempt certificates, and allowing for witnesses in hearings. The one substantive change was to allow elementary-level students and not just secondary and professional students. Salyer, *Laws Harsh as Tigers,* 164–66. The use of Boxer indemnities to pay for scholarships was intended to underwrite China's modernization. Most students were required to study engineering, mining, or agriculture. The number of Chinese students in the United States grew from fifty in 1903 to 292 in 1910 and 990 in 1918. Hsu, *Good Immigrants,* 47–48. On merchants: Ng, *Treatment of the Exempt Classes,* 13.

The *Ju Toy* decision (1905), which virtually eliminated the use of habeas corpus for court review and allowed for virtually unchecked administrative discretion in immigration decisions, led to a bureaucratization of procedures that relied on documentation and interrogation. Ironically, that turn encouraged the use of false documents and memorization and the proliferation of "paper sons" claiming derivative citizenship of Chinese allegedly born in the United States. On *Ju Toy*: Salyer, *Laws Harsh as Tigers,* chap. 4, esp. 113–15. On paper sons and bureaucratization of admissions: Ngai, *Impossible Subjects,* chap. 6; McKeown, *Melancholy Order,* chaps. 9–10.

22. Gerth, *China Made,* 4–9; Wang, *In Search of Justice,* 194. See also Wong, *China's Boycott Movement.*

23. Remer, *Chinese Boycotts,* 37–39.

24. Ibid., 230–32.

EPILOGUE: THE SPECTER OF THE YELLOW PERIL, REDUX

1. "1000 illegal miners busted," GhanaWeb, January 30, 2018, https://www.ghanaweb.com/GhanaHomePage/NewsArchive/1000-illegal-miners-busted-622033?fbclid=IwAR2Rvkkh-aUYgc-qc-FIsvpMjNCvoKRRNhW7k1kax7OjSzewq-aqfCWH_oo; Boafo et al., "Illicit Chinese Mining."

2. Boafo et al., "Illicit Chinese Mining"; Botchwey et al., "South-South Irregular Migration."

3. Yang Jiao, "Chinese Illegal Gold Miners in Ghana" (blogpost), China-Africa Research Initiative, Johns Hopkins University, June 21, 2013, http://www.chinaafricarealstory.com/2013/06/guest-post-chinese-illegal-gold-miners.html.

4. Ibid.

5. The other top gold producers are (in order) Australia, Russia, the United States, and Canada. U.S. Geological Survey, annual report 2019. Gold consumption for jewelry in 2019: by China 629 tons and by India, 191 tons. "Elevated Gold Prices for 2019 amid Renewed Investor Interest," *Value Walk,* January 29, 2020. https://www.valuewalk.com/2020/01/elevated-gold-prices-2019.

6. "China's Impact on African Mining Cannot be Underestimated." *Investing in African Mining,* October 16, 2019. https://www.miningindaba.com/Articles/chinese-investment-in-african-mining-what-you.

7. Mariana Sow, "Figures of the Week: Chinese Investment in Africa," *Brookings*, September 6, 2018. https://www.brookings.edu/blog/africa-in-focus/2018/09/06/figures-of-the-week-chinese-investment-in-africa; Lee, "Specter of Global China"; "Chinese Investment in Africa," China Africa Research Initiative, Johns Hopkins University, http://www.sais-cari.org/chinese-investment-in-africa.

8. "The Pandemic is Hurting China's Belt and Road Initiative," *Economist,* June 4, 2020, https://www.economist.com/china/2020/06/04/the-pandemic-is-hurting-chinas-belt-and-road-initiative; Economy, *Third Revolution,* chap. 7; Christine Gerbode, "Dreams of a Green Silk Road, Part 1: Responsible Development Across Borders" (blogpost), Duke University, December 5, 2018, https://blogs.nicholas.duke.edu/between-the-lines/dreams-of-a-green-silk-road-part-1-responsible-development-across-borders/; Lee, "Specter of Global China."

9. Wang, "Discourse of Unequal Treaties"; Ku, "Abolition of Unequal Treaties." Australia repealed its White Australia law in 1973. South Africa began recruiting immigrants from Taiwan in the 1970s.

10. Mao Zedong, Opening address at the First Plenary Session of the Chinese People's Political Consultative Conference, September 21, 1949. Riskin, "China's Human Development"; Karl, *China's Revolutions,* 110–34.

11. Riskin, "Seven Questions." According to the standard of poverty defined by the World Bank, China still had 835 million people living in poverty in 1981. Alan Piazza, "Poverty and Living Standards Since 1949," *Oxford Bibliographies,* June 8, 2017, https://www.oxfordbibliographies.com/view/document/obo-9780199920082/obo-9780199920082-0080.xml.

12. For a summary of Deng- and Xi-era economic policies see Karl, *China's Revolutions,* 177–92; Economy, *Third Revolution,* chap. 1. On China Development Bank financing urbanization: Sanderson and Forsythe, *China's Superbank,* chap. 1. For 2019, the U.S. gross domestic product was $21.48 trillion, and China's GDP was $14.17 trillion; followed by Japan, Germany, UK, India. "Top 20 Largest Economies," *Investopedia,* https://www.investopedia.com/insights/worlds-top-economies.

13. Karl, *China's Revolutions,* 176–77.

14. Sugihara, "Global Industrialization"; Sugihara, "Multiple Paths to Industrialization"; Arrighi, *Adam Smith in Beijing*; Zelin, "Structures During Qing Period." The "industrious revolution" in East Asia differs from the consumption-driven model conceptualized in early modern Europe by DeVries, "Industrial and Industrious Revolution." The East Asia "industrious revolution" literature is in part a response to the "great divergence" scholarship of Pomeranz, *Great Divergence,* and Rosenthal and Wong, *Before and Beyond Divergence,* among others. Critical political economic histories include Abu-Lughod, *Before European Hegemony*; Rodney, *How Europe Underdeveloped Africa*; Wallerstein, *Modern World System*; Robinson, *On Racial Capitalism*; Frank, *Capitalism and Underdevelopment*; Frank, *ReOrient*. On the persistence of Eurocentric economic norms in the Great Divergence literature: Karl, *Magic of Concepts.*

15. Arrighi, *Adam Smith in Beijing;* Sugihara, "Global Industrialization."

16. "USA: Percent of World GDP," Global Economy (World Bank data), https://www
   .theglobaleconomy.com/usa/gdp_share; Isabella Weber, "Could the US and Chinese Economies Really 'Decouple'?" *Guardian*, February 11, 2020.

17. Andrew Chatzky and James McBride, "China's Massive Belt and Road Initiative," Council on Foreign Relations, January 28, 2020, https://www.cfr.org/
   backgrounder/chinas-massive-belt-and-road-initiative; "The Pandemic is Hurting
   China's Belt and Road Initiative," *Economist*, June 4, 2020; Sanderson and Forsythe,
   China's Superbank, chaps. 3–4; "China's Assistance in the Construction of the
   Tanzania-Zambia Railway," Ministry of Foreign Affairs, People's Republic of China,
   https://www.fmprc.gov.cn/mfa_eng/ziliao_665539/3602_665543/3604_665547/
   t18009.shtml.

18. Kimberly Amadeo, "US Imports by Year, Top Five Countries," *Balance* (February 26,
   2020). https://www.thebalance.com/u-s-imports-by-year-and-by-country-3306259.

19. U.S. Department of Commerce, Bureau of Economic Analysis, *U.S. International
   Transactions, Fourth Quarter and Year 2019*, March 19, 2020, https://www.bea
   .gov/news/2020/us-international-transactions-fourth-quarter-and-year-2019; U.S.
   Department of the Treasury, *Monthly Statement of the Public Debt of the United States*,
   March 31, 2020, https://www.treasurydirect.gov/govt/reports/pd/mspd/2020/
   opds032020.pdf; U.S. Treasury, *Major Foreign Holders of Treasury Securities*, May 15,
   2020, https://ticdata.treasury.gov/Publish/mfh.txt; Eswar Prasad, "The U.S.-China
   Economic Relationship: Shifts and Twists in the Balance of Power," testimony to
   the U.S.-China Economic and Security Review Commission Hearing on U.S. Debt
   to China: Implications and Repercussions, March 10, 2020, https://www.brookings
   .edu/wp-content/uploads/2016/06/20100225_us_china_debt_prasad-1.pdf.

20. "China Current Account to GDP," Trading Economics (n.d.), https://
   tradingeconomics.com/china/current-account-to-gdp; U.S. Treasury, *Major Holders of US Treasury Securities*, September 2019, https://ticdata.treasury.gov/Publish/
   mfh.txt.

21. Lee, *My Country Versus Me*; Wang, "Beyond Identity and Racial Politics"; Ashley
   Yeager, "US Looks to Block Chinese Grad Students and Researchers' Visas," *Scientist*, May 28, 2020, https://www.the-scientist.com/news-opinion/us-looks-to-block
   -chinese-grad-students-and-researchers-visas-67591; Association of American University Professors, "National Security, the Assault on Science, and Academic Freedom," December 2017, https://www.aaup.org/sites/default/files/JA18_National
   Security.pdf.

22. Songtian Lin, "South Africa and China Are Beneficial Partners," *Independent
   Online* (South Africa), February 27, 2018, https://www.iol.co.za/pretoria-news/
   south-africa-and-china-are-beneficial-partners-13508542.

23. Australia, Department of Foreign Affairs and Trade, "China Country Brief, Bilateral Relations," https://www.dfat.gov.au/geo/china/Pages/china-country-brief#:~:tex
   t=China%20is%20Australia's%20largest%20two,per%20cent%20year%20on%20
   year); Su-LinTan, "Why Has the China-Australia Relationship Deteriorated into What
   Some Are Calling 'Trade War 2.0'?" *South China Morning Post*, July 2, 2020, https://

www.scmp.com/economy/china-economy/article/3091182/why-has-china-australia
-relationship-deteriorated-what-some.

24. U.S. Trade Representative, "People's Republic of China, US-China Trade Facts"
    (n.d.),   https://ustr.gov/countries-regions/china-mongolia-taiwan/peoples-republic
    -china#:~:text=U.S.%20goods%20imports%20from%20China,overall%20U.S.%20
    imports%20in%202018.

Bibliography

PRIMARY SOURCES

Archives and Libraries

Academia Sinica, Taipei
> Institute of Modern History, Records of Qing Foreign Ministry

Bendigo Regional Archival Centre, Bendigo, Victoria

California Historical Society, San Francisco

California State Archives, Sacramento

California State Library, Sacramento

California State University, Chico
> Special Collections, Northeast California

Claremont Colleges Library, Claremont, California
> Special Collections, William Honnold Papers

Golden Dragon Museum, Bendigo, Victoria

Huntington Library, San Marino, California

Library of Congress, Washington, D.C.

Museum of Chinese Australian History, Melbourne

National Archives (UK), Kew
> Cabinet Office Files
> Records of the Colonial Office
> Records of the Foreign Office

National Archives (South Africa)
> Public Records of former Transvaal Province and its Predecessors, Pretoria
> Western Cape Archives and Record Service, Cape Town

National Library of Australia, Canberra
New York Public Library
Public Record Office of Victoria
    Ballarat
    North Melbourne
State Library of New South Wales, Sydney
State Library of Victoria, Melbourne
University of California, Berkeley
    Bancroft Library
    Earth Sciences and Maps Library
    Ethnic Studies Library
University of Cambridge, University Library
    Conservative Central Office
    Liberal Publication Department
    Imperial South Africa Association
University of Oxford, Bodleian Library
    Alfred, Viscount Milner Papers
    George Farrar and Family Papers
    Central Mining and Investment Corporation Papers
Wells Fargo and Company, Corporate Archives, San Francisco
Wuyi Overseas Chinese Museum, Jiangmen, Guangdong, China
Yuba County Library, Marysville, California

Newspapers and Periodicals

Age (Melbourne)
Aiguo bao (Chinese Times, Melbourne)
Anhui suhua bao (Tokyo)
Anti-Slavery Reporter (London)
Argus (Melbourne)
Australian (Sydney)
Beiguo chunqiu (Northern Annals, Beijing)
Bendigo Advertiser (Victoria)
Brisbane Courier (Queensland)
Bulletin (Sydney)
Butte Record (Oroville, California)
California Star (San Francisco)
Californian (San Francisco)
China Review (Hong Kong)
Chispa (Sonora, California)
Covered Wagon (Shasta, California)
Daily Alta California (San Francisco)
Diggin's (Oroville, California)

Dongfang zazhi (Eastern Miscellany, Shanghai)

Donghuabao (Chinese Times, Melbourne)

Economist

Empire (Sydney)

Empire Review (London)

Engineering and Mining Journal (New York)

Fortnightly Review (London)

Friend of China (Hong Kong)

Hangzhou baihuabao (Hangzhou Daily)

Independent Review (London)

Jiaohui xinbao (Church News, Shanghai)

Journal of the American Asiatic Association (New York)

Los Angeles Herald

Macmillan's (London)

Manchester Guardian (UK)

Mining and Scientific Press (San Francisco)

Mountain Messenger (LaPorte, California)

New York Times

Nineteenth Century and After (London)

North American Review

North Queensland Register (Townsville, Queensland)

Oriental (Dongya xinlu, San Francisco)

Overland Monthly and Out West (San Francisco)

Polynesian (Honolulu)

Provenance (North Melbourne, Victoria)

Queenslander (Brisbane, Queensland)

Rand Daily Mail (Johannesburg)

Sacramento Daily Union

Saturday Review (London)

Sonoma Democrat (California)

Sonora Herald (California)

Speaker: The Liberal Review (London)

Sydney Morning Herald

Telegraph (Brisbane, Queensland)

Times (London)

Transvaal Leader (Johannesburg)

Xinbao (Shanghai)

Xinmin congbao (New Citizen, Yokohama)

Waijiao bao (Diplomatic Review, Beijing)

Wanguo gongbao (Review of the Times, Shanghai)

West Australian (Perth, Western Australia)

Western Mail (Perth, Western Australia)

Worker (Brisbane, Queensland)

Zhongwai xinwen qiri bao (Seven Days, Hong Kong)
Zhongxi ribao (China West Daily, San Francisco)

Government Serial Publications and Reports

AUSTRALIA

Australasia. *Correspondence relating to Chinese Immigration into the Australasian Colonies presented to both Houses of Parliament by Command of Her Majesty.* UK Parliamentary Papers. C.5448. London, 1888.

New South Wales. Legislative Council. *Report from the Committee on Immigration, with the Appendix, Minutes of Evidence, and Replies to Circular Letter on the Aborigines.* Sydney, 1841.

Victoria. *Parliamentary Papers.* Melbourne, 1855–98.

———. *Reports of the Mining Surveyors and Registrars.* Melbourne, 1867–87.

———. *Returns of the Census of the Population of Victoria, 1857.*

GREAT BRITAIN

Great Britain. Emigration Commission. *Colonization Circular.* G. E. Eyre and W. Spottiswoode, 1866.

U.K. Parliament. *Parliamentary Papers,* https://www.parliament.uk/about/how/publications/parliamentary/

SOUTH AFRICA

Africa. *Correspondence respecting the Introduction of Chinese Labour into the Transvaal.* UK Parliamentary Papers. Cd. 1945. London, 1904.

Transvaal. *Annual Report of the Foreign Labour Department 1905–6.* UK Parliamentary Papers. Cd. 3338. London, 1907.

———. *Correspondence Relating to Labour in the Transvaal Mines.* UK Parliamentary Papers. Cd. 2183, 2401, 2785, 2786, 2819, 3024. London, 1904–6.

———. *Correspondence Relating to Legislation Affecting Asiatics in the Transvaal.* UK Parliamentary Papers. Cd. 3308, 3887, 3892, 4327, 4584, 5363. London, 1907–10.

———. *Handbook of Ordinances, Proclamations, Regulations and Instructions, Connected with the Importation of Foreign Labour into the Transvaal.* Pretoria, 1906.

———. *Report of the Mining Industry Commission, 1907–8.* Pretoria, 1908.

Transvaal Labour Commission. *Reports of the Transvaal Labour Commission.* UK. Parliamentary Papers. Cd. 1896–97. London, 1904.

Transvaal and Orange Free State. Chamber of Mines. *Annual Report.* Pretoria, 1900–10.

———. *The Mining Industry: Evidence and Report of the Industrial Commission of Enquiry.* Johannesburg, 1897.

Transvaal and Orange River Colony. *Correspondence Related to Affairs in the Transvaal and Orange River Colony.* UK Parliamentary Papers. Cd. 1895, 2563, 3528. London, 1904–7.

Zuid-Afrikaanse Republiek (ZAR). Witwatersrand Chamber of Mines. *The Mining Industry, Evidence and Report of the Industrial Commission of Enquiry.* Johannesburg, 1897.

UNITED STATES

Browne, J. Ross. *Mineral Resources of the States and Territories.* Washington, D.C.: U.S. Department of the Treasury, 1867, 1868, 1869.

California. Bureau of Mines. *Annual Report of the State Mineralogist.* Sacramento, 1880–1916.

———. Legislature. Committee on Mines and Mining Interests. *Report.* In *Journals of the Assembly and Senate of the State of California,* 4th sess. (1853), appendix, doc. 28. Sacramento, 1853.

———. Joint Select Committee. *Report Relative to the Chinese Population of the State of California.* In *Journals of the Assembly and Senate of the State of California,* 13th sess., appendix 23. Sacramento, 1862.

———. *Journals of the Assembly and Senate of the State of California.* Sacramento, 1850–90.

———. Senate. *Chinese Immigration, Its Social, Moral and Political Effects. Report and Testimony Taken before a Committee of the Senate of the State of California.* Sacramento, 1876.

———. *State Census of 1852.* Ancestry.com.

Raymond, Rossiter W. *Statistics of Mines and Mining in the States and Territories West of the Rocky Mountains.* Washington, D.C.: U.S. Department of the Treasury, 1869–77.

U.S. Bureau of the Census. *Decennial Population Census of the United States.* Washington, D.C.: 1850–1900. Ancestry.com.

———. *Selected Nonpopulation Schedules, 1850–80.* Ancestry.com.

U.S. Congress. *Congressional Record.* Washington, D.C., 1870–90.

U.S. Department of State. Office of the Historian. *Foreign Relations of the United States, China and Chinese Legation of the United States, 1885–86.* https://history.state.gov/historicaldocuments.

U.S. Geological Survey. *Annual Report, 2019.*

U.S. Senate. Joint Special Committee to Investigate Chinese Immigration. *Report of the Joint Special Committee to Investigate Chinese Immigration,* 44th Cong., 2d sess., February 27, 1877. Washington, D.C., 1877.

Online Collections

California Digital Newspaper Collection. Center for Bibliographical Studies and Research. University of California at Riverside, http://cdnc.ucr.edu

Center for Research Libraries. Chicago, https://www.crl.edu/electronic-resources/collections

Chinese Heritage of Australian Federation Project. La Trobe University, http://www.chaf.lib.latrobe.edu.au/

CNBKSY. Quan guo bao kan suo yin. Shanghai Library, https://www.cnbksy.com

Eureka! The Rush for Gold. Library of New South Wales, http://www.sl.nsw.gov.au/stories/eureka-rush-gold/rumours-gold

Trove. National Library of Australia, https://trove.nla.gov.au/
    Historical Records of Australia
    Newspapers and Gazettes

Published Primary Sources

Ah Ket, William. "The Chinese and the Factories Act." Melbourne, 1906.

Ai, Zhouchang, ed. *Zhong fei guan xi shi wen xuan, 1500–1918, Di 1 ban.* (Documentary History of China-South Africa Relations) Shanghai: East China Normal University Press, 1989.

Aldus, Don. *Coolie Traffic and Kidnapping.* London: McCorquodale & Co., 1876.

Allsop, Thomas, ed. *California and Its Gold Mines: Being a Series of Recent Communications from the Mining Districts.* London: Groombridge & Sons, 1853.

An Analysis of the Chinese Question Consisting of a Special Message of the Governor and, in Reply Thereto, Two Letters of the Chinamen and a Memorial of the Citizens of San Francisco. San Francisco: *San Francisco Herald,* 1852.

"An Asiatic." *The "China Question" Dispassionately Considered.* London: Edward Stanford, 1857.

Anderson, George. "Chinese Exchange and Chinese Foreign Trade." *Journal of American Asiatic Association* 5 (August 1905): 199–202.

Anderson, Hugh. *Eureka: Victorian Parliamentary Papers Votes and Proceedings 1854–1867.* Melbourne: Hill of Content, 1969.

Bancroft, Hubert Howe. *History of California,* 7 vols. San Francisco: History Company, 1890.

Bee, Frederick A. *The Other Side of the Chinese Question: To the People of the United States and the Honorable the Senate and House of Representatives Testimony of California's Leading Citizens; Read and Judge.* San Francisco: Woodward & Co., 1886.

Borthwick, John David. *Three Years in California, 1851–1854, with Eight Illustrations by the Author.* Edinburgh: W. Blackwood & Sons, 1857.

Brooks, B. S. *Brief of the Legislation and Adjudication Touching the Chinese Question Referred to the Joint Commission of Both Houses of Congress.* San Francisco: Women's Co-operative Printing Union, 1877.

Brooks, Charles Wolcott. "The Chinese Labor Problem," *Overland Monthly and Out West* 3 (November 1869): 407–19.

Brown, D. Mackenzie. *China Trade Days in California; Selected Letters from the Thompson Papers, 1832–1863.* Berkeley: University of California Press, 1947.

Browne, J. H. Balfour. *South Africa: A Glance at Current Conditions and Politics.* London, 1905.

Browne, J. Ross. *Resources of the Pacific Slope: A Statistical and Descriptive Summary.* San Francisco: H. H. Bancroft, 1869.

Buchanan, W. F. *Australia to the Rescue: A Hundred Years' Progress in New South Wales.* London: Gilbert and Rivington, 1890.

Buck, Franklin A. *A Yankee Trader in the Gold Rush,* edited by Katherine A. White. Boston: Houghton Mifflin, 1930.

Burns, John. "Slavery in South Africa," *Independent Review,* May 1904, pp. 594–611.

Burt, Thomas. *A Visit to the Transvaal; Labour: White, Black, and Yellow.* Newcastle-upon-Tyne: Co-operative Printing Society, 1905.

Buxton, Sydney. *Chinese Labour: The Transvaal Ordinance Analysed Together with the British Guiana Ordinance.* London: Liberal Publication Department, 1904.

California Miners' Association. *California Mines and Minerals.* Press of L. Roesch Co., 1899.

Canfield, Chauncey, ed. *Diary of a Forty-Niner*. Boston: Houghton Mifflin, 1920.

Chen Hansheng, ed. *Huagong chuguo shiliao huibian* (Documentary History of Chinese Labor Emigration), 10 vols. Beijing: Zhonghua Shuju, 1980–85.

Cheong, Cheok Hong. *Chinese Remonstrance to the Parliament and People of Victoria*. Melbourne: Wm. Marshall & Co., 1888.

Chew, Lee. "Biography of a Chinaman," *Independent* 15 (February 19, 1903): 417–23.

Chico Anti-Chinese League. *Chico Anti-Chinese League Minute Book*, 1894.

Clifford, John. *God's Greater Britain, Letters and Addresses*. London: Clark, 1899.

Colquhoun, Archibald R. *China in Transformation*. New York: Harper & Bros., 1912.

———. *The Mastery of the Pacific*. New York: Macmillan, 1902.

Comstock, J. L. *A History of the Precious Metals from the Earliest Periods to the Present Time*. Hartford, Conn.: Belknap & Hamersley, 1849.

Condit, Ira. *The Chinaman as We See Him, and Fifty Years of Work for Him*. Chicago: F. H. Revell Co., 1900.

Coolidge, Mary Roberts. *Chinese Immigration*. New York: Holt & Co., 1909.

Crawford, J. Dundas. *Notes by Mr. Crawford on Chinese Immigration in the Australian Colonies*. Great Britain Foreign Office Confidential Prints FO 3742. London: HMSO, 1877.

Creswell, Frederic H. P. *The Chinese Labour Question from Within: Facts, Criticisms, and Suggestions; Impeachment of a Disastrous Policy*. London: P. S. King & Son, 1905.

Cuba Commission. *Report of the Commission Sent by China to Ascertain the Condition of Chinese Coolies in Cuba*. Shanghai: Imperial Maritime Customs Press, 1878.

Curle, J. H. *Gold Mines of the World*, 3rd ed. London: Routledge, 1905.

———. *Our Testing Time; Will the White Race Win Through?* New York: George H. Doran Co., 1926.

Davis, D. H., and John A. Silsby. *Shanghai Vernacular: Chinese-English Dictionary*. Shanghai: American Presbyterian Mission Press, 1900.

Del Mar, Alexander. *Monograph on the History of Money in China: From the Earliest Times to the Present*. San Francisco: J. R. Brodie & Co., 1881.

Derby, George Horatio, Gary Clayton Anderson, Laura L. Anderson, and Arthur H. Clark Co., eds. *The Army Surveys of Gold Rush California: Reports of Topographical Engineers, 1849–1851*. Norman: University of Oklahoma Press, 2015.

Des Voeux, Sir G. William. "Chinese Labour in the Transvaal: A Justification." *Nineteenth Century and After* 59 (April 1906): 581–94.

D'Ewes, J. *China, Australia and the Pacific Islands, in the Years 1855–56*. London: Richard Bentley, 1857.

Dilke, Charles Wentworth. *Greater Britain*. London: Macmillan, 1869.

———. *Problems of Greater Britain*. London: Macmillan, 1890.

Dressler, Albert. *California Chinese Chatter*. San Francisco: n.p., 1927.

Durand, R. A. "Indentured Labour Under British Rule," *Monthly Review* 23 (May 1906): 39–46.

Edelman, George W. *Guide to the Value of California Gold*. Philadelphia: G. S. Appleton, 1850.

Edkins, Joseph. *Banking and Prices in China*. Shanghai: Presbyterian Mission Press, 1905.

Egenhoff, Elisabeth L., ed. *The Elephant as They Saw It; a Collection of Contemporary Pictures and Statements on Gold Mining in California*. San Francisco, 1949.

Egerton, Hugh Edward. *A Short History of British Colonial Policy*, 3rd ed. London: Methuen, 1910.

Eitel, Ernest John. *China and the Far Eastern Question: A Study in Political Geography*. Adelaide: W. K. Thomas, 1900.

———. *Europe in China*. London: Luzac, 1895.

"Eyewitness." *John Chinaman on the Rand*. London: R. A. Everett, 1905.

Farrar, George. "The South African Labour Problem: Speech by George Farrar at a meeting held on the East Rand Proprietary Mines, on March 31st, 1903." London: W.W. Sprague, 1903.

Fauchery, Antoine. *Letters from a Miner in Australia*, translated by A. R. Chisholm. Melbourne: Georgian House, 1965.

Field, Stephen J. *Personal Reminiscences of Early Days in California*. N.p., 1893.

Fong, Walter N. "Chinese Six Companies." *Overland Monthly*, May 1894.

Frodsham, J. D., ed. *The First Chinese Embassy to the West: The Journals of Kuo-Sung-T'ao, Liu Hsi-Hung and Chang Te-Yi*. Oxford: Clarendon Press, 1974.

George, Henry. "Chinese in California." *New York Tribune*, May 1, 1869.

———. *Complete Works*, 10 vols. New York: Doubleday, 1904.

George, Henry, Jr. *The Life of Henry George*. New York: Doubleday & McClure, 1900.

Gervasoni, Clare. *Castlemaine Petitions: Petitioners for a Castlemaine Municipality and Petitioners Against the Chinese Residence License*. Ballarat, Victoria: Goldfield Heritage Books, 1998.

Gibson, Otis. *"Chinaman or White Man, Which?": Reply to Father Buchard*. San Francisco: Alta, 1873.

———. *The Chinese in America*. Cincinnati: Hitchcock & Walden, 1877.

Gompers, Samuel, and Herman Gutstadt. *Meat vs. Rice. American Manhood Against Asiatic Coolieism, Which Shall Survive?* San Francisco: American Federation of Labor, 1902.

Hanna, H. C., Charles Conalt, and Jeremiah Jenks. *Gold Standard in International Trade. Report on the Introduction of the Gold Exchange Standard into China, the Philippine Islands, Panama, and Other Silver-Using Countries and on the Stability of Exchange*. Commission on International Exchange. Washington, D.C.: Government Printing Office, 1905.

Haskins, Charles Warren. *The Argonauts of California, Being the Reminiscences of Scenes and Incidents That Occurred in California in Early Mining Days*. New York: Fords, Howard & Hulbert, 1890.

History of Tuolumne County, California, Compiled From The Most Authentic Records. San Francisco: B.F. Alley, 1882.

Hittell, Theodore Henry. *History of California*. 4 vols. San Francisco: N.J. Stone, 1898.

Horsfall, David. *A Year on Bendigo Goldfield (Courier of the Mines)*. Bendigo: Australian Institute of Genealogical Studies, Bendigo Area, 1856.

Huang Zunxian. "Expulsion of the Immigrants." Translated by J. D. Schmidt. In *Land Without Ghosts: Chinese Impressions of America from the Mid-Nineteenth Century to the Present*, edited by David Akrush and Leo Ouyang Lee. Berkeley: University of California Press, 1989.

————. *Renjinglu shicao jianzhu* (In the Human Realm), annotated and edited by Qian Esun. Shanghai, 1981.

Hunter, W. C. *The "Fan Kwae" at Canton: Before the Treaty Days, 1825–1844*. London: K. Paul & Trench, 1882.

Jebb, Richard. *Studies in Colonial Nationalism*. London: E. Arnold, 1905.

Jenkins, Edward. *The Coolie, His Rights and Wrongs Notes of a Journey to British Guiana, with a Review of the System and of the Recent Commission of Inquiry*. London: Strahan, 1871.

Jenks, Jeremiah. "Considerations on a New Monetary System of China." *Journal of the American Asiatic Association* 5 (February 1905): 12–20.

Jin, Kok Hu, ed. *Hung Men Handbook*. Bendigo, Victoria: Golden Dragon Museum, 2002.

Jindaishi ziliao (Documented History of Modern Chinese History). 131 vols. Beijing: Zhonghua Shuju, 1954–.

Johnson, Sun. *The Self Educator*. Sydney: National Library of Australia, 1892.

Just, P. *Australia, or, Notes Taken during a Residence in the Colonies from the Gold Discovery in 1851 till 1857*. Dundee, Scotland: Durham & Thomson, 1859.

Keynes, John Maynard. *General Theory of Employment, Interest, and Money*. New York: Harcourt Brace, 1965, 1936.

————. *Indian Currency and Finance*. London: Macmillan, 1913.

Kinkead, J. C., Recorder. *Book of Records for Miners Depot*. Miner's Depot, Calif., 1855.

Kinloch-Cooke, Clement. *Chinese Labour (in the Transvaal): A Study of Its Moral, Economic, and Imperial Aspects*, rev. ed. London: Macmillan, 1906.

Kip, Leonard. *California Sketches with Recollections of the Gold Mines*. Albany: E. H. Pease, 1850.

Lai Chun-chuen and Wilberforce Eames. *Remarks of the Chinese Merchants of San Francisco, upon Governor Bigler's Message, and Some Common Objections: With Some Explanations of the Character of the Chinese Companies, and the Laboring Class in California*. San Francisco: Whitton, Towne, 1855.

Lay, G. Tradescant. *The Chinese as They Are: Their Moral, Social, and Literary Character: A New Analysis of the Language: With Succinct Views of Their Principal Arts and Sciences*. London: W. Ball, 1841.

Layres, Augustus. *Critical Analysis of the Evidence for and against Chinese Immigration*. San Francisco: A.F. Woodbridge, 1877.

Leland, Charles Godfrey. *Pidgin-English Sing-Song; or, Songs and Stories in the China-English Dialect, with a Vocabulary*. London: Trübner, 1876.

Li Anshan, ed. *Fei zhou huaqiao huaren she hui shi zi liao xuan ji, 1800–2005* (Social History of Overseas Chinese in Africa: Selected Documents, 1800–2005). Beijing University Center for the Study of Overseas Chinese: Hong Kong Press for Social Sciences, 2006.

————. *History of Overseas Chinese to Africa to 1911*. New York: Diasporic Africa Press, 2012.

Liang Qichao. *Xin dalu youji* (Travelogue of the New Continent). 1904; Beijing: Commercial Press, 2014.

Lin Shu, trans. *Heinu yu tian lu* (A Black Slave's Cry to Heaven [*Uncle Tom's Cabin*]). 1901; Beijing: Zhaohua Press, 2017.

Loomis, Augustus. "The Chinese Companies." *Overland Monthly and Out West Magazine*, September 1868, pp. 221–27.

Lopp, James Keith. *An Analysis of the Characteristics and Causes of Anti-Chinese Sentiment in Butte County 1849–1887*, n.p., n.d.

Louis Ah Mouy. *The Chinese Question Analyzed: With a Full Statement of Facts / by One Who Knows Them*. Melbourne: W. Fairfax, 1857.

Lowe Kong Meng, Cheok Hong Cheong, and Louis Ah Mouy, *The Chinese Question in Australia, 1878–1879*. Melbourne: F. F. Bailliere, 1879.

Lucett, Edward. *Rovings in the Pacific, from 1837 to 1849: With a Glance at California*. New York: AMS Press, 1979.

Mechanics' State Council. "Communication from the Mechanics' State Council of California in Relation to Chinese Immigration." *Journal of the Assembly and Senate of the State of California,*, 17th sess., 1868, appendix.

"Memorial of Chinese Laborers, Resident at Rock Springs, Wyoming Territory, to the Chinese Consul at New York" (1885). In *Chink!*, edited by Cheng-Tsu Wu, 152–64. New York: World Publishing, 1972.

"Memorial of the Six Chinese Companies. An Address to the Senate and House of Representatives of the U.S.; Testimonies of California's Leading Citizens before the Joint Special Congressional Committee; Read and Judge Us." San Francisco: Alta, 1877.

Milner, Alfred, Viscount. *The Milner Papers*, ed. Cecil Headlam. 2 vols. London: Caswell, 1931–33.

Morrison, G. E. *An Australian in China: Being the Narrative of a Quiet Journey Across China to Burma*. London: Horace Cox, 1895.

Morse, Hosea B. *Chronicles of the East India Company*, vol. 1. Oxford, UK: Clarendon Press, 1926.

———. *International Relations of the Chinese Empire*, 3 vols. New York: Longmans, 1910–18.

———. *The Trade and Administration of the Chinese Empire*. London: Longmans, Green, 1908.

Nanfeizhou jinkuang huagong xintu (Illustrated Guide to Chinese Labor in South African Gold Mines). Tianjin: Tianjin Publishing, 1906.

"Nanfeizhou nüedai huaqiao canzhuang shu" (An Account of the Miserable Conditions of the Chinese in South Africa), *Xinmin congbao* 3, no. 1 (1904).

"Nanfeizhou di er tongxin" (A Second Letter from South Africa), *Xinmin congbao* 3, no. 6 (1904).

Navarro, Ramón Gil. *Gold Rush Diary*, edited by María Ferreyra. Lincoln: University of Nebraska Press, 2000.

Neame, Lawrence Elwin. *The Asiatic Danger in the Colonies*. London: G. Routledge, 1907.

Ng, Poon Chew. *The Treatment of the Exempt Classes of Chinese in the United States*. San Francisco: n.p., January 1908.

Olmsted, Frederick Law. *The Papers of Frederick Law Olmstead*, vol. 5, *The California Frontier, 1863–1865*. Baltimore: Johns Hopkins University Press, 1990.

Pan, Shü-lun. *Trade of the United States with China*. New York: China Trade Bureau, 1924.

Patterson, J. A. *The Gold Fields of Victoria in 1862*. Melbourne: Wilson & Mackinnon, 1862.

Pearson, Charles Henry. *National Life and Character*. London: Macmillan, 1894.

Penrose, R. A. F., Jr. "The Witwatersrand Gold Region, Transvaal, South Africa, as Seen in Recent Mining Developments," *Journal of Geology* 15 (November–December 1907): 735–49

Phillips, Lionel. *All That Glittered: Selected Correspondence of Lionel Phillips, 1890–1924*, edited by Maryna Fraser and Allan Jeeves. Cape Town: Oxford University Press, 1977.

———. *Transvaal Problems: Some Notes on Current Politics*. London: J. Murray, 1905.

Potts, John. *One Year of Anti-Chinese Work in Queensland, with Incidents of Travel*. Brisbane: Davison & Metcalf, 1888.

Qingji huagong chuguo shiliao 1863–1910 (Chinese Labor Emigration During the Qing Dynasty). Taipei: Institute of Modern History Series, Academia Sinica, 1995.

Reed, Mary. *China: Short Sketch of the China Inland Mission, Location of Australian Missionaries, the Truth about Opium etc.* Melbourne: Mason, Firth & M'Cutcheon, 1892.

Ritchie, Leitch. *The British World in the East*. London: W. H. Allen, 1846.

Roosevelt, Theodore. *Letters of Theodore Roosevelt*, edited by Elting Morison. 4 vols. Cambridge, Mass.: Harvard University Press, 1951–54.

Rusling, James F. *Across America: The Great West and Pacific Coast*. New York: Sheldon, 1877.

Schumacher, Robert W. *A Transvaal View of the Chinese Labour Question*. Westminster [London]: Imperial South African Association, 1906.

Seeley, John Robert. *The Expansion of England: Two Courses of Lectures*. London: Macmillan, 1883.

Seward, George Frederick. *Chinese Immigration, in Its Social and Economical Aspects*. New York: Charles Scribner's Sons, 1881.

Shinn, Charles Howard. *Land Laws of Mining Districts*. Baltimore: Johns Hopkins University Press, 1884.

———. *Mining Camps: A Study in American Frontier Government*. New York: Charles Scribner's Sons, 1884.

"Sinensis." *China, the Sleep and the Awakening: A Reply to Marquis Tseng*. Hong Kong: China Mail, 1887.

Sirr, Henry Charles. *China and the Chinese: Their Religion, Character, Customs and Manufactures: The Evils Arising from the Opium Trade*. London: W.S. Orr, 1849.

Smith, W. L. G. *Observations on China and the Chinese*. New York: Carleton, 1863.

Smyth, R. Brough. *The Gold Fields and Mineral Districts of Victoria, with Notes on the Modes of Occurrence of Gold and Other Metals and Minerals*. Melbourne: J. Ferres, 1869.

Speer, William. *China and California: Their Relations, Past and Present*. San Francisco: Marvin & Hitchcock, 1853.

———. *An Humble Plea, Addressed to the Legislature of California, in Behalf of the Immigrants from the Empire of China to This State*. San Francisco: Office of the *Oriental*, 1856.

——— *The Oldest and Newest Empire: China and the United States*. Cincinnati: National Publishing, 1870.

Stilwell, Benjamin M., and J. Ross Browne, eds. *The Mariposa Estate: Its Past, Present and Future*. New York: Russell's American Steam Printing House, 1868.

Stoddart, Thomas Robertson. *Annals of Tuolumne County.* Sonora, Calif.: Mother Lode Press, 1963.

Sumner, Charles A. *Chinese Immigration: Speech of Hon. Charles A. Sumner, of California, in the House of Representatives, Saturday, May 3, 1884.* Washington, D. C.: Government Printing Office, 1884.

Thom, Robert. *Mining Report of Tuolumne County.* Sonora, Calif., 1914.

Thomson, Edward. *Our Oriental Missions . . .* Cincinnati: Hitchcock & Walden, 1870.

Torgashev, Boris Pavlovich. *Mining Labor in China.* Shanghai: Bureau of Industrial and Commercial Information, Ministry of Industry, Commerce, and Labor, 1930.

Treaties, Conventions, etc., between China and Foreign States, 2nd ed. Shanghai: Statistical Department of the Inspectorate General of Customs, 1917.

Tseng, Marquis (Zeng, Jizi). "China—The Sleep and the Awakening," *Asiatic Quarterly Review* 3 (January–April 1887): 1–10.

Williams, C. E. *Yuba and Sutter Counties: Their Resources, Advantages and Opportunities.* San Francisco: Bacon, 1887.

Williams, Samuel Wells. *Our Relations with the Chinese Empire.* Chinese Immigration Pamphlets. San Francisco, 1877.

Withers, William Bramwell. *The History of Ballarat, from the First Pastoral Settlement to the Present Time,* 2nd ed. Ballarat: F. W. Niven, 1887.

Wong Sam and Assistants. *An English-Chinese Phrase Book, Together with the Vocabulary of Trade, Law, etc., Also, A Complete List of Wells, Fargo & Co's Offices in California, Nevada, etc.* San Francisco: Wells, Fargo & Co., 1875.

"Wu gao zhi min" (A People with Nowhere to Turn). *Xinmin congbao* 3, no. 11 (1904).

Wu Ting-Fang. "Mutual Helpfulness between China and the United States." *North American Review* (July 1900): 1–13.

Xie Zixiu. *Youli Nanfeizhou Ji* (South Africa Travel Journal), 1905. In *Huagong chuguo shiliao* (Documentary History of Chinese Labor Emigration), ed. Chen Hangshen, 9:278–89. Beijing: Zhonghua Shuju, 1985.

Xue Fucheng. *The European Diary of Hsieh Fucheng: Envoy Extraordinary of Imperial China.* Translated by Helen Hsieh Chien. New York: St. Martin's Press, 1993.

Young, Rev. William. *Report on the Conditions of the Chinese Population in Victoria, Presented to both Houses of Parliament by his Excellency's Command.* Victoria Parliament, 1868, no. 56.

Zhang Deyi. *Diary of a Chinese Diplomat,* translated by Simon Johnstone. Beijing: Panda Books, 1992.

———. *Gaoben hang hai shu qi huibian* (Strange Tales from Over the Ocean), 3 vols. 1868–1905; Beijing: Beijing Tu Shu Guan Chu Ban She, 1996.

Zhu, Rui-sheng, *Guangzhao yingyu* (English Through the Vernaculars of the Canton and Shuihing Prefectures), rev. ed. Chinese Museum of Melbourne. Guangzhao: n.p., 1862.

Theses and Other Unpublished Documents

Griffiths, Philip Gavin. "The Making of White Australia: Ruling Class Agendas, 1876–1888." PhD diss., Australian National University, 2006.

Hall, Mary Frances Millard, and Sylvester "Mike" Millard. "History of California Pioneer and Chinese Interpreter Jerome Millard." Unpublished typescript, 1973.

Harris, Karen. "History of Chinese in South Africa to 2012." PhD diss., University of South Africa, 1998.

Hitchcock, Charles Richard. "Oroville, California: A Study of Diversity in the California Mining Country." PhD diss., University of California at Berkeley, 1998.

Huangfu, Zhengzheng. "Internalizing the West: Qing Envoys and Ministers in Europe, 1866–1893." PhD diss., University of San Diego, 2012.

Lovejoy, Valerie. "Fortune Seekers of Dai Gum San: First Generation Chinese on the Bendigo Goldfield, 1854–1882." PhD diss., LaTrobe University, 2009.

Monaco, James Edward. "The Changing Ethnic Character of a California Gold Mining Community: Butte County, 1848–1880." MA thesis, California State University at Chico, 1986.

Ormston, Robert. "The Rise and Fall of a Frontier Mining Town: Cooktown 1870–1885." PhD diss., University of Queensland, 1996.

Rasmussen, Amanda. "Chinese in Nation and Community: Bendigo 1870s–1920s." PhD diss., LaTrobe University, 2009.

Southern, Ann. "Chinese in the Mines." Shasta County Library, Redding, Calif., n.d.

Valentine, David W. "Historical and Archeological Excavations at 26PE2137: American Canyon, Pershing County, Nevada." MA thesis, University of Nevada at Las Vegas, 1999.

Williams, Stephen. "The Chinese in the California Mines, 1848–1860." MA thesis, Stanford University, 1930.

Yong, Liu. "The Dutch East India Company's Tea Trade with China, 1757–1791." PhD diss., University of Leiden, 1974.

SECONDARY LITERATURE

Articles and Chapters

Allen, Robert C., Jean-Pascal Bassino, Debin Ma, Christine Moll-Murata, and Jan Luiten Van Zanden. "Wages, Prices, and Living Standards in China, 1738–1925: In Comparison with Europe, Japan, and India." *Economic History Review* 64, S1 (2011): 8–38.

Anderson, Warwick. "Coolie Therapeutics: Labor, Race, and Medical Science in Tropical Australia." *International Labor and Working Class History* 91 (Spring 2017): 46–53.

Barron, Beverly. "Celestial Empire." *Chispa* 13, no. 4 (1974): 453–56.

Battellino, Ric. "Mining Booms and the Australian Economy." *Bulletin of the Reserve Bank of Australia* (March 2010): 63–69.

Beck, John H. "Henry George and Immigration." *American Journal of Economics and Sociology* 71 (October 2012): 966–87.

Beckert, Sven. "American Danger: United States Empire, Eurafrica, and the Territorialization of American Capitalism." *American Historical Review* 122 (2017): 1137–70.

Bibb, Leland E. "China Houses: Chinese Prefabricated Structures in the California Gold Rush." *Asian American Comparative Collection Newsletter* 27 (March 2010).

Boafo, James, Sebastian Angzoorokuu Paalo, and Senyo Dotsey. "Illicit Chinese Small-Scale Mining in Ghana: Beyond Institutional Weakness?" *Sustainability* 11 (2019).

Bonner, Philip. "South African Society and Culture, 1910–1948." In *Cambridge History of South Africa*, edited by Robert Ross, Anne Lelk Mager, and Bill Nasson, 2:254–318. New York: Cambridge University Press, 2011.

Botchwey, Gabriel, Gordon Crawford, Nicolas Loubere, and Jixia Lu. "South-South Irregular Migration: The Impacts of China's Informal Gold Rush to Ghana." *International Migration* 57, no. 4 (August 2019): 310–28.

Bowen, Alister. "The Merchants: Chinese Social Organization in Colonial Australia." *Australian Historical Studies* 42, no. 1 (2011): 25–44.

Cai, Shaoqing. "From Mutual Aid to Public Interest: Chinese Secret Societies in Australia." In *After the Rush: Regulation, Participation, and Chinese Communities in Australia, 1860–1940*, edited by Sophie Couchman, John Fitzgerald, and Paul Macgregor, 133–51. Kingsbury, Vic.: *Otherland Literary Journal*, 2004.

Carruthers, Bruce G., and Sarah Babb. "The Color of Money and the Nature of Value: Greenbacks and Gold in Postbellum America." *American Journal of Sociology* 101 (May 1996): 1556–91.

Carstens, Sharon A. "Chinese Culture and Polity in Nineteenth-Century Malaya: The Case of Yap Ah Loy." In *"Secret Societies" Reconsidered: Perspectives on the Social History of Modern South China and Southeast Asia*, edited by David Ownby and Mary Somers Heidhues, 120–52. Armonk, NY: M.E. Sharpe, 1993.

Chan, Fee. "Early Chinese in Oroville." *Diggin's* 7 (Winter 1963): 8–12.

Chan, Sucheng. "Chinese American Entrepreneur: The California Career of Chin Lung." *Chinese America History and Perspectives* 1987 (San Francisco): 73–86.

———. "Chinese Livelihood in Rural California: The Impact of Economic Change, 1860–1880." In *Working People of California*, edited by Daniel Cornford, 57–83. Berkeley: University of California Press, 1995.

———. "A People of Exceptional Character: Ethnic Diversity, Nativism, and Racism in the California Gold Rush." *California History* 79 (Summer 2000): 44–85.

Chua, J. Y. "'An Open and Public Scandal' in the Transvaal: The 1906 Bucknill Inquiry in a Global Context." *Journal of History and Sexuality* 29 (2020): 135–61.

Chung, Sue Fawn. "Between Two Worlds: The Zhigongdang and Chinese American Funerary Rituals." In *The Chinese in America: A History from Gold Mountain to the New Millennium*, edited by Susie Lan Cassel, 217–38. Walnut Creek, Calif.: AltaMira, 2002.

Cloud, Patricia, and David W. Galenson. "Chinese Immigration and Contract Labor in the Late Nineteenth Century." *Explorations in Economic History* 24 (1987): 22–42.

———. "Chinese Immigration: Reply to Charles McClain." *Explorations in Economic History* 28, no. 2 (1991): 239–47.

Clyde, Paul. "The China Policy of J. Ross Browne, American Minister at Peking, 1868–1869." *Pacific Historical Review* 1, no. 1 (1932): 312–23.

Collyer, W. R. "Straits Settlements: Malacca Lands." *Journal of the Society of Comparative Legislation* 4, no. 1 (1902): 82–84.

Comber, Jillian. "Chinese Sites on the Palmer Goldfield, Far North Queensland." In *His-*

tories of the Chinese in Australasia and the South Pacific, edited by Paul Macgregor. Melbourne: Museum of Chinese Australian History, 1995.

Cooper-Ainsworth, Barbara. "The Chinese in Ballarat." In *Histories of the Chinese in Australasia and the South Pacific*, edited by Paul Macgregor. Melbourne: Museum of Chinese Australian History, 1995.

Costello, Julia. "Calaveras Chinese." CalaverasHistory.org, http://www.calaverashistory .org/chinese.

Curthoys, Ann. "Conflict and Consensus: The Seamen's Strike of 1878." In *Who Are Our Enemies? Racism and the Working Class in Australia*, edited by Ann Curthoys and Andrew Markus, 48–65. Sydney, 1978.

——. "'Men of All Nations, Except Chinamen': Europeans and Chinese on the Goldfields of New South Wales." In *Gold: Forgotten Histories and Lost Objects of Australia*, edited by I. McCalman, A. Cook, and A. Reeves, 103–23. Cambridge: Cambridge University Press, 2001.

Daunton, Martin. "Britain and Globalization Since 1850: Creating a Global Order, 1850–1914." *Transactions of the Royal Historical Society* 16 (2006): 1–38.

David, A. Paul, and Gavin Wright, "Increasing Returns and the Genesis of American Resource Abundance." *Industrial and Corporate Change* 6, no. 2 (1997): 203–45.

Delius, Peter. "Migrant Labour and the Pedi, 1840–80." In *Economy and Society in Pre-Industrial South Africa*, edited by Shula Marks and Anthony Atmore, 293–312. London: Longman, 1980.

Denny, Elizabeth. "Mud, Sludge and Town Water: Civic Action in Creswick's Chinatown." *Provenance: Journal of Public Record Office Victoria* 11 (2012).

Denoon, Donald. "Capital and Capitalists in the Transvaal in the 1890s and 1900s." *Historical Journal* 23, no. 1 (1980): 111–32.

Denoon, Donald, with Marivic Wyndham. "Australia and the Western Pacific." In *The Oxford History of the British Empire*, vol. 3, *The Nineteenth Century*, edited by Andrew Porter, 546–72. New York: Oxford University Press, 1999.

DeVries, Jan. "The Industrial Revolution and the Industrious Revolution." *Journal of Economic History* 54, no. 2 (1994): 249–70.

Dubow, Saul. "Colonial Nationalism, the Milner Kindergarten, and the Rise of 'South Africanism.'" *History Workshop* 43, no. 1 (1997): 53–85.

——. "South Africa and South Africans: Nationality, Belonging, Citizenship." In *Cambridge History of South Africa*, edited by Robert Ross, Anne Kelk Mager, and Bill Nasson, 2:17–65. New York: Cambridge University Press, 2011.

Eichengreen, Barry, and Peter Temin. "The Gold Standard and the Great Depression." *Contemporary European History* 9, no. 2 (2000): 183–207.

Engelken, Dagmar. "A White Man's Country? The Chinese Labour Controversy in the Transvaal." In *Wages of Whiteness and Racist Symbolic Capital*, edited by Wulf D Hund, Jeremy Krikler, and David Roediger, 161–94. New Brunswick, N.J.: Transaction, 2010.

Epprecht, Marc. "'Unnatural Vice' in South Africa: The 1907 Commission of Enquiry." *International Journal of African Historical Studies* 34, no. 1 (2001): 121–40.

Erickson, Charlotte. "The Encouragement of Emigration by British Trade Unions, 1850–1900." *Population Studies* 3, no. 3 (1949): 248–73.

Erthington, Norman, Patrick Harries, and Bernard K. Mbenga, "From Colonial Hegemonies to Imperial Conquest." In *Cambridge History of South Africa*, edited by Carolyn Hamilton, Bernard Mbenga, and Robert Ross, 1:319–91. Cambridge: Cambridge University Press, 2010.

Evans, Raymond, and Robert Ørsted-Jensen, "'I Cannot Say the Numbers That Were Killed': Assessing Violent Mortality on the Queensland Frontier." Paper presented at the Australian Historical Association, University of Queensland, July 2014.

Fahey, Charles. "Peopling the Victorian Goldfields: From Boom to Bust, 1851–1901." *Australian Economic History Review* 50 (July 2010): 148–61.

Finnane, Mark. "'Habeas Corpus Mongols'—Chinese Litigants and the Politics of Immigration in 1888." *Australian Historical Studies* 45, no. 2 (2014): 165–83.

Fitzgerald, John. "'To Advance Australia Fairly:' Chinese Voices at Federation." In *After the Rush: Regulation, Participation, and Chinese Communities in Australia, 1860–1940*, edited by Sophie Couchman, John Fitzgerald, and Paul Macgregor, 59–74. Kingsbury, Vic.: *Otherland Literary Journal*, 2004.

Flynn, Dennis O., and Arturo Giráldez. "Born with a Silver Spoon: The Origin of World Trade in 1571." *Journal of World History* 2 (1995): 201–21.

———. "Cycles of Silver: Global Economic Unity through the Late Eighteenth Century." *Journal of World History* 13 (2002): 391–427.

Freund, Bill. "South Africa: The Union Years, 1910–1948." *Cambridge History of South Africa*, edited by Robert Ross, Anne Lelk Mager, and Bill Nasson, 2:211–53. New York: Cambridge University Press, 2011.

Gardella, Robert. "Contracting Business Partnerships in Late Qing and Republican China: Paradigms and Patterns." In *Contract and Property in Early Modern China: Rational Choice in Political Science*, edited by Madeleine Zelin, Robert Gardella, and Jonathan K. Ocko, 327–47. Stanford: Stanford University Press, 2004.

Gonzalez, Michael J. "'My Brother's Keeper': Mexicans and the Hunt for Prosperity in California, 1848–2000." In *Riches for All: The California Gold Rush and the World*, edited by Kenneth N. Owens, 118–41. Lincoln: University of Nebraska Press, 2002.

Goodman, Bryna. "The Locality as Microcosm of the Nation? Native Place Networks and Early Urban Nationalism in China." *Modern China* 21, no. 4 (1995): 387–419.

Goodman, David, "Making an Edgier History of Gold." In *Gold: Forgotten Histories and Lost Objects of Australia*, edited by Iain McCalman, 23–36. New York: Cambridge University Press, 2011.

Gottschang, Thomas R. "Economic Change, Disasters, and Migration: The Historical Case of Manchuria." *Economic Development and Cultural Change* 35, no. 3 (1987): 461–90.

Greer, Richard A. "California Gold—Some Reports to Hawai'i." *Hawaiian Journal of History* 4 (1970): 157–73.

Griffiths, Paul. "The Strategic Fears of the Ruling Class: The Construction of Queensland's Chinese Immigrants Regulation Act of 1877." *Australian Journal of Politics and History* 58, no. 1 (2011): 1–19.

Guoth, Nicholas, and Paul Macgregor. "Getting Chinese Gold off the Victorian Goldfields." *Chinese Southern Diaspora Studies* 8 (2019): 129–50.

Guterl, Matthew, and Christine Skwiot. "Atlantic and Pacific Crossings: Race, Empire and the 'Labor Problem' in the Late Nineteenth Century." *Radical History Review* 91 (Winter 2005): 40–61.

Hagan, James, and Andrew Wells. "The British and Rubber in Malaya, c1890–1940." University of Wollongong Research Online, 2005, https://ro.uow.edu.au/artspapers/1602.

Hamashita, Takeshi. "Geopolitics of Hong Kong Economy." In *Rethinking Hong Kong: New Paradigms, New Perspectives*, edited by Elizabeth Sinn, Wong Siu-lun, and Chan Wing-hoi, 101–44. Hong Kong: University of Hong Kong Press, 2009.

———. "The Intra-Regional System in East Asia in Modern Times." In *Network Power: Japan and Asia*, edited by Peter Katzenstein and Takashi Shiraishi, 113–34. Ithaca, N.Y.: Cornell University Press, 1997.

Harris, Karen. "Private and Confidential: The Chinese Mine Labourers and 'Unnatural Crime.'" *South African Historical Journal* 50, no. 1 (2004): 115–33.

———. "'Strange Bedfellows': Gandhi and Chinese Passive Resistance 1906–1911." *Journal of Natal and Zulu History* 31 (2013): 14–38.

Heidhues, Mary F. Somers. "Chinese Organizations in West Borneo and Bangka: Kongsis and *Hui*." In *"Secret Societies" Reconsidered: Perspectives on the Social History of Modern South China and Southeast Asia*, edited by David Ownby and Mary Somers Heidhues, 68–88. Armonk N.Y.: M.E. Sharpe, 1993.

Higginson, John. "Privileging the Machines: American Engineers, Indentured Chinese and White Workers in South Africa's Deep Level Gold Mines, 1901–1907." *International Review of Social History* 52, no. 1 (2007): 1–34.

Hoover, Mildred Brooke, Hero Eugene Rensch, and Ethel Grace Rensch. *Historic Spots in California*, 3rd ed. Stanford: Stanford University Press, 1966.

Houston, A. W. "Chinese Gold Diggers." *Covered Wagon* (June 1946): 27–28.

Howe, Anthony. "Free Trade and Global Order: The Rise and Fall of a Victorian Vision." In *Victorian Visions of Global Order*, edited by Duncan Bell, 26–46. New York: Cambridge University Press, 2007.

Hsu, Madeline. "Decoupling Peripheries from the Center: The Dangers of Diaspora in Chinese Migration Studies." *Diaspora: Journal of Transnational Studies* 20, no. 1 (2011): 204–15.

———. "Exporting Homosociality: Culture and Community in Chinatown America, 1882–1943." In *Cities in Motion: Interior, Coast, and Diaspora in Transnational China*, edited by Wen-hsin Yeh, David Strand, and Sherman Cochran, 219–46. Berkeley: University of California Press, 2007.

Hu DeHart, Evelyn. "Chinese Coolie Labor in Cuba in the Nineteenth Century: Free Labor or Neo-Slavery?" *Contributions in Black Studies* 12 (1994): article no. 5.

———. "From Slavery to Freedom: Chinese Coolies on the Sugar Plantations of Nineteenth Century Cuba." *Labour History* (Canberra) (2017): 31–51.

Hunter, Boyd. "The Aboriginal Legacy." In *Cambridge Economic History of Australia*, edited by Simon Ville and Glenn Withers, 73–96. New York: Cambridge University Press, 2014.

Huynh, Tu T. "'We Are Not a Docile People': Chinese Resistance and Exclusion in the

Re-Imagining of Whiteness in South Africa, 1903–1910." *Journal of Chinese Overseas* 8, no. 2 (2002): 137–68.

Hyslop, Jonathan. "The Imperial Working Class Makes Itself 'White': White Labourism in Britain, Australia, and South Africa Before the First World War." *Journal of Historical Sociology* 12, no. 4 (1999): 398–421.

Ingham, Geoffrey. "Money is a Social Relation." *Review of Social Economy* 54, no. 4 (1996): 507–29.

Jones, Timothy G. "Ping Que: Mining Magnate of the Northern Territory 1854–1886." *Journal of Chinese Australia* 1 (May 2005).

Jung, Maureen. "Capitalism Comes to the Diggings." *California History* 77, no. 4 (1998): 52–77.

Kamachi, Noriko. "American Influences on Chinese Reform Thought: Huang Tsun-hsien in California, 1882–1885." *Pacific Historical Review* 47, no. 2 (1978): 239–60.

Katz, Elaine. "The Underground Route to Mining: Afrikaners and the Witwatersrand Gold Mining Industry from 1902 to the 1907 Miners' Strike." *Journal of African History* 36, no. 3 (1995): 467–89.

Keller, Wolfgang, Li Ben, and Carol H. Shiue. "China's Foreign Trade: Perspectives from the Past 150 Years." *World Economy* 34, no. 6 (2011): 853–92.

Kian, Kwee Hui. "Chinese Economic Dominance in Southeast Asia: A *Longue Duree* Perspective." *Comparative Studies in Society and History* 55, no. 1 (2013): 5–34.

King, Frank H. H. "The Boxer Indemnities—'Nothing but Bad.'" *Modern Asian Studies* 40, no. 3 (2006): 663–89.

Kirkman, Noreen. "Chinese Miners on the Palmer." *Journal of Royal Historical Society of Queensland* 13, no. 2 (1986): 49–62.

Kobrin, Rebecca. "A Credit to Their Nation: East European Jewish Immigrant 'Bankers,' Credit Access, and the Transnational Business of Mass Migration, 1873–1914." In *Immigrant Entrepreneurship: The German-American Experience Since 1700*, edited by Hartmut Berghoff and Uwe Spiekermann, 69–90. Washington, D.C.: German Historical Institute, 2016.

———. "Currents and Currency: Jewish Immigrant 'Bankers' and the Transnational Business of Mass Migration, 1873–1914." In *Transnational Traditions: New Perspectives on Jewish History*, edited by Ava Kahn and Adam Mendelsohn, 87–104. Detroit: Wayne State University Press, 2014.

Kramer, Paul A. "Imperial Openings: Civilization, Exemption, and the Geopolitics of Mobility in the History of Chinese Exclusion, 1868–1910." *Journal of the Gilded Age and Progressive Era* 14, no. 3 (2015): 317–47.

Ku, Charlotte. "Abolition of China's Unequal Treaties and the Search for Regional Stability in Asia, 1919–1943." *Texas A&M Law Scholarship* 12 (1994): 67–86.

Kuroda, Akinobu. "Anonymous Currencies or Named Debts? Comparison of Currencies, Local Credits, and Units of Account Between China, England, and Japan in the Pre-Industrial Era." *Socio-Economic Review* 11, no. 1 (2012): 57–80.

Kyi, Anna. "'The Most Determined, Sustained Diggers' Resistance Campaign': Chinese Protests Against the Victorian Government's Anti-Chinese Legislation, 1855–1862." *Provenance: Journal of the Public Record Office Victoria* 8 (2009).

Lai, Cheng-Chung, Joshua Jr-shian Gau, and Tai-kuang Ho. "Professor Jeremiah Jenks of Cornell University and the 1903 Chinese Monetary Reform." *Hitotsubashi Journal of Economics* 50 (2009): 35–46.

Lai, Him Mark. "Potato King and Film Producer, Flower Growers, Professionals, and Activists: The Huang Liang Du Community in Northern California." *Chinese America: History and Perspectives* (1998): 1–24.

Lake, Marilyn. "Challenging the 'Slave-Driving Employers': Understanding Victoria's 1896 Minimum Wage through a World-History Approach." *Australian Historical Studies* 45, no. 1 (2014): 87–102.

———. "The Chinese Empire Encounters the British Empire and Its 'Colonial Dependencies': Melbourne, 1887." In *Chinese Australians: Politics, Engagement and Resistance*, edited by Sophie Couchman and Kate Bagnall, 98–116. Leiden: Brill, 2015.

Lee, Ching Kwan. "The Specter of Global China." *New Left Review* 89 (September–October 2014): 29–65.

Legassick, Martin. "The Frontier Tradition in South African Historiography." In *Economy and Society in Pre-Industrial South Africa*, edited by Shula Marks and Anthony Atmore, 44–79. London: Longman, 1980.

Limbaugh, Ronald H. "Chinese of Knight's Ferry, 1850–1920: A Preliminary Study." *California History* 72, no. 2 (1993): 106–28.

———. "Making Old Tools Work Better: Pragmatic Adaptation and Innovation." *California History* 77, no. 4 (1998): 24–51.

Limerick, Patricia Nelson. "The Gold Rush and the Shaping of the American West." *California History* 77, no. 1 (1998): 30–41.

Lockard, Craig A. "Chinese Migration and Settlement in Southeast Asia Before 1850: Making Fields from the Sea." *History Compass* 11, no. 9 (2013): 765–81.

Lorence, James J. "Business and Reform: The American Asiatic Association and the Exclusion Laws, 1905–1907." *Pacific Historical Review* 39 (1970): 421–38.

Lovejoy, Valerie. "The Things that Unite: Inquests into Chinese Deaths on the Bendigo Goldfields, 1854–65." *Provenance: Journal of Public Record Office Victoria* 6 (2007).

Loy-Wilson, Sophie. "Coolie Alibis: Seizing Gold from Chinese Miners in New South Wales." *International Labor and Working Class History* 91 (Spring 2017): 28–45.

———. "Rural Geographies and Chinese Empires: Chinese Shopkeepers and Shop-Life in Australia." *Australian Historical Studies* 45, no. 3 (2014): 407–24.

Ma, L. Eve Armentrout. "The Big Business Ventures of Chinese in North America, 1850–1930." In *The Chinese American Experience*, edited by Genny Lim, 101–12. San Francisco: Chinese Historical Society, 1984.

Macgregor, Paul. "Chinese Political Values in Colonial Victoria: Lowe Kong Meng and the Legacy of the July 1880 Election." In *Chinese Australians: Politics, Engagement and Resistance*, edited by Sophie Couchman and Kate Bagnall, 53–97. Leiden: Brill, 2015.

———. "Lowe Kong Meng and Chinese Engagement in the International Trade of Colonial Victoria." Provenance: *Journal of Public Record Office Victoria* 11 (2012).

Malchow, Howard L. "Trade Unions and Emigration in Late Victorian England: A National Lobby for State Aid." *Journal of British Studies* 15, no. 2 (1976): 92–116.

Manhattan, Kris. "Plantation Dispossessions: The Global Travel of Racial Capitalism." In *American Capitalism: New Histories*, edited by Sven Beckert and Christine Desan, 361–87. New York: Columbia University Press, 2018.

Mantena, Karuna. "Crisis of Liberal Imperialism." In *Victorian Visions of Global Order*, edited by Duncan Bell, 113–35. New York: Cambridge University Press, 2007.

Marks, Shula. "Cultures of Subordination and Subversion." *Social History* 14, no. 2 (1989): 225–31.

———. "War and Union, 1899–1910." In *Cambridge History of South Africa*, edited by Robert Ross, Anne Lelk Mager, and Bill Nasson, 2:157–210. New York: Cambridge University Press, 2011.

Marks, Shula, and Stanley Trapido. "Lord Milner and the South African State." *History Workshop* 8 (Autumn 1979): 50–80.

———. "Lord Milner and the South African State Reconsidered." In *Imperialism, the State, and the Third World*, edited by Michael Twaddle, 80–94. London: British Academic Press, 1992.

Markus, Andrew. "Divided We Fall: The Chinese and the Melbourne Furniture Trade Union, 1870–1900." *Labour History* 26 (May 1974): 1–10.

Martínez, Julia. "The End of Indenture? Asian Workers in the Australian Pearling Industry, 1901–1972." *International Labor and Working Class History* 67 (Spring 2005): 125–47.

———. "'Unwanted Scraps' or 'An Alert, Resolute, Resentful People'? Chinese Railroad Workers in the French Congo." *International Labor and Working Class History* 91 (Spring 2017): 79–98.

Matson, J. N. "The Common Law Abroad: English and Indigenous Laws in the British Commonwealth." *International and Comparative Law Quarterly* 42, no. 4 (1993): 753–79.

Matsuoka, Koji. "China's Currency Reform and its Significance." *Kyoto University Economic Review* 11 (1936): 75–98.

McCarthy, Justin. "Tales from the Empire City: Chinese Miners in the Pine Creek Region, Northern Territory 1872–1915." In *Histories of the Chinese in Australasia and the South Pacific*, edited by Paul Macgregor, 191–202. Melbourne: Museum of Chinese Australian History, 1993.

McClain, Charles. "Chinese Immigration: A Comment on Cloud and Galenson." *Explorations in Economic History* 27, no. 3 (1990): 363–78.

McCulloch, Samuel Clyde. "Sir George Gipps and Eastern Australia's Policy Toward the Aborigine, 1838–46." *Journal of Modern History* 33, no. 3 (1961): 261–69.

McGillivery, Angus R. "Convict Settlers, Seamen's Greens, and Imperial Designs at Port Jackson: A Maritime Perspective of British Settler Agriculture." *Agricultural History* 78, no. 3 (2004): 261–88.

McGowan, Barry. "The Economics and Organisation of Chinese Mining in Colonial Australia." *Australian Economic History Review* 45 (July 2005): 119–38.

McKee, Delbert. "The Chinese Boycott of 1905–1906 Reconsidered: The Role of Chinese Americans." *Pacific Historical Review* 55, no. 2 (1986): 165–91.

McKeown, Adam. "Global Migration, 1846–1940." *Journal of World History* 15, no. 2 (2004): 155–89.

———. "Transnational Chinese Families and Chinese Exclusion, 1875–1943." *Journal of American Ethnic History* 18, no. 2 (1999): 73–110.

Mei, June. "Socioeconomic Origins of Emigration: Guangdong to California, 1850–1882." *Modern China* 5, no. 4 (1979): 463–99.

Meissner, Christopher M. "A New World Order: Explaining the International Diffusion of the Gold Standard, 1870–1913." *Journal of International Economics* 66, no. 2 (2005): 385–406.

Meissner, Daniel J. "Bridging the Pacific: California and the China Flour Trade." *California History* 76, no. 4 (1997): 82–93.

———. "The 1905 Anti-American Boycott: A Nationalist Myth?" *Journal of American–East Asia Relations* 10, no. 3–4 (2001): 175–96.

Messner, Andrew. "Popular Constitutionalism and Chinese Protest on the Victorian Goldfields." *Journal of Australian Colonial History* 2, no. 2 (2000): 63–69.

Mitchell, Bruce. "Hargraves, Edward Hammond (1816–1891)." *Australian Dictionary of Biography*. Melbourne: Melbourne University Press, 1972.

Mitchell, H. "The Gold Standard in the Nineteenth Century." *Canadian Journal of Economics and Political Science* 17 (August 1951): 369–76.

Moodie, T. Dunbar, Vivienne Ndatshe, and British Sibuyi. "Migrancy and Male Sexuality on the South African Gold Mines." *Journal of Southern African Studies* 14, no. 2 (1988): 228–56.

Murphy, Martin J. "'White Gold' or 'White Blood'? The Rubber Plantations of Colonial Indochina, 1910–1940." *Journal of Peasant Studies* 19, no. 3–4 (1992): 41–67.

Nauright, John. "Cornish Miners in the Witwatersrand Gold Mines in South Africa, c. 1890–1904." *Cornish History* (2004): 1–32.

Nicolini, Dolores Yescas. "When East Met West: The Chinese Presence in Tuolumne County." *Chispa* 24, no. 3 (January–March 1985): 809–13.

Nicolini, Dolores Yescas, Richard Yescas, and Roberta McDow. "Chinese Camp." *Pacific Historian* 16 (Summer 1972): 47–67.

Ohlsson, Tony. "The Origins of White Australia: The Coolie Question 1837–43." *Journal of the Royal Australian Historical Society* 97, no. 2 (2011): 203–19.

O'Malley, Michael, "Specie and Species: Race and the Money Question in Nineteenth-Century America." *American Historical Review* 99, no. 2 (1994): 369–95.

Park, Yoon Jung. "Chinese Migrants in Latin America/Caribbean and Africa, Then and Now." *Journal of Overseas Chinese* 13, no. 2 (2017): 163–79.

Passananti, T. P. "The Politics of Silver and Gold in an Age of Globalization: The Origins of Mexico's Monetary Reform of 1905." *América Latina en la Historia Económica* 15 (2008): 67–95.

Paul, Rodman W. "The Origin of the Chinese Issue in California." *Journal of American History* 25, no. 2 (1938): 181–96.

Peng Jiali. "Qingdai yingguo wei nanfei jinkuang zhaomu huagong shimo" (Introduction of Chinese Gold Mining Laborers to British South Africa During the Qing Dynasty). *Lishi yanjiu* (Historical Research) 3 (1983).

Pérez Rosales, Vicente. "Diary of a Journey to California, 1848–1849." In *We Were 49ers!*

Chilean Accounts of the California Gold Rush, edited and translated by Edwin A. Beil-harz and Carlos U. López, 3–100. Pasadena, Calif.: Ward Ritchie Press, 1976.

Ransmeier, Johanna. "Body-Price." In *Sex, Power, and Slavery*, edited by Gwyn Campbell and Elizabeth Elbourne, 319–44. Athens: Ohio University Press, 2014.

Rasmussen, Amanda. "The Rise of Labor: A Chinese Australian Participates in Bendigo Local Politics at a Formative Moment, 1904–1905," *Journal of Chinese Overseas* 9, no. 2 (2015): 174–202.

Rawls, James J. "Gold Diggers: Indian Miners in the California Gold Rush." *California Historical Quarterly* 55, no. 1 (1976): 28–45.

Reeves, Keir. "Sojourners or a New Diaspora? Economic Implications of the Movement of Chinese Miners to the South-west Pacific Goldfields." *Australian Economic History Review* 50, no. 2 (2010): 178–92.

Reid, Anthony. "Chinese on the Mining Frontier in Southeast Asia." In *Chinese Circulations: Capital, Commodities, and Networks in Southeast Asia*, edited by Eric Tagliacozzo and Wen-chin Chang, 21–36. Durham, N.C.: Duke University Press, 2011.

Ricards, Sherman L., and George M. Blackburn. "The Sydney Ducks: A Demographic Analysis." *Pacific Historical Review* 42, no. 1 (1973): 20–31.

Richardson, Peter. "Coolies and Randlords: The North Randfontein Chinese Miners' 'Strike' of 1905." *Journal of Southern African Studies* 2, no. 2 (1976): 151–77.

———. "The Recruiting of Chinese Indentured Labour for the South African Gold-Mines, 1903–1908." *Journal of African History* 18, no. 1 (1977): 85–108.

Richardson, Peter, and Jean-Jacques Van Helten. "The Development of the South African Gold Mining Industry, 1895–1918." *Economic History Review* 37, no. 3 (1984): 319–40.

Riskin, Carl. "China's Human Development after Socialism." In *Cambridge History of Communism*, edited by Juliane Fürst, Silvio Pons, and Mark Selden, 3:474–501. New York: Cambridge University Press, 2017.

———. "Seven Questions about the Chinese Famine of 1959–1961." *China Economic Review* 9, no. 2 (1998): 111–24.

Rohe, Randall. "After the Gold Rush: Chinese Mining in the Far West, 1850–1890." In *Chinese on the American Frontier*, edited by Arlif Dirlik, 3–26. Lanham, Md.: Rowman and Littlefield, 2001.

———. "The Chinese and Hydraulic Mining in the Far West." *Mining History Association Annual* (1994): 73–91.

———. "Chinese Mining and Settlement at the Lava Beds, California." *Mining History Journal* (1996): 51–60.

Rule, Pauline. "The Transformative Effect of Australian Experience on the Life of Ho A Mei, Hong Kong Community Leader and Entrepreneur." In *Chinese Australians: Politics, Engagement, and Resistance*, edited by Sophie Couchman and Kate Bagnall, 22–52. Leiden: Brill, 2015.

Saunders, Christopher, and Iain Smith. "Southern Africa 1795–1910." In *The Oxford History of the British Empire*, vol. 3, *The Nineteenth Century*, edited by Andrew Porter, 597–623. New York: Oxford University Press, 1999.

St. John, Rachel. "The Unpredictable America of William Gwin: Expansion, Secession, and the Unstable Borders of Nineteenth Century America." *Journal of the Civil War Era* 6, no. 1 (2016): 56–84.

Schell, William, Jr. "Silver Symbiosis: ReOrienting Mexican Economic History." *Hispanic American Historical Review* 81, no. 1 (2001): 89–133.

Schran, Peter. "The Minor Significance of Commercial Relations between the United States and China." In *America's China Trade in Historical Perspective*, ed. Ernest May and John Fairbank, 237–58. Cambridge, Mass.: Harvard University Press, 1986.

Shi Jirui (Schmidt, Jerry D.). "Jinshan sannian ku: Huang Zunxian shimei yanjiu de xin cailiao" (Three Hard Years on Golden Hill: New Sources for the Study of Huang Zunxian), translated by Liu Qian. *Journal of South China Normal University* (Social Science Edition) 3 (May 2018): 5–17.

Sinn, Elizabeth. "Beyond 'Tianxia': The 'Zhongwai Xinwen Qiribao' (Hong Kong 1871–1872) and the Construction of a Transnational Chinese Community." *China Review* 4, no. 1 (2004): 89–122.

Sisson, Kelly J. "Bound for California: Chilean Contract Workers and 'Patrones' in the California Gold Rush, 1848–1852." *Southern California Quarterly* 90 (October 2008): 259–305.

Spoehr, Alexander. "Hawai'i and the Gold Rush: George Allan of the Hudson's Bay Company Reports on His 1848 Pursuit of Captain John Sutter." *Hawaii Journal of History* 26 (1992): 123–32.

Standart, Mary Collette. "The Sonoran Migration to California, 1848–1856: A Study in Prejudice." *Southern California Quarterly* 58 (1976): 333–57.

Stapp, Darby. "The Documentary Record of an Overseas Chinese Mining Camp." In *Hidden Heritage: Historical Archaeology of the Overseas Chinese*, edited by Patricia Wegers, 3–32. Amityville, N.Y: Baywood, 1993.

Sugihara, Kaoru. "Global Industrialization: A Multipolar Perspective." In *Cambridge World History*, edited by J. R. McNeill and K. Pomeranz, 8:106–35. New York: Cambridge University Press, 2015.

———. "Multiple Paths to Industrialization: A Global Context of the Rise of Emerging States." In *Paths to the Emerging State in Asia and Africa*, edited by K. Otsuka and Kaoru Sugihara, 244–78. Singapore: Springer, 2019.

———. "Patterns of Chinese Emigration to Southeast Asia, 1869–1939." In *Japan, China and the Growth of the Asian International Economy, 1850–1949*, edited by Kaoru Sugihara, 244–72. New York: Oxford University Press, 2005.

Sun, E-Tu Zen. "Mining Labor in the Ch'ing Period." In *Approaches to Modern Chinese History*, edited by Albert Feuerwerker, Rhoads Murphey, and Mary Clabaugh Wright, 45–67. Berkeley: University of California Press, 1967.

Trapido, Stanley. "Imperialism, Settler Identities, and Colonial Capitalism: The Hundred-Year Origins of the 1899 South African War." In *Cambridge History of South Africa*, edited by Robert Ross, Anne Kelk Mager, and Bill Nasson, 2:66–101. New York: Cambridge University Press, 2011.

Valentine, David. "Chinese Placer Mining in the U.S.: An Example from American Canyon, Nevada." In *The Chinese in America: A History from Gold Mountain to the New*

Millennium, edited by Susie Lan Cassel, 37–53. Walnut Creek, Calif.: Alta Mira Press, 2002.

Van Helten, Jean-Jacques. "Empire and High Finance: South Africa and the International Gold Standard 1890–1914." *Journal of African History* 23, no. 4 (1982): 529–48.

Ville, Simon. "Business Development in Colonial Australia." *Australian Economic History Review* 38, no. 1 (1998): 16–41.

Wang, Aiyun. "Ershi shiji chu nanfei huagong shijian chu tan" (Preliminary Study of Chinese Emigrant Labor to South Africa in the Early Twentieth Century). *Nankai xuebao*, no. 2 (1996).

Wang, Dong. "The Discourse of Unequal Treaties in Modern China." *Pacific Affairs* 76, no. 3 (2003): 399–425.

Wang, L. Ling-chi. "Beyond Identity and Racial Politics: Asian Americans and the Campaign Fund-raising Controversy." *Asian Law Journal* 5, no. 12 (1998): 329–40.

Wilson, Andrew. "Andrew Wilson's 'Jottings' on Civil War California." Edited by John Haskell Kemble. *California Historical Society Quarterly* 32, no. 3 (1953): 209–24.

Wilton, Janis. "Chinese Stores in Rural Australia." In *Asian Department Stores*, edited by Kerrie L. MacPherson, 90–113. Honolulu: University of Hawaii Press, 1998.

Wolfe, Patrick. "Settler Colonialism and the Elimination of the Native." *Journal of Genocide Research* 8, no. 4 (2006): 387–409.

Woo, Wesley S. "Presbyterian Mission: Christianizing and Civilizing the Chinese in Nineteenth Century California." *American Presbyterians* 68, no. 3 (1990): 167–78.

Wunder, John R. "Chinese in Trouble: Criminal Law and Race on the Trans-Mississippi West Frontier." *Western Historical Quarterly* 17, no. 1 (1986): 25–41.

Zelin, Madeline. "A Critique of Rights of Property in Prewar China." In *Contract and Property in Early Modern China*, edited by Madeline Zelin, Jonathan Ocko, and Robert Gardella, 17–36. Stanford: Stanford University Press, 2004.

———. "The Structures of the Chinese Economy During the Qing Period." In *Perspectives on Modern China: Four Anniversaries*, edited by Kenneth Lieberthal, Joyce Kallgren, Roderick MacFarquhar, and Eric Wakeman, Jr., 31–67. Armonk, N.Y.: M.E. Sharpe, 1991.

Books

Aarim-Heriot, Najia. *Chinese Immigrants, African Americans, and Racial Anxiety in the United States, 1848–82*. Urbana: University of Illinois Press, 2003.

Abu-Lughod, Janet L. *Before European Hegemony: The World System 1250–1350*. New York: Oxford University Press, 1989.

Accone, Darryl. *All Under Heaven: The Story of a Chinese Family in South Africa*. Claremont, South Africa, 2004.

Adelman, Paul. *Gladstone, Disraeli and Later Victorian Politics*, 3rd ed. London: Longman, 1997.

Alborn, Timothy, *All that Glittered: Britain's Most Precious Metal from Adam Smith to the Gold Rush*. New York: Oxford University Press, 2019.

Ally, Russell. *Gold and Empire: The Bank of England and South Africa's Gold Producers*. Johannesburg: Witwatersrand University Press, 1994.

Anderson, Hugh. *Colonial Minstrel*. Melbourne: F. W. Cheshire, 1960.

Anderson, Warwick. *The Cultivation of Whiteness: Science, Health, and Racial Destiny in Australia*. Carlton South, Vic.: Melbourne University Press, 2002.

Arkush, David, and Leo Ouyang Lee. *Land Without Ghosts: Chinese Impressions of America from the Mid-Nineteenth Century to the Present*. Berkeley: University of California Press, 1989.

Arrighi, Giovanni. *Adam Smith in Beijing: Lineages of the Twenty-First Century*. New York: Verso, 2007.

Atkinson, David. *The Burden of White Supremacy: Containing Asian Migration in the British Empire and the United States*. Chapel Hill: University of North Carolina Press, 2016.

Auerbach, Sascha. *Race, Law, and "the Chinese Puzzle" in Imperial Britain*. New York: Palgrave Macmillan, 2009.

Bakken, Gordon Morris. *Law in the Western United States*. Norman: University of Oklahoma Press, 2000.

———. *Practicing Law in Frontier California*. Lincoln: University of Nebraska Press, 1991.

Ballantyne, Tony. *Webs of Empire: Locating New Zealand's Colonial Past*. Vancouver, British Columbia: University of British Columbia Press, 2014.

Banivanua-Mar, Tracey. *Violence and Colonial Dialogue: The Australian-Pacific Indentured Labor Trade*. Honolulu: University of Hawaii Press, 2007.

Barth, Gunther. *Bitter Strength: A History of Chinese in the United States, 1850–1870*. Cambridge, Mass.: Harvard University Press, 1964.

Bate, Weston. *Lucky City: The First Generation at Ballarat, 1851–1901*. Carlton, Vic.: Melbourne University Press, 2003.

Bederman, Gail. *Manliness and Civilization: A Cultural History of Gender and Race, 1880–1917*. Chicago: University of Chicago Press, 1995.

Belich, James. *Replenishing the Earth: The Settler Revolution and the Rise of the Anglo-World, 1783–1939*. New York: Oxford University Press, 2009.

Bell, Duncan. *The Idea of Greater Britain: Empire and the Future of World Order, 1860–1900*. Princeton: Princeton University Press, 2007.

———. *Reordering the World*. Princeton: Princeton University Press, 2016.

Bello, David. *Opium and the Limits of Empire: Drug Prohibition in the Chinese Interior, 1729–1850*. Cambridge, Mass.: Harvard University Press, 2005.

Benton, Gregor, and Hong Liu. *Dear China: Emigrant Letters and Remittances*. Berkeley: University of California Press, 2018.

Benton, Lauren. *A Search for Sovereignty: Law and Geography in European Empires, 1400–1900*. New York: Cambridge University Press, 2009.

Bernhardt, Kathryn. *Women and Property in China, 960–1949*. Stanford: Stanford University Press, 1999.

Birrell, Ralph W. *Staking a Claim: Gold and the Development of Victorian Mining Law*. Carlton South, Vic.: Melbourne University Press, 1998.

Bloomfield, Anne, with Benjamin F. H. Ananian and Philip P. Choy. *History of Chinese Camp: Cultural Resources Inventory*. San Francisco: Tuolumne County Historic Preservation Commission, 1994.

Boyle, R. W. *Gold: History and Genesis of Deposits*. New York: Van Nostrand Reinhold, 1984.

Brands, H. W. *The Age of Gold: The California Gold Rush and the New American Dream*. New York: Anchor Books, 2003.

Brass, Tom, and Marcel van der Linden, eds. *Free and Unfree Labour: The Debate Continues*. New York: Peter Lang, 1997.

Bright, Rachel. *Chinese Labour in South Africa, 1902–10: Race, Violence, and Global Spectacle*. Basingstoke, Hampshire: Palgrave Macmillan, 2013.

Broadbent, James, Suzanne Rickard, and Margaret Steven. *India, China, Australia: Trade and Society, 1788–1850*. Sydney: Historic Houses Trust of New South Wales, 2003.

Buckbee, Edna Bryan. *The Saga of Old Toulumne*. New York: Press of the Pioneers, 1935.

Buckbee, Edna Bryan, and Wallace Motloch. *Calaveras County: Gold Rush Stories*. San Andreas, Calif.: Calaveras County Historical Society, 2005.

Buxbaum, David. *Family Law and Customary Law in Asia: A Contemporary Legal Perspective*. Hague: Martinus Nijhoff, 1968.

Bytheway, Simon James, and Mark Metzler. *Central Banks and Gold: How Tokyo, London, and New York Shaped the Modern World*. Ithaca, N.Y.: Cornell University Press, 2016.

Campbell, Persia. *Chinese Coolie Emigration to Countries Within the British Empire*. London: PS King, 1923.

Cahir, Fred. *Black Gold: Aboriginal People on the Goldfields of Victoria, 1850–1870*. Australian National University E-Press, 2012.

Carey, Jane, and Claire McLisky. *Creating White Australia*. Sydney: Sydney University Press, 2009.

Carlson, Ellsworth C. *The Kaiping Mines, 1877–1912*, 2nd ed. Cambridge, Mass.: Harvard University Press, 1971.

Chan, Shelly. *Diaspora's Homeland: Modern China in the Age of Global Migration*. Durham: Duke University Press, 2018.

Chan, Sucheng. *This Bittersweet Soil: The Chinese in California Agriculture 1860–1910*. Berkeley: University of California Press, 1986.

Chang, Gordon H. *Ghosts of Gold Mountain: The Epic Story of the Chinese Who Built the Transcontinental Railroad*. Boston: Houghton Mifflin Harcourt, 2019.

Chang, Gordon H., and Shelly Fishkin, eds. *The Chinese and the Iron Road*. Stanford: Stanford University Press, 2019.

Chen, Da. *Chinese Migrations, with Special Reference to Labor Conditions*. Washington, D.C.: Government Printing Office, 1923.

Chen, Yong. *Chinese San Francisco, 1850–1943: A Transpacific Community*. Stanford, Calif.: Stanford University Press, 2000.

Chesneaux, Jean. *Secret Societies in China in the Nineteenth and Twentieth Centuries*. Ann Arbor: University of Michigan Press, 1971.

Chiu, Ping. *Chinese Labor in California, 1850–1880, an Economic Study*. Madison: State Historical Society of Wisconsin, 1963.

Chou, Wah-shan. *Tongzhi: Politics of Same-Sex Eroticism in Chinese Societies*. New York: Haworth Press, 2000.

Chu, Yiu Kong. *The Triads as Business*. New York: Routledge, 2000.

Chung, Sue Fawn. *Chinese in the Woods: Logging and Lumbering in the American West.* Urbana: University of Illinois Press, 2015.

———. *In Pursuit of Gold: Chinese American Miners and Merchants in the American West.* Urbana: University of Illinois Press, 2011.

Clarke, P. F. *Hope and Glory: Britain, 1900–2000,* 2nd ed. London : Penguin, 2004.

Cohen, Robin. *Global Diasporas: An Introduction.* New York: Routledge, 1997.

Couchman, Sophie, and Kate Bagnall, eds. *Chinese Australians: Politics, Engagement and Resistance.* Leiden: Brill, 2015.

Couchman, Sophie, John Fitzgerald, and Paul Macgregor, eds. *After the Rush: Regulation, Participation and Chinese Communities in Australia, 1860–1940.* Fitzroy, Vic.: Arena, 2004.

Craddock, P. T. *Early Metal Mining and Production.* Washington, D.C: Smithsonian Institution Press, 1995.

Cronin, Kathryn. *Colonial Casualties: Chinese in Early Victoria.* Melbourne: University of Melbourne Press, 1982.

Davenport, Jade. *Digging Deep: A History of Mining in South Africa, 1852–2002.* Johannesburg: Jonathan Ball, 2013.

Davies, Glyn. *A History of Money from Ancient Times to the Present Day.* Cardiff: University of Wales Press, 1994.

De Cecco, Marcello. *The International Gold Standard: Money and Empire.* London: Pinter, 1984.

De León, Arnoldo. *Racial Frontiers: Africans, Chinese and Mexicans in Western America, 1848–1890.* Albuquerque: University of New Mexico Press, 2002.

Denoon, Donald. *A Grand Illusion; The Failure of Imperial Policy in the Transvaal Colony During the Period of Reconstruction, 1900–1905.* London: Longman, 1973.

———. *Settler Capitalism: The Dynamics of Dependent Development in the Southern Hemisphere.* Oxford: Oxford University Press, 1983.

———. *Southern Africa Since 1800.* London: Longman, 1984.

Desan, Christine. *Making Money: Coin, Currency and the Coming of Capitalism.* New York: Oxford University Press, 2014.

Deverell, William. *Railroad Crossing: Californians and the Railroad, 1850–1910.* Berkeley: University of California Press, 1994.

Docker, Edward Wybergh. *The Blackbirders: The Recruiting of South Seas Labour for Queensland, 1863–1907.* Sydney: Angus & Robertson, 1970.

Dodd, Nigel. *The Social Life of Money.* Princeton: Princeton University Press, 2014.

Duara, Prasenjit. *Rescuing History from the Nation: Questioning Narratives of Modern China.* Chicago: University of Chicago Press, 1995.

Dubow, Saul. *A Commonwealth of Knowledge: Science, Sensibility, and White South Africa, 1820–2000.* New York: Oxford University Press, 2006.

———. *Racial Segregation and the Origins of Apartheid in South Africa, 1919–36.* New York: St. Martin's Press, 1989.

Economy, Elizabeth. *The Third Revolution: Xi Jinping and the New Chinese State.* New York: Oxford University Press, 2018.

Eichengreen, Barry. *Globalizing Capital: A History of the International Monetary System.* Princeton: Princeton University Press, 1996.

Eichengreen, Barry, and Marc Flandreau, eds. *The Gold Standard in Theory and History*. New York: Routledge, 1997.

Ellison, William Henry. *A Self-Governing Dominion: California 1849–1860*. Berkeley: University of California Press, 1950.

Evans, Ivan. *Cultures of Violence*. Manchester: Manchester University Press, 2009.

Evans, Raymond, ed. *Race Relations in Colonial Queensland*, 3rd ed. St. Lucia: University of Queensland Press, 1993.

Farkas, Lani Ah Tye. *Bury My Bones in America: The Saga of a Chinese Family in California, 1852–1996: From San Francisco to the Sierra Gold Mines*. Nevada City, Calif.: Carl Mautz, 1998.

Fitzgerald, John. *Big White Lie: Chinese Australians in White Australia*. Sydney: University of New South Wales Press, 2007.

Fitzsimons, Peter. *Eureka: The Unfinished Revolution*. N. Sydney, Aus.: Random House, 2012.

Flandreau, Marc. *The Glitter of Gold: France, Bimetallism, and the Emergence of the International Gold Standard, 1848–1873*. New York: Oxford University Press, 2004.

Flandreau, Marc, ed. *The Money Doctors: The Experience of International Financial Advising*. New York: Routledge, 2003.

Follett, Richard J., Eric Foner, and Walter Johnson. *Slavery's Ghost: The Problem of Freedom in the Age of Emancipation*. Baltimore: Johns Hopkins University Press, 2011.

Frank, Andre Gunder. *Capitalism and Underdevelopment in Latin America: Historical Studies of Chile and Brazil*. New York: Monthly Review Press, 1967.

———. *ReOrient: Global Economy in the Asian Age*. Berkeley: University of California Press, 1998.

Gabaccia, Donna R., and Dirk Hoerder, eds. *Connecting Seas and Connected Ocean Rims: Indian, Atlantic, and Pacific Oceans and China Seas Migrations from the 1830s to the 1930s*. Studies in Global Social History. Leiden: Brill, 2011.

Ganter, Regina. *Mixed Relations: Asian-Aboriginal Contact in North Australia*. Perth: University of Western Australia Publishing, 2006.

Gates, Paul W. *History of Public Land Law Development*. Washington, D.C.: Public Land Law Review Commission, 1968.

Gerth, Karl. *China Made: Consumer Culture and the Creation of the Nation*. Cambridge, Mass.: Harvard University Press, 2003.

Gilberg, M. E. *Auburn, a California Mining Camp Comes of Age*. Newcastle, Calif.: Gilmar Press, 1986.

Ghosh, Amitav. *Sea of Poppies*. New York: Picador, 2008.

Golden Dragon Museum. *Chinese Memorials and Memories: The White Hills Cemetery-Bendigo*. Bendigo, Vic.: Bart-n-Print, 2001.

Gomez, Edmund Terence, and Xinhuang Xiao. *Chinese Business in Southeast Asia: Contesting Cultural Explanations, Researching Entrepreneurship*, new ed. London: Routledge Curzon, 2004.

Goodman, Bryna. *Native Place, City, and Nation: Regional Networks and Identities in Shanghai, 1853–1937*. Berkeley: University of California Press, 1995.

Goodman, David. *Gold Seeking: Victoria and California in the 1850s.* St. Leonards, NSW: Allen & Unwin, 1994.

Gott, Richard. *Britain's Empire: Resistance, Repression and Revolt.* London: Verso, 2011.

Grant, Kevin. *A Civilised Savagery: Britain and the New Slaveries in Africa, 1884–1926.* London: Routledge, 2005.

Greenland, Powell. *Hydraulic Mining in California: A Tarnished Legacy.* Western Lands and Waters Series. Spokane, Wash: A.H. Clark, 2001.

Gudde, Erwin Gustav. *California Gold Camps: A Geographical and Historical Dictionary of Camps, Towns, and Localities Where Gold Was Found and Mined, Wayside Stations and Trading Centers.* Berkeley: University of California Press, 1975.

Haddad, John R. *America's First Adventure in China: Trade, Treaties, Opium, and Salvation.* Philadelphia: Temple University Press, 2013.

Hahamovitch, Cindy. *No Man's Land: Jamaican Guest Workers in America and the Global History of Disposable Labor.* Princeton: Princeton University Press, 2011.

Hall, R. A., Jr. *Pidgin and Creole Languages.* Ithaca, N.Y.: Cornell University Press, 1966.

Hamill, John. *The Strange Career of Mr. Hoover under Two Flags.* New York: W. Faro, 1931.

Heidhues, Mary F. Somers. *Banga Tin and Mentok Pepper: Chinese Settlement on an Indonesian Island.* Singapore: Institute of Southeast Asian Studies, 1992.

———. *Golddiggers, Farmers and Traders in the Chinese Districts of West Kalimantan, Indonesia.* Ithaca, N.Y.: Cornell University Press, 2003.

Hicks, Patricia. *Stories of a Gold Miner: Trinity County, California, 1848–1861.* Weaverville, Calif: n.p., 1989.

Higginson, John. *Collective Violence and the Agrarian Origins of South African Apartheid, 1900–1948.* New York: Cambridge University Press, 2014.

Hirota, Hidetaka. *Expelling the Poor: Atlantic Seaboard States and the Origins of American Immigration Policy.* New York: Oxford University Press, 2017.

Hobsbawm, Eric J. *Industry and Empire: From 1750 to the Present Day.* 1968; London: Penguin Books, 1999.

Hsiao, Liang-lin. *China's Foreign Trade Statistics 1864–1949.* Cambridge, Mass.: East Asian Research Center, Harvard University, 1974.

Hsu, Madeline. *Dreaming of Gold, Dreaming of Home: Transnationalism and Migration Between the United States and South China.* Stanford: Stanford University Press, 2000.

———. *The Good Immigrants: How the Yellow Peril Became the Model Minority.* Princeton: Princeton University Press, 2015.

Huang, Philip. *Peasant Economy and Social Change in North China.* Stanford: Stanford University Press, 1985.

Huck, Arthur. *Chinese in Australia.* Melbourne: Longmans, 1968.

Hunt, Michael H. *Making of a Special Relationship: The United States and China to 1914.* New York: Columbia University Press, 1983.

Huttenback, Robert A. *Racism and Empire: White Settlers and Colored Immigrants in the British Self-Governing Colonies, 1830–1910.* Ithaca, N.Y.: Cornell University Press, 1976.

Igler, David. *The Great Ocean: Pacific Worlds from Captain Cook to the Gold Rush*. New York: Oxford University Press, 2013.

Irving, Helen. *To Constitute a Nation: A Cultural History of Australia's Constitution*. New York: Cambridge University Press, 1997.

Isenberg, Andrew. *Mining California: An Ecological History*. New York: Hill & Wang, 2005.

Jackson, James C. *Chinese in the West Borneo Goldfields: A Study in Cultural Geography*. Occasional Papers in Geography. Hull, UK: University of Hull, 1970.

Jackson, Joseph Henry. *Anybody's Gold: The Story of California's Mining Towns*. San Francisco: Chronicle Books, 1970.

James, Ronald L. *Ruins of a World: Chinese Gold Mining at the Mon-Tung Site in the Snake River Canyon*. Idaho Cultural Resource Series. Washington, D.C.: Bureau of Land Management, 1995.

Jiangmenshi dang'an ju, Jiangmenshi zazhi ban, Wuyi Daxue Guangdong Qiaoxiang Wenhua Yanjiu Zhongxin, eds. *Qingxi qiaoxiang: Wuyi yinxin dang'an tu'ce* (Maintaining Connections with an Overseas Chinese Village: Archival Photographs of Silver Letters from Wuyi). Jiangmen, Guangdong: Jiangmenshi Dang'an Ju, 2010.

Jing, Su. *Landlord and Labor in Late Imperial China: Case Studies from Shandong*. Cambridge, Mass: Harvard University Press, 1978.

Johnson, Susan Lee. *Roaring Camp: The Social World of the California Gold Rush*. New York: W. W. Norton, 2000.

Jones, Gavin Roger. *Strange Talk: The Politics of Dialect Literature in Gilded Age America*. Berkeley: University of California Press, 1999.

Jones, Timothy G. *Chinese in the Northern Territory*. Darwin: Northern Territory University Press, 1997.

Jung, Moon-Ho. *Coolies and Cane: Race, Labor, and Sugar in the Age of Emancipation*. Baltimore: Johns Hopkins University Press, 2006.

Kaiping Shi Wenwuju, ed. *Kaiping Yinxin* (Silver Letters from Kaiping). Guangzhou: Guangdong Lüyou Chubanshe, 2014.

Kanazawa, Mark. *Golden Rules: The Origins of California Water Law in the Gold Rush*. Chicago: University of Chicago Press, 2015.

Karl, Rebecca. *China's Revolutions in the Modern World: A Brief Interpretive History*. New York: Verso, 2020.

———. *The Magic of Concepts: History and the Economic in Twentieth-Century China*. Durham, N.C.: Duke University Press, 2017.

———. *Staging the World: Chinese Nationalism at the Turn of the Twentieth Century*. Durham, N.C.: Duke University Press, 2002.

Karl, Rebecca, and Peter Zarrow, eds. *Rethinking the 1898 Reform Period: Political and Cultural Change in Late Qing China*. Cambridge, Mass.: Harvard University Press, 2002.

Karuka, Manu. *Empire's Tracks: Indigenous Nations, Chinese Workers, and the Transcontinental Railroad*. Berkeley: University of California Press, 2019.

Kaske, Elisabeth. *The Politics of Language in Chinese Education, 1895–1919*. Leiden: Brill, 2008.

Katz, Elaine. *A Trade Union Aristocracy: A History of White Workers in the Transvaal and the General Strike of 1913*. Johannesburg: University of Witwatersrand, 1976.

————. *White Death: Silicosis on the Witwatersrand Gold Mines, 1886–1910.* Johannesburg: Witwatersrand University Press, 1994.

Keesing, Nancy. *Gold Fever: The Australian Goldfields, 1851 to the 1890s.* Sydney: Angus & Robertson, 1967.

Kelley, Robert Lloyd. *Gold vs. Grain: The Hydraulic Mining Controversy in California's Sacramento Valley; a Chapter in the Decline of the Concept of Laissez Faire.* Glendale, Calif.: A.H. Clark, 1959.

Kennedy, Brian. *A Tale of Two Mining Cities: Johannesburg and Broken Hill, 1885–1925.* Carlton, Vic.: International Scholarly Books, 1984.

Klotz, Audie. *Migration and National Identity in South Africa, 1860–2010.* New York: Cambridge University Press, 2013.

Ko, Dorothy. *Teachers of the Inner Chambers: Women and Culture in Seventeenth-Century China.* Stanford: Stanford University Press, 1994.

Kuhn, Philip. *Chinese Among Others: Emigration in Modern Times.* Lanham, Md.: Rowman & Littlefield, 2008.

Kuo, Mei-fen. *Making Chinese Australia: Urban Elites, Newspapers, and the Formation of Chinese-Australian Identity.* Clayton, Vic.: Monash, 2013.

Kurashige, Lon. *Two Faces of Exclusion: The Untold History of Anti-Asian Racism in the United States.* Chapel Hill: University of North Carolina Press, 2016.

Lai, Him Mark. *Becoming Chinese American: A History of Communities and Institutions.* Walnut Creek, Calif.: Rowman Alta Mira, 2004.

Lake, Marilyn, and Henry Reynolds. *Drawing the Global Colour Line: White Men's Countries and the International Challenge of Racial Equality.* New York: Cambridge University Press, 2008.

Lattimore, Owen. *Studies in Frontier History; Collected Papers, 1928–1958.* New York: Oxford University Press, 1962.

Lee, Robert. *Orientals: Asian Americans in Popular Culture.* Philadelphia: Temple University Press, 1999.

Lee, Wen Ho, with Helen Zia. *My Country Versus Me: The First-Hand Account of the Los Alamos Scientist Who Was Falsely Accused of Being a Spy.* New York: Hyperion, 2001.

LeFeber, Walter. *The New Empire: An Interpretation of American Expansion.* 1963; Ithaca, N.Y.: Cornell University Press, 1998.

Levy, Norman. *The Foundations of the South African Cheap Labour System.* International Library of Sociology. Boston: Routledge & Kegan Paul, 1982.

Lew-Williams, Beth. *The Chinese Must Go: Violence, Exclusion, and the Making of the Alien in America.* Cambridge, Mass.: Harvard University Press, 2018.

Li, Baida, ed. *Shijie jiyi yichan: Taishan yinxin dang'an ji yanjiu* (World Heritage Memories: Taishan Silver Letters—Archives and Research). Guangzhou: Jinan University Press, 2017.

Limbaugh, Ronald H., and Willard P. Fuller. *Calaveras Gold: The Impact of Mining on a Mother Lode County.* Reno: University of Nevada Press, 2004.

Liu, Andrew. *Tea War: A History of Capitalism in China and India.* New Haven, Conn.: Yale University Press, 2020.

Liu, Haiming. *From Canton Restaurant to Panda Express: A History of Chinese Food in the United States.* New Brunswick, N.J.: Rutgers University Press, 2015.

Liu, Jin. *Taishan lishi wenhua ji: Taishan yinxin* (Anthology of Taishan History and Culture: Silver Letters of Taishan). Beijing: Zhongguo Huaqiao Chubanshe, 2007.

———. *Wuyi yinxin* (Silver Letters from Wuyi). Guangzhou: Guangdong Renmin Chubanshe, 2009.

Liu, Lydia H. *The Clash of Empires: The Invention of Modern China in Modern Worldmaking.* Cambridge, Mass.: Harvard University Press, 2004.

Loh, Francis Kok Wah. *Beyond the Tin Mines: Coolies, Squatters, and New Villagers in the Kinta Valley, Malaysia, 1880–1980.* Singapore: Oxford University Press, 1988.

Look Lai, Walton. *Indentured Labor, Caribbean Sugar: Chinese and Indian Migrants to the British West Indies, 1838–1918.* Baltimore: Johns Hopkins University Press, 1993.

Louis, William Roger, Alaine M. Low, Nicholas P. Canny, and P. J. Marshall, eds. *The Oxford History of the British Empire,* vol. 1, *The Origins of Empire.* Oxford: Oxford University Press, 1998.

Lynch, Martin. *Mining in World History.* London: Reaktion Books, 2002.

Ma, L. Eve Armentrout. *Revolutionaries, Monarchists, and Chinatowns.* Honolulu: University of Hawaii Press, 1990.

MacPherson, Kerrie L., ed. *Asian Department Stores.* 1998; New York: Routledge, 2013.

Madley, Benjamin, *An American Genocide: The United States and the California Indian Catastrophe.* New Haven, Conn.: Yale University Press, 2016.

Mann, Ralph. *After the Gold Rush: Society in Grass Valley and Nevada City, California, 1849–1870.* Stanford: Stanford University Press, 1982.

Mansfield, George C. *Butte: The Story of a California County.* Oroville, Calif., 1919.

Mantena, Karuna. *Alibis of Empire: Henry Maine and the Ends of Liberal Imperialism.* Princeton: Princeton University Press, 2010.

Marks, Shula, and Anthony Atmore, eds. *Economy and Society in Pre-Industrial South Africa.* London: Longman, 1980.

Marks, Shula, and Peter Richardson, eds. *International Labour Migration: Historical Perspectives.* London: Institute of Commonwealth Studies, 1984.

Marks, Shula, and Stanley Trapido, eds. *The Politics of Race, Class, and Nationalism in Twentieth-Century South Africa.* New York: Longman, 1987.

Markus, Andrew. *Australian Race Relations.* Sydney: Allen & Unwin, 1994.

———. *Fear and Hatred: Purifying Australia and California, 1850–1901.* Sydney: Hale & Iremonger, 1979.

Martínez, Julia, and Adrian Vickers. *The Pearl Frontier: Indonesian Labor and Indigenous Encounters in Australia's Northern Trading Network.* Honolulu: University of Hawaii Press, 2015.

Mather, R. E. *Gold Camp Desperadoes: A Study of Violence, Crime, and Punishment on the Mining Frontier.* San Jose, Calif.: History West, 1990.

May, Ernest, and John Fairbank, eds. *America's China Trade in Historical Perspective.* Cambridge, Mass.: Harvard University Press, 1986.

May, Philip Ross. *Origins of Hydraulic Mining in California.* Oakland, Calif.: Holmes, 1970.

McArthur, Scott. *The Enemy Never Came: The Civil War in the Pacific Northwest.* Caldwell, Idaho: Caxton Press, 2012.

McCalman, Iain, Alexander Cook, and Andrew Reeves, eds. *Gold: Forgotten Histories and Lost Objects of Australia*. Cambridge: Cambridge University Press, 2001.

McDonnell, Jeanne Farr. *Juana Briones of Nineteenth-Century California*. Tucson: University of Arizona Press, 2008.

McKanna, Clare Vernon. *Race and Homicide in Nineteenth-Century California*. Las Vegas: University of Nevada Press, 2002.

McKeown, Adam. *Chinese Migrant Networks and Cultural Change: Peru, Chicago, Hawaii, 1900–1936*. Chicago: University of Chicago Press, 2000.

———. *Melancholy Order: Asian Migration and the Globalization of Borders*. New York: Columbia University Press, 2008.

McPhee, John. *Assembling California*. New York: Farrar, Straus & Giroux, 1994.

Meagher, Arnold. *The Coolie Trade: The Traffic of Chinese Laborers to Latin America, 1847–1874*. n.p., 2008.

Meredith, Martin. *Diamonds, Gold, and War: The British, the Boers, and the Making of South Africa*. New York: Public Affairs, 2007.

Merritt, Jane T. *The Trouble with Tea: The Politics of Consumption in the Eighteenth-Century Global Economy*. Baltimore: Johns Hopkins University Press, 2017.

Metzler, Mark. *Lever of Empire: The International Gold Standard and the Crisis of Liberalism in Pre-war Japan*. Berkeley: University of California Press, 2006.

Miles, Robert. *Capitalism and Unfree Labour: Anomaly or Necessity?* London: Tavistock, 1987.

Minke, Pauline. *Chinese in the Mother Lode, 1850–1870*. San Francisco: R & E Research Associates, 1974.

Mintz, Sidney. *Sweetness and Power: The Place of Sugar in Modern History*. New York: Penguin Books, 1985.

Monaghan, Jay. *Australians and the Gold Rush: California and Down Under, 1849–1864*. Berkeley: University of California Press, 1966.

Mountford, Benjamin. *Britain, China, and Colonial Australia*. New York: Oxford University Press, 2016.

Mountford, Benjamin, and Stephen Tuffnell, eds. *A Global History of Gold Rushes*. Berkeley: University of California Press, 2018.

Murray, Dian H. *The Origins of the Tiandihui: The Chinese Triads in Legend and History*. Stanford: Stanford University Press, 1994.

Muthu, Sankar. *Empire and Modern Political Thought*. New York: Cambridge University Press, 2012.

Nadeau, Remi A. *Ghost Towns and Mining Camps of California: A History and Guide*, 4th ed. Santa Barbara, Calif: Crest, 1992.

Nevins, Allan. *Frémont, the West's Greatest Adventurer*. New York: Harper & Bros., 1928.

Ngai, Mae. *Impossible Subjects: Illegal Aliens and the Making of Modern America*. Princeton: Princeton University Press, 2004.

———. *The Lucky Ones: One Family and the Extraordinary Invention of Chinese America*. Boston: Houghton Mifflin Harcourt, 2010.

Nish, Ian. *Anglo-Japanese Alliance: The Diplomacy of Two Island Empires, 1894–1907*. London: Athlone, 1966.

Northrop, David. *Indentured Labor in the Age of Imperialism.* New York: Cambridge University Press, 1995.

Osterhammel, Jürgen. *The Transformation of the World: A Global History of the Nineteenth Century.* Princeton: Princeton University Press, 2017.

Otte, Thomas G. *China Question: Great Power Rivalry and British Isolation, 1894–1905.* New York: Oxford University Press, 2007.

Owens, Kenneth, ed. *Riches for All: The California Gold Rush and the World.* Lincoln: University of Nebraska Press, 2002.

Ownby, David. *Brotherhoods and Secret Societies in Early and Mid-Qing China: The Formation of a Tradition.* Stanford: Stanford University Press, 1996.

Ownby, David, and Mary F. Somers Heidhues, eds. *"Secret Societies" Reconsidered: Perspectives on the Social History of Early Modern South China and Southeast Asia.* Armonk, N.Y.: M.E. Sharpe, 1993.

Paden, Irene Dakin. *The Big Oak Flat Road: An Account of Freighting from Stockton to Yosemite Valley.* San Francisco: Yosemite Natural History Association, 1959.

Pan, Lynn. *The Encyclopedia of the Chinese Overseas.* Cambridge, Mass.: Harvard University Press, 1999.

Pan, Shü-lun. *The Trade of the United States with China.* New York: China Trade Bureau, 1924.

Parthasarathi, Prasannan. *Why Europe Grew Rich and Asia Did Not: Global Economic Divergence, 1600–1850.* New York: Cambridge University Press, 2011.

Pascoe, Peggy. *Relations of Rescue: The Search for Female Moral Authority in the American West, 1874–1939.* New York: Oxford University Press, 1990.

Paul, Rodman W. *California Gold; the Beginning of Mining in the Far West.* Cambridge: Harvard University Press, 1947.

Payton, Philip. *The Making of Modern Cornwall: Historical Experience and the Persistence of "Difference."* Redruth, Cornwall: Dyllansow Truran, 1994.

Peck, Gunther. *Reinventing Free Labor: Padrones and Immigrant Workers in the North American West, 1880–1930.* New York: Cambridge University Press, 2000.

Pelling, Henry. *Popular Politics and Society in Late Victorian Britain: Essays.* London: Macmillan, 1968.

Pelling, Henry, and Alastair J. Reid. *A Short History of the Labour Party.* New York: St. Martin's, 1996.

Peterson, Richard H. *The Bonanza Kings: The Social Origins and Business Behavior of Western Mining Entrepreneurs, 1870–1900.* Norman: University of Oklahoma Press, 1991.

———. *Manifest Destiny in the Mines: A Cultural Interpretation of Anti-Mexican Nativism in California, 1848–1853.* San Francisco: R & E Research Associates, 1975.

Pfaelzer, Jean. *Driven Out: The Forgotten War Against Chinese Americans.* New York: Random House, 2007.

Pitt, Leonard, *The Decline of the Californios: A Social History of the Spanish-Speaking Californians, 1846–1890.* Berkeley: University of California Press, 1966.

Pomeranz, Kenneth. *The Great Divergence: China, Europe and the Making of the Modern World Economy.* Princeton: Princeton University Press, 2000.

Porter, Andrew. *"Cultural Imperialism" and Missionary Enterprise.* Cambridge: North Atlantic Missionary Project, 1996.

Porter, Andrew, and William Roger Lewis, eds. *The Oxford History of the British Empire,* vol. 3, *The Nineteenth Century.* New York: Oxford University Press, 1999.

Price, Charles Archibald. *The Great White Walls Are Built: Restrictive Immigration to North America and Australasia 1836–1888.* Canberra: Australian National University Press, 1974.

Qin, Yucheng. *The Diplomacy of Nationalism: The Six Companies and China's Policy toward Exclusion.* Honolulu: University of Hawaii Press, 2009.

Qu, Tonzu. *Han Social Structure.* Seattle: University of Washington Press, 1972.

Quaife, G. R. *Gold and Colonial Society, 1851–1870.* North Melbourne, Vic.: Cassell Australia, 1975.

Quinn, Arthur. *The Rivals: William Gwin, David Broderick, and the Birth of California.* New York: Crown, 1994.

Reid, Anthony, ed. *Sojourners and Settlers: Histories of Southeast Asia and the Chinese.* Honolulu: University of Hawaii Press, 2001.

Reid, John Phillip. *Policing the Elephant: Crime, Punishment, and Social Behavior on the Overland Trail.* San Marino, Calif.: Huntington Library, 1997.

Remer, C. F. *Foreign Investment in China.* New York: Macmillan, 1933.

———. *A Study of Chinese Boycotts.* Baltimore: Johns Hopkins University Press, 1933.

Reynolds, Henry, ed. *Dispossession: Black Australians and White Invaders.* Crow's Nest, NSW: Allen and Unwin, 1989.

———. *Race Relations in North Queensland.* Townsville: James Cook University of North Queensland, 1978.

Rhoads, Edward J. M. *Stepping Forth into the World: The Chinese Educational Mission to the United States, 1872–1881.* Hong Kong: Hong Kong University Press, 2011.

Richardson, Peter. *Chinese Mine Labour in the Transvaal.* London: Macmillan, 1982.

Rifkin, Mark. *Manifesting America: The Imperial Construction of U.S. National Space.* New York: Oxford University Press, 2009.

Robinson, Cedric. *On Racial Capitalism, Black Internationalism, and Cultures of Resistance.* London: Pluto, 2019.

Robinson, Ronald, and John Gallagher. *Africa and the Victorians: The Climax of Imperialism in the Dark Continent.* New York: Anchor Books, 1961.

Rodney, Walter. *How Europe Underdeveloped Africa.* Washington, D.C.: Howard University Press, 1972.

Rohrbough, Malcolm J. *Days of Gold: The California Gold Rush and the American Nation.* Berkeley: University of California Press, 1997.

Rosenberg, Emily. *Financial Missionaries to the World.* Durham, N.C.: Duke University Press, 1999.

Rosenthal, Jean-Laurent, and Roy Bin Wong. *Before and Beyond Divergence: The Politics of Economic Change in China and Europe.* Cambridge, Mass.: Harvard University Press, 2011.

Rudolph, Jennifer M. *Negotiated Power in Late Imperial China: The Zongli Yamen and the Politics of Reform.* Ithaca, N.Y.: Cornell University Press, 2008.

Ruskola, Teemu. *Legal Orientalism: China, the United States, and Modern Law*. Cambridge, Mass.: Harvard University Press, 2013.

Russell, A. K. *Liberal Landslide: The General Election of 1906*. Hamden, Conn.: Archon Books, 1973.

Salyer, Lucy E. *Laws Harsh as Tigers: Chinese Immigrants and the Shaping of Modern Immigration Law*. Chapel Hill: University of North Carolina Press, 1995.

Sandemeyer, Elmer Clarence. *The Anti-Chinese Movement in California*. Urbana: University of Illinois Press, 1973.

Sanderson, Henry, and Michael Forsythe. *China's Superbank: Debt, Oil and Influence: How China Development Bank is Rewriting the Rules of Finance*. Hoboken, N.J.: Bloomberg Press, 2013.

Saunders, Kay, ed. *Indentured Labour in the British Empire, 1834–1920*. London: Croom Helm, 1984.

Saxton, Alexander. *The Indispensable Enemy*. Berkeley: University of California Press, 1971.

Schmidt, J. D. *In the Human Realm: The Poetry of Huang Zunxian*. Cambridge, Mass.: Harvard University Press, 1994.

Scott, James C. *The Art of Not Being Governed: An Anarchist History of Upland Southeast Asia*. New Haven, Conn.: Yale University Press, 2009.

Semmel, Bernard. *Imperialism and Social Reform: English Social-Imperial Thought, 1895–1914*. Cambridge, Mass.: Harvard University Press, 1960.

Serle, Geoffrey. *The Golden Age: A History of the Colony of Victoria, 1851–1861*. Melbourne: Melbourne University Press, 1963.

Shah, Nayan. *Contagious Divides: Epidemics and Race in San Francisco's Chinatown*. Berkeley: University of California Press, 2001.

Sheafer, Silvia Anne. *Chinese and the Gold Rush*. Whittier, Calif.: Journal, 1979.

Shelton, Tamara Venit. *A Squatter's Republic: Land the Politics of Monopoly in California, 1850–1900*. Berkeley: University of California Press, 2013.

Shen, Yuanfang. *Dragon Seed in the Antipodes: Chinese-Australian Autobiographies*. Carlton, Vic.: Melbourne University Press, 2001.

Shih, Shu-mei, Chien-hsin Tsai, and Brian Bernards, eds. *Sinophone Studies: A Critical Reader*. New York: Columbia University Press, 2013.

Shover, Michele J. *Chico's Lemm Ranch Murders and the Anti-Chinese Campaign of 1877*. Chico: Association for Northern California Records and Research, 1998.

Shuck, Oscar, ed. *History of the Bench and Bar of California: Being Biographies of Many Remarkable Men*. San Francisco: Bench and Bar, 1912.

Simmel, Georg. *Philosophy of Money*, third edition, ed. David Frisby. London and NY: Routledge, 2004, 1907.

Singh, Daleep. *From Dutch South Africa to Republic of South Africa, 1652–1994: The Story of Three and a Half Centuries of Imperialism*. New Delhi: Allied, 2010.

Sinn, Elizabeth. *Pacific Crossing: California Gold, Chinese Migration, and the Making of Hong Kong*. Hong Kong: Hong Kong University Press, 2013.

———. *Rethinking Hong Kong: New Paradigms, New Perspectives*. Hong Kong: Hong Kong University Press, 2009.

Skidelsky, Robert. *Money and Government: A Challenge to Mainstream Economics.* New York: Penguin Books, 2019.

Skinner, G. William. *Chinese Society in Thailand: An Analytical History.* Ithaca, N.Y.: Cornell University Press, 1957.

———. *Leadership and Power in the Chinese Community of Thailand.* Association for Asian Studies. Ithaca: Cornell University Press, 1958.

Skjeie, Sheila M. "California, Racism, and the Fifteenth Amendment: 1849–1870." In *California and the Coming of the Fifteenth Amendment,* edited by Sheila Skjeie and Ralph E. Shaffer. Pomona: California Polytechnic University, 2005.

Smith, Dottie. *History of the Chinese in Shasta County.* Redding, Calif.: Shasta Historical Society, n.d.

Smith, Iain. *The Origins of the South African War, 1899–1902.* New York: Longman, 1996.

Smith, Stacey L. *Freedom's Frontier: California and the Struggle over Unfree Labor, Emancipation, and Reconstruction.* Chapel Hill: University of North Carolina Press, 2013.

Sommer, Matthew Harvey. *Polyandry and Wife-Selling in Qing Dynasty China: Survival Strategies and Judicial Interventions.* Oakland: University of California Press, 2015.

———. *Sex, Law, and Society in Late Imperial China.* Stanford: Stanford University Press, 2000.

Sparks, Theresa A. *China Gold.* Fresno: Academy Library Guild, 1954.

Spence, Jonathan. *God's Chinese Son: The Taiping Heavenly Kingdom of Hong Xiuquan.* New York: W. W. Norton, 1996.

Spude, Catherine Holder, ed. *Eldorado!: The Archaeology of Gold Mining in the Far North.* Lincoln: University of Nebraska Press, 2011.

Stanley, Amy Dru. *From Bondage to Contract: Wage Labor, Marriage, and the Market in the Age of Slave Emancipation.* Cambridge: Cambridge University Press, 1998.

Stanley, Jerry. *Digger: The Tragic Fate of the California Indians from the Missions to the Gold Rush.* New York: Crown, 1997.

Stephens, John J. *Fueling the Empire: South Africa's Gold and the Road to War.* Hoboken, N.J.: Wiley, 2003.

Stoler, Ann Laura, ed. *Imperial Debris: On Ruins and Ruination.* Durham, N.C.: Duke University Press, 2013.

Sugihara, Kaoru, ed. *Japan, China, and the Growth of the Asian International Economy, 1850–1949.* New York: Oxford University Press, 2005.

Sun, E-tu Zen, ed. and trans. *Chinese Social History: Translations of Selected Studies.* 1956; New York: Octagon Books, 1966.

Tagliacozzo, Eric. *Chinese Circulations: Capital, Commodities, and Networks in Southeast Asia.* Durham, N.C.: Duke University Press, 2011.

Talbitzer, Bill. *Echoes of the Gold Rush: Tales of the Northern Mines.* Oroville, Calif: Oroville Features, 1985.

Tandeter, Enrique. *Coercion and Market: Silver Mining in Colonial Potosí, 1692–1826.* Albuquerque: University of New Mexico Press, 1993.

Tandeter, Enrique, ed. *The Market of Potosí at the End of the Eighteenth Century.* London: University of London, 1987.

Tanner, Duncan. *Political Change and the Labour Party, 1900–1918.* Cambridge: Cambridge University Press, 1990.

Tanner, Duncan, ed. *Debating Nationhood and Governance in Britain, 1885–1945: Perspectives From the "Four Nations."* Manchester: Manchester University Press, 2006.

Taylor, Philip. *The Distant Magnet: European Emigration to the U.S.A.* New York: Harper & Row, 1971.

Thomason, Sarah Grey, and Terrence Kaufman. *Language Contact, Creolization, and Genetic Linguistics.* Berkeley: University of California Press, 1988.

Tinker, Hugh. *A New System of Slavery: The Export of Indian Labour Overseas.* London: Oxford University Press, 1993.

Todd, A. C. *The Cornish Miner in America: The Contribution to the Mining History of the United States by Emigrant Cornish Miners—the Men Called Cousin Jacks.* Truro, Cornwall: Barton, 1967.

Tom, Brian, and Lawrence Tom. *Marysville's Chinatown.* San Francisco: Images of America, 2008.

Tordoff, Judith D. *Analysis, Evaluation, Effect Determination and Mitigation Plan for Two Chinese Mining Sites in Butte County, California.* Sacramento: Public Anthropological Research, 1986.

Trafzer, Clifford E., and Joel R. Hyer, eds. *Exterminate Them! Written Accounts of the Murder, Rape, and Enslavement of Native Americans During the California Gold Rush.* East Lansing: Michigan State University Press, 1999.

Trocki, Carl A. *Opium and Empire: Chinese Society in Colonial Singapore, 1800–1910.* Ithaca, N.Y.: Cornell University Press, 1990.

Tutino, John. *The Mexican Heartland: How Communities Shaped Capitalism, a Nation, and World History, 1500–2000.* Princeton: Princeton University Press, 2018.

Twain, Mark. *Gold Miners and Guttersnipes: Tales of California.* San Francisco: Chronicle Books, 1991.

Tweedie, Sandra. *Trading Partners: Australia and Asia, 1790–1993.* Sydney: University of NSW Press, 1994.

Umbeck, John R. *A Theory of Property Rights: With Application to the California Gold Rush.* Ames: Iowa State University Press, 1981.

Van Onselen, Charles. *New Babylon, New Nineveh: Everyday Life on the Witwatersrand, 1886–1914.* Johannesburg: Jonathan Ball, 2001.

Vaughan, Trudy. *Archaeological Investigations at a Sacramento River Miningcamp (CA-SHA-1450), Shasta County, California.* Redding: City of Redding and U.S. Bureau of Land Management, 1986.

Vaught, David. *After the Gold Rush: Tarnished Dreams in the Sacramento Valley.* Baltimore: Johns Hopkins University Press, 2007.

Von Glahn, Richard. *Economic History of China.* New York: Cambridge University Press, 2016.

———. *Fountain of Fortune: Money and Monetary Policy in China, 1000–1700.* Berkeley: University of California Press, 1996.

Walker, David. *Anxious Nation: Australia and the Rise of Asia, 1850–1939*. St. Lucia: University of Queensland Press, 1999.

Wallerstein, Immanuel. *The Modern World System*, 4 vols. New York: Academic Press, 1977–2011.

Wang, Guanhua. *In Search of Justice: The 1905–1906 Chinese Anti-American Boycott*. Cambridge, Mass.: Harvard University Press, 2001.

Wang Gungwu. *The Chinese Overseas: From Earthbound China to the Quest for Autonomy*. Cambridge, Mass.: Harvard University Press, 2000.

———. *Don't Leave Home: Migration and the Chinese*. Singapore: Times Academic Press, 2001.

———. *The Nanhai Trade: The Early History of Chinese Trade in the South China Sea*. Singapore: Times Academic Press, 1998.

Wang Gungwu and Chin-Keong Ng, eds. *Maritime China in Transition 1750–1850*. Wiesbaden, Germany: Otto Harrassowitz Verlag, 2004.

Wang, Sing-wu. *The Organization of Chinese Emigration, 1848–1888, with special reference to Chinese Emigration to Australia*. San Francisco: Chinese Materials Center, 1978.

Welsh, Lionel. *Vermilion and Gold: Vignettes of Chinese Life in Ballarat*. Sandy Bay, Tasmania: Banyan Press, 1985.

Westad, Odd Arne. *Restless Empire: China and the World Since 1750*. New York: Basic, 2012.

Willard, Myra. *History of the White Australia Policy to 1920*, 2nd ed. London: Cass, 1967.

Williams, William Appleman. *The Tragedy of American Diplomacy*. 1959; New York: Dell, 1962.

Wolfe, Patrick. *Settler Colonialism and the Transformation of Anthropology: The Politics and Poetics of an Ethnographic Event*. New York: Cassell, 1999.

Wong, Edlie. *Racial Reconstruction: Black Inclusion, Chinese Exclusion, and the Fictions of Citizenship*. New York: NYU Press, 2015.

Wong, Roy Bin. *China Transformed: Historical Change and the Limits of European Experience*. Ithaca, N.Y.: Cornell University Press, 1997.

Wong Lin Ken. *The Malayan Tin Industry to 1914*. Tucson: University of Arizona Press, 1965.

Wong Sin Kiong. *China's Anti-American Boycott Movement in 1905: A Study in Urban Protest*. New York: Peter Lang, 2002.

Worden, Nigel. *Making of Modern South Africa: Conquest, Segregation, and Apartheid*. Cambridge, Mass.: Blackwell, 1994.

Xu Dixin and Wu Chengming, eds. *Chinese Capitalism, 1522–1840*, trans. C. A. Curwen. New York: St. Martin's Press, 2000.

Xu Guoqi. *Chinese and Americans: A Shared History*. Cambridge, Mass.: Harvard University Press, 2014.

Yang, William. *Australian Chinese*. Canberra: National Portrait Gallery, 2001.

Yap, Melanie, and Dianne Leong Man. *Colour, Confusion and Concessions: The History of the Chinese in South Africa*. Hong Kong: Hong Kong University Press, 1996.

Yen Ching-Hwang. *Coolies and Mandarins: China's Protection of Overseas Chinese During the Late Ching Period, 1851–1911*. Singapore: Singapore University Press, 1985.

Yin, Xiao-huang. *Chinese American Literature Since the 1850s*. Urbana: University of Illinois Press, 2000.

Yong, C. F. *The New Gold Mountain: The Chinese in Australia, 1901–1921*. Richmond, S. Australia: Raphael Arts, 1977.

Yuan, Bingling. *Chinese Democracies: A Study of the Kongsis of West Borneo, 1776–1884*. Leiden: Universiteit Leiden, 2000.

Yun, Lisa. *The Coolie Speaks: Chinese Indentured Laborers and African Slaves in Cuba*. Philadelphia: Temple University Press, 2008.

Yung, Judy. *Unbound Feet: A Social History of Chinese Women in San Francisco*. Berkeley: University of California Press, 1995.

Zarrow, Peter. *After Empire: The Conceptual Transformation of the Chinese State, 1885–1924*. Stanford: Stanford University Press, 2012.

———. *China in War and Revolution, 1895–1949*. London: Routledge, 2005.

Zo, Kil Young. *Chinese Emigration into the United States, 1850–1880*. 1971; New York: Arno Press, 1978.

Credits

I thank the editors and publishers for permission to republish early versions of Chapters 1 and 2: "Chinese Gold Miners and the Chinese Question in Nineteenth Century California and Victoria," *Journal of American History* 101 no. 4 (March 2015): 1092–105 and "The Chinese Question: The Gold Rushes and Global Politics, 1849–1910," in *A Global History of Gold Rushes,* ed. Benjamin Mountford and Stephen Tuffnell (Berkeley: University of California Press, 2018): 109–20. Chapters 3 and 4: "The True Story of Ah Jake: Language and Justice in Late-Nineteenth-Century Sierra County, California," in *Cultures in Motion,* ed. Daniel T. Rodgers, Bhavani Raman, and Helmut Reimitz (Princeton: Princeton University Press, 2014): 59–78. Chapter 5: "Chinese Miners, Headmen, and Protectors on the Victorian Goldfields, 1853–1863." *Australian Historical Studies* 42, no. 1 (March 2011): 10–24, permission of Taylor and Francis. Chapters 8–11: "Trouble on the Rand: The Chinese Question and the Apogee of White Settlerism," *International Labor and Working Class History* 91 (Spring 2017): 59–78, permission of Cambridge University Press.

Excerpts from Huang Zunxian's poem, "The Expulsion of the Immigrants," trans. by J. D. Schmidt, in *Land Without Ghosts,* ed. R. David Arkush and Leo O. Lee, are published with the permission of J. D. Schmidt.

IMAGE CREDITS

Section I

1. Courtesy of the California History Room, California State Library, Sacramento, California
2. Museum No. 8151 Chinese Coach, Semmens Collection, Creswick Museum, Victoria
3. PIC Drawer 6199 #S2788, National Library of Australia

4. Nevada Historical Society
5. H32956, Pictures Collection, State Library Victoria
6. Courtesy of the California History Room, California State Library, Sacramento, California
7. Courtesy of the Department of Special Collections, Stanford University Libraries
8. Carleton E. Watkins Stereograph Collection, The Huntington Library, San Marino, California
9. Roy D. Graves Pictorial Collection, BANC PIC 1905.17500—ALB, The Bancroft Library, University of California, Berkeley
10. IAN27/09/66/4, Illustrated Newspaper File, State Library Victoria
11. Gum San Chinese Heritage Centre, Ararat, Victoria
12. IAN18/07/68/SUPP/5, Illustrated Newspaper File, State Library Victoria

Section II

13. F.W. Niven & Co., PIC Volume 156 #U3861 NK3770/8, National Library of Australia
14. IAN01/12/75/188, Illustrated Newspaper File, State Library Victoria
15. HarpWeek
16. LC-USZ62-96518, Library of Congress
17. State Library of New South Wales
18. State Library of New South Wales
19. Wikimedia Commons
20. Courtesy of Tong Bingxue
21. Niday Picture Library / Alamy Stock Photo
22. J2098, Jeffreys Collection, Western Cape Archives and Records Service
23. Historia / Shutterstock
24. London School of Economics Library
25. 1/2-019165-F, McNeur Collection, Alexander Turnbull Library, National Library of New Zealand

Index